REA's Test Prep Books Are The Best!

(a sample of the <u>hundreds of letters</u> REA receives each year)

" Your Fundamentals of Engineering Exam book was the absolute best preparation I could have had for the exam, and it is one of the major reasons I did so well and passed the FE on my first try. "

Student, Sweetwater, TN

" My students report your chapters of review as the most valuable single resource they used for review and preparation. "

Teacher, American Fork, UT

" Your book was such a better value and was so much more complete than anything your competition has produced (and I have them all!) "

Teacher, Virginia Beach, VA

" Compared to the other books that my fellow students had, your book was the most useful in helping me get a great score. "

Student, North Hollywood, CA

" Your book was responsible for my success on the exam, which helped me get into the college of my choice... I will look for REA the next time I need help. "

Student, Chesterfield, MO

" Just a short note to say thanks for the great support your book gave me in helping me pass the test... I'm on my way to a B.S. degree because of you! "

Student, Orlando, FL

(more on next page)

(continued from front page)

" I just wanted to thank you for helping me get a great score
on the AP U.S. History exam... Thank you for making great test preps! "
Student, Los Angeles, CA

" I did well because of your wonderful prep books... I just wanted to thank
you for helping me prepare for these tests. "
Student, San Diego, CA

" I used your book to prepare for the test and found that the advice and the
sample tests were highly relevant... Without using any other material, I earned
very high scores and will be going to the graduate school of my choice. "
Student, New Orleans, LA

" What I found in your book was a wealth of information sufficient to shore up
my basic skills in math and verbal... The section on analytical analysis was
excellent. The practice tests were challenging and the answer explanations most
helpful. It certainly is the Best Test Prep for the GRE! "
Student, Pullman, WA

" I really appreciate the help from your excellent book. Please keep up
the great work. "
Student, Albuquerque, NM

" I am writing to thank you for your test preparation... your book helped me
immeasurably and I have nothing but praise for your GRE preparation."
Student, Benton Harbor, MI

(more on back page)

The Best Test Preparation & Review Course

FE/EIT

Fundamentals of Engineering / Engineer-in-Training

PM Exam in General Engineering

John Presti, P.E., B.S.
Massachusetts Institute of Technology

George Wetzel, M.S.
University of Texas-Austin

James Colaizzi, Ph.D.
Rutgers University

And the Staff of REA
Dr. M. Fogiel, Director

Research & Education Association
61 Ethel Road West
Piscataway, New Jersey 08854

The Best Test Preparation & Review Course for the FE/EIT
(Fundamentals of Engineering/Engineer-in-Training)
PM Exam in General Engineering

Printed in the United States of America

Library of Congress Control Number 2002106969

International Standard Book Number 0-87891-261-4

Research & Education Association
61 Ethel Road West
Piscataway, New Jersey 08854
E-mail: info@rea.com

ABOUT RESEARCH & EDUCATION ASSOCIATION

Research & Education Association (REA) is an organization of educators, scientists, and engineers specializing in various academic fields. Founded in 1959 with the purpose of disseminating the most recently developed scientific information to groups in industry, high schools and universities, Research & Education Association has become a successful and highly respected publisher of study aids, test preps, handbooks, and reference works.

REA's Test Preparation series includes study guides for all academic levels in almost all disciplines. Research & Education Association publishes test preps for students who have not yet completed high school, as well as high school students preparing to enter college. Students from countries around the world seeking to attend college in the United States will find the assistance they need in REA's publications. For college students seeking advanced degrees, REA publishes test preps for many major graduate school admission examinations in a wide variety of disciplines, including engineering, law, and medicine. Students at every level, in every field, with every ambition can find what they are looking for among REA's publications.

Unlike most test preparation books—which present only a few practice tests that bear little resemblance to the actual exams—REA's series presents tests that accurately depict the official exams in both degree of difficulty and types of questions. REA's practice tests are always based upon the most recently administered exams, and include every type of question that can be expected on the actual exams.

REA's publications and educational materials are highly regarded and continually receive an unprecedented amount of praise from professionals, instructors, librarians, parents, and students. Our authors are as diverse as the fields represented in the books we publish. They are well known in their respective disciplines and serve on the faculties of prestigious high schools, colleges, and universities throughout the United States and Canada.

ACKNOWLEDGMENTS

In addition to our authors, we would like to thank the following: Dr. Max Fogiel, President, for his overall guidance, which brought this publication to completion; Nicole Mimnaugh, New Book Development Manager, for directing the editorial staff throughout each phase of the project; Kelli A. Wilkins, Assistant Editorial Manager, for coordinating development of the book; Mark Zipkin, Editorial Assistant, for coordinating revisions; Gary DaGiau for his editorial contributions; and Martin Perzan for typesetting the manuscript.

CONTENTS

FE/EIT

FE: PM General Engineering Exam

CHAPTER 1

You Can Succeed on the FE: PM General Engineering Exam

CHAPTER 1

YOU CAN SUCCEED ON THE FE: PM GENERAL ENGINEERING EXAM

By reviewing and studying this book, you can succeed on the Fundamentals of Engineering Examination PM Portion in General Engineering. The FE is an eight-hour exam designed to test knowledge of a wide variety of engineering disciplines. The FE was formerly known as the EIT (Engineer-in-Training) exam. The FE Exam format and title have now replaced the EIT completely.

The purpose of REA's *Best Test Preparation and Review Course for the FE: PM General Engineering Exam* is to prepare you sufficiently for the afternoon portion of the FE exam by providing 12 review chapters, including sample problems in each review, and two practice tests. The review chapters and practice tests reflect the scope and difficulty level of the actual FE: PM Exam. The reviews provide examples with thorough solutions throughout the text. The practice tests provide simulated FE exams with detailed explanations of answers. While using just the reviews or the practice tests is helpful, an effective study plan should incorporate both a review of concepts and repeated practice with simulated tests under exam conditions.

ABOUT THE TEST

The Fundamentals of Engineering Exam (FE) is one part in the four-step process toward becoming a professional engineer (PE). Graduating from an approved four-year engineering program and passing the FE qualifies you for your certification as an "Engineer-in-Training" or an "Engineer Intern." The final two steps towards licensing as a P.E. involve completion of four years of additional engineering experience and passing the Principles and Practices of Engineering Examination administered by the National Council of Examiners for Engineering and Surveying (NCEES). Registration as a professional engineer is deemed both highly rewarding and beneficial in the engineering community.

In order to register for the FE, contact your state's Board of Examiners for Professional Engineers and Land Surveyors. To determine the location for the board in your state, contact the main NCEES office at the following address:

National Council of Examiners for Engineering and Surveying
P.O. Box 1686
Clemson, SC 29633-1686
(864) 654-6824
Website: http://www.ncees.org

TEST FORMAT

The FE consists of two distinct sections. One section is given in the morning (FE: AM) while the other is administered in the afternoon (FE: PM). Students have the option of taking one of six discipline-specific modules, or a general module, in the afternoon. This book will prepare you for the general module.

The FE: PM is a *supplied-reference exam,* and students are not permitted to bring reference material into the test center. Instead, you will be mailed a reference guide when you register for the exam. This guide will provide all the charts, graphs, tables, and formulae you will need. The same book will be given to you in the test center during the test administration.

You will have four hours to complete the exam. The FE: PM consists of 60 questions covering 12 different engineering subjects. The subjects and their corresponding percentages of questions are shown on the next page.

FE: PM GENERAL ENGINEERING SUBJECT DISTRIBUTION

Subject	Percentage of Problems
Chemistry	7.5
Computers	5
Dynamics	7.5
Electrical Circuits	10
Engineering Economics	5
Ethics	5
Fluid Mechanics	7.5
Material Science/Structure of Matter	5
Mathematics	20
Mechanics of Materials	7.5
Statics	10
Thermodynamics	10

Our review book covers all of these topics thoroughly. Each topic is explained in detail, with example problems, diagrams, charts, and formulae.

You may want to take a practice exam at various studying stages to measure your strengths and weaknesses. This will help you to determine which topics need more study. Take one test when you finish studying so that you may see how much you have improved. For studying suggestions that will help you to make the best use of your time, see the "Study Schedule" presented after this chapter.

SCORING THE EXAM

Your FE: PM score is based upon the number of correct answers you choose. No points are taken off for incorrect answers. A single score of 0 to 100 is given for the entire test, which includes both the AM and PM sections. Both the AM and PM sections have an equal weight. The grade given is on a pass/fail basis. Passing and failing scores may vary from state to state, although 70 is the national reference point for passing. Thus, the general reference point for the FE: PM section alone would be 35.

The pass/fail margin is not a percentage of correct answers, nor a percentage of students who scored lower than you. This number fluctuates from year to year and is reset with every test administration. It is based on previous exam administrations and relates your score to those of previous FE examinees.

Because this grading system is so variable, there is no real way for you to know exactly what you got on the test. For the purpose of grading the practice tests in this book, however, REA provides the following formula to enable you to calculate a realistic score on each FE: PM practice test:

$$\left[\frac{\text{No. of questions answered correctly on the FE: PM}}{120}\right] \times 100 \ = \ \text{your score}$$

Remember, this formula is meant for the computation of your raw score for the practice tests in this book. It does not, and cannot, equate to your grade on the actual FE examination.

TEST-TAKING STRATEGIES

How to Beat the Clock

Every second counts, and you will want to use the available test time for each section in the most efficient manner. Here's how:

1. Bring a watch! This will allow you to monitor your time.

2. Become familiar with the test directions. You will save valuable time if you already understand the directions on the day of the test.

3. Pace yourself. Work steadily and quickly. Do not spend too much time on any one question. Remember, you can always return to the problems that gave you the most difficulty. Try to answer the easiest questions first, then return to the ones you missed.

Guessing Strategy

1. When all else fails, guess! The score you achieve depends on the number of correct answers. There is no penalty for wrong answers, so it is a good idea to choose an answer for all of the questions.

2. If you guess, try to eliminate choices you know to be wrong. This will allow you to make an educated guess. Here are some examples of what to look for when eliminating answer choices:

   Thermodynamics—check for signs of heat transfer and work

   Fluid Mechanics—check for signs of pressure reading

   Statics—check for direction of forces and compression/tension units.

3. Begin with the subject areas you know best. This will give you more time and will also build your confidence. If you use this strategy, pay careful attention to your answer sheet; you do not want to mismatch the ovals and answers. It may be a good idea to check the problem number and oval number *each time* you mark down an answer.

4. Break each problem down into its simplest components. Approach each part one step at a time. Use diagrams and drawings whenever possible, and do not wait until you get a final answer to assign units. If you decide to move onto another problem, this method will allow you to resume your work without too much difficulty.

HOW TO STUDY FOR THE FE: PM EXAM

Two groups of people take the FE examination: college seniors in undergraduate programs and graduate engineers who decide that professional registration is necessary for future growth. Both groups begin their Professional Engineer career with a comprehensive exam covering the entirety of their engineering curriculum. How does one prepare for an exam of such magnitude and importance?

Time is the most important factor when preparing for the FE: PM. Time management is necessary to ensure that each section is reviewed prior to the exam. Once the decision to test has been made, determine how much time you have to study. Divide this time amongst your topics, and make up a schedule which outlines the beginning and ending dates for study of each exam topic and include time for a final practice test followed by a brief review. Set aside extra time for the more difficult subjects, and include a buffer for unexpected events such as college exams or business trips. There is never enough time to prepare, so make the most of the time that you have.

You can determine which subject areas require the most time in several ways. Look at your college grades: those courses with the lowest grades probably need the most study. Those subjects outside your major are generally the least used and most easily forgotten. These will require a good deal of review to bring you up to speed. Some of the subjects may not be familiar at all because you were not required to study them in college. These subjects may be impossible to learn before the examination, although some can be self-taught. One such subject is engineering economics; the mathematics may be not exceptionally difficult to you and most of the concepts are common sense.

Another way to determine your weakest areas is to take one of the practice tests provided in this book. The included simulated exams will help you assess your strengths and weaknesses. By determining which type of questions you answered incorrectly on the practice tests, you find the areas that need the most work. Be careful not to neglect the other subjects in your review; do not rule out any subject area until you have reviewed it to some degree.

You may also find that a negative attitude is your biggest stumbling block. Many students do not realize the volume of material they have covered in four years of college. Some begin to study and are immediately overwhelmed because they do not have a plan. It is important that you get a good start and that you are positive as you review and study the material.

You will need some way to measure your preparedness, either with problems from books or with a review book that has sample test questions similar to the ones on the FE: PM General Engineering Exam. This book contains sample problems in each section which can be used before, during, or after you review the material to measure your understanding of the subject matter. If you are a wizard in thermodynamics, for example, and are confident in your ability to solve problems, select a few and see what happens. You may want to perform at least a cursory review of the material before jumping into problem solving, since there is always something to learn. If you do well on these initial problems, then momentum has been established. If you do poorly, you might develop a negative attitude as mentioned above. Being positive is essential as you move through the subject areas.

The question that comes to mind at this point is: "How do I review the material?" Before we get into the material itself, let us establish rules which lead to **good study habits**. Time was previously mentioned as the most important issue. When you decide to study you will need blocks of uninterrupted time so that you can get something accomplished. Two hours should be the minimum time block allotted, while four hours should be the maximum. Schedule five-minute breaks into your study period and stay with your schedule. Cramming for the FE can give you poor results, including short-term memory and confusion when synthesis is required.

Next, you need to work in a quiet place, on a flat surface that is not cluttered with other papers or work that needs to be completed before the next day. **Eliminate distractions**—they will rob you of time while you pay attention to them. **Do not eat while you study**; few of us can do two things at once and do them both well. Eating does require a lot of attention and disrupts study. Eating a sensible meal before you study resolves the "eating while you work" problem. We encourage you to have a large glass of water available since water quenches your thirst and fills the void which makes you want to get up and find something to eat. In addition, **you should be well rested when you study**. Late nights and early mornings are good for some, especially if you have a family, but the best results are associated with adequate rest.

Lastly, **study on weekend mornings while most people are still asleep**. This allows for a quiet environment and gives you the remainder of the day to do other things. If you must study at night, we suggest two-hour blocks ending before 11 p.m.

Do not spend time memorizing charts, graphs, and formulae; the FE is a supplied reference exam, and you will be provided a booklet of equations and other essential information during the test. This reference material will be sent to you prior to your examination date. You can use the supplied reference book as a guide while studying, since it will give you an indication of the depth of study you will need to pursue. Furthermore, familiarity with the book will alleviate some test anxiety since you will be given the same book to use during the actual exam.

While you review for the test, use the review book supplied by the NCEES, paper, pencil, and a calculator. Texts can be used, but reliance on them should be avoided. The object of the review is to identify what you know, the positive, and that which requires work, the negative. As you review, move past those equations and concepts that you understand and annotate on the paper those concepts that require more work. Using this method you can review a large quantity of material in a short time and reduce the apparent workload to a manageable amount. Now go back to your time schedule and allocate the remaining time according to the needs of the subject under consideration. Return to the material that requires work and review it or study it until your are satisfied that you can solve problems covering this material. When you have finished the review, you are ready to solve problems.

Solving problems requires practice. To use the problems in this book effectively, you should cover the solution and try to solve the problem on your own. If this is not possible, map out a strategy to answer the problem and then check to see if you have the correct procedure. Remember, that most problems that are not solved correctly were never started correctly. Merely reviewing the solution will not help you to start the problem when you see it again at a later date. Read the problems carefully and in parts. Many people teach that reading the whole problem gives the best overview of what is to come; however, solutions are developed from small clues that are in parts of a sentence. For example, "An engine operates on an Otto cycle," tells a great deal about the thermodynamic processes, the maximum temperature, the compression ratio, and the theoretical thermal efficiency. **Read the problem and break it into manageable parts.** Next, **try to avoid numbers until the problem is well formulated.** Too often, numbers are substituted into equations early and become show stoppers. You will need numbers, just use them after the algebra has been completed. **Be mechanical**, list the knowns, the requirements of the problem, and check off those bits of knowledge you have as they appear. Checking off the intermediate answers and information you know is a positive attitude builder. Continue to solve problems until you are confident or you exceed the time allowed in you schedule for that subject area.

As soon as you complete one subject, move to the next. Retain all of you notes as you complete each section. You will need these for your final overall review right before the exam. After you have completed the entire review, you may want to take a practice test. Taking practice exams will test your understanding of all the engineering subject areas and will help you identify sections that need additional study. With the test and the notes that you retained from the subject reviews, you can determine weak areas requiring some additional work.

You should be ready for the exam if you follow these guidelines:

* Program your time wisely.

* Maintain a positive attitude.

* Develop good study habits.

* Review the material smartly and maximize the learning process.

* Do practice problems and practice tests.

* Review again to finalize your preparation.

GOOD LUCK!

STUDY SCHEDULE

The following is a suggested eight-week study schedule for the Fundamentals of Engineering: PM General Engineering Exam. You may want to condense or expand the schedule depending on the amount of time remaining before the test. Set aside some time each week, and work straight through the activity without rushing. By following a structured schedule, you will be able to complete an adequate amount of studying, and be more confident and prepared on the day of the exam.

Week 1	Acquaint yourself with this FE: PM General Engineering Test Preparation Book by reading the first chapter: "You Can Succeed on the FE: PM General Engineering Exam." Take Practice Test 1. When you score the test, be sure to look for areas where you missed many questions. Pay special attention to these areas when you read the review chapters.
Week 2	Begin reviewing Chapters 2 and 3. As you read the chapters, try to solve the examples without aid of the solutions. Use the solutions to guide you through any questions you missed.
Week 3	Study and review Chapters 4 and 5. Take notes as you read the chapters; you may even want to write concepts on index cards and thumb through them during the day. As you read the chapters, try to solve the examples without the aid of the solutions.
Week 4	Review any notes you have taken over the last few weeks. Study Chapters 6 and 7. As you read the chapters, try to solve the examples without the aid of the solutions.
Week 5	Study Chapters 8 and 9 while continuing to review your notes. As you read the chapters, try to solve the examples without the aid of the solutions.
Week 6	Study Chapters 10 and 11. As you read the chapters, try to solve the examples without the aid of the solutions to guide you through any questions you missed.

Week 7	Study Chapter 12. As you read, try to solve the examples without the aid of the solutions. Use the solutions to guide you through any questions you missed.
Week 8	Take Practice Test 2. When you score the text, be sure to look for any improvement in the areas that you missed in Practice Test 1. If you missed any questions in any particular area, go back and review those areas. Be patient and deliberate as you review; with careful study, you can only improve.

FE/EIT

FE: PM General Engineering Exam

CHAPTER 2

Ethics

CHAPTER 2

ETHICS

Engineering ethics encompasses moral issues confronting individuals and organizations involved in engineering, and related issues of conduct, character, ideals, and relationships.

The National Society of Professional Engineers (NSPE) established the Board of Ethical Review in the 1950s to review factual situations involving ethical dilemmas submitted by engineers, public officials, and members of the public. These dilemma situations are reviewed by the Board and considered in light of the language of the NSPE Code of Ethics, Board of Ethical Review precedents, and the practical experiences of seven professional engineers selected from each of NSPE's separated geographical regions who serve on the Board.

Upon completion of deliberation, the Board issues written opinions that contain a description of the facts, pertinent Code citations, relevant questions, detailed discussions, and conclusions.

NSPE CODE OF ETHICS FOR ENGINEERS

Preamble

Engineering is an important and learned profession. The members of the profession recognize that their work has a direct and vital impact on the quality of life for all people. Accordingly, the services provided by engineers require honesty, impartiality, fairness, and equity, and must be dedicated to the protection of public health, safety, and welfare. In the practice of their profession, engineers must perform under a standard of professional behavior which requires adherence to the highest principles of ethical conduct on behalf of the public, clients, employers, and the profession.

I.   Fundamental Canons

Engineers, in the fulfillment of their professional duties, shall:

1. Hold paramount the safety, health, and welfare of the public in the performance of their professional duties.

2. Perform services only in the areas of their competence.

3. Issue public statements only in an objective and truthful manner.

4. Act in professional matters for each employer or client as faithful agents or trustees.

5. Avoid deceptive acts in the solicitation of professional employment.

II.   Rules of Practice

1. Engineers shall hold paramount the safety, health, and welfare of the public in the performance of their professional duties.

    a. Engineers shall at all times recognize that their primary obligation is to protect the safety, health, property, and welfare of the public. If their professional judgment is overruled under circumstances where safety, health, property, or welfare of the public are endangered, they shall notify their employer or client and such authority as may be appropriate.

    b. Engineers shall approve only those engineering documents which are safe for public health, property, and welfare in conformity with accepted standard.

    c. Engineers shall not reveal facts, data, or information obtained in a professional capacity without the prior consent of the client or employer except as authorized or required by law of this Code.

    d. Engineers shall not permit the use of their name or firm name nor associate in business ventures with any person or firm which they have reason to believe is engaging in fraudulent or dishonest business or professional practices.

    e. Engineers having knowledge of any alleged violation of

this Code shall cooperate with the proper authorities in furnishing such information or assistance as may be required.

2. Engineers shall perform services only in the areas of their competence.

    a. Engineers shall undertake assignments only when qualified by education or experience in the specific technical fields involved.

    b. Engineers shall not affix their signatures to any plans or documents dealing with subject matter in which they lack competence, nor to any plan or document not prepared under their direction and control.

    c. Engineers may accept assignments and assume responsibility for coordination of an entire project and sign and seal the engineering documents for the entire project, provided that each technical segment is signed and sealed only by the qualified engineers who prepared the segment.

3. Engineers shall issue public statements only in an objective and truthful manner.

    a. Engineers shall be objective and truthful in professional reports, statements, or testimony. They shall include all relevant and pertinent information in such reports, statements, or testimony.

    b. Engineers may express publicly a professional opinion on technical subjects only when that opinion is founded upon adequate knowledge of the facts and competence in the subject matter.

    c. Engineers shall issue no statements, criticisms, or arguments on technical matters which are inspired or paid for by interested parties, unless they have prefaced the comments by explicitly identifying the interested parties on whose behalf they are speaking, and by revealing the existence of any interest the engineer may have in the matter.

4. Engineers shall act in professional matters for each employer or client as faithful agents or trustees.

    a. Engineers shall disclose all known or potential conflicts of interest to their employers or clients by promptly informing them of any business association, interest, or other circumstances which could influence or appear to influence their judgment or the quality of their services.

b. Engineers shall not accept compensation, financial or otherwise, from more than one party for services on the same project, or for services pertaining to the same project, unless the circumstances are fully disclosed to, and agreed to by, all parties.

c. Engineers shall not solicit or accept financial or other valuable consideration, directly or indirectly, from contractors, their agents, or other parties in connection with work for employers or clients for which they are responsible.

d. Engineers in public service as members, advisors, or employees of a government or quasi-governmental body or department shall not participate in decisions with respect to professional services solicited or provided by them or their organization in private or public engineering practice.

e. Engineers shall not solicit or accept a professional contract from a governmental body on which a principal or officer of their organization serves as a member.

5. Engineers shall avoid deceptive acts in the solicitation of professional employment.

a. Engineers shall not falsify or permit misrepresentation of their, or their associates', academic or professional qualifications. They shall not misrepresent or exaggerate their degree of responsibility in or for the subject matter of prior assignments. Brochures or other presentations incidental to the solicitation of employment shall not misrepresent pertinent facts concerning employers, employees, associates, joint ventures, or past accomplishments with the intent and purpose of enhancing their qualifications and their work.

b. Engineers shall not offer, give, solicit, or receive, either directly or indirectly, any political contribution in any amount intended to influence the award of a contract by public authority, or which may be reasonably construed by the public of having the effect or intent to influence the award of a contract. They shall not offer any gift or other valuable consideration in order to secure work. They shall not pay a commission, percentage, or brokerage fee in order to secure work except to a bona fide employee or bona fide established commercial or marketing agency retained by them.

III. Professional Obligations

1. Engineers shall be guided in all their professional relations by the highest standards of integrity.

    a. Engineers shall admit and accept their own errors when proven wrong and refrain from distorting or altering the facts in an attempt to justify their decisions.

    b. Engineers shall advise their clients or employers when they believe a project will not be successful.

    c. Engineers shall not accept outside employment to the detriment of their regular work or interest. Before accepting any outside employment, they will notify their employers.

    d. Engineers shall not attempt to attract an engineer from another employer by false or misleading pretenses.

    e. Engineers shall not actively participate in strikes, picket lines, or other collective coercive action.

    f. Engineers shall avoid any act tending to promote their own interest at the expense of the dignity and integrity of the profession.

2. Engineers shall at all times strive to serve the public interest.

    a. Engineers shall seek opportunities to be of constructive service in civic affairs and work for the advancement of safety, health, and well-being of their community.

    b. Engineers shall not complete, sign, or seal plans and/or specifications that are not of a design safe to the public safety, health, and welfare and in conformity with accepted engineering standards. If the client or employer insists on such unprofessional conduct, they shall notify the proper authorities and withdraw from further service on the project.

    c. Engineers shall endeavor to extend public knowledge and appreciation of engineering and its achievements and to protect the engineering profession from misrepresentation and misunderstanding.

3. Engineers shall avoid all conduct or practice which is likely to discredit the profession or deceive the public.

   a. Engineers shall avoid the use of statements containing a material misrepresentation of fact or omitting a material fact necessary to keep statements from being misleading or intended likely to create an unjustified expectation, or statements containing prediction of future success.

   b. Consistent with the foregoing, Engineers may advertise for recruitment of personnel.

   c. Consistent with the foregoing, Engineers may prepare articles for the lay or technical press, but such articles shall not imply credit to the author for work performed by others.

4. Engineers shall not disclose confidential information concerning the business affairs or technical processes of any present or former client or employer without his consent.

   a. Engineers in the employ of others shall not enter promotional efforts or negotiations for work, or make arrangements for other employment as a principal, or practice in connection with a specific project for which the Engineer has gained particular and specialized knowledge.

   b. Engineers shall not, without the consent of all interested parties, participate in or represent any adversary interest in connection with a specific project or proceeding in which the Engineer has gained particular specialized knowledge on behalf of a former client or employer.

5. Engineers shall not be influenced in their professional duties by conflicting interests.

   a. Engineers shall not accept financial or other considerations, including free engineering designs, from material or equipment suppliers for specifying their project.

   b. Engineers shall not accept commissions or allowances, directly or indirectly, from contractors or other parties dealing with clients or employers of the Engineer in connection with work for which the Engineer is responsible.

6. Engineers shall uphold the principle of appropriate and adequate compensation for those engaged in engineering work.

a. Engineers shall not accept remuneration from either an employee or employment agency for giving employment.

b. Engineers when employing other engineers, shall offer salary according to professional qualifications.

7. Engineers shall not attempt to obtain employment or advancement or professional engagements by untruthfully criticizing other engineers, or by other improper or questionable methods.

a. Engineers shall not request, propose, or accept a professional commission on a contingent basis under circumstances in which their professional judgment may be compromised.

b. Engineers in salaried positions shall accept part-time engineering work only to the extent consistent with policies of the employer and in accordance with ethical considerations.

c. Engineers shall not use equipment, supplies, laboratory, or office facilities of an employer to carry on outside private practice without consent.

8. Engineers shall not attempt to injure, maliciously or falsely, directly or indirectly, the professional reputation, prospects, practice, or employment of other engineers, nor untruthfully criticize other engineers' work. Engineers who believe others are guilty of unethical or illegal practice shall present such information to the proper authority for action.

a. Engineers in private practice shall not review the work of another engineer for the same client, except with the knowledge of such engineer, or unless the connection of such engineer with the work has been terminated.

b. Engineers in governmental, industrial, or educational employ are entitled to review and evaluate the work of other engineers when so required by their employment duties.

c. Engineers in sales or industrial employ are entitled to make engineering comparisons of represented products with products of other suppliers.

9. Engineers shall accept responsibility for their professional activities; provided, however, that the Engineer may seek indemnification for professional services arising out of their practice for other than gross negligence, where the Engineer's interest cannot otherwise be protected.

a. Engineers shall conform with state registration laws in the practice of engineering.

b. Engineers shall not use association with a non-engineer, a corporation, or partnership as a "cloak" for unethical acts, but must accept personal responsibility for all professional acts.

10. Engineers shall give credit for engineering work to those to whom credit is due, and will recognize the proprietary interests of others.

a. Engineers shall, whenever possible, name the person or persons who may be individually responsible for designs, inventions, writings, or other accomplishments.

b. Engineers using designs supplied by a client recognize that the design remain the property of the client and may not be duplicated by the Engineers for others without express permission.

c. Engineers, before undertaking work for others in connection with which the Engineer may make improvements, plan, designs, inventions, or other records which may justify copyrights or patents, should enter into a positive agreement regarding ownership.

d. Engineers' designs, data, records, and notes referring exclusively to an employer's work are the employer's property.

11. Engineers shall cooperate in extending the effectiveness of the profession by interchanging information and experience with other engineers and students, and will endeavor to provide opportunity for the professional development and advancement of engineers under their supervision.

a. Engineers shall encourage engineering employees' efforts to improve their education.

b. Engineers shall encourage engineering employees to attend and present papers at professional and technical society meetings.

c. Engineers shall urge engineering employees to become registered at the earliest possible date.

d. Engineers shall assign a Professional Engineer duties of a nature to utilize full training and experience, insofar as possible, and delegate lesser functions to subprofessionals or to technicians.

e. Engineers shall provide a prospective engineering employee with complete information on working conditions and proposed status of employment, and after employment will keep employees informed of changes.

CASES AND JUDGMENTS

The following cases and judgments have been adapted from the NSPE Board of Ethical Review (BER):

NSPE Case 76–4

Public Welfare – Knowledge of Information Damaging to the Client's Interest

FACTS:

The XYZ Corporation has been advised by a State Pollution Control Authority that it has 60 days to apply for a permit to discharge manufacturing wastes into a receiving body of water. XYZ is also advised of the minimum standard that must be met.

In an effort to convince the authority that the receiving body of water after receiving the manufacturing wastes will still meet established environmental standards, the corporation employs Engineer Doe to perform consulting engineering services and submit a detailed report.

After completion of his studies but before completion of any written report, Doe concludes that the discharge from the plant will lower the quality of the receiving body of water below established standards. He further concludes that corrective action will be very costly. Doe verbally advises the XYZ Corporation of his findings. Subsequently, the corporation terminates the contract with Doe with full payment for services performed, and instructs Doe not to render a written report to the corporation.

Thereafter, Doe learns that the authority has called a public hearing and that the XYZ Corporation has presented data to support its view that the present discharge meets minimum standards.

QUESTION:

Does Doe have an ethical obligation to report his findings to the authority upon learning of the hearing?

REFERENCES:

Code of Ethics – Section 1 – "The Engineer will be guided in all his professional relations by the highest standards of integrity, and will act in professional matters for each client or employer as a faithful agent or trustee."

Section 1(c) – "He will advise his client or employer when he believes a project will not be successful."

Section 2 – "The Engineer will have proper regard for the safety, health, and welfare of the public in the performance of his professional duties. If his engineering judgment is overruled by nontechnical authority, he will clearly point out the consequences. He will notify the proper authority of any observed conditions which endanger public safety and health."

Section 2(a) – "He will regard his duty to the public welfare as paramount."

Section 2(c) – "He will not complete, sign, or seal plans and/or specifications that are not of a design safe to the public health and welfare and in conformity with accepted engineering standards. If the client or employer insists on such unprofessional conduct, he shall notify the proper authorities and withdraw from further service on the project."

Section 7 – "The Engineer will not disclose confidential information concerning the business affairs or technical processes of any present or former client or employer without his consent."

DISCUSSION:

Section 1 of the Code is clear in providing that the engineer "will act in professional matters for each client or employer as a faithful agent or trustee." In this spirit Engineer Doe has advised the XYZ Corporation that the results of his studies indicate that the established standards will in his opinion be violated. His verbal advice to the corporation would seem to meet the letter and spirit of Section 1 and 1(c).

The termination of Doe's contract with full payment for services rendered is a business decision which we will presume is permitted by the terms of the engineering services contract between Doe and his client.

Doe, however, has reason to question why the corporation specifically stipulates that he not render a written report. Upon learning of the hearing, he is squarely confronted with his obligations to the public concerning its safety, health, and welfare. Section 2(a) requires that his duty to the public be paramount. In this case, it is presumed that a failure to meet the minimum standards established by law is detrimental to the public health and safety.

Prior to this case, the Board has not had occasion to interpret Section 2(c) of the Code. That portion of Section 2(c) that requires the engineer to report any request for "unprofessional" conduct to "proper authorities" is particularly pertinent in this situation. The client's action instructing Doe to not render a written report, when coupled with XYZ's testimony at the hearing, raises the question of Doe's obligation under Section 2(c). The Board interprets the language in the context of the facts to mean that it would now be "unprofessional conduct" for Doe to not take further action to protect the public interest.

It is not material, in the Board's view, that the subject matter does not involve plans and specifications as stipulated in Section 2(c). The Board interprets "plans and specifications" in this section to include all engineering instruments of service. That particular reference must be read in light of the overall thrust of Sections 2 and 2(a), both of which indicate clearly that the paramount duty of the engineer is to protect the public safety, health, and welfare in a broad context. As has been noted in a prior case, even though involving unrelated facts and circumstances, "It is basic to the entire concept of a profession that its members will devote their interests to the public welfare, as is made abundantly clear in Section 2 and Section 2(a) of the Code."

Section 7 of the Code does not give the Board pause because the action of the engineer in advising the proper authority of the apparent danger to the public interest will not in this case be disclosing the technical processes or business affairs of the client.

CONCLUSION:

Doe has an ethical obligation to report his findings to the authority upon learning of the hearing.

Note: This opinion is based on data submitted to the Board of Ethical Review and does not necessarily represent all of the pertinent facts when applied to a specific case. This opinion is for educational purposes only and should not be construed as expressing any opinion on the ethics of specific individuals. This opinion may be reprinted without further permission, provided that this statement is included before or after the text of the case.

NSPE Case No. 80-4

Participation of Engineer with Competing Firms for the Same Contract

FACTS:

Engineer Able, on behalf of the firm of which he is a principal, submitted a statement of qualifications to a governmental agency for a project. In due course, he was notified that his firm was on the "short list" for consideration along with several other firms, but it was indicated to him that his firm did not appear to have qualifications in some specialized aspects of the requirements, and that it might be advisable for the firm to consider a joint venture with another firm with such capabilities. Engineer Able thereupon contacted Engineer Baker, a principal of a firm with the background required for the specialized requirements, and inquired if the Baker firm would be interested in a joint venture if Able was awarded the job. The Baker firm responded in the affirmative.

Thereafter, Engineer Carlson, a principal in a firm that was also on the "short list," contacted Engineer Baker and indicated the same requirement for a joint venture for specialized services, and also asked if the Baker firm would be willing to engage in a joint venture if the Carlson firm was selected for the assignment. Baker also responded in the affirmative to Carlson but did not notify Able of his response to Carlson.

QUESTION:

Is it ethical for Engineer Baker to agree to participate in a joint venture arrangement with more than one of the firms since he did not make a full disclosure to all of the firms?

REFERENCES:

Code of Ethics – Section 1 – "The Engineer will be guided in all his professional relations by the highest standards of integrity, and will act in professional matters for each client or employer as a faithful agent or trustee."

Section 8 – "The Engineer shall disclose all known or potential conflicts of interest to his employer or client by promptly informing them of any business connections, interests, or other circumstances which could influence his judgment or the quality of his services, or which might reasonably be construed by others as constituting a conflict of interest."

DISCUSSION:

As is often the case in a particularized set of facts, the Code does not specifically address the question, but we have the latitude to read related sections of the Code to apply within reasonable limits. On that basis, Section 8 on conflicts of interest and Section 1 on professional integrity are stated broadly enough to provide a basis for an opinion.

The thrust of Section 8 is to require full and complete disclosure of known or potential conflicts of interest, but it does not necessarily rule out such conflicts if they exist. If there was objection by any party, the ethical question would have to be determined under the pertinent facts of that case.

The Board did not have to reach that question in this case, however, because there is not a conflict of interest under the facts before us. The Code does not define "conflict of interest." At the very least, however, it means that "a professional person may not take action or make decisions which would divide his loyalties or interests from those of his employer or client."

In this case there is no potential or actual division of loyalty as to either the Able or Carlson firm on the part of Baker. Assuming that Baker is willing to work out a joint venture agreement with either firm which might secure the contract, his loyalty would be centered only with the one selected firm. As a joint venturer, in fact, he would be a party to a single legal entity (the joint venture) for the one contract.

Technically, the disclosure requirement of Section 8 would not mandate that Baker advise Able of the contact from Carlson or advise Carlson that he had talked to Able because at this point Baker does not have a "client," as such.

However, the requirement of Section 1 for highest standards of integrity makes it ethically necessary for Baker to contact both of the firms and advise each that he had indicated his willingness to participate in a joint venture with either. In this connection we consider that the agreement of Baker to work with Able constitutes a relationship of trust which should not be diluted by establishing a similar and possibly competitive relationship with Carlson unless disclosure is made to all concerned.

CONCLUSION:

It is unethical for Engineer Baker to agree to participate in a joint venture agreement with more than one of several firms being considered for an engineering engagement since he did not make a disclosure to all of the firms.

NSPE Case No. 69–13

Engineer's Disclosure of Potential Conflict of Interest

FACTS:

Engineer A is retained by the state to perform certain feasibility studies relating to a possible highway spur. The state is considering the possibility of constructing the highway spur through an area that is adjacent to a residential community in which Engineer A's residence is located. After learning of the proposed location for the spur, Engineer A discloses to the state the fact that his residential property may be affected by the new spur and fully discloses the potential conflict with the state. The state does not object to Engineer A performing the work. Engineer A proceeds with his feasibility study and ultimately recommends that the spur be constructed. The highway spur is constructed.

QUESTION:

Was it ethical for Engineer A to perform the feasibility study despite the fact that his land may be affected thereby?

REFERENCES:

Code of Ethics – Section II.4: "Engineers shall act in professional matters for each employer or client as faithful agents or trustees."

Section II.4.a: "Engineers shall disclose all known or potential conflicts of interest to their employers or clients by promptly informing them of any business association, interest, or other circumstances which could influence or appear to influence their judgment or the quality of their services."

DISCUSSION:

The Board has noted on numerous occasions that the ethical duty of the engineer in areas of conflict of interest is to inform the client of those business connections or interests that may influence the judgment and quality of the engineering services. Those decisions have been consistent with the provisions of Section II.4.a. of the NSPE Code of Ethics cited above.

While that provision of the Code has been interpreted many times over the years, it is, as are all Code provisions, subject to constant examination and reinterpretation. For any code of ethics to have meaning, it must be a living, breathing document which responds to situations that evolve and develop.

This Board has generally interpreted that Code provision in a strict manner. Previously, the Board reviewed a situation where an engineer was an officer in an incorporated engineering consulting firm that was engaged primarily in civil engineering projects for clients. Early in the engineer's life, he had acquired a tract of land by inheritance, which was in an area being developed for residential and industrial use. The engineer's firm had been retained to study and recommend a water and sewer system in the general area of his land interest. The question faced by the Board under those facts was, "May the engineer ethically design a water and sewer system in the general area of his land interest?" The Board ruled that the engineer could not ethically design the system under those circumstances.

The Board acknowledged that the question was a difficult one to resolve, pointing to the fact that there was no conflict of interest when the engineer entered his practice but that the conflict developed in the normal course of his practice. It became apparent that his study and recommendation could lead to the location of a water and sewer system that might cause a considerable appreciation in the value of his land depending upon the exact location of certain system elements in proximity to his land. The Board stated that while the engineer must make full disclosure of his personal interest to his client before proceeding with the project, such disclosure was not enough under the Code. The Board stated, "He can avoid such a conflict under these facts either by disposing of his land holdings prior to undertaking the commission or by declining to perform the services if it is not feasible or desirable for him to dispose of his land at the particular time." The Board concluded by saying: "This is a harsh result, but so long as men are in their motivations somewhat 'lower than angels,' it is a necessary conclusion to achieve compliance with both the letter and the spirit of the Code of Ethics. The real test of ethical conduct is not when compliance with the Code comports with the interests of those it is intended to govern, but when compliance is adverse to personal interests."

In its reading of the Code of Ethics, the Board took a strict view of the meaning of the Code provisions then in force, which stated:

"8. The Engineer will endeavor to avoid a conflict of interest with his employer or client, but when unavoidable, the Engineer shall fully disclose the circumstances to his employer or client."

"8(a). The Engineer will inform his client or employer of any business connections, interests, or circumstances which may be deemed as influencing his judgment or the quality of his services to his client or employer."

It is clear from a reading of that case that the Board focused its attention on the first clause of Section 8 stating that "The engineer will endeavor to avoid a conflict of interest with his employer or client." Undoubtedly, the Board reasoned that this was the basic obligation of the engineer in this context, and that any qualification of that obligation would dilute the essential meaning and intent of that obligation. Therefore, the Board did not choose to rely upon the remaining provisions contained in Sections 8 and 8(a) in reaching its decision. Instead, the Board determined that under the facts it would not be sufficient for the engineer to make full disclosure of his personal interest to the client in order to properly address the potential conflict-of-interest question.

While the reasoning of the Board is extremely important in understanding the ethical dimensions of the instant case, the decision becomes less significant in view of the fact that the Code provisions under which the decision was rendered have been crucially altered. (See Code Sections II.4. and II.4.a., the successor provisions to Section 8.)

As one can readily see, the phrase "engineer will endeavor to avoid a conflict of interest with his employer or client…" is no longer contained in the applicable Code provision. Clearly, the reason for that omission is certainly not out of a lack of desire within the engineering profession for an ethical proscription relating to conflicts of interest. Truly, ethical dilemmas relating to conflicts of interest are some of the most significant issues facing the engineering profession today.

Nevertheless, the provision in the Code relating to conflicts of interest was amended and those changes impact upon the manner in which this Board regards the previous case, as well as the manner in which the Board interprets the Code. It is evident that had Sections II.4. and II.4.a. been in effect at the time the Board decided the prior case, the Board may well have reached a different result.

While it is not the Board's role to speculate upon the intent of this significant change in the NSPE Code of Ethics, the Board does think that some expression in that regard would assist readers in understanding the basis for the change. In no sense should this change be interpreted in any way to suggest a retreat by this Board or the Code of Ethics from a deep concern for dilemmas relating to conflicts of interest. Rather, it is the modifications in the Code that reflect recognition of the fact that conflicts of interest emerge in a multitude of degrees and circumstances and that a blanket, unqualified expression prohibiting engineers to avoid all activities that raise the shadow of a conflict of interest is not a workable approach.

It is often a question of degree as to what does and does not constitute a significant conflict of interest. Obvious and significant conflicts of interest are easily identifiable and should always be avoided. These difficult, multifaceted situations require discussion and consideration as they are complex and sometimes irresolvable. A code should address and provide guidance for these kinds of conflicts of interest. The new Code provisions sought to establish the ethical obligation to engage in dialogue with a client or employer on the difficult questions relating to conflicts of interest. It was for this reason that the Code provisions were altered.

Turning to the facts of the instant case, the ethical obligations contained in Section II.4.a. do not require the engineer to "avoid" any and all situations that may or may not raise the specter of a conflict of interest. Such an interpretation of the Code would leave engineers with neither any real understanding of the ethical issues nor any guidance as to how to deal with the problem. The basic purpose of a code of ethics is to provide the engineering profession with a better awareness and understanding of ethical issues that impact upon the public. Only through interacting with the public and clients will engineers be able to comprehend the true dimensions of ethical issues.

The Board assumes that, under the facts of this case, the state agency involved has a fully qualified staff which will ultimately review the recommendation of the engineer. Therefore, Engineer A's discussion with the client prior to performing the services and disclosing the possible conflict of interest came within the ethical guidelines of the Code and was a proper course to take in dealing with the conflict. In this case the Board did not state that the engineer can only avoid such a conflict either by "disposing of his land and holdings prior to undertaking the commission or by declining to perform the services if it is not feasible or desirable for him to dispose of his land at the particular time."

CONCLUSION:

It was not unethical for Engineer A to perform the feasibility study despite the fact that his land may be affected thereby.

NSPE Case No. 78–7

Commission Basis of Payment Under a Marketing Agreement

FACTS:

John Doe, P.E., has been engaged extensively in recent years in a variety of engineering activities in the international market. He determines that on the basis of his experience, familiarity with the special requirements of engineering work in other countries, and personal contacts with officials of certain foreign countries he could better serve the interests of the engineering profession, as well as his own economic interests, by representing United States firms that wish to engage in international engineering and lack a background in the special fields of knowledge required for that purpose, or which do not have the resources to develop the necessary skills to successfully enter that field.

Recognizing the inability of many U.S. firms to commit themselves to a substantial capital outlay to develop their potential in the international market pending the award of a contract, Doe drafts a plan, called a "Marketing Agreement," under which he offers his services to represent U.S. firms interested in obtaining international work. The agreement calls for Doe to provide information and develop contacts within stated geographical areas, to evaluate potential projects for the firms he represents, to coordinate project development, arrange contract terms between the client and the represented firm, and provide such other special services as the represented firms may authorize.

For these services Doe is to be paid a basic fee, the amount of which is to be negotiated on an individual firm basis, a monthly retainer fee of a negotiated amount on an individual firm basis, and a "marketing fee" of a negotiated percentage of the fees actually collected by the firm he represents for projects that were "marketed" by Doe.

QUESTION:

Is it ethical for an engineering firm to enter into such a "Marketing Agreement" with Doe?

REFERENCE:

Code of Ethics – Section II(b) – "He will not pay, or offer to pay, either directly or indirectly, any commission, political contribution, or a gift, or other consideration in order to secure work, exclusive of securing salaried positions through employment agencies."

DISCUSSION:

It is presumed that the case does not violate federal laws or laws of the country involved. It is clear that the "commercial marketing firm" involved is an individual professional engineer offering his services on a commission basis, in part.

In an earlier Board decision, a paramount factor was that a sales representative of an engineering firm to be paid on a combined salary-commission basis was not an engineer. In that case it was concluded that the firm could utilize the sales promotion of a nonengineer, provided he did not discuss engineering aspects of the project. The Board's comment on the commission payment issue was that "…this method of compensation is undesirable since it could lead to loss of confidence by the public in the professional nature of engineering services."

Extending that comment however, the Board said that the use of a commercial marketing firm would offend the Code of Ethics because "…the engineering firm has control over the conduct of an employee, whereas it has little or no control over the conduct of an outside marketing firm which operates on a commercial basis. The danger is thus much enhanced that a commercial marketing firm may more readily in its zeal to earn its compensation engage in conduct which may adversely reflect upon the dignity or honor of the profession."

Three members of the Board of Ethical Review, while signing that opinion, expressed "additional views" to the effect that "…in the context of modern business practices as required by our complex society and the increasing number of U.S. firms exporting their technical expertise on a global basis, there is a serious question as to whether the present language of the code is unduly restrictive while offering at best a limited measure of protection of the public interest." The members of the BER subscribing to the additional views suggested that the issue should be reviewed for a possible change in the pertinent Code language or concept. To date, however, Section II(b) of the Code has not been revised.

When the prohibition of commission fees as a basis to secure work is read in conjunction with other parts of Section II(b), i.e., political contributions or gifts, it would appear that the original purpose and intent were to foreclose circumstances which might arouse doubt or suspicion of impropriety in securing engineering assignments.

It is clear, however, that Section II(b) prohibits the payment of "any" commission in order to secure work (other than salaried positions), thereby ruling out the permissibility of a commission basis coupled with definite sums as a retainer fee or basic fee.

CONCLUSION:

It is not ethical for an engineering firm to enter into such a "marketing agreement" with Doe.

NSPE Case No. 92–9

Use of Disadvantaged Firm After Learning of Impropriety

FACTS:

Engineer A is a principal in a large consulting engineering firm specializing in civil and structural engineering. Engineer A's firm does a large percentage of its engineering work for public agencies at the state, federal, and local levels. Engineer A is frequently encouraged by representatives of those agencies to consider retaining the services of small, minority, or women-owned design firms as sub-consultants to the firm, particularly on publicly funded projects.

For about a year, Engineer A's firm has retained the services of Engineer B's firm, a disadvantaged firm of a type described above, on several public and private projects. Engineer A's firm has gotten a good deal of public relations benefit as a result of its retention of Engineer B's firm, particularly among its public and private clients. The work of Engineer B's firm is adequate but not of high quality. In addition, Engineer B suddenly began charging Engineer A much higher fees in recent months, particularly after an article appeared in a local publication that was very complementary of Engineer A's efforts to retain disadvantaged firms.

QUESTION:

What would be the proper action for Engineer A to take under the circumstances?

REFERENCES:

Preamble: "Engineering is an important and learned profession. The members of the profession recognize that their work has a direct and vital impact on the quality of life for all people. Accordingly, the services provided by engineers require honesty, impartiality, fairness, and equity, and must be dedicated to the protection of the public health, safety and welfare. In the practice of their profession, engineers must perform under a standard of professional behavior which requires adherence to the highest principles of ethical conduct on behalf of the public, clients, employers, and the profession."

Section II.2.a: "Engineers shall undertake assignments only when qualified by education or experience in the specific technical fields involved."

Section III.6: "Engineers shall uphold the principle of appropriate and adequate compensation for those engaged in engineering work."

DISCUSSION:

Over the past several years a significant amount of socioeconomic legislation and regulation has been enacted at the federal, state, and local levels to promote the retention of businesses that had been heretofore underrepresented in the procurement process. As a result, many engineering firms have been encouraged both by public and private clients to establish goals to retain qualified employees and consultants representative of such underrepresented groups.

This Board has never had occasion to examine a case in the context of such a program. As a general proposition, the Board believes the Code of Ethics is generally supportive of the establishment of voluntary programs that provide engineers with the opportunity to be of constructive service in community affairs and to work for its advancement and wellbeing. Many governmental and private procurement procedures take into account such factors consistent with their procurement requirements and standards.

Having made these general observations, we turn to the case before us. It appears that while the philosophy of establishing voluntary targets or goals for the retention of disadvantaged firms is not inconsistent with the objective of the Code of Ethics, the continued retention of a firm that is abusing its relationship with its client may be at odds with the intent of the Code. In order for an engineer to ethically engage in a joint venture, the engineer must maintain a careful scrutiny of the operation of the firm of the other engineer to assure, to the extent possible, that unethical conduct will not develop during and with respect to the joint venture. If an engineer's scrutiny of the operation of the firm reveals improper action, the engineer has an ethical obligation to disassociate with that firm in a manner that would not be prejudicial to his client.

Regarding Engineer B's unjustified escalation of his firm's fees and charges, the key to avoiding a misunderstanding in this area is through careful negotiation and discussion and through a "give and take" procedure. In the context of the present case, this type of negotiation was lacking. As it appears under the facts, Engineer B unilaterally imposed an escalation of his firm's fees and charges. Instead, Engineer B had an obligation to negotiate any future increases in his fees and charges with Engineer A's firm.

CONCLUSION:

Engineer A has an obligation to discuss and negotiate with Engineer B in an effort to improve the quality and relative value of Engineer B's services. If a mutual agreement cannot be reached concerning the terms and conditions of service, Engineer A should terminate his relationship with Engineer B and in the future continue to strive to retain qualified employees and consultants representative of such under-represented groups.

NSPE Case No. 75–11

Credit for Engineering Work Research Data

FACTS:

The XYZ Company headed by Engineer A offered to provide funding to professors in the chemistry department of a major university for research on removing poisonous heavy metals (copper, lead, nickel, zinc, chromium) from waste streams. The university then agreed to contract with XYZ Company to give the company exclusive use of the technology developed in the field of water treatment and wastewater stream treatment. Under the agreement, XYZ Company will provide a royalty to the university from profits derived from the use of the technology. Also, a group of the university professors organized QRS, a separate company to exploit applications of the technology other than the treatment of water and wastewater. At the same time that the university research was being conducted, XYZ continued to conduct research in the same area. Performance figures and conclusions were developed. XYZ freely shared the figures and conclusions with QRS.

At the university, Engineer B, a professor of civil engineering, wanted to conduct research and develop a paper relating to the use of the technology to treat sewage. Engineer B contacted the professors in the university's chemistry department. The chemistry professors provided XYZ's data to Engineer B for use in the research and paper. The professors did not reveal to Engineer B that the data was generated by Engineer A and XYZ Company.

Engineer B's paper was published in a major journal. Engineer A's data was displayed prominently in the paper, and the work of XYZ constituted a major portion of the journal. The paper credits two of the chemistry professors as major authors along with Engineer B. No credit was given to Engineer A or XYZ as the source of the data, the funds that supported the research. After publication, Engineer B learns about the actual source of the data and its finding.

QUESTION:

Does Engineer B have an obligation under the Code of Ethics to clarify the source of the data contained in the paper?

REFERENCES:

Section III.10: "Engineers shall give credit for engineering work to those to whom credit is due, and will recognize the proprietary interests of others."

Section III.10a: "Engineers shall, whenever possible, name the person or persons who may be individually responsible for designs, inventions, writings, or other accomplishments."

DISCUSSION:

The issue of providing credit for research work performed by others is a vital matter in this day and age. Its importance is more than merely crediting contributions of individuals who have performed work in an area of engineering and scientific research. In actual fact, funding decisions for research and development of various technologies are vitally affected by the credit and acknowledgments.

Engineer B did not knowingly fail to credit Engineer A or XYZ Company for its contributions to the research which formed the basis of his paper. Instead, Engineer B assumed that the material he received from the other professors was developed solely by those professors.

The Board concluded that Engineer B did not knowingly and deliberately fail to credit Engineer A or XYZ for its contributions to the research. However, had Engineer B made more of an effort to substantiate the sources contained in his paper, he may have been able to identify those sources. Also of concern is the conduct of the chemistry professors, who, for whatever reason(s), misled Engineer B by failing to reveal the sources of the data. While not technically covered by this Code, the conduct of the chemistry professors is clearly deplorable and is unacceptable under the philosophical standards embodied in the Code of Ethics.

Finally, the Board suggested Engineer B prepare and request that the journal publish a clarification of the matter explaining how the matter occurred along with an apology for any misunderstanding which may have arisen as a result of the publication of the paper.

CONCLUSION:

Engineer B has an obligation to request that the journal publish a clarification of the matter explaining how the matter occurred along with an apology for any misunderstanding which may have arisen as a result of the publication of the paper.

FE/EIT

FE: PM General Engineering Exam

CHAPTER 3

Mathematics

CHAPTER 3

MATHEMATICS

Mathematics is the most important basic tool for engineers. The fundamental elements of mathematics—algebra, geometry, vectors, calculus, and differential equations—are encountered frequently in the solution of engineering problems.

ALGEBRAIC CONCEPTS

Basic algebraic concepts include: factoring of polynomial terms, the solution of simultaneous equations, the solution of quadratic equations, the use of polar coordinates, trigonometric functions, logarithms, and complex numbers.

Factoring

Factoring most frequently takes the form of "removing" common factors from a series of terms in a mathematical expression, that is, from a polynomial. With more complex expressions, the factoring of polynomials is encountered. Though the factoring of polynomials is essentially using division, it is more intuitive in that it requires that one, or more, of the factors be determined by a "trial and error" process.

To illustrate, look at the polynomial $X^2 + 9 \times X + 20$. If there are factors for this polynomial, they are binomials of the form $(a \pm b)$. Thus:

- The first term in each must be X (to get X^2).
  Thus: $(X + \underline{\hspace{1em}}) \times (X + \underline{\hspace{1em}})$

- The second terms must be factors of 20. Try +2 and +10.
  $(X + 2) \times (X + 10)$

- Check these factors by determining the middle term, which calculates to $12 \times X$, which is not correct (it should be $9 \times X$).

- Try +4 and +5 as factors of 20. Thus, $(X + 4) \times (X + 5)$.

- Check these factors by determining the middle term, which calculates to $9 \times X$, which is correct.

Simultaneous Equations

Equations with more than one variable are solved simultaneously, requiring at least the same number of independent equations as there are variables for the solution. There are various techniques used to solve such equations. These techniques include "elimination of one variable," "addition and subtraction," and "substitution."

For a set of equations with two variables, the "elimination of one variable" technique consists of solving each of the equations for one of the variables and equating the results to solve for the remaining variable. To illustrate, look at the set of equations $2X + Y = 10$ and $3X - Y = 5$. First, solve each for the variable Y, obtaining $Y = 10 - 2X$ and $Y = 3X - 5$. Then equate $Y = Y$ and substitute the right side of each of the latter equations for their respective Y's. This yields the equation $10 - 2X = 3X - 5$. Now solving this equation, with the single variable X, by addition, subtraction, and division of the appropriate terms yields the result of $X = 3$. To solve for the remaining variable, Y, substitute the value 3 for X in either of the original equations, yielding the solution of $Y = 4$.

The technique of addition and subtraction consists of adding, or combining the equations such that the sum of the coefficients of one of the variables is equal to 0, and thus eliminating that variable in the equations. The resultant equation is then solved for the remaining variable. To illustrate: Look at the two equations, $2X + Y = 10$ and $3X - Y = 5$. By adding the right side to the right side and the left side to the left side, gives: $2X + 3X + Y - Y = 10 + 5$. Combining like terms gives $5X = 15$, or $X = 3$. Likewise, to solve for the remaining variable, Y, substitute the value 3 for X in either of the original equations, yielding the solution of $Y = 4$.

The technique of substitution consists of solving one of the equations for one of the variables in terms of the other variables, and substituting that value of the former variable into the other equations, which thus becomes an equation of one remaining variable. To illustrate: solving the first equation $2X + Y = 10$ for Y yields $Y = 10 - 2X$. Substituting this value of Y into the second equation, $3X - Y = 5$, yields $3X - (10 - 2X) = 5$.

Solving this equation, with the single variable X, by addition, subtraction, and division of the appropriate terms yields the result of $X = 3$. To solve for the remaining variable, Y, again substitute the value 3 for X in either of the original equations, yielding the solution of $Y = 4$.

For sets of equations with three or more variables, this procedure is repeated eliminating one variable at a time, until a single variable remains. The solution of this variable is then substituted in a previous equation to determine the second variable. The solution for the two variables is then substituted into an earlier equation to solve for the third variable, and so forth for any remaining variables.

Quadratic Equations

Quadratic equations are equations in which the highest exponent of the variable is 2. There are several techniques for solving quadratics, but they all use the various techniques of factoring polynomials. When solving a quadratic equation, it is important to remember the principle that when the product of two or more factors equals 0, then one or more of the factors equals 0.

Certain quadratics can be factored into two (or more) terms, each containing variables with an exponent of 1. When the quadratic expression also is equal to 0, then each of the factors can be equated to 0, effecting a simple solution to each of the factors. Other quadratics can be factored into two equal terms, each containing a variable with the exponent of 1. Each of these factors can also be equated to 0 effecting a simple solution to each of the factors.

This technique has been used to develop a solution to a general quadratic equation in the form: $a \times X^2 + b \times X + c = 0$, where

a, b, and c are the coefficients.

The solution to this general equation is:

$$X = \{-b \pm [b^2 - 4 \times ac]^{1/2}\}/(2a).$$

Using the equation $x^2 - 5x + 4 = 0$ as an example, the coefficients are: $a = 1$, $b = -5$, and $c = 4$. Substituting these into the general solution yields:

$$x = \{-(-5) \pm [(-5)^2 - 4 \times 1 \times 4]^{1/2}\}/(2 \times 1)$$

$$x = \{+5 \pm [25 - 16]^{1/2}\}/(2) = (5 \pm 3)/2$$

$$x = 8/2 = 4, \text{ and } x = 2/2 = 1$$

Polar Coordinates

Any curve can be expressed in polar coordinates. That is, the coordinates of each point on a curve can be defined in terms of its distance from the origin of Cartesian coordinates (X, Y) and the angle from the positive X axis. Thus, for any curve:

$$x = r \times \cos\theta \text{ and } y = r \times \sin\theta$$

where: x = the position of a point along the X axis; y = the position of a point along the Y axis; r = the linear distance of a point from the origin; θ = the angle between the positive X axis and the line connecting the point on the curve and the origin.

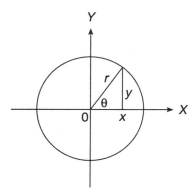

It can be seen from this relationship that r can be visualized as the hypotenuse of a triangle formed by itself and the distances from the X and Y axes, with its magnitude determined using the Pythagorean Theorem.

Trigonometric Functions

Trigonometric functions are simply the ratios of sides of a right triangle to each other, where the ratios are unique for each angle, and therefore define each angle. The values of these trigonometric functions have been calculated and tabulated and are readily available in engineering handbooks, on calculators, and in computers. For a right triangle with legs a and b and a hypotenuse c, with angle α opposite leg a and angle β opposite leg b, the basic trigonometric functions, or ratios, sine (sin), cosine (cos), tangent (tan), and cotangent (cot) are:

$$\sin(\alpha) = \frac{a}{c}; \sin(\beta) = \frac{b}{c}; \qquad \cos(\alpha) = \frac{b}{c}; \cos(\beta) = \frac{a}{c}$$

$$\tan(\alpha) = \frac{a}{b}; \tan(\beta) = \frac{b}{a}; \qquad \cot(\alpha) = \frac{b}{a}; \cot(\beta) = \frac{a}{b}$$

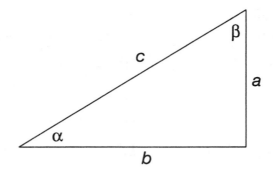

Trigonometric functions encountered in various engineering situations are merely algebraic manipulations of these ratios.

Logarithms

Logarithms are exponents of a number, in which the number is referred to as the base of the logarithm. Multiplying algebraic monomials of the same base consists of adding or subtracting the exponents. Thus, by expressing numbers as powers of a base number, one is able to multiply and divide these numbers by merely adding or subtracting the exponents of the base number, in which exponents are called logarithms.

The two most frequently used logarithms are called *common logarithms* and *natural logarithms*. Common logarithms use the number 10 as a base. Thus, common logarithms are no more than exponents of the number 10. Natural logarithms use an infinite series, represented by *e*, as a base. The number *e* is one of the most important numbers in mathematics and is approximately equal to 2.718. (It is more precisely equal to the sum of the series:

$$1 + \sum \frac{1}{(n!)}$$

where *n* ranges from 1 to infinity.) This number occurs frequently in describing many physical phenomena. It is essential in calculus and in the solution of differential equations.

Complex Numbers

Complex numbers are algebraic expressions in which at least one term is "imaginary." This is defined as a term that contains the square root of −1, usually indicted by the letter *i*. Though complex numbers behave similarly to polynomials with *i* being treated as any other variable, there are certain properties and characteristics that are unique to complex numbers.

- Powers of *i*: Like any polynomial, when it is multiplied by another, i results in powers of i^2, i^3, i^4, and so on. These powers of i can be evaluated by remembering that i is merely $(-1)^{1/2}$. Thus:

$$i^2 = [(-1)^{1/2}]^2 = -1$$

$$i^3 = [(-1)^{1/2}]^3 = -1 \times i \text{ or } -i$$

$$i^4 = [(-1)^{1/2}]^4 = (-1) \times (-1) \text{ or } +1$$

$$i^5 = i^4 \times (-1)^{1/2} = +1 \times i \text{ or } i$$

- Complex numbers are equal if, and only if, the real part of one is equal to the real part of the other, and the imaginary part of one is equal to the imaginary part of the other. This can be stated as

$a + bi = c + di$ if and only if $a = c$ and $b = d$.

- The sum or difference of complex numbers $a + bi$ and $c + di$ is the complex number

$$(a + c) + (b + d)i.$$

- The product of complex numbers $a + bi$ and $c + di$ is the complex number

$$(ac - bd) + (ad + bc)i.$$

(Note: $bi \times di = bd \times i^2 = bd \times (-1) = -bd$.)

VECTORS

Some numbers are limited to a property called "magnitude." These numbers are called *scalar* quantities and they are used to represent physical entities as length and mass. Other numbers have the properties of "magnitude" and "direction." These numbers are called *vector* quantities and they are used to represent physical concepts such as force and velocity. Vectors are represented by arrows whose direction represents the direction of the vector, and whose length represents its magnitude. Algebraically, a two-dimensional vector is represented as:

$$v = a \times i + b \times j$$

where:

$a \times i =$ the component of the vector parallel to the X axis

$b \times j =$ the component of the vector parallel to the Y axis

(The magnitude of this vector is equal to $(a^2 + b^2)^{1/2}$ and the slope of the angle between the vector and the X axis is equal to a/b.)

It is also important to remember that vectors add by adding the legs parallel to the X axis to each other, and the legs parallel to the Y axis to each other. Algebraically stated:

$$v_1 = a_1 \times i + b_1 \times j \text{ and } v_2 = a_2 \times i + b_2 \times j$$

yield the new vector, v_3

$$v_3 = (v_1 + v_2) = (a_1 + a_2) \times i + (b_1 + b_2) \times j$$

CALCULUS CONCEPTS

Calculus has been called the mathematics of limits. It is based on the definition of a *derivative*, which is defined in terms of a limit. Basic calculus concepts include differentiation, integration, infinite series, and transformations.

Differentiation and Integration

The derivative of a function at any point is equal to the instantaneous rate of change of that function with respect to the independent variable at that point. It represents the slope of the tangent to the curve, which graphically represents that function, at that specific point.

A derivative of a function is algebraically defined as:

$$f'(x_1) = \text{limit(as } x_2 \rightarrow x_1) \text{ of } \frac{f(x_2) - f(x_1)}{x_2 - x_1}$$

where:

$f'(x_1)$ = derivative of a function of the independent variable, x_1, at that point

$f(x_2)$ = the function evaluated at the point x_2

$f(x_1)$ = the function evaluated at the point x_1

Calculus also includes the concept of integration, which can be viewed as the reverse of differentiation. Integration of a function represents the summation of infinitely small area elements under the curve, usually with specified limits of the independent variable. Integration of a function is a more intuitive process than differentiation. However, it is generally defined as:

$$U^n \times dU = \frac{U^{(n+1)}}{(n+1) + C}$$

where: U^n = a function raised to the nth power and C = the constant of integration.

Infinite Series

A series is a sequence of mathematical expressions with an orderly procession from one term in the sequence to the next. Basic generic sequences include arithmetic series, geometric series, and power series. Series can be *divergent*, *convergent*, or *oscillating*. A divergent series is one where the sum of the terms increases without limit as the number of terms included increases. A convergent series is one where the sum of the series approaches a specific value as the number of terms in the series approaches infinity. An oscillating series is one where the sum of the series does not approach a specific value as the number of terms in the series approaches infinity, but rather oscillates between a finite upper and lower limit.

PROBLEM 1:

Find:

$$\lim_{x \to \infty} (x\sqrt{x^2 + 1} - x^2).$$

SOLUTION:

We can find this limit by three different methods. For the first method, let:

$$\lim_{x \to \infty} (x\sqrt{x^2 + 1} - x^2) = \lim_{x \to \infty} (x\sqrt{x^2 + 1} - x^2)\left(\frac{x\sqrt{x^2 + 1} + x^2}{x\sqrt{x^2 + 1} + x^2}\right)$$

$$= \lim_{x \to \infty} \frac{x^2}{x\sqrt{x^2 + 1} + x^2}$$

since:

$$= \lim_{x \to \infty} \frac{1}{\left(\sqrt{1 + \frac{1}{x^2}} + 1\right)} = \frac{1}{2}$$

$$\lim_{n \to \infty} \frac{1}{n^2} = 0$$

For the second method, we use the following theorem:

$$f(x), g(x) \in C^{n+1} \text{ for } a \le x \le b.$$

In addition, let $f^{(k)}(a) = g^{(k)}(a) = 0$ for $k = 0, 1, \ldots, n$ and let $g^{(n+1)}(a) \ne 0$. Then:

$$\lim_{x \to a^+} \frac{f(x)}{g(x)} = \frac{f^{(n+1)}(a)}{g^{(n+1)}(a)}$$

To be able to apply this theorem to the given problem, we must replace x by $\frac{1}{y}$ and let y approach zero. Then:

$$\lim_{x \to \infty} (x\sqrt{x^2 + 1} - x^2) = \lim_{y \to 0} \left(\frac{1}{y}\sqrt{\frac{1}{y^2} + 1} - \frac{1}{y^2} \right) \qquad (1)$$

$$= \lim_{y \to 0} \left(\frac{\sqrt{y^2 + 1} - 1}{y^2} \right)$$

Now, let $f(y) = (y^2 + 1)^{1/2} - 1$ and $g(y) = y^2$. Then:

$$f'(y) = y(y^2 + 1)^{-1/2}, \; g'(y) = 2y$$

$$f''(y) = (y^2 + 1)^{-1/2} - y^2(y^2 + 1)^{-3/2}, \; g''(y) = 2$$

Here, $n = 1$ since $f(0), g(0), f'(0), g'(0)$ each equal zero. Hence:

$$\lim_{y \to 0} \frac{f(y)}{g(y)} = \frac{f''(a)}{g''(a)}$$

where a is equal to 0. Hence:

$$\lim_{y \to 0} \frac{f(y)}{g(y)} = \frac{f''(0)}{g''(0)} = \frac{1}{2}$$

Thus, by (1):

$$\lim_{x \to \infty} (x\sqrt{x^2 + 1} - x^2) = \frac{1}{2}$$

For the third method, expand the function in powers of $1/x$. Hence:

$$\lim_{x \to \infty} x\sqrt{x^2 + 1} - x^2 = \lim_{x \to \infty} x^2 \left[\left(1 + \frac{1}{x^2} \right)^{\frac{1}{2}} - 1 \right]$$

(by the binomial theorem)

$$= \lim_{x \to \infty} x^2 \left(\frac{1}{2x^2} - \frac{1}{8x^4} + ... \right)$$

$$= \lim_{x \to \infty} \left(\frac{1}{2} - \frac{1}{8x^2} + ... \right) = \frac{1}{2}$$

Since:

$$\lim_{n \to \infty} \frac{1}{n^p} = 0 \text{ for } p > 0,$$

and:

$$\lim_{n \to \infty} (S_{n_1} + S_{n_2} + ...) = S_1 + S_2 + ...$$

given that:

$$\lim_{n \to \infty} S_{n_i} = S_i$$

PROBLEM 2:

Determine if the series

$$\frac{1}{2} + \frac{1}{3} + \frac{1}{2^2} + \frac{1}{3^2} + \frac{1}{2^3} + \frac{1}{3^3} + ...$$

is convergent or divergent.

SOLUTION:

The series can be rewritten as the sum of the sequence of numbers given by

$$a_n = \begin{cases} \dfrac{1}{2^{(n+1)/2}} & \text{if } n \text{ is odd } (n > 0) \\ \dfrac{1}{3^{n/2}} & \text{if } n \text{ is even } (n > 0) \end{cases}$$

Now the ratio test states: If

$$a_k > 0 \text{ and } \lim_{k \to \infty} \frac{a_k + 1}{a_k} = \ell < 1, \text{ then:}$$

$$\sum_{k=1}^{\infty} a_k$$

converges. Similarly, if:

$$\lim_{k \to \infty} \frac{a_k + 1}{a_k} = \ell \ (1 < \ell \le \infty)$$

then:

$$\sum_{k=1}^{\infty} a_k \text{ diverges.}$$

If $\ell = 1$, the test fails. Therefore, applying this test gives:

If a_n is odd:

$$\lim_{n\to\infty} \frac{a_n + 1}{a_n} = \lim_{n\to\infty} \frac{\dfrac{-1}{3^{n/2}}}{\dfrac{1}{2^{(n+1)/2}}} = \lim_{n\to\infty} \frac{2^{(n+1)/2}}{3^{n/2}} = \lim_{n\to\infty}\left(\frac{2}{3}\right)^{n/2} 2^{1/2} = 0$$

If a_n is even:

$$\lim_{n\to\infty} \frac{a_n + 1}{a_n} = \lim_{n\to\infty} \frac{\dfrac{1}{2^{(n+1)/2}}}{\dfrac{1}{3^{n/2}}} = \lim_{n\to\infty}\left(\frac{3}{2}\right)^{n/2} 2 1/2$$

and no limit exists.

Hence, the ratio test gives two different values, one <1 and the other >1; therefore, the test fails to determine if the series is convergent. Thus, another test, known as the root test, is now applied. This test states that:

$$\sum_{k=1}^{\infty} a_k$$

is a series of nonnegative terms, and let:

$$\lim_{n\to\infty}\left(\sqrt[n]{a_n}\right) = S, \text{ where } 0 \leq S \leq \infty$$

If:

1) $0 \leq S < 1$, the series converges.

2) $1 < S \leq \infty$, the series diverges.

3) $S = 1$, the series may converge or diverge.

If a_n is odd, applying this test yields:

$$\lim_{n\to\infty} \sqrt[n]{a_n} = \lim_{n\to\infty} \sqrt[n]{\frac{1}{2^{(n+1)/2}}} = \lim_{n\to\infty} \sqrt[n]{\frac{1}{2^{n/2}}} \sqrt[n]{\frac{1}{2^{1/2}}}$$

$$= \lim_{n\to\infty} \frac{1}{\sqrt{2}} \frac{1}{2^{1/2n}} = \frac{1}{\sqrt{2}} < 1$$

If a_n is even:

$$\lim_{n\to\infty} \sqrt[n]{a_n} = \lim_{n\to\infty} \sqrt[n]{\frac{1}{3^{n/2}}} = \frac{1}{\sqrt{3}} < 1$$

Thus, since for both cases, the

$$\lim_{n\to\infty} \sqrt[n]{a_n} < 1,$$

the series coverges.

Certain specific types of convergent infinite series can be used to define or approximate functions that describe certain physical situations that cannot otherwise be easily described using predefined or tabulated functions. The Taylor series is often used for polynomial type series over a specific range. For more complex series over a large range, the Fourier series is used. The process whereby these series are used is frequently referred to as an "expansion," such as a Taylor expansion or a Fourier expansion. Such expansions are illustrated in the following examples.

PROBLEM 3:

Derive the series expansion

$$\sin^{-1} x = x + \frac{1}{2}\frac{x^3}{3} + \frac{1}{2}\times\frac{3}{4}\frac{x^5}{5} + \frac{1\times3\times5}{2\times4\times6}\frac{x^7}{7} + \dots$$

SOLUTION:

To derive the given series for $\sin^{-1}x$, we need the following theorem where f is a function defined by:

$$f(x) = \sum_{n=0}^{\infty} a_n x^n$$

where $R \neq 0$ for the power series. Then f is continuous in the open interval of convergence of the series. Moreover, if a and b are points of this interval:

$$\int_a^b f(x)dx = \sum_{n=0}^{\infty} a_n \frac{b^{n+1} - a^{n+1}}{n+1} \tag{1}$$

That is, the integral of the function is equal to the series obtained by integrating the original power series term by term, i.e.:

$$\int_a^b f(x)dx = \sum_{n=0}^{\infty} a_n \int_a^b x^n dx$$

To apply this theorem we start with the fact that:

$$\sin^{-1} x = \int_0^x \frac{dt}{\sqrt{1-t^2}} \qquad (2)$$

Now (2) is valid if $|x| \le 1$; however, the integral is improper if $x = \pm 1$ since the integrand becomes infinite at $t = \pm 1$. Now by the binomial theorem:

$$(1+x)^r = 1 + rx + \frac{r(r-1)}{2!}x^2 + \ldots + \frac{r(r-1) \ldots (r-n+1)}{n!}x^n + \ldots$$

when $|x| < 1$, and where r is any real number.

We replace x by $-t^2$ and let $r = -\frac{1}{2}$ to yield:

$$(1-t^2)^{-1/2} = 1 - \frac{1}{2}(-t^2) + \frac{\left(-\frac{1}{2}\right)\left(-\frac{3}{2}\right)}{2!}(-t^2)^2 +$$

$$\frac{\left(-\frac{1}{2}\right)\left(-\frac{3}{2}\right)\left(-\frac{5}{2}\right)}{3!}(-t^2)^3 + \ldots$$

$$= 1 + \frac{1}{2}t^2 + \frac{1\times3}{2\times4}t^4 + \frac{1\times3\times5}{2\times4\times6}t^6 + \ldots$$

where this result is valid if $|t| < 1$. Therefore, the series has radius of convergence $R = 1$. Thus, by the theorem we may integrate the series from $t = 0$ to $t = x$ if $|x| < 1$. That is:

$$\sin^{-1} x = \int_0^x \frac{dt}{\sqrt{1-t^2}} = \int_0^x dt + \int_0^x \frac{t^2}{2}dt + \int_0^x \frac{1\times3 t^4}{2\times4}dt + \ldots$$

$$= x + \frac{1}{2}\frac{x^3}{3} + \frac{1\times3}{2\times4}\frac{x^5}{5} + \frac{1\times3\times5}{2\times4\times6}\frac{x^7}{7} + \ldots$$

if $|x| < 1$. This is the desired expansion.

PROBLEM 4:

Find the Fourier series of the function $f(x) = e^x$, $-\pi < x < \pi$.

SOLUTION:

The given function is defined on the familiar interval $(-\pi, \pi)$. A good habit to acquire is to recall the most general definition of a Fourier series of a function and then use the particular values given in the problem in this definition. Thus, recall that the Fourier series of a function $f(x)$, which has a period $2c$ and defined on some domain D of the real numbers, $f:D \to R$, is given by:

$$f(x) \sim \frac{a_0}{2} + \sum_{n=1}^{\infty} \left[a_n \cos\left(\frac{\pi n x}{c}\right) + b_n \sin\left(\frac{\pi n x}{c}\right) \right] \tag{1}$$

where the coefficients are given by:

$$a_n = \frac{1}{c} \int_a^{a+2c} f(x) \cos\left(\frac{\pi n x}{c}\right) dx \tag{2}$$

$$b_n = \frac{1}{c} \int_a^{a+2c} f(x) \sin\left(\frac{\pi n x}{c}\right) dx \tag{3}$$

where a is any number such that the interval $(a, a+2c)$ is contained in D. In the case at hand, $f(x) = e^x$, $x \epsilon(-\pi, \pi)$ is only defined on an interval of length 2π. Hence, (1) represents the periodic extension of f over the whole real axis. (Note that f is not periodic within that interval, so 2π is the only period that can be assigned any meaning here.) Therefore, in equations (1)–(3) the substitutions to be made for this particular function are:

$$c = \pi; \; a = -\pi; \; f(x) = e^x. \tag{4}$$

Using (4), the coefficients become:

$$a_0 = \frac{1}{\pi} \int_{-\pi}^{\pi} e^x dx = \frac{2}{\pi} \frac{e^\pi - e^{-\pi}}{2} = \frac{2}{\pi} \sin h\pi$$

$$a_n = \frac{1}{\pi} \int_{-\pi}^{\pi} e^x \cos nx \, dx = \frac{1}{\pi} \left[e^x \frac{(\cos nx + n \sin nx)}{n^2 + 1} \right]_{-\pi}^{\pi}$$

$$= (-1)^n \frac{e^\pi - e^{-\pi}}{(n^2 + 1)\pi} = (-1)^n \frac{2 \sin h\pi}{(n^2 + 1)\pi}$$

$$b_n = \frac{1}{\pi} \int_{-\pi}^{\pi} e^x \sin nx \, dx = \frac{1}{\pi} \left[e^x \frac{(\sin nx - n \cos nx)}{n + 1} \right]_{-\pi}^{\pi}$$

$$= (-1)^{n+1} \frac{e^{\pi} - e^{-\pi}}{(n^2 + 1)\pi} n$$

$$= -\frac{(-1)^n 2n \, \sinh \pi}{(n^2 + 1)\pi}$$

Substituting these values back into the Fourier expression, (1), with the substitutions of (3) gives:

$$f(x) \sim \frac{a_0}{2} + \sum_{n=1}^{\infty} (a_n \cos nx + b_n \sin nx)$$

$$= \frac{\sinh \pi}{\pi} + \sum_{n=1}^{\infty} \left[\frac{(-1)^n 2 \, \sinh \pi}{(n^2 + 1)\,\pi} \cos nx - \frac{(-1)^n 2n \, \sinh \pi}{(n^2 + 1)\,\pi} \sin nx \right]$$

$$= \frac{\sinh \pi}{\pi} \left\{ 1 + 2 \sum_{n=1}^{\infty} \left[\frac{(-1)^n}{n^2 + 1} (\cos nx - n \sin nx) \right] \right\} \tag{5}$$

Note that the symbol ~ is used in (5) since no determination of the convergence of the series to the function has yet been made. This will be done later and it will be shown that ~ may be replaced by =.

DIFFERENTIAL EQUATIONS

Equations which contain one or more derivatives, or differentials, are called *differential equations*. These are classified by three characteristics—*type, order*, and *degree*.

There are two *types,* namely, ordinary differential equations or partial differential equations. Ordinary equations are those where the dependent variable, Y, is a function of a single independent variable, X. However, if the dependent variable, Y, is a function of two or more independent variables, X and T, then partial derivative of Y may occur and the equation would be a partial differential equation.

The *order* of a differential equation is that of the highest order derivative that appears in the equation. A second order equation would contain a second derivative, but none higher. A third order equation would contain a third derivative, but none higher, and so forth.

The *degree* of a differential equation is the highest exponent of the highest order derivative which appears in the equation. Differential equations can be any combination of the above characteristics.

In addition to being classified in accordance with the above characteristics, they are also classified according to basic types for which there are differing solution techniques. These types include: homogeneous equations, first order – linear, linear equations with constant coefficients, and second order – linear – homogeneous – with constant coefficients.

The techniques for solving the various types of differential equations which are encountered in engineering problems are illustrated in the following examples:

Technique for Separable Differential Equations

PROBLEM 5:

Solve the differential equation

$$2(y-1)dx + (x^2 \sin y)dy = 0$$

SOLUTION:

Rewrite the differential form as an equation in derivative form.

$$\frac{dy}{dx} = \frac{-2(y-1)}{x^2 \sin y} \text{ for } x \neq 0$$

This equation is separable if we can write it in the form:

$$\frac{dy}{dx} = f(x)\, g(y)$$

Thus:

$$\frac{dy}{dx} = \left(\frac{-2}{x^2}\right)\left(\frac{y-1}{\sin y}\right)$$

and the equation is indeed separable.

$$\frac{\sin y}{y-1}dy = \frac{-2}{x^2}dx \text{ for } y \neq 1$$

Integration gives:

$$\int \frac{\sin y}{y-1}dy = \frac{2}{x} + c$$

where the expression on the left is not an elementary integral and must be evaluated by numerical methods if the limits of integration are given. *C* is an arbitrary constant of integration.

Note that we excluded the cases where $x = 0$ and where $y = 1$. Substitution in the original equation reveals that $x \int 0$ and $y \int 1$ are also solutions:

$$2(y - 1)d(0) + (0^2 \sin y)dy = 0 + 0 = 0$$

and

$$2(1 - 1)dx + (x^2 \sin 1)d(1) = 0 + 0 = 0$$

These last two solutions were lost in the separation progess.

Technique of the Transformation of Variables

PROBLEM 6:

Solve the first-order differential equation

$$e^{-y}\left(\frac{dy}{dx} + 1\right) = xe^x \tag{1}$$

SOLUTION:

Given an equation like (1), the best mode of attack is to isolate dy/dx. Thus, we have:

$$\frac{dy}{dx} = (xe^x e^y) - 1$$

In this form, it is not possible to separate the variables. If we rewrite the equation in the form

$$\frac{dy}{dx} + 1 = xe^x e^y = xe^{x+y}$$

and then make the substitution $u = x + y$, it is possible to obtain a separable equation.

$$u = x + y \; ; \; \frac{du}{dx} = \frac{dx}{dx} + \frac{dy}{dx} = 1 + \frac{dy}{dx} = xe^u$$

Thus:

$$\frac{du}{dx} = xe^u \; ; \; \frac{du}{e^u} = x \, dx$$

Integrating:

$$\int \frac{du}{e^u} = \int x \, dx \; ; \quad -e^{-u} = \frac{x^2}{2} + c_1$$

where c_1 is an arbitrary constant. We can write this as $e^{-u} + \dfrac{x^2}{2} = c$ where $c = -c_1$. Now we substitute $u = x + y$:

$$e^{-(x+y)} + \frac{x^2}{2} = c$$

Taking logarithms,

$$-(x + y)\ln e = \ln\left(c - \frac{x^2}{2}\right)$$

or

$$y = -\ln\left(c - \frac{x^2}{2}\right) - x$$

PROBLEM 7:

Solve $(x + \sin y)dx + (x \cos y - 2y)dy = 0$.

SOLUTION:

Rewriting the equation as:

$$\frac{dy}{dx} = -\frac{(x + \sin y)}{(x \cos y - 2y)}$$

we see that it is not possible to separate the variables so that

$$\frac{dy}{dx} = f(x)g(y).$$

Nor is the equation homogeneous. But checking for exactness, we find that

$$\frac{\partial}{\partial y}(x + \sin y) = \cos y = \frac{\partial}{\partial x}(x \cos y - 2y).$$

Therefore, the solution of the equation is a function $F(x, y) = c$ such that its total differential is given by:

$$dF = (x + \sin y)dx + (x \cos y - 2y)dy.$$

To find $F(x, y)$, $\int(x + \sin y)dx$ (treating y as a constant) gives

$$\frac{x^2}{2} + x \sin y + \varphi(y).$$

Now we must have

$$\frac{\partial}{\partial y}\left(\frac{x^2}{2} + x\sin y + \varphi(y)\right) = (x \cos y - 2y)$$

Therefore,

$$x \cos y + \varphi'(y) = x \cos y - 2y \text{ and } \varphi'(y) = -2y, \; \varphi(y) = -\int 2y\, dy$$

$$= -y^2 + c$$

The solution to the problem is:

$$F(x, y) = \frac{x^2}{2} + x\sin y - y^2 = c$$

This is an implicit solution of y; it is not possible to solve explicitly for y.

Technique for Homogeneous Differential Equations

PROBLEM 8:

Solve $2xy\, dy = (y^2 - x^2)dx$

SOLUTION:

This equation has homogeneous coefficients of the second degree. Homogeneous equations are of the form

$$f(xt, yt) = t^n f(x, y)$$

for all $t > 0$. Quantity n is called the degree. For example, if we let $f(x, y) = 2xy$ and $g(x, y) = y^2 - x^2$, then:

$$f(xt, yt) = 2xtyt = t^2(2xy) = t^2 f(x, y)$$

and

$$g(xt, yt) = (yt)^2 - (xt)^2 = t^2(y^2 - x^2) = t^2 g(x, y)$$

Separation of variables appears to be possible if we set $y = vx$ in this

$$\frac{d^2y}{dx^2} + 2\frac{dy}{dx} + y = m^2ce^{mx} + 2mce^{mx} + ce^{mx} = 0$$

or
$$ce^{mx}(m^2 + 2m + 1) = 0$$

Assuming e^{mx} to be different from zero, and considering $c = 0$ leads to a trivial solution, the only nontrivial solution occurs when:

$$m^2 + 2m + 1 = 0$$
or
$$(m + 1)^2 = 0$$

with a repeated root: $m = -1$.

Since a multiple root occurs here, in order to obtain a complete solution, we seek another linearly independent expression that satisfies the obtained auxiliary equation besides ce^{mx}. To get this, we take $y = c_2xe^{mx}$ and hence:

$$xc_2e^{mx}(m^2 + 2m + 1) + c_1e^{mx}(m^2 + 2m + 1) = 0$$

Thus:
$$y = (c_1 + c_2x)e^{mx}$$

is the desired general solution.

Using $m = -1$ as a root, the general solution of the differential equation is:

$$y = (c_1 + c_2x)e^{-x}$$

LAPLACE TRANSFORMS

The Laplace transform is a method that reduces the solution of certain differential equations to algebraic equations. They are most effective in the solution of linear and partial differential equations, which meet certain conditions of continuity and boundary conditions. Depending on the area of engineering, the algebraic equations are usually expressed in terms of the variables s or p, and the technique is sometimes referred to as "working" in the s plane, or the p plane.

The Laplace transform is obtained by multiplying both sides of a differential equation by the factor $e^{-pt}dt$, where t is the independent variable in the differential equation and where p is the algebraic variable. Alternatively, $e^{-st}dt$ can be used, where t is the independent variable in the differential equation and where s is the variable.

The Laplace transforms for many of the mathematical expressions

kind of equation. If we put $y = vx$, then $dy = v\,dx + x\,dv$. The equation becomes:

$$2x \times vx(v\,dx + x\,dv) = (v^2x^2 - x^2)dx$$

or

$$(v^2 + 1)dx + 2xv\,dv = 0$$

Separating variables, we get:

$$\frac{dx}{x} + \frac{2v\,dv}{v^2 + 1} = 0$$

Integrating, we have:

$$\ln x + \ln(v^2 + 1) = \ln C$$

$$\ln\,[x(v^2 + 1)] = \ln C$$

Therefore, $\quad x\left[\dfrac{y^2}{x^2} + 1\right] = C$, and $y^2 + x^2 = Cx$

Transposing Cx to the left-hand side of the general solution and completing the square, we obtain:

$$y^2 + \left(x - \frac{C}{2}\right)^2 = \frac{C^2}{4}$$

which represents a family of circles centered at $(C/2, 0)$ with radii of $C/2$.

Technique of Integrating Factors

PROBLEM 9:

Solve the equation:

$$(1 + 3x \sin y)dx - x^2 \cos y\,dy = 0$$

SOLUTION:

Since the equation is nonlinear and inexact, we must find an integrating factor to make it exact.

First, however, note that $\cos y\,dy$ is $\dfrac{d}{dy}$ (sin y). Hence, the substitution $\omega = \sin y$ suggests itself. Then:

$$(1 + 3x\omega)\,dx - x^2\,d\omega = 0 \text{ or } \frac{d\omega}{dx} - \frac{3\omega}{x} = \frac{1}{x^2}$$

This is a linear equation whose integrating factor is given by $\exp\int -\dfrac{3}{x}dx$

or $e^{\ln\left|x^{-3}\right|}$ which is $\dfrac{1}{x^3}$.

Then:
$$x^{-3}\frac{d\omega}{dx} \;-\; \frac{3}{x^4}\omega \;=\; \frac{1}{x^5}$$

Here:
$$x^{-3}\frac{d\omega}{dx} \;-\; \frac{3}{x^4}\omega \text{ is } \frac{d}{dx}(x^{-3}\omega)$$

Thus:
$$\frac{d}{dx}(x^{-3}\omega) = \frac{1}{x^5}$$

Integrating:
$$x^{-3}\omega \;=\; -\frac{1}{4}x^{-4}+\frac{1}{4}c$$

or
$$4x\omega = cx^4 - 1$$

Now insert the original term, $\sin y = \omega$; $4x\sin y = cx^4 - 1$ which is the required solution.

Technique for Homogeneous Differential Equations with Constant Coefficients

PROBLEM 10:

Solve the equation:

$$\frac{d^2y}{dx^2} + 2\frac{dy}{dx} + y \;=\; 0$$

SOLUTION:

Assume $y = ce^{mx}$ is the solution for the differential equation. Then, since

$$\frac{dy}{dx} = mce^{mx} \text{ and } \frac{d^2y}{dx^2} = m^2ce^{mx},$$

substituting for the given equation gives:

found in differential equations have already been calculated and tabulated. They are readily available in engineering and mathematical handbooks.

PROBLEM 11:

Find the Laplace transform of

$$f(t) = t^n$$

where n is a positive integer.

SOLUTION:

Using L as the Laplace transform operator with

$$L\{f(t)\} = \int_0^\infty e^{-st} f(t)dt$$

and first considering real s, we find:

$$L\{t^n\} = \int_0^\infty (e^{-st})(t^n)dt = \lim_{R\to\infty} \int_0^R t^n e^{-st} dt$$

For $s = 0$:

$$L\{t^n\} = \lim_{R\to\infty} \int_0^R t^n e^{0t} dt = \lim_{R\to\infty} \int_0^R t^n dt$$

$$= \lim_{R\to\infty} \frac{R^{n+1}}{n+1} = \infty$$

hence, $L\{t^n\}$

$$G(s) = \lim_{R\to\infty} \left. -\left(\frac{1}{s}e^{-st}\right)\right|_{t=0}^R$$

$$= \lim_{R\to\infty} \frac{1}{s}\left(1 - e^{-Rs}\right) = \frac{1}{s} - \lim_{R\to\infty} \frac{e^{-Rs}}{s} \qquad (1)$$

If $s < 0$, then $-Rs > 0$ for positive R; hence, e^{-Rs} approaches infinity as R approaches infinity, and the integral diverges. If $s > 0$, then $-Rs < 0$ for positive R; hence, e^{-Rs} approaches zero as R approaches infinity, and the integral converges to $1/s$.

Extending the domain of the Laplace transform to complex values of s, we evaluate the expression of e^{-Rs} by Euler's formula:

$$e^{-Rs} = e^{-R(Re\{s\}) - iR(Im\{s\})}$$

$$= e^{-R(Re\{s\})} [\cos[-R(Im\{s\})] + i \sin[-R(Im\{s\})]] \qquad (2)$$

where $Re\{s\}$ is the real part of s, $Im\{s\}$ is the imaginary part of s, and $i \equiv \sqrt{-1}$ is the imaginary constant. The cosine and sine functions are bounded; hence, expression (2) diverges as $R \to \infty$, for $Re\{s\} < 0$, and converges to zero for $Re\{s\} > 0$. In the case where $s \neq 0$ and $Re\{s\} = 0$, we have:

$$e^{-R(Re\{s\})} = 1$$

hence,

$$e^{-Rs} = \cos[-R(Im\{s\})] + i\,\sin[-R(Im\{s\})]$$

which is a nonconstant periodic function, thus, e^{-Rs} does not converge to any value as $R \to \infty$.

Since e^{-Rs} is the only expression that varies with R in equality (1), its convergence properties for $R \to \infty$ determine the convergence properties of $G(s)$. Thus, in general, $G(s)$ converges to $1/s$ for $Re\{s\} > 0$ and diverges otherwise.

Using L as the Laplace transform operator, with

$$L\{f(t)\} = F(s) \equiv \int_0^\infty e^{-st} f(t)\, dt$$

we take the Laplace transform of $f(t)$ for $t \geq 0$, noting that it does not exist for $s = 0$. Thus, for $s \neq 0$ and integrating by parts:

$$L\{t^n\} = \lim_{R \to \infty} \left\{ \frac{-t^n e^{-st}}{s} \Big|_{t=0}^{R} + \frac{n}{s} \int_0^R e^{-st} t^{n-1} dt \right\}$$

$$= \lim_{R \to \infty} \left\{ \frac{-R^n e^{-sR}}{s} + \frac{n}{s} \int_0^R e^{-st} t^{n-1}\, dt \right\}$$

$$= \lim_{R \to \infty} \left(\frac{-R^n e^{-sR}}{s} \right) + \frac{n}{s} \lim_{R \to \infty} \left(\int_0^R e^{-st} t^{n-1}\, dt \right)$$

$$= \lim_{R \to \infty} \left(\frac{-R^n e^{-sR}}{s} \right) + \frac{n}{s} L\{t^{n-1}\} \tag{1}$$

For $s \leq 0$ the argument of the limit in expression (1) diverges as $R \to \infty$; hence,

$$L\{t^n\}$$

does not exist. For $s > 0$ rewrite (1) as:

$$L\{t^n\} = \lim_{R\to\infty}\left(\frac{-R^n}{se^{sR}}\right) + \frac{n}{s}\,L\{t^{n-1}\} \qquad (2)$$

Since both the numerator and denominator in the argument of the limit in equation (2) approach ∞ as $R\to\infty$, we can apply L'Hospital's rule:

$$\lim_{R\to\infty}\left(\frac{-R^n}{se^{sR}}\right) = \lim_{R\to\infty}\left[\frac{d/dR(-R^n)}{d/dR(se^{sR})}\right] = \lim_{R\to\infty}\left(\frac{-nR^{n-1}}{s^2e^{sR}}\right) \qquad (3)$$

As long as the numerator and denominator of the argument of our limit approach ∞ as $R\to\infty$, we can iteratively apply L'Hospital's rule to equality (3):

$$\lim_{R\to\infty}\left(\frac{-R^n}{se^{sR}}\right) = \lim_{R\to\infty}\left(\frac{-nR^{n-1}}{s^2e^{sR}}\right) = \lim_{R\to\infty}\left[\frac{-n(n-1)R^{n-2}}{s^3e^{sR}}\right]$$

$$= \ldots = \lim_{R\to\infty}\left[\frac{-n(n-1)(n-2)\ldots(2)(1)R^{n-n}}{s^{n+1}e^{sR}}\right]$$

$$= (-1)\lim_{R\to\infty}\left[\frac{n!}{s^{n+1}e^{sR}}\right] = 0$$

Substituting this result in equation (2):

$$L\{t^n\} = \frac{n}{s}L\{t^{n-1}\} \quad \text{for } s > 0 \qquad (4)$$

Substituting $(n-1)$ for n in equation (4), we find:

$$L\{t^{n-1}\} = \frac{n-1}{s}L\{t^{n-2}\}$$

Substituting this result back into equation (4):

$$L\{t^n\} = \frac{n}{s}\left(\frac{n-1}{s}L\{t^{n-2}\}\right) = \frac{n(n-1)}{s^2}L\{t^{n-2}\}$$

By iterating this process, we obtain:

$$L\{t^n\} = \frac{n(n-1)(n-2)\ldots(2)(1)}{s^n}L\{t^0\} = \frac{n!}{s^n}L\{1\}$$

$$= \frac{n!}{s^n} \lim_{R \to \infty} \int_0^R e^{-st}(1)dt$$

since $s > 0$ converges to:

$$L\{t^n\} = \frac{n!}{s^n} \lim_{R \to \infty} \left(\frac{1 - e^{-sR}}{s} \right) = \frac{n!}{s^n} \times \frac{1}{s}$$

$$= \frac{n!}{s^{n+1}} \quad \text{for } s > 0 \tag{5}$$

If s is complex, a similar computation will give the same result as (5), except that the condition on s will now be *Re* $s > 0$.

After the algebraic equation resulting from a Laplacian transformation has been determined, it must then be converted back into an expression in terms of the original independent variable. The final step is referred to as the determination of the *inverse Laplace transform*. These inverse transformations are made using the tables of Laplace transform in reverse. In the cases where the inverse transform cannot be found listed in the tables, it may be possible to break the transform down into the product of two or more transforms.

PROBLEM 12:

Find the inverse Laplace transforms.

(a) $L^{-1}\left\{ \dfrac{2s}{(s^2 + 1)^2} \right\}$

(b) $L^{-1}\left\{ \dfrac{1}{\sqrt{s}} \right\}$

SOLUTION:

(a) In a table of Laplace transforms, we find:

$$L\{t \sin bt\} = \frac{2bs}{(s^2 + b^2)^2}$$

where b is a constant; hence, taking $b = 1$, we find:

$$L\{t \sin t\} = \frac{2s}{(s^2 + 1)^2}$$

Therefore, by definition of the inverse Laplace transform:

$$L^{-1}\left\{\frac{2s}{(s^2+1)^2}\right\} = t\sin t$$

(b)   In a table of Laplace transforms, we find:

$$L\left\{\frac{1}{\sqrt{t}}\right\} = \frac{\sqrt{\pi}}{\sqrt{s}}$$

Thus, by definition of the inverse Laplace transform:

$$L^{-1}\left\{\frac{\sqrt{\pi}}{\sqrt{s}}\right\} = \frac{1}{\sqrt{t}}$$

Since L^{-1} is a linear operator:

$$L^{-1}\left\{\frac{1}{\sqrt{s}}\right\} = \frac{1}{\sqrt{\pi}}L^{-1}\left\{\frac{\sqrt{\pi}}{\sqrt{s}}\right\} = \frac{1}{\sqrt{\pi}}\times\frac{1}{\sqrt{t}}$$

PROBLEM 13:

A beam of rigidity *EI* is clamped at one end and is loaded as shown in the figure; the weight of the beam is neglected. Find the deflection of the beam, $y(x)$, where, for the coordinate system shown, the following differential relations are known to hold.

$$\frac{d^2 y(x)}{dx^2} = -\frac{1}{EI}m(x), \tag{1}$$

where $y(x)$ is the deflection of the beam at point (x), and $m(x)$ is the bending moment [counterclockwise torque of all (external) forces to the right of point x],

$$\frac{dm(x)}{dx} = t(x), \tag{2}$$

where $t(x)$ is the shearing force (resultant of all vertical forces to the right of point x,

$$\frac{dt(x)}{dx} = -q(x), \tag{3}$$

where $q(x)$ is the load per unit length at point x.

Inversion yields

$$y(x) = L^{-1}\{Y(s)\} = L^{-1}\left\{\frac{q_0}{EI}\frac{1}{s^5}\right\} - L^{-1}\left\{\frac{q_0}{EI}\frac{e^{-sL/2}}{s^5}\right\}$$

$$+ L^{-1}\left\{\frac{q_0 L^2}{8EI}\frac{1}{s^3}\right\} - L^{-1}\left\{\frac{q_0 L}{2EI}\frac{1}{s^4}\right\}$$

or

$$y(x) = \frac{q_0}{24EI}x^4 - \frac{q_0}{24EI}\left(x - \frac{L}{2}\right)^4 \alpha\left(x - \frac{L}{2}\right) + \frac{q_0 L^2}{16EI}x^2 - \frac{q_0 L}{12EI}x^3.$$

It is more convenient to rewrite this solution in the form

$$y(x) = \begin{cases} \dfrac{q_0}{EI}\left(\dfrac{x^4}{24} - \dfrac{Lx^3}{12} + \dfrac{L^2 x^2}{16}\right) & \left(0 \le x < \dfrac{L}{2}\right) \\[2ex] \dfrac{q_0}{EI}\left(\dfrac{L^3 x}{48} - \dfrac{L^4}{384}\right) & \left(\dfrac{L}{2} < x \le L\right) \end{cases}$$

from which, for instance, it is clearly seen that the right half of the beam will remain straight, a fact anticipated on physical grounds.

FE/EIT

FE: PM General Engineering Exam

CHAPTER 4

Chemistry

CHAPTER 4

CHEMISTRY

The science of chemistry is composed of two major categories, inorganic chemistry and organic chemistry. Organic chemistry is basically the chemistry of the element carbon and its compounds, while inorganic chemistry encompasses all other elements and compounds.

CHEMICAL EQUATIONS

The reactions of chemicals with one another are expressed by chemical equations, which give information about the reactants, about the products, and about their relative molar proportions. Chemical equations can be written on different levels of detail, using various "short-hand" conventions.

For aqueous solutions, chemicals which are strong electrolytes are usually written in their dissociated forms, that is, as the ionic species, while weak electrolytes and non-electrolytes are usually written in their undissociated form. For example, the chemical reaction of aqueous silver nitrate ($AgNO_3$) and sodium chloride ($NaCl$) to produce the precipitate silver chloride ($AgCl$):

$$Ag^+ + (NO_3)^- + Na^+ + Cl^- \rightleftharpoons AgCl(s) + Na^+ + (NO_3)^-$$

The equation can be written as a "net" equation as follows:

$$Ag^+ + Cl^- \rightleftharpoons AgCl(s)$$

It should be noted that the sodium ions (Na^+) and the nitrate ions ($NO_3)^-$ remain unchanged in the above reaction. Also, H_2O is not included. Since they do not participate in the reaction, they need not be shown in the equation.

For non-aqueous reactions, the reactants and products are usually written in their molecular form such as:

$$2H_2 + O_2 \rightleftharpoons 2H_2O.$$

The aqueous ions or the molecule shown in chemical equations can also have parenthetical indications of the state in which they exist. Commonly used indicators are:

(aq) = dissociated form of the ion is in an aqueous solution

(s) = the molecule is a precipitate, or is in the solid state

(l) = the molecule is in the liquid state

(g) = the molecule is in the gaseous state

Unless otherwise noted, the species are assumed to be at standard temperature (273°K) and pressure (1 atmosphere).

Finally, chemical equations are not complete until they are properly balanced. The law of the conservation of matter must be observed. It must be remembered that *all* atoms must be accounted for as well as *all* the charges (also called valences). For example, look at the unbalanced chemical reaction:

$$\_PCl_3 + \_H_2O \rightarrow \_P(OH)_3 + \_HCl$$

To balance this equation, balance one element at a time. There is 1 phosphorous (P) on each side, which balances. There are 3 chlorines (Cl) on the left and only 1 on the right side; therefore, put a 3 in front of the hydrogen chloride (HCl) to indicate 3 atoms of Cl. The 3 HCl's now result in 6 hydrogens (H) on the right side of the equation and only 2 on the left side. Thus, 3 water (H_2O) are needed to balance the hydrogen molecules. With the chlorine and hydrogen atoms balanced, there are 3 oxygen atoms on each side, which is balanced. Thus, the balanced equation reads:

$$PCl_3 + 3H_2O \rightarrow P(OH)_3 + 3HCl$$

PROBLEM 1:

Balance the following by filling in missing species and proper coefficient:

(1) $NaOH +$ _____ $\rightarrow NaHSO_4 + HOH$

(2) $PCl_3 +$ _____ $3HOH \rightarrow$ _____ $+ 3HCl$

(3) $CH +$ _____ $\rightarrow CCl_4 + 4HCl$

SOLUTION:

To balance chemical equations, it is noted that *all* atoms (and charges) must be accounted for. The use of coefficients in front of compounds is a means to this end. Thus,

$$NaOH + \underline{\hspace{1cm}} \rightarrow NaHSO_4 + HOH \qquad (1)$$

On the right side of the equation, you have 1 Na, 3 H's, 5 O's, and 1 S. This same number of elements must appear on the left side. However, on the left side, there exists only 1 Na, 1 O, and 1 H. You are missing 2 H's, 1 S, and 4 O's. The missing species is H_2SO_4, sulfuric acid. You could have anticipated this since a strong base (NaOH) reacting with a strong acid yields a salt ($NaHSO_4$) and water. The point is, however, that H_2SO_4 balances the equation by supplying all the missing atoms.

$$PCl_3 + 3HOH \rightarrow \underline{\hspace{1cm}} + 3HCl \qquad (2)$$

Here, the left side has 1 P, 3 Cl's, 6 H's, and 3 O's. The right side has 3 H's, and 3 Cl's. You are missing 1 P, 3 O's, and 3 hydrogens. Therefore, $P(OH)_3$ is formed.

$$CH_4 + \underline{\hspace{1cm}} \rightarrow CCl_4 + 4HCl \qquad (3)$$

Here, there are 1 C, 8 Cl's, and 4 H's on the right and 1 C and 4 H's on the left. The missing compound, therefore, contains 8 Cl's and thus it is $4Cl_2$. It is known that it is $4Cl_2$ rather than Cl_8 or $8Cl$ because elemental chlorine gas is a diatomic, or two atom, molecule.

STOICHIOMETRY

Stoichiometry is the arithmetic of chemistry that involves measuring the relative amounts and proportions of reactants and of products in chemical reactions. The basic unit of quantity measurement in stoichiometry is the *mole* (sometimes spelled *mol*). A mole of a substance contains approximately 6.2×10^{23} (Avogadro's number) atoms or molecules of that substance. By definition:

1 mole = 1 unit of mass/molecular weight (or atomic weight).

If the mass is expressed in grams, the mole are referred to as gram-moles (to which Avogadro's number applies); if expressed in kilograms, the moles are referred to as kilogram-moles; if expressed as pounds, the moles are referred to as pound-moles, and so forth. As examples: 1) the element carbon (C) has an atomic weight of 12, thus, 1 gram-mole of carbon contains 12 grams, and 1 pound-mole of carbon contains 12 pounds;

and O_2 present. The number of moles is found by dividing the number of grams present by molecular weight:

$$\text{number of moles} = \frac{\text{number of grams}}{\text{M.W.}}$$

For O_2: M.W. = 32

$$\text{Number of moles} = \frac{6.0 \text{ g}}{32.0 \text{ g/mole}} = 1.875 \times 10^{-1} \text{ moles}$$

For SO_2: M.W. = 64

$$\text{Number of moles} = \frac{25.0 \text{ g}}{64.0 \text{ g/mole}} = 3.91 \times 10^{-1} \text{ moles}$$

Because 2 moles of SO_2 are needed to react with 1 mole of O_2, 3.75×10^{-1} moles of SO_2 will react with 1.875×10^{-1} moles of O_2. This means that $3.91 \times 10^{-1} - 3.75 \times 10^{-1}$ moles or 0.16×10^{-1} moles of SO_2 will remain unreacted. In this case, O_2 is called the limiting reagent because it determines the number of moles of SO_3 formed. There will be twice as many moles of SO_3 formed as there are O_2 reacting.

$$\text{Number of moles of } SO_3 \text{ formed} = 2 \times 1.875 \times 10^{-1} \text{ moles}$$

$$= 3.75 \times 10^{-1} \text{ moles}$$

The weight is found by multiplying the number of moles formed by the molecular weight (M.W. of SO_3 = 80).

weight of $SO_3 = 3.75 \times 10^{-1}$ moles $\times 80$ g/mole $= 30.0$ g

SOLUTIONS

A *solution* is a homogeneous mixture of substances. They may be gaseous, liquid, or solid solutions. However, liquid solutions are the most frequently encountered by the engineer. The amount of a substance is the combination of a solute and solvent. The *solute* is the material dissolved in another substance, called the *solvent*. The quantity of solute in a solution is called the *concentration*.

The property of a substance that allows it to dissolve in a given solvent is called its *solubility*. The solubility of most solids in liquids increases with temperature, but the solubility of gases in liquids usually decreases with temperature. The change in solubility due to a change in temperature is expressed by the following equation:

2) the substance water (H_2O) has a molecular weight of 18 (the atomic weight of oxygen, 16, and two hydrogen atoms with an atomic weight of one each); thus, 1 gram-mole of water contains 18 grams, and 1 pound-mole of water contains 18 pounds.

Another concept used in stoichiometry is called *equivalent weights*, which are the amount of a substance that reacts completely with another in a chemical reaction. In *electrolytic* reactions, the equivalent weight is that weight of the substance that receives or donates one mole of electrons at the electrode. In *oxidation-reduction* reactions, the equivalent weight is that weight of the substance that gains or loses one mole of electrons. In *acid-base* reactions, the equivalent weight is that quantity of acid that supplies or loses one mole of H^+, or of one mole of the base equivalent, OH^-. As an example of equivalent weight:

$Fe^{3+} + e^- = Fe^{2+}$; one equivalent weight per mole, equal to 56 grams per equivalent

$Fe^{3+} + 3e^- = Fe^\circ$; three equivalent weight per mole, equal to $(1/3)(56)$ = 18.7 grams per equivalent

Stoichiometry requires that all chemical equations be properly balanced. The coefficients in these equations provide the ratios in which the number of moles of one substance reacts with another, and the ratios of products to each other and to the reactants. In actual situations the reactants and products are not usually set up using the exact stoichiometric ratios. Some reactants will be present in amounts exceeding their stoichiometric ratios, and will not be completely consumed in the reaction. Chemical reactions can proceed only as far as the least abundant reactant, referred to as the *limiting reagent*, will allow. The limiting reagent determines the amount of product formed. Thus, the stoichiometric calculations must be based on the quantity of the limiting reagent.

The amount of a product is often somewhat less than the amount which is indicated by the stoichiometry of the pertinent chemical equation. This maximum amount of a product which can be produced by a chemical reaction when the reaction goes to completion is called the *theoretical yield*. It is determined by the equilibrium between the reactants and the products.

PROBLEM 2:

Calculate the mole fractions of ethyl alcohol, C_2H_5OH, and water in a solution made by dissolving 9.2 g of alcohol in 18 g of H_2O. The M.W. of $H_2O = 18$ and the M.W. of $C_2H_5OH = 46$.

SOLUTION:

Mole fraction problems are similar to percent composition problems. A mole fraction of a compound tells us what fraction of 1 mole of solution is due to that particular compound. Hence,

$$\text{mole fraction of solute} = \frac{\text{moles of solute}}{\text{moles of solute} + \text{moles of solvent}}$$

The solute is the substance being dissolved into, or added to, the solution. The solvent is the solution to which the solute is added.

The equation for calculating mole fractions is:

$$\frac{\text{moles A}}{\text{moles A} + \text{moles B}} = \text{mole fraction A}$$

Moles are defined as grams/molecular weight (M.W.). Therefore, first find the number of moles of each compound present and then use the above equation.

$$\text{moles of } C_2H_5OH \quad = \frac{9.2 \text{ g}}{46.0 \text{ g/mole}} = 0.2 \text{ mole}$$

$$\text{moles of } H_2O \quad = \frac{18 \text{ g}}{18 \text{ g/mole}} = 1 \text{ mole}$$

$$\text{mole fraction of } C_2H_5OH \quad = \frac{0.2}{1 + 0.2} = 0.167$$

$$\text{mole fraction of } H_2O \quad = \frac{1}{1 + 0.2} = 0.833$$

Note the sum of the mole fractions is equal to 1.

PROBLEM 3:

What is the maximum weight of SO_3 that could be made from 25.0 g of SO_2 and 6.0 g of O_2 by the following reaction?

$$2SO_2 + O_2 \rightarrow 2SO_3$$

SOLUTION:

From the reaction, one knows that for every 2 moles of SO_3 formed, 2 moles of SO_2 and 1 mole of O_2 must react. Thus, to find the amount of SO_3 that can be formed, one must first know the number of moles of SO_2

SOLUTION:

To balance chemical equations, it is noted that *all* atoms (and charges) must be accounted for. The use of coefficients in front of compounds is a means to this end. Thus,

$$NaOH + \underline{\hspace{2cm}} \rightarrow NaHSO_4 + HOH \tag{1}$$

On the right side of the equation, you have 1 Na, 3 H's, 5 O's, and 1 S. This same number of elements must appear on the left side. However, on the left side, there exists only 1 Na, 1 O, and 1 H. You are missing 2 H's, 1 S, and 4 O's. The missing species is H_2SO_4, sulfuric acid. You could have anticipated this since a strong base (NaOH) reacting with a strong acid yields a salt ($NaHSO_4$) and water. The point is, however, that H_2SO_4 balances the equation by supplying all the missing atoms.

$$PCl_3 + 3HOH \rightarrow \underline{\hspace{2cm}} + 3HCl \tag{2}$$

Here, the left side has 1 P, 3 Cl's, 6 H's, and 3 O's. The right side has 3 H's, and 3 Cl's. You are missing 1 P, 3 O's, and 3 hydrogens. Therefore, $P(OH)_3$ is formed.

$$CH_4 + \underline{\hspace{2cm}} \rightarrow CCl_4 + 4HCl \tag{3}$$

Here, there are 1 C, 8 Cl's, and 4 H's on the right and 1 C and 4 H's on the left. The missing compound, therefore, contains 8 Cl's and thus it is $4Cl_2$. It is known that it is $4Cl_2$ rather than Cl_8 or $8Cl$ because elemental chlorine gas is a diatomic, or two atom, molecule.

STOICHIOMETRY

Stoichiometry is the arithmetic of chemistry that involves measuring the relative amounts and proportions of reactants and of products in chemical reactions. The basic unit of quantity measurement in stoichiometry is the *mole* (sometimes spelled *mol*). A mole of a substance contains approximately 6.2×10^{23} (Avogadro's number) atoms or molecules of that substance. By definition:

1 mole = 1 unit of mass/molecular weight (or atomic weight).

If the mass is expressed in grams, the mole are referred to as gram-moles (to which Avogadro's number applies); if expressed in kilograms, the moles are referred to as kilogram-moles; if expressed as pounds, the moles are referred to as pound-moles, and so forth. As examples: 1) the element carbon (C) has an atomic weight of 12, thus, 1 gram-mole of carbon contains 12 grams, and 1 pound-mole of carbon contains 12 pounds;

and O_2 present. The number of moles is found by dividing the number of grams present by molecular weight:

$$\text{number of moles} = \frac{\text{number of grams}}{\text{M.W.}}$$

For O_2: M.W. = 32

$$\text{Number of moles} = \frac{6.0 \text{ g}}{32.0 \text{ g/mole}} = 1.875 \times 10^{-1} \text{ moles}$$

For SO_2: M.W. = 64

$$\text{Number of moles} = \frac{25.0 \text{ g}}{64.0 \text{ g/mole}} = 3.91 \times 10^{-1} \text{ moles}$$

Because 2 moles of SO_2 are needed to react with 1 mole of O_2, 3.75×10^{-1} moles of SO_2 will react with 1.875×10^{-1} moles of O_2. This means that $3.91 \times 10^{-1} - 3.75 \times 10^{-1}$ moles or 0.16×10^{-1} moles of SO_2 will remain unreacted. In this case, O_2 is called the limiting reagent because it determines the number of moles of SO_3 formed. There will be twice as many moles of SO_3 formed as there are O_2 reacting.

Number of moles of SO_3 formed = $2 \times 1.875 \times 10^{-1}$ moles

$$= 3.75 \times 10^{-1} \text{ moles}$$

The weight is found by multiplying the number of moles formed by the molecular weight (M.W. of SO_3 = 80).

weight of SO_3 = 3.75×10^{-1} moles $\times$ 80 g/mole = 30.0 g

SOLUTIONS

A *solution* is a homogeneous mixture of substances. They may be gaseous, liquid, or solid solutions. However, liquid solutions are the most frequently encountered by the engineer. The amount of a substance is the combination of a solute and solvent. The *solute* is the material dissolved in another substance, called the *solvent*. The quantity of solute in a solution is called the *concentration*.

The property of a substance that allows it to dissolve in a given solvent is called its *solubility*. The solubility of most solids in liquids increases with temperature, but the solubility of gases in liquids usually decreases with temperature. The change in solubility due to a change in temperature is expressed by the following equation:

$$\log \frac{K_2}{K_1} = \frac{-\Delta H^0}{2.303R} \left(\frac{1}{T_2} - \frac{1}{T_1} \right)$$

where: K_2 = the solubility constant at temperature T_2

K_1 = the solubility constant at temperature T_1

ΔH^0 = enthalpy change when the solute dissolves into the solvent (a positive ΔH indicates that the solubility increases with increasing temperature.)

R = the universal gas constant

A positive ΔH indicates that the solubility increases with increasing temperature. Though pressure has little effect on the solubility of solid or liquids into liquids, the solubility of gases always increases with increasing pressure. The freezing point, the boiling point, and vapor pressure of a solution differ from those of the pure solvent. In addition, the osmotic pressure also changes when adding solute to a pure solvent.

The equilibrium constant for sparingly soluble substances is called the *solubility product*, K_{sp}. Using the following equation as an example:

$$Ag_2CrO_4(s) \rightleftharpoons 2Ag^+ + (CrO_4)^{2-}, \quad \text{with } K_{sp} = 8.5 \times 10^{-8}.$$

The solubility constant for this equation is defined as the arithmetic product of the concentrations of the substances on the right side of the equation divided by the arithmetic product of the concentrations of the substances on the left side of the equation, with each term raised to the power of the coefficient of a balanced equation. In this case:

$$K_{eq} = \frac{[Ag^+]^2 \times [(CrO_4)^{2-}]}{[Ag_2CrO_4(s)]}$$

where the values in the brackets, [ ], are the concentrations of the species indicated, and the concentration of the solid species is equal to 1. With this latter condition, the formula reduces to:

$$K_{sp} = [Ag+]^2 \times [(CrO_4)^{2-}] = 8.5 \times 10^{-8}.$$

The concentrations of the sparingly soluble ions can be determined using this above formula and the stoichiometry of the reaction. In this example it shows the concentration of the silver ion to be two times the concentration of the chromate ion. Thus, if the variable X is assigned to the concentration of the chromate, the concentration of the silver ion is $2X$.

Substituting these variables into the formula $[2X]^2 \times [X] = 8.5 \times 10^{-8}$, and solving for X:

$$X = 2.76 \times 10^{-3}$$

PROBLEM 4:

The following reaction:

$$2H_2S(g) \rightleftharpoons 2H_2(g) + S_2(g)$$

was allowed to proceed to equilibrium. The contents of the two-liter reaction vessel were then subjected to analysis and found to contain 1.0 mole H_2S, 0.20 mole H_2, and .80 mole S_2. What is the equilibrium constant K_{eq} for this reaction?

SOLUTION:

This problem involves substitution into the equilibrium constant expression for this reaction:

$$K_{eq} = \frac{[H_2]^2[S_2]}{[H_2S]^2}$$

The equilibrium concentration of the reactant and products are $[H_2S] =$ 1.0 mole/2 liters = 0.50 M, $[H_2] = 0.20$ mole/2 liters = 0.10 M, and $[S_2] =$ 0.80 mole/2 liters = 0.40 M. Hence, the value of the equilibrium constant is

$$K_{eq} = \frac{[H_2]^2[S_2]}{[H_2S]^2} = \frac{(0.10)^2(0.40)}{(0.50)^2} = 0.016$$

for this reaction.

EQUILIBRIUM

A system, or chemical reaction, is in *equilibrium* when both the forward and reverse reactions proceed at the same rate. If a system is disturbed by an external stress, for example, by changes in temperature, pressure, or concentration of constituents, it adjusts to a new equilibrium.

The equilibrium for a reaction:

$$aA + bB \rightleftharpoons eE + fF,$$

is defined by the equilibrium constant, K_{eq}:

$$K_{eq} = \frac{[E]^e[F]^f}{[A]^a[B]^b}$$

This relationship is known as the *mass action equation*. It is important to note that pure solids or pure liquids have concentrations of 1, and do not appear in the mass action expression. Also, if a reaction involves gases, the concentrations of the gases are expressed in partial pressures.

In addition to determining the concentrations of the reactants and products, the equilibrium constant can be used in certain other ways:

1. The value of the K_{eq} provides an indication as to the direction of a reversible reaction. Very large values indicate large concentrations of products and that the reaction favors the products. Conversely, very small values favor the reactants.

2. Kinetic information can be gathered by analyzing the mass action expression of a reversible reaction. The rate of the general chemical equation, $aA + bB \rightleftharpoons eE + fF$ can be expressed as:

   $$\text{rate}_{\text{forward}} = k_f[A]^a[B]^b \quad \text{and} \quad \text{rate}_{\text{reverse}} = k_r[E]^e[F]^f$$

   where k_f and k_r are rate constants for the forward and reverse reactions, respectively.

3. For thermodynamics, the equilibrium constant can be used to evaluate the Gibbs free energy function as follows:

   $$\Delta G^o = -RT[\ln K_{eq}]$$

   where: R is the universal gas constant,

   T is the absolute temperature, and

   $\ln K_{eq}$ is the natural logarithm of the equilibrium constant.

ACIDS AND BASES

Though there are several definitions of acids and bases, for most engineering purposes, acids are substances that ionize in water yielding an H^+ ion, and bases are substances that ionize in water yielding an OH^- ion. Acids and bases are often examined in terms of the acid-base equilibria in aqueous solutions. This can be expressed by the chemical equation:

$$H_2O \rightleftharpoons H^+ + OH^-$$

with the equilibrium constant, $K_w = [H^+][OH^-] = 1.0 \times 10^{-14}$

Acid and base concentrations are usually expressed in terms of pH, which is related to the equilibrium constant as follows:

$$pH = -\log[H^+]; \quad pOH = -\log[OH^-]; \quad pK_w = pH + pOH = 14.0$$

Thus a neutral solution is one where the pH = 7, and pOH = 7. Solutions with a pH less than 7 are considered "acid," and solutions with a pH greater that 7 are considered basic, or alkaline.

When soluble salts composed of a positive ion (which would form a strong base) and a negative ion (which would form a weak acid) are dissolved in water, the resultant solution will be basic. Conversely, when soluble salts composed of a positive ion (which would form a weak base) and a negative ion (which would form a strong acid) are dissolved in water, the resultant solution will be acidic. This phenomenon is called *hydrolysis.*

Buffer solutions are equilibrium systems, usually of weakly acidic or weakly basic substances, that resist changes in acidity. They maintain a constant pH when small amounts of acid or base are added to them, either by direct addition or by the hydrolysis of salts of weak acids or weak bases.

Titration is a process used to determine the amount of a solution of known concentration that is required to react completely with a sample of unknown concentration that is being analyzed. The concentration units used in titration are "normality" and "equivalents." An equivalent is defined as a substance that releases one mole of hydrogen ions, H^+, or hydroxyl ions, OH^-. A standard solution that has a concentration of 1 equivalent per liter has a Normality of 1 and is referred to as a 1N solution.

Another term related to acid-base chemistry is the term *amphoteric.* An amphoteric substance is one that may act as an acid or a base. Such a substance (for example, aluminum hydroxide, $Al(OH)_3$) can donate a hydrogen ion or a hydroxyl ion depending on the pH of the solute.

PROBLEM 5:

The ionization constant for acetic acid is 1.8×10^{-5}.

(1) Calculate the concentration of H^+ ions in a 0.10 molar solution of acetic acid.

(2) Calculate the concentration of H^+ ions in a 0.10 molar solution

of acetic acid in which the concentration of acetate ions has been increased to 1.0 molar by adding sodium acetate.

SOLUTION:

(1) The ionization constant (K_a) is defined as the concentration of H^+ ions times the concentration of the conjugate base ions of a given acid divided by the concentration of unionized acid. For an acid, HA:

$$K_a = \frac{[H^+][A^-]}{[HA]}$$

where K_a is the ionization constant, $[H^+]$ is the concentration of H^+ ions, $[A^-]$ is the concentration of the conjugate base ions, and $[HA]$ is the concentration of the unionized acid. The K_a for acetic acid is stated as

$$K_a = \frac{[H^+][\text{acetate ion}]}{[\text{acetic acid}]} = 1.8 \times 10^{-5}$$

The chemical formula for acetic acid is $HC_2H_3O_2$. When it is ionized, one H^+ is formed and one $C_2H_3O^-$ (acetate) is formed; thus, the concentration of H^+ equals the concentration of $C_2H_3O^-$:

$$[H^+] = [C_2H_3O^-]$$

The concentration of un-ionized acid is decreased when ionization occurs. The new concentration is equal to the concentration of H^+ subtracted from the concentration of un-ionized acid:

$$[HC_2H_3O] = 0.10 - [H^+]$$

Since $[H^+]$ is small relative to 0.10, it may be assumed that $0.10 - [H^+]$ is approximately equal to 0.10:

$$0.10 - [H^+] \cong 0.10$$

Using this assumption, and the fact that $[H^+] = [C_2H_3O^-]$, K_a can be written as:

$$K_a = \frac{[H^+][H^+]}{0.10} = 1.8 \times 10^{-5}$$

Solving for the concentration of H^+:

$$[H^+]^2 = (1.0 \times 10^{-1})(1.8 \times 10^{-5}) = 1.8 \times 10^{-6}$$

$$[H^+] = \sqrt{1.8 \times 10^{-6}} = 1.3 \times 10^{-3}\,M.$$

ELECTROCHEMISTRY

Reactions that do not occur spontaneously can be forced to occur by supplying energy through an external source of energy, in this case electricity. These are called *electrolytic* reactions, which take place in electrolytic cells where electrical energy is converted into chemical energy. Another type of electrochemical cell is the galvanic, or voltaic, cell. In galvanic cells, chemical energy is converted to electrical energy. Since the energy conversion process occurs in the opposite direction in galvanic cells as compared to electrolytic cells, the anodes and cathodes are switched. In galvanic cells, the anode is negative, and the cathode positive. Electrons flow from the negative electrode to the positive electrode.

The force driving the electrons is called the electromotive force, EMF, and is measured as voltage. The quantity of electrons transferred in a reaction is measured in coulombs, and the flow rate of coulombs, or current, is measured in amperes. As an example, the cell potential, or EMF, for a zinc/copper cell may be written:

$$E^0{}_{cell} = E^0{}_{Cu} + E^0{}_{Zn}$$

where E^0 are the standard reduction potentials, which are generally provided in tables of reduction potentials in various engineering handbooks.

PROBLEM 7:

For the following oxidation-reduction reaction, 1) write out the two half-reactions and balance the equation, 2) calculate ΔE^0, and 3) determine whether the reaction will proceed spontaneously as written:

$$Fe^{2+} + MnO_4^- + H^+ \rightarrow Mn^{2+} + Fe^{3+} + H_2O$$

(1) $Fe^{3+} + e^- \rightleftharpoons Fe^{2+}$, $E^0 = 0.77eV$ (electronvolt)

(2) $MnO_4^- + 8H^+ + 5e \rightleftharpoons Mn^{2+} + 4H_2O$, $E^0 = 1.51eV$

SOLUTION:

(1) The two half-reactions of an oxidation–reduction reaction are the equations for the oxidation process (loss of electrons) and the reduction process (gain of electrons). The overall reaction begins with Fe^{2+} and results in Fe^{3+}. It had to lose an electron to accomplish this. Thus, there is oxidation:

$$Fe^{2+} \rightarrow Fe^{3+} + e^-.$$

The concentration of H^+ is thus 1.3×10^{-3}M.

(2)   When the acetate concentration is increased, the concentration of H^+ is lowered to maintain the K_a. The K_a for acetic acid is stated as:

$$K_a = \frac{[H^+][C_2H_3O^-]}{[HC_2H_3O]} = 1.8 \times 10^{-5}$$

As previously shown for acetic acid equilibria in a solution of 0.10 molar acid, the concentration of acid after ionization is:

$$[HC_2H_3O] = 0.10 - [H^+]$$

Because $[H^+]$ is very small compared to 0.10, $0.10 - [H^+] \cong 0.10$ and:

$$[HC_2H_2O] = 0.10 \text{ M}$$

In this problem, we are told that the concentration of acetate is held constant at 1.0 molar by addition of sodium acetate. Because we know the concentrations of the acetate and the acid, the concentration of H^+ can be found:

$$\frac{[H^+][C_2H_3O^-]}{[HC_2H_3O]} = 1.8 \times 10^{-5}$$

$$\frac{[H^+][1.0]}{[0.10]} = 1.8 \times 10^{-5}$$

$$[H^+] = 1.8 \times 10^{-6} \text{ M}$$

OXIDATION–REDUCTION

Oxidation is a reaction in which atoms undergo a loss of electrons to become more positive. Conversely, *reduction* is a reaction in which atoms undergo a gain of electrons to become more negative. The charge on an atom resulting from the gain or loss of electrons (from its neutral state) is called its *oxidation number*.

Chemical reactions must have all oxidations balanced by reductions, electron for electron. Such reactions are referred to as *redox* reactions. Redox equations can be balanced by the Oxidation Number Change method or by the Ion-Electron (or "half-reaction") method.

In the Oxidation Number Change method, the oxidation numbers are assigned to each atom in the equation. It is important to note which atoms undergo a change in oxidation number and then make the number of electrons gained be equal to the number of electrons lost. In the Ion-Electron method, it is necessary to determine which atoms undergo a change in oxidation state by the gain or loss of electrons, then to write one equation for each of those elements showing the gain or loss of electrons. The analysis requires that the number of electrons shown in each of the two half-reactions are equal by multiplying one of the equations by the appropriate factor, and then combining the equations together to obtain a balanced overall equation.

PROBLEM 6:

For the following voltaic cell, write the half-reactions, designating which is oxidation and which is reduction. Write the cell reaction and calculate the voltage (E^0) of the cell from the given electrodes. The cell is:

$$Cu;Cu^{+2} \| Ag^{+1};Ag$$

SOLUTION:

In a voltaic cell, the flow of electrons creates a current. Their flow is regulated by two types of reactions that occur concurrently—oxidation and reduction. Oxidation is a process where electrons are lost and reduction where electrons are gained. The equations for these are the half-reactions. From the cell diagram, the direction of the reaction is always left to right.

$$Cu \rightleftharpoons Cu^{2+} + 2e^- \qquad \text{oxidation}$$

$$2Ag^+ + 2e^- \rightleftharpoons 2Ag \qquad \text{reduction}$$

Therefore, the combined cell reaction is

$$Cu + 2Ag^+ \rightleftharpoons Cu^{2+} + 2Ag.$$

To calculate the total E^0, look up the value for the E^0 of both half-reactions as reductions. To obtain E^0 for oxidation, reverse the sign of the reduction E_0. Then, substitute into $E^0_{cell} = E^0_{red} + E^0_{ox}$. Thus:

$$E^0_{cell} = -(E^0_{red}Cu) + E^0_{red}Ag^{+1}$$

$$= -0.34 + .12$$

$$= 0.46 \text{ volt}$$

of acetic acid in which the concentration of acetate ions has been increased to 1.0 molar by adding sodium acetate.

SOLUTION:

(1) The ionization constant (K_a) is defined as the concentration of H^+ ions times the concentration of the conjugate base ions of a given acid divided by the concentration of unionized acid. For an acid, HA:

$$K_a = \frac{[H^+][A^-]}{[HA]}$$

where K_a is the ionization constant, $[H^+]$ is the concentration of H^+ ions, $[A^-]$ is the concentration of the conjugate base ions, and $[HA]$ is the concentration of the unionized acid. The K_a for acetic acid is stated as

$$K_a = \frac{[H^+][\text{acetate ion}]}{[\text{acetic acid}]} = 1.8 \times 10^{-5}$$

The chemical formula for acetic acid is $HC_2H_3O_2$. When it is ionized, one H^+ is formed and one $C_2H_3O^-$ (acetate) is formed; thus, the concentration of H^+ equals the concentration of $C_2H_3O^-$:

$$[H^+] = [C_2H_3O^-]$$

The concentration of un-ionized acid is decreased when ionization occurs. The new concentration is equal to the concentration of H^+ subtracted from the concentration of un-ionized acid:

$$[HC_2H_3O] = 0.10 - [H^+]$$

Since $[H^+]$ is small relative to 0.10, it may be assumed that $0.10 - [H^+]$ is approximately equal to 0.10:

$$0.10 - [H^+] \cong 0.10$$

Using this assumption, and the fact that $[H^+] = [C_2H_3O^-]$, K_a can be written as:

$$K_a = \frac{[H^+][H^+]}{0.10} = 1.8 \times 10^{-5}$$

Solving for the concentration of H^+:

$$[H^+]^2 = (1.0 \times 10^{-1})(1.8 \times 10^{-5}) = 1.8 \times 10^{-6}$$

$$[H^+] = \sqrt{1.8 \times 10^{-6}} = 1.3 \times 10^{-3} M.$$

ELECTROCHEMISTRY

Reactions that do not occur spontaneously can be forced to occur by supplying energy through an external source of energy, in this case electricity. These are called *electrolytic* reactions, which take place in electrolytic cells where electrical energy is converted into chemical energy. Another type of electrochemical cell is the galvanic, or voltaic, cell. In galvanic cells, chemical energy is converted to electrical energy. Since the energy conversion process occurs in the opposite direction in galvanic cells as compared to electrolytic cells, the anodes and cathodes are switched. In galvanic cells, the anode is negative, and the cathode positive. Electrons flow from the negative electrode to the positive electrode.

The force driving the electrons is called the electromotive force, EMF, and is measured as voltage. The quantity of electrons transferred in a reaction is measured in coulombs, and the flow rate of coulombs, or current, is measured in amperes. As an example, the cell potential, or EMF, for a zinc/copper cell may be written:

$$E^0{}_{cell} = E^0{}_{Cu} + E^0{}_{Zn}$$

where E^0 are the standard reduction potentials, which are generally provided in tables of reduction potentials in various engineering handbooks.

PROBLEM 7:

For the following oxidation-reduction reaction, 1) write out the two half-reactions and balance the equation, 2) calculate ΔE^0, and 3) determine whether the reaction will proceed spontaneously as written:

$$Fe^{2+} + MnO_4^- + H^+ \rightarrow Mn^{2+} + Fe^{3+} + H_2O$$

(1) $Fe^{3+} + e^- \rightleftharpoons Fe^{2+}$, $E^0 = 0.77eV$ (electronvolt)

(2) $MnO_4^- + 8H^+ + 5e \rightleftharpoons Mn^{2+} + 4H_2O$, $E^0 = 1.51eV$

SOLUTION:

(1)   The two half-reactions of an oxidation–reduction reaction are the equations for the oxidation process (loss of electrons) and the reduction process (gain of electrons). The overall reaction begins with Fe^{2+} and results in Fe^{3+}. It had to lose an electron to accomplish this. Thus, there is oxidation:

$$Fe^{2+} \rightarrow Fe^{3+} + e^-.$$

Note: This is the reverse of the reaction given with $E^0 = 0.77eV$. As such, the oxidation reaction in this problem has $E^0 = -0.77eV$. The reduction must be

$$MnO_4^- + 8H^+ + 5e^- \rightarrow Mn^{2+} + 4H_2O,$$

since in the overall reaction, you see $MnO_4^- + H^+$ go to Mn^{2+} (the Mn^{7+} is reduced to Mn^{2+}), which suggests a gain of electrons. This is the same reaction as the one given in the problem, $E^0 = 1.51eV$. To balance the overall reaction, add the oxidation reaction to the reduction reaction, such that all electron charges disappear. If you multiply the oxidation reaction by 5, you obtain:

$$5Fe^{2+} \rightarrow 5Fe^{3+} + 5e^-$$

$$MnO_4^- + 8H^+ + 5e^- \rightarrow Mn^{2+} + 4H_2O$$

$$5Fe^{2+} + MnO_4^- + 8H^+ \rightarrow 5Fe^{3+} \; Mn^{2+} + 4H^2O$$

Note: Since both equations contained $5e^-$ on different sides, they canceled out. This explains why the oxidation reaction is multiplied by five, resulting in the balanced equation.

(2) The ΔE^0 for the overall reaction is the sum of the E^0 for the half-reactions, i.e.:

$$\Delta E^0 = E_{red} + E_{oxid}$$

E_{red} and E_{oxid} are both given, thus:

$$\Delta E^0 = 1.51 - 0.77 = 0.74eV$$

(3) A reaction will only proceed spontaneously when $\Delta E^0 =$ a positive value. A positive ΔE^0 has been calculated, which means the reaction proceeds spontaneously.

KINETICS

Kinetics is the study of the rates of chemical reactions. Rates are usually expressed in terms of the change in the concentration of one of the molecules, either a reactant or a product, per unit time. The factors that influence reaction rates include: the nature of the intra-molecular bonds of the molecules involved, the surface area of the reactants, the concentration of the reactants and products, and the temperature.

Reaction rates are related to temperature and energy by the Arrhenius equation:

$$k = Ae^{\frac{-E}{RT}}$$

where: k = the rate constant

A = Arrhenius constant

E = the activation energy

R = the universal gas constant

T = the absolute temperature

In general, the value for the Arrhenius constant, A, is usually determined empirically, by measuring the rates at different temperatures. There has been some success, however, in predicting the Arrhenius constant from theoretical considerations. Also, values have been tabulated for common reactions.

The activation energy E is the energy input to the system necessary to cause a reaction to proceed. After that point the reaction will proceed, releasing energy, to the equilibrium level of the products. In an exothermic process, the energy released by the formation of the products is greater than the activation energy.

The order of the reaction describes its kinetics:

Zero Order: The reaction rate remains constant regardless of changes in the concentration of the reactants.

First Order: The reaction rate is directly proportional to the concentration of the reactant (i.e., if the concentration of the reactants double, the reaction rate doubles).

Second Order: The reaction rate is directly proportional to the square of the concentration of the reactant (i.e., if the concentration of the reactants double, the reaction rate quadruples).

Third Order: The reaction rate is directly proportional to the cube of the concentration of the reactant (i.e., if the concentration of the reactants double, the reaction rate increases by a factor of eight).

PROBLEM 8:

(1) A reaction proceeds five times as fast at 60°C as it does at 30°C. Estimate its energy of activation. (2) For a gas phase reaction with E_A =

40,000 cal/mole, estimate the change in rate constant due to a temperature change from 1,000°C to 2,000°C.

SOLUTION:

The actual activation energy E_A can be related to the rate constants k_1 (at temperature T_1) and k_2 (at temperature T_2) by the Arrhenius equation:

$$\log \frac{k_2}{k_1} = -\frac{E_a}{2.303R}\left(\frac{1}{T_2} - \frac{1}{T_1}\right)$$

where R = universal gas constant.

(1) It is given that the reaction proceeds five times as fast at 60°C as it does at 30°C. Therefore, if k_1 = rate constant at 30°C = 303°K (degrees Kelvin) with T_1 = 303K, then $k_2 = 5k_1$ at 60°C = 333°K with T_2 = 333°K. Since R is given, substitute these values into the Arrhenius equation and solve for E_A. Rewriting and substituting:

$$E_a = \frac{-2.303R}{\dfrac{1}{T_2} - \dfrac{1}{T_1}} \log\frac{k_2}{k_1} = \frac{(-2.303)(1.987)\left(\dfrac{1\text{ kcal}}{1,000\text{ cal}}\right)}{\left(\dfrac{1}{333} - \dfrac{1}{303}\right)} \log 5$$

$$= (15.4 \text{ kcal/mole})(0.699) = 10.8 \text{ kcal/mole}$$

Note: 1 kcal/1,000 cal is a conversion factor to obtain the correct units.

To answer (2) find $\dfrac{k_2}{k_1}$ from the Arrhenius equation. Rewriting and substituting:

$$\frac{k_2}{k_1} = \text{anti} \log\left(\frac{E_a}{2.303R}\left(\frac{1}{T_2} - \frac{1}{T_1}\right)\right)$$

$$= \text{anti} \log\left(\frac{-40,000}{(2.303)(1.987)}\left(\frac{1}{2,273} - \frac{1}{1,273}\right)\right)$$

$$= \text{anti} \log 3.02 = 1.05 \times 10^3$$

That is, the rate should be about 1,050 times as great at 2,000°C as at 1,000°C.

ORGANIC CHEMISTRY

Organic chemistry is basically the chemistry of the element carbon, C, and its compounds. Many of these compounds contain the element hydrogen and are therefore called hydrocarbons. Carbon has four bonding sites, and may form single, double, and triple bond compounds as well as ring-like structured compounds or longer hydrocarbon chains. Organic compounds can have the same chemical composition, yet have very different structures and properties. Such molecules are called *isomers*. Organic compounds fall into various basic categories. The nature and structure of organic molecules are indicated by their nomenclature, with prefixes and suffixes indicating substitutions, functional groups, and bonding type. For example, all organic molecules in the alkane category end with the suffix "-ane," and the prefix depends on the number of carbons in the longest continuous chain of the molecule.

Alkanes are hydrocarbons that contain only single bonds. Their structural formula is C_nH_{2n+2}. They are referred to as saturated compounds (meaning that they have no multiple bonds), and may take the form of straight chains or rings. Alkanes are generally non-polar, unreactive molecules. Their boiling point, melting point, density, and viscosity increase as the length of the carbon chain increases.

Alkenes are hydrocarbons with one or more carbon-to-carbon double bonds. Their structural formula is C_nH_{2n}. All compounds in this category end with the suffix "-ene," and the location of the double bond is usually indicated in the name. Many of the reactions of alkenes focus on the double bond. "Addition reactions" saturate the double bond, while "cleavage reactions" break the double bond and create two new molecules.

Alkynes are hydrocarbons with one or more triple bonds. Their structural formula is C_nH_{2n-2}. All compounds in this category end with the suffix "-yne." Alkynes undergo the same types of addition and cleavage reactions as alkenes.

Organic molecules may also form cyclic structured molecules. One of the more important types of cyclic organics are *aromatic* compounds. These are six-membered carbon rings with alternating double and single bonds. The basic aromatic compound is benzene with the chemical formula, C_6H_6.

There are many other organic compounds that are created by functional groups added-on to the basic hydrocarbon structure. These functional groups determine the chemical properties of the organic compound.

These compounds include alcohols, ethers, aldehydes, ketones, and carboxylic acids.

PROBLEM 9:

Four liters of octane gasoline weigh 3.19 kg. Calculate the volume of air required for its complete combustion at STP.

SOLUTION:

To answer this problem, you need to write the balanced equation for the combustion of octane gasoline. This means knowing the molecular formula of octane gasoline and what is meant by combustion. Octane is a saturated hydrocarbon, i.e., it is an alkane. A saturated hydrocarbon means a compound that contains only single bonds between the carbon-to-carbon and carbon-to-hydrogen bonds. Alkanes have the general formula C_nH_{2n+2}, where N = number of carbon atoms. Since the prefix "oct" means eight, there are 8 carbon atoms, which indicates that 18 hydrogen atoms are present. Thus, gasoline octane has the formula C_8H_{18}. Now, combustion is the reaction of an organic compound with oxygen to produce CO_2 and H_2O. With this in mind you can write the balanced equation for the reaction:

$$2C_8H_{18} + 25O_2 \rightarrow 16CO_2 + 18H_2O$$

To determine the volume of air required for combustion, you need the volume of O_2 required, since 21 percent of air is oxygen (O_2). To find the amount of O_2 involved, use the fact that at STP (standard temperature and pressure) 1 mole of any gas occupies 22.4 liters. Thus, if you know how many moles of O_2 were required, you would know its volume. You can find the number of moles by using stoichiometry. You have 3.19 kg or 3,190 g (1,000 g = 1 kg) of octane gasoline. The molecular weight (M.W.) of octane is 114 grams/mole. Thus, since:

$$\text{mole} = \frac{\text{grams (weight)}}{\text{M.W.}}, \text{ you have } \frac{3,190}{114} = 27.98 \text{ moles of gasoline.}$$

From the equation's coefficients, you see that for every 2 moles of gasoline, 25 moles of O_2 are required. Thus, for this number of moles of gasoline, you need:

$$(27.98)\frac{25}{2} = 349.75 \text{ moles of } O_2$$

Recalling that 1 mole of gas occupies 22.4 liters at STP, 349.75 moles of

O_2 occupies $(349.75)(22.4) = 7,834.40$ liters. Oxygen is 21% of the air. Thus, the amount of air required is:

$$\frac{7,834.40 \text{ liters}}{0.21 \text{ liters } O_2} O_2 = 37,306.7 \text{ liters air}$$

FE/EIT

FE: PM General Engineering Exam

CHAPTER 5

Thermodynamics

CHAPTER 5

THERMODYNAMICS

Thermodynamics is the engineering discipline concerning the transformation of energy from one form to another and the availability of energy to perform work. The field is based primarily on three basic laws. The First Law is concerned with the balance of various types of energy in a given system. The Second Law is concerned with the availability of that energy to do work and the concept of *entropy*. The Third Law, developed from the concept of *free energy*, involves the determination of chemical equilibrium and kinetics, and properties of materials not readily measurable.

THE FIRST LAW

The First Law of thermodynamics is analogous to the concept of conservation of mass. As with that concept, the First Law of thermodynamics can be thought of as the law of conservation of energy and it can be stated by the word equation:

increase in energy (accumulation) = heat absorbed (input)
– work done (output)

The First Law is stated mathematically as:

$$dU = dQ - dW - dKE - dPE$$

where: dU = is the incremental increase in internal energy of the system

dQ = the incremental quantity of heat absorbed by the system

dW = the incremental quantity work done by the system

dKE = the incremental increase of kinetic energy of the system *dPE* = the incremental increase of potential energy of the system

For a system that goes from state *A* to state *B* the First Law equation may be written as:

$$U_B - U_A = Q - W - KE - PE$$

The values for any changes in the internal energy, ΔU, are determined entirely from the initial and final states of the system as defined by temperature, pressure, volume, mass, and chemical composition. ΔU is not dependent on the path followed by the system in getting from state *A* to state *B*. (This property is sometimes referred to as a *point* function.) The values for any changes in kinetic energy and potential energy, ΔKE and ΔPE, are also determined entirely from the initial and final states of the system as defined by velocity, mass, and physical position or condition, and are not dependent on the path followed by the system in getting from state *A* to state *B*. However, while the term $(Q - W)$ is also dependent only on the initial and final states of a system, the individual quantities Q and W *are* dependent upon the path by which the system gets from state *A* to state *B*. (This property is sometimes referred to as a *path* function.)

To illustrate, if the pressure of a system is represented by p and the volume by V, the work done by expansion or compression against another pressure differing by the incremental amount of *dp*, is then:

$$dW = pdV \qquad \text{or} \qquad W = {}_A\!\int^B pdV$$

which simply says that the work done is equal to the areas under the curve, or "path," followed by the system on a pressure-volume phase diagram.

The changes in kinetic energy, ΔKE, and potential energy, ΔPE, of a system are defined in the usual manner. That is:

$$\Delta KE = (\tfrac{1}{2}mv^2)_B - (\tfrac{1}{2}mv^2)_A, \text{ and } \Delta PE = (mgh)_B - (mgh)_A.$$

PROBLEM 1:

Determine the final equilibrium state when 2 lbm of saturated liquid mercury at 1 psia is mixed with 4 lbm of mercury vapor at 1 psia and 1,400°F. During the process the pressure in the cylinder is kept constant and no energy is lost between the cylinder and mercury.

SOLUTION:

Since the amount of liquid might change during the process, the liquid or only vapor cannot be taken as the control mass. Instead take the

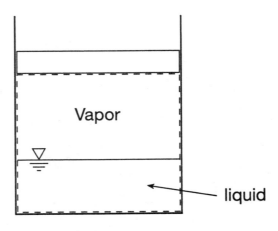

Figure 1
The control mass

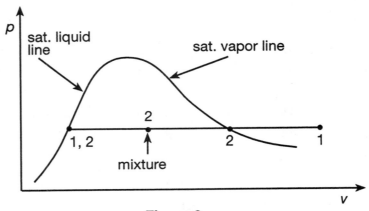

Figure 2
The process representation

entire 6 lbm of mercury. By assumption, no energy transfers as heat occurs, but the volume is expected to change, resulting in an energy transfer as work. The only energy stored within the control mass is the internal energy of the mercury; the energy balance, made over the time for the process to take place, is therefore (Figures 1 and 2):

$$W \quad = \quad \Delta U$$
energy input $\qquad$ increase in energy storage

where $\Delta U = U_2 - U_1$

The work calculation is made easy by the fact that the pressure is constant. When the piston moves an amount dx, the energy transfer as work from the environment to the control mass is:

$$dW = PAdx = -P\,dV$$

Integrating:

$$W = \int_1^2 -PdV = P(V_1 - V_2)$$

Combining with the energy balance to obtain:

$$U_2 + PV_2 = U_1 + PV_1 \qquad (1)$$

		Enthalpy, Btu/lbm		
P, psia	T,°F	Sat. liq.	Evap.	Sat. vap.
0.010	233.57	6.668	127.732	134.400
0.020	259.88	7.532	127.614	135.146
0.030	276.22	8.068	127.540	135.608
0.050	297.97	8.778	127.442	136.220
0.100	329.73	9.814	127.300	137.114
0.200	364.25	10.936	127.144	138.080
0.300	385.92	11.639	127.047	138.086
0.400	401.98	12.159	126.975	139.134
0.500	415.00	12.568	126.916	139.484
0.600	425.82	12.929	126.868	139.797
0.800	443.50	13.500	126.788	140.288
1.00	457.72	13.959	126.724	140.683
2.00	504.93	15.476	126.512	141.988
3.00	535.25	16.439	126.377	142.816
5.00	575.70	17.741	126.193	143.934

Figure 3
Properties of saturated mercury

To evaluate the initial terms assume that the liquid is in an equilibrium state and the vapor is in an equilibrium state, even though they are not in equilibrium with one another. The graphical and tabular equations of state, the chart listing the properties of saturated mercury and the table for the thermodynamic properties of saturated mercury may then be employed for each phase. Since the available equation-of-state information is in terms of the enthalpy property, express the right-hand side of equation (1) as:

$$U_1 + PV_1 = M_{l_1} u_{l_1} + M_{v_1} u_{v_1} + P\left(M_{l_1} v_{l_1} + M_{v_1} v_{v_1}\right)$$
$$= M_{l_1} h_{l_1} + M_{v_1} h_{v_1}$$

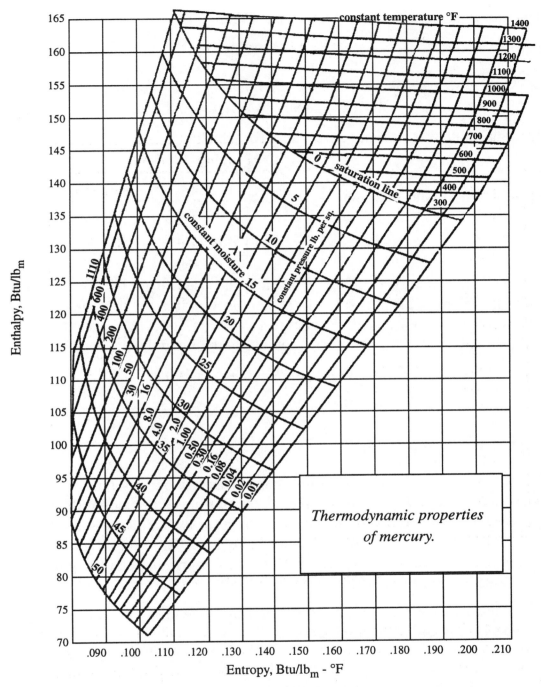

Figure 4
Thermodynamic properties of mercury

Now, from the tables, the initial liquid enthalpy is (saturated liquid at 1 psia):

$$h_{l_1} = 13.96 \text{ Btu/lbm}$$

$$T_1 = 457.7°F$$

The initial vapor enthalpy is found from Figure 4 as:

$$h_{v_1} = 164 \text{ Btu/lbm.}$$

Substituting the numbers:

$$U_1 + PV_1 = 2 \times 13.96 + 4 \times 164 = 684 \text{ Btu.}$$

The final state is a state of equilibrium, for which:

$$U_2 + PV_2 = M(u + Pv)_2 = Mh_2.$$

The enthalpy in the final state is therefore:

$$h_2 = \frac{684 \text{ Btu}}{6 \text{ lbm}} = 114 \text{ Btu/lbm}$$

The final pressure and enthalpy may be used to fix the final state. Upon inspection of Figure 4 the final state is a mixture of saturated liquid and vapor at 1 psia and the moisture $(1 - x)$ is about 21 percent (0.79 quality). Alternatively, the information in Figure 3 could have been used.

$$114 = (1 - x_2) \times 13.96 + x_2 \times 140.7$$

$$x_2 = 0.79$$

THE SECOND LAW

All systems or processes left to themselves without any outside influences move, either rapidly or slowly, toward a state of rest or equilibrium. The further removed a system or process is from its equilibrium state, the greater the amount of useful work that can be done. The Second Law gives a quantitative measure of the amount of useful work that can be obtained from any system or process.

The Second Law is formally defined by the entropy equation which can be stated in the word equation:

$$\text{increase in entropy} = \frac{\text{head used}}{\text{absolute temperature}}$$

The Second Law is stated mathematically as:

$$dS = \frac{dQ}{T}$$

where: dS = the incremental increase in entropy of the system

dQ = the incremental quantity of heat used by the system

T = the absolute temperature of the system

For ideal reversible processes, the sum of all changes in entropy is equal to zero.

Mathematically:

$$\Sigma dS_i = \frac{\Sigma dQ_1}{T_1}$$

Since all actual processes are irreversible to some extent, the sum of all changes in entropy for these processes increases. This increase in entropy represents losses and inefficiencies of the system or process. Entropy is also a point function, that is, it is determined entirely from the initial and final states, and is not dependent on the path of the process.

Heat Engine

A heat engine is a system that takes heat from a high temperature source, converts as much of the heat as possible to useful work, and discharges the remaining heat to a lower temperature reservoir. Simultaneously solving the First Law equation and the Second Law equation for a heat engine yields the Carnot equation for heat engines, which is the maximum amount of work obtainable from a given amount of heat when operating between two temperatures. It is mathematically expressed as:

$$\frac{W}{Q_1} = \frac{T_1 - T_2}{T_1}$$

where: W = amount of work done

Q_1 = quantity of heat input to the system from the higher temperature heat source

T_1 = absolute temperature of the heat source

T_2 = absolute temperature of the heat sink

The $(T_1 - T_2)/T_1$ term is often referred to as the *Carnot efficiency*. It is the maximum efficiency obtainable between the temperature of the source and the temperature of the sink. Though the Carnot equation is used here to describe the work done by a "heat potential," that is, a temperature differential, it is also applicable to other potentials including pressure differentials and voltage differentials.

A heat engine working in reverse is called *a refrigeration machine*.

Work is put into the system, and the heat is pumped from the lower temperature sink up to the higher temperature reservoir. When such a device is used to accomplish cooling with the heat at the higher temperature wasted, it is called a *refrigeration device*. The same process is used for an air-conditioning device. When such a machine is used as a heating device, with the heat at the lower temperature pumped to a higher temperature (i.e., potential) and used for heating, it is called a *heat pump*. However, thermodynamically, the two processes are the same.

The effectiveness of a reverse heat engine, refrigeration device, or heat pump is measured by a coefficient of performance (COP) rather than by efficiency. The COP for a refrigeration system is the ratio of the heat removed from the lower temperature end (the product for a refrigerator), while the COP for a heat pump system is the ratio of the heat discharged into the higher temperature end (the product for a heat pump). They are defined as follows:

$$COP_R = \frac{Q_L}{W} = \frac{Q_L}{Q_H - Q_L} \qquad \text{(refrigerator)}$$

$$COP_{HP} = \frac{Q_H}{W} = \frac{Q_H}{Q_L - Q_H} \qquad \text{(heat pump)}$$

where: COP_R = coefficient of performance for a refrigerating system

COP_{HP} = coefficient of performance for a heat pump system

W = amount of work input

Q_L = quantity of heat input to the system from the *lower* temperature heat source

Q_H = quantity of heat output from the system at the *higher* temperature heat source

The maximum work, W, that can be done by a system is also called the *availability*. This maximum work is achieved when the work and the overall process are reversible. However, all processes and systems have a certain amount of irreversibility because of heat losses and friction. The irreversibility manifests itself as an increase in entropy, and it can be expressed as the difference between the theoretical reversible work and the actual work accomplished. Algebraically, it is expressed as:

$$I = W_{\text{rev}} - W_{\text{act}}$$

where: I = irreversibility;

W_{rev} = reversible work

W_{act} = actual work

Cycles

The basic heat engine system operates as a Carnot cycle, which is a system consisting of reversible processes. Since it is reversible, a system based on a Carnot heat engine can act as a refrigerator or heat pump. A Carnot cycle operating between a high temperature reservoir and a low temperature reservoir consists of four processes as shown:

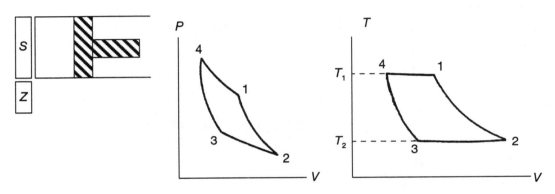

Figure 5
Carnot cycle on *P–V* and *T–V* diagrams

1 to 2   A *reversible adiabatic process*, an expansion in which the temperature of the working fluid decreases from the higher temperature to the lower temperature (T_2), with a corresponding decrease in pressure.

2 to 3   A *reversible isothermal process*, where heat is transferred to or from the low temperature reservoir.

3 to 4   A *reversible adiabatic process*, a compression in which the temperature of the working fluid increases from the lower temperature (T_2) to the higher temperature (T_1), with a corresponding decrease in pressure.

4 to 1   A *reversible isothermal process*, where heat is transferred to or from the high temperature reservoir.

The amount of work output from a Carnot cycle heat engine is a path function and is represented by the area enclosed by the above four processes on a pressure-volume phase diagram for the working fluid.

PROBLEM 2:

A container that has a volume of 0.1 m³ is fitted with a plunger enclosing a volume of steam at 0.4 MPa. Calculate the amount of heat transferred and the work done when the steam is heated to 300°C at constant pressure.

SOLUTION:

For this system changes in kinetic and potential energy are not significant. Therefore:

$$Q = m(u_2 - u_1) + W$$

$$W = \int_1^2 P\,dV = P\int_1^2 dV = P(V_2 - V_1) = m(P_2 v_2 - P_1 v_1)$$

Therefore:

$$Q = m(u_2 - u_1) + m(P_2 v_2 - P_1 v_1) = m(h_2 - h_1)$$

$$v_1 = \frac{V_1}{m} = \frac{0.1}{0.5} = 0.2 = 0.001084 + x_1(0.4614)$$

$$x_1 = \frac{0.1989}{0.4614} = 0.4311$$

Then:

$$h_1 = h_f + x_1 h_{fg}$$

$$= 604.74 + 0.4311 \times 2{,}133.8 = 1{,}524.6$$

$$h_2 = 3{,}066.8$$

$$Q = 0.5(3{,}066.8 - 1{,}524.6) = 771.1 \text{ kJ}$$

$$W = mP(v_2 - v_1) = 0.5 \times 400(0.6548 - 0.2)$$

$$= 91.0 \text{ kJ}$$

Therefore:

$$U_2 - U_1 = Q - W = 771.1 - 91.0 = 680.1 \text{ kJ}$$

The heat transfer can be calculated from u_1 and u_2 by using:

$$Q = m(u_2 - u_1) + W$$

$$u_1 = u_f + x_1 u_{fg}$$

$$= 604.31 + 0.4311 \times 1{,}949.3 = 1{,}444.6$$

$$u_2 = 2,804.8$$

and,

$$Q = .5(2,804.8 - 1,444.6) + 91.0 = 771.1 \text{ kJ}$$

Power Cycles

There are two major categories of cycles: power cycles and refrigeration cycles. Power cycles are divided into two categories: vapor power cycles (e.g., steam turbine cycles) and air-standard cycles (e.g., gas turbine cycles).

The idealized vapor (steam) power cycle is called the Rankine cycle. A simple steam plant that operates on the Rankine cycle consists of a boiler, a steam turbine, a condenser, and a water return pump. The Rankine cycle is considered a closed cycle in that the exhaust steam from the turbine is returned to the boiler via the condenser and boiler feed water pump. It is usually represented on a temperature-enthalpy graph. The basic four processes that comprise the Rankine cycle are:

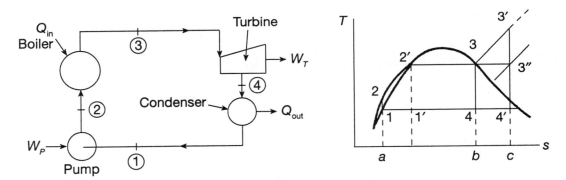

Figure 6
Simple steam power plant that operates on the Rankine cycle

1 to 2   A *reversible adiabatic (isentropic)* pumping of the boiler feed water into the boiler.

2 to 3   *Constant pressure heat addition*, from the combustion in the furnace to the boiler.

3 to 4   A *reversible isentropic expansion* through the steam turbine.

4 to 1   *Constant pressure heat rejection* from the condenser to the ambient.

The Rankine cycle efficiency can be increased by several techniques including lowering the exhaust pressure from the turbine, increasing the boiler pressure, superheating the steam before it enters the turbine, preheating the boiler feed water using extraction steam, or a combination of these techniques.

PROBLEM 3:

Steam at 3 MPa, 300°C leaves the boiler and enters the high-pressure turbine (in a reheat cycle) and is expanded to 300 kPa. The steam is then reheated to 300°C and expanded in the second stage turbine to 10 kPA. What is the efficiency of the cycle if it is assumed to be internally reversible?

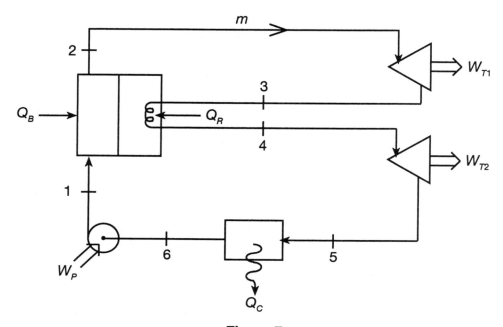

Figure 7
Schematic of heating cycle

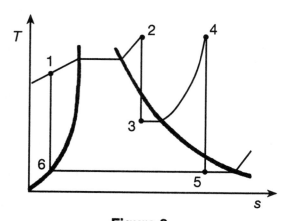

Figure 8
T–s diagram for heating cycle

SOLUTION:

The efficiency η can be obtained from the following equation:

$$\eta = \frac{\dot{W}_{t_1} + \dot{W}_{t_2} - \dot{W}_p}{\dot{Q}_b - \dot{Q}_r} \qquad (1)$$

To calculate $\dot{W}_{t_1}$ assume that the turbine is adiabatic and neglect kinetic and potential energy changes. Applying the First Law to the turbine:

$$\dot{W}_{t_1} = \dot{m}(h_2 - h_3).$$

From the steam tables:

$$h_2 = 2{,}993.5 \text{ kJ/kg}$$

$$s_2 = 6.5390 \text{ kJ/kg} - \text{K}$$

To find h_3, for the internally reversible adiabatic process $2 \to 3$:

$$s_2 = s_3 = 6.5390 \text{ kJ/kg} - \text{K}$$

At state 3:

$$s_{f_3} = 1.6718 \text{ kJ/kg} - \text{K} \qquad h_{f_3} = 561.47 \text{ kJ/kg}$$

$$s_{fg_3} = 5.3201 \text{ kJ/kg} - \text{K} \qquad h_{fg_3} = 2{,}163.8 \text{ kJ/kg}$$

$$s_{g_3} = 6.9919 \text{ kJ/kg} - \text{K} \qquad h_{g_3} = 2{,}725.3 \text{ kJ/kg}$$

$$s_2 = s_3 = s_{f_3} + x_3 s_{fg_3}$$

$$6.5390 = 1.6718 + x_3(5.3201)$$

$$x_3 = 0.915$$

$$h_3 = h_{f_3} + x_3 h_{fg_3}$$

$$h_3 = 561.47 + 0.915(2{,}163.8)$$

$$h_3 = 2{,}541 \text{ kJ/kg}$$

$$\frac{\dot{W}_{t_1}}{\dot{m}} = h_2 - h_3$$

$$= 2{,}993.5 - 2{,}541$$

$$= 452 \text{ kJ/kg}$$

Similarly, to find $\dot{W}_{t_2}$:

$$\dot{W}_{t_2} = \dot{m}(h_4 - h_5)$$

From the steam tables:

$$h_4 = 3{,}069.3 \text{ kJ/kg}$$

$$s_4 = 7.7022 \text{ kJ/kg} - \text{K}$$

To find h_5, note that:

$$s_4 = s_5$$

At state 5:

$$s_{f_5} = 0.6493 \text{ kJ/kg} - \text{K}$$

$$h_{f_5} = 191.83 \text{ kJ/kg}$$

$$s_{fg_5} = 7.5009 \text{ kJ/kg} - \text{K}$$

$$h_{fg_5} = 2{,}392.8 \text{ kJ/kg}$$

$$s_{g_5} = 8.1502 \text{ kJ/kg} - \text{K}$$

$$h_{g_5} = 2{,}584.7 \text{ kJ/kg}$$

$$s_4 = s_5 = s_{f_5} + x_5 s_{fg_5}$$

$$x_5 = 0.949$$

$$h_5 = h_{f_5} + x_5 h_{fg_5}$$

$$h_5 = 191.83 + 0.949(2{,}392.8)$$

$$h_5 = 2{,}463 \text{ kJ/kg}$$

Therefore, $\quad \dfrac{\dot{W}_{t_2}}{\dot{m}} = h_4 - h_5$

$$= 3069.3 - 2463$$

$$= 606 \text{ kJ/kg}$$

To obtain $\dot{W}_p$, assume that $\dot{W}_p = \dot{m} v_6 (p_1 - p_6)$.

From the steam tables:

$$v_6 = v_{f_6}$$

$$= 1.0102 \times 10^{-3} \text{m}^3/\text{kg}$$

Thus:

$$\frac{\dot{W}_p}{\dot{m}} = 1.0102(30 - 0.1)10^5 \times 10^{-6}$$

$$= 3.0 \text{ kJ/kg}$$

To obtain $\dot{Q}_b$, use:

$$\dot{Q}_b = \dot{m}(h_2 - h_1)$$

$$h_1 = h_6 + \frac{\dot{W}_p}{\dot{m}}$$

$$= 191.8 + 3.0$$

$$= 194.8 \text{ kJ/kg}$$

$$\frac{\dot{Q}_b}{\dot{m}} = 2{,}993.5 - 194.8$$

$$= 2{,}799 \text{ kJ/kg}$$

To find $\dot{Q}_r$:

$$\dot{Q}_r = \dot{m}(h_4 - h_3)$$

$$\frac{\dot{Q}_r}{\dot{m}} = 3{,}069.3 - 2{,}542$$

$$= 527 \text{ kJ/kg}$$

From equation (1) then:

$$\eta = \frac{452 + 606 - 3}{2{,}799 + 527}$$

$$= 0.317$$

The idealized air-standard power cycle is called the Otto cycle. A simple gas turbine that operates on the Otto cycle consists of a compressor, a combustion chamber, and an expansion/exhaust turbine. The Otto cycle is considered an "open" cycle in that the exhaust gas (air) is not put directly back into the intake duct, but rather fresh air is used. The basic four processes which comprise the Otto cycle are:

1 to 2 A *constant volume heat addition*, in the burner chamber resulting in a pressure increase.

2 to 3 An *isentropic expansion* through the exhaust turbine.

3 to 4 A *constant volume heat rejection*, out the tailpipe to the ambient atmosphere.

4 to 1 An *isentropic compression* of the atmospheric air from the ambient atmosphere into the combustion chamber.

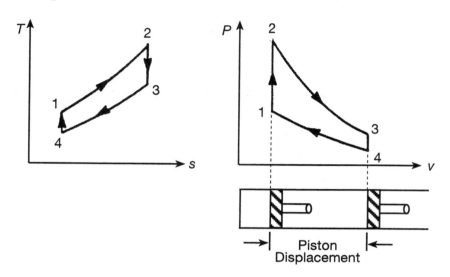

Figure 9
Air-standard Otto cycle

PROBLEM 4:

1.   One kilogram of air at 101.35 kPa, 21°C is compressed in an Otto cycle with a compression ratio of 7 to 1. During the combustion process, 953.66 kJ of heat is added to the air. Compute (a) the specific volume, pressure, and temperature at the four points in the cycle, (b) the air standard efficiency, and (c) the mep (mean effective pressure) and hp of the engine, if it uses 1 kg/min of air.

2.   Calculate the efficiency for a Carnot cycle operating between the maximum and minimum temperatures of the Otto cycle.

SOLUTION:

1(a)   At state 1:

$$P_1 = 101.35 \text{ kPa}$$

$$T_1 = 294 \text{K}$$

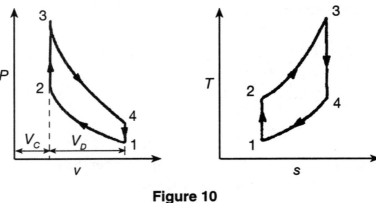

Figure 10
Otto cycle

The specific volume, v_1, is determined by using the perfect gas equation of state:

$$v_1 = \frac{RT_1}{P_1}$$

$$= \frac{0.287(294)}{101.35}$$

$$= 0.8325 \text{ m}^3/\text{kg}$$

At 2, the specific volume can be obtained by using the compression ratio:

$$\frac{v_2}{v_1} = \frac{1}{7}$$

or:

$$v_2 = \frac{v_1}{7}$$

$$= \frac{0.8325}{7}$$

$$= 0.1189 \text{ m}^3/\text{kg}$$

The pressure (P_2) is obtained from the isentropic relation:

$$P_2 = P_1 \left(\frac{v_1}{v_2}\right)^k$$

$$= 101.35 \left(\frac{0.8325}{0.1189}\right)^{1.4}$$

$$= 1{,}545.6 \text{ kPa}$$

The temperature (T_2) is:

$$T_2 = T_1 \left(\frac{v_1}{v_2} \right)^{k-1}$$

$$= 294 \left(\frac{0.8325}{0.1189} \right)^{1.4-1}$$

$$= 640.4 \text{ K}$$

State 3, $v_3 = v_2 = 0.1189$ m³/kg. The temperature here can be calculated from the quantity of heat supplied since:

$$Q_{in} = mc_v(T_3 - T_2)$$

or solving for T_3:

$$T_3 = \frac{Q_{in}}{mc_v} + T_2$$

$$= \frac{953.66}{1(0.7243)} + 640.4$$

$$= 1,957.1 \text{K}$$

The pressure (P_3) is:

$$P_3 = \frac{RT_3}{v_3}$$

$$= \frac{0.287(1,957.1)}{0.1189}$$

$$= 4.724 \text{ kPa}$$

At state 4:

$$v_4 = v_1 = 0.8325 \text{ m}^3/\text{kg}$$

and the pressure is:

$$P_4 = P_3 \left(\frac{v_3}{v_4} \right)^k$$

$$= 4,724 \left(\frac{0.1189}{0.8325} \right)^{1.4}$$

$$= 309.7 \text{ kPa}$$

The temperature T_4 is:

$$T_4 = T_3 \left(\frac{v_3}{v_4} \right)^{k-1}$$

$$= 1{,}957.1 \left(\frac{0.1189}{0.8325} \right)^{1.4-1}$$

$$= 898.5 \text{K}$$

(b)   The efficiency of the Otto cycle is defined as:

$$\eta = \frac{Q_{in} - Q_{out}}{Q_{in}} \times 100 \qquad (1)$$

where:

$$Q_{in} = 953.66 \text{ kJ}$$

and

$$Q_{out} = mc_v(T_4 - T_1)$$

$$= 1(0.7243)(898.5 - 294)$$

$$= 437.8 \text{ kJ}$$

Therefore:

$$\eta = \frac{953.66 - 437.8}{953.66} \times 100$$

$$= 54\%$$

(c)   The mep is:

$$\text{mep} = \frac{W_{net}}{v_1 - v_2}$$

where:

$$W_{net} = q_{in} - q_{out}$$

$$= 953.66 - 437.8$$

$$= 515.86 \text{ kJ}$$

Thus:

$$\text{mep} = \frac{515.86}{0.8325 - 0.1189} = 722.9 \text{ kPa}$$

The horsepower is:

$$\text{hp} = \dot{m}W_{net} = 515.86\,\text{kW}$$

$$= 5.3\,\text{hp}$$

2) The maximum and minimum temperatures of the Otto cycle are:

$$T_{max} = 1,957.1\,\text{K}$$

$$T_{min} = 294\,\text{K}$$

The Carnot cycle efficiency is:

$$\eta = \frac{T_{max} - T_{min}}{T_{max}} \times 100$$

$$= \frac{1,957.1 - 294}{1,957.1} \times 100$$

$$= 85\%$$

which is comparatively higher than the Otto cycle efficiency.

Another idealized air-standard power cycle is called the Brayton cycle. A simple gas turbine that operates on the Brayton cycle can be either an open cycle like the Otto cycle, or it can be a closed cycle. In the closed cycle configuration, the gas quality is not depleted during the heat addition stage. In the open cycle process heat input is accomplished by burning the fuel in the process fluid. Air is then depleted of oxygen. The Brayton cycle machine also consists of a compressor, a heat addition chamber, and an expansion/exhaust turbine.

PROBLEM 5:

The adiabatic efficiencies of the compressor and turbine used in an air-standard Brayton cycle are 85% and 90%, respectively. If the cycle operates between 14.7 and 55 psia and if the maximum and minimum temperatures are 1,500°F and 80°F, respectively, compute the thermal efficiency of the cycle. Assume constant specific heats.

SOLUTION:

Use the accompanying figure to refer to the different states of the cycle. The thermal efficiency of the cycle is calculated using the formula:

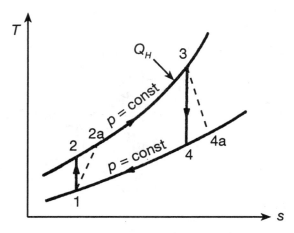

Figure 11
Brayton cycle

$$\eta_{th} = \frac{W_{act}}{Q_H} \qquad (1)$$

where:

$$W_{act} = W_{turb.} + W_{comp.} \qquad (2)$$

For this problem, the processes in the turbine and compressor are not reversible, and so the work done will be less than the work if the processes were reversible. Using the given efficiencies, it can be written:

$$W_{act}\Big|_{turb.} = \eta_{turb.} \times W_{theo.}\Big|_{turb.} \qquad (3)$$

and:

$$W_{act}\Big|_{comp.} = \frac{W_{theo.}\big|_{comp.}}{\eta_{comp.}} \qquad (4)$$

where:

$$W_{theo.}\big|_{turb.} = h_3 - h_4 = c_p(T_3 - T_4) \qquad (5)$$

and:

$$-W_{theo.}\big|_{comp.} = h_2 - h_1 = c_p(T_2 - T_1) \qquad (6)$$

To find the temperatures at states 2 and 4, use the isentropic relation:

$$\frac{T_a}{T_b} = \left(\frac{P_a}{P_b}\right)^{\frac{k-1}{k}}$$

At state 2:

$$T_2 = T_1\left(\frac{P_2}{P_1}\right)^{\frac{k-1}{k}}$$

$$= 540\left(\frac{55}{14.7}\right)^{0.286}$$

$$= 787.6°R$$

At state 4:

$$T_4 = T_3\left(\frac{P_4}{P_3}\right)^{\frac{k-1}{k}}$$

$$= 1,960\left(\frac{14.7}{55}\right)^{0.286}$$

$$= 1,343.9°R$$

With these values, and $c_p = 0.24$ Btu/lbm – °R, from equations (5) and (6):

$$w_{theo.}\big|_{turb.} = 0.24(1,960 - 1,343.9)$$

$$= 147.9 \text{ Btu/lbm}$$

and:

$$-w_{theo.}\big|_{comp.} = 0.24(787.6 - 540)$$

$$= 59.42 \text{ Btu/lbm}$$

Substituting into equations (3) and (4):

$$w_{act}\big|_{turb.} = 0.90(147.9) = 133.1 \text{ Btu/lbm}$$

$$-w_{act}\big|_{comp.} = \frac{59.42}{0.85} = 69.9 \text{ Btu/lbm}$$

From equation (2), then:

$$w_{act} = 133.1 - 69.9 = 63.2 \text{ Btu/lbm}$$

The only term unknown in equation (1) is the heat added to the system during process 2–3 (Q_H). However:

$$Q_H = h_3 - h_{2a} - c_p(T_3 - T_{2a}) \qquad (7)$$

where T_{2a} is the actual temperature at state 2, and can be found using the efficiency of the compressor. Hence:

$$\eta_{comp} = \frac{T_2 - T_1}{T_{2a} - T_1} = 0.85$$

or

$$T_{2a} = \left(\frac{T_2 - T}{0.85}\right) + T_1$$

$$= \left(\frac{787.6 - 540}{0.85}\right) + 540$$

$$= 831.3°R$$

Equation (7) then gives:

$$Q_H = 0.24(1960 - 831.3)$$

$$= 270.89$$

Finally, using equation (1), the efficiency of the cycle is calculated as:

$$\eta_{th} = \frac{63.2}{270.89} = 0.233$$

or

$$\eta_{th} = 23.3\%$$

The Diesel cycle is thermodynamically the same as the Otto cycle (usually associated with the gas turbine), though the equipment is quite different. The four process steps for the Diesel cycle with its related mechanical actions are:

1 to 2 A *constant volume heat addition*, resulting in a pressure increase.

2 to 3 An *isentropic expansion*, pushing the piston down in the cylinder.

3 to 4 A *constant volume heat rejection*, by the piston moving up the cylinder.

4 to 1 An *isentropic compression* of the atmospheric air, by the piston moving back up the cylinder after drawing in atmospheric air on the down stroke.

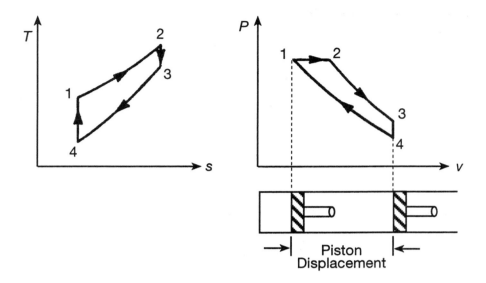

Figure 12
The Diesel cycle

PROBLEM 6:

Consider an air-standard Diesel cycle. At the beginning of compression the temperature is 300K and the pressure is 101.35 kPa. If the compression ratio is 15 and during the process 1,860 kJ/kg of air are added as heat, calculate: (a) the maximum cycle pressure and temperature, (b) the thermal efficiency of the cycle, and (c) the mep.

SOLUTION:

(a)   Using the ideal gas equation of state:

$$Pv = RT \tag{1}$$

The specific volume at state d is:

$$v_d = \frac{RT_d}{P_d}$$

$$= \frac{0.287(300)}{101.35}$$

$$= 0.8495 \text{ m}^3\text{/kg}$$

Process $c \rightarrow d$ is an isochoric (constant volume) process. Hence:

$$v_c = v_d = 0.8495 \text{ m}^3\text{/kg}$$

The compression ratio is:

$$r_v = \frac{v_d}{v_a} = 15$$

or

$$= \frac{v_d}{15}$$

$$= \frac{0.8495}{15}$$

$$= 0.0566 \text{ m}^3/\text{kg}$$

Process $d \to a$ is an isentropic process. Therefore:

$$\frac{T_a}{T_d} = \left(\frac{v_d}{v_a}\right)^{k-1}$$

or

$$T_a = 300 \left(\frac{0.8495}{0.0566}\right)^{1.4-1}$$

$$= 886.5\text{K}$$

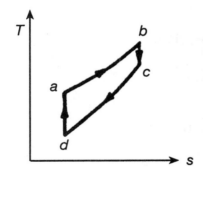
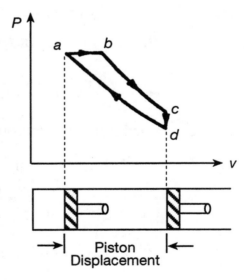

Figure 13
Diesel cycle

Also,

$$\frac{P_a}{P_d} = \left(\frac{v_d}{v_a}\right)^{k}$$

or

$$P_a = 101.35 \left(\frac{0.8495}{0.0566}\right)^{1.4}$$

$$= 4,495 \text{ kPa}$$

Therefore, $P_{max} = P_a = 4,495 \text{ kPa}$

The maximum temperature can be obtained as follows. From the First Law, assuming constant specific heats, the heat supplied is:

$$Q_{in} = Q_{ab} = C_p(T_b - T_a)$$

or

$$T_b = \frac{Q_{ab}}{C_p} + T_a$$

$$= \frac{1,860}{1.0035} + 886.5$$

$$= 2,740 \text{K}$$

Therefore, $T_{max} = T_b = 2,740 \text{K}$

(b)   The thermal efficiency of the Diesel cycle is:

$$\eta_{th} = 1 - \frac{(T_c - T_d)}{k(T_b - T_a)} \tag{2}$$

T_c can be obtained from the isentropic relation:

$$\frac{T_b}{T_c} = \left(\frac{v_c}{v_b}\right)^{k-1} \tag{3}$$

where:

$$v_b = \frac{RT_b}{P_b} \text{ from equation (1)}$$

$$= \frac{0.287(2,740)}{4,495}$$

$$= 0.1749 \text{ m}^3/\text{kg}$$

Substituting into (3):

$$\frac{T_b}{T_c} = \left(\frac{0.8495}{0.1749}\right)^{1.4-1}$$

or

$$\frac{T_b}{T_c} = 1.88$$

Solving for T_c:

$$T_c = \frac{2,740}{1.88}$$

$$= 1,457.5\text{K}$$

From equation (2), then:

$$\eta_{th} = 1 - \frac{(1,457.5 - 300)}{1.4(2,740 - 886.5)}$$

$$= 1 - \frac{1,157.5}{2,594.9}$$

$$= 0.554$$

(c)   The mean effective pressure (mep) is defined as:

$$\text{mep} = \frac{W_{\text{net}}}{v_d - v_a} \qquad (4)$$

where:

$$W_{\text{net}} = \eta_{th}\, Q_{\text{in}}$$

$$= 0.554(1,860)$$

$$= 1,030.44 \text{ kJ/kg}$$

Substituting into (4):

$$\text{mep} = \frac{1,030.44}{(0.8495 - 0.0566)}$$

$$= 1,299.6 \text{ kPa}$$

Refrigeration Cycles

The vapor compression refrigeration cycle is essentially the same as the Rankine cycle, but in reverse. This refrigeration cycle consists of the following processes:

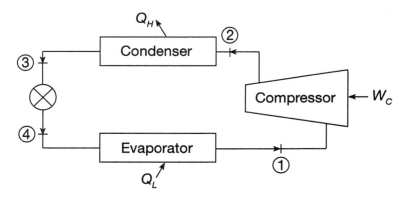

Figure 14.1
The ideal vapor compression refrigeration cycle

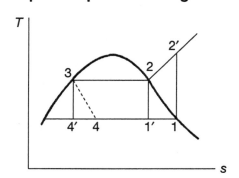

Figure 14.2
The ideal vapor compression refrigeration cycle

1 to 2   An *isentropic compression*, in which the working fluid is increased in temperature and pressure.

2 to 3   A *constant pressure heat rejection*, whereby heat is removed from the working fluid (and discharged into a higher temperature sink).

3 to 4   An *adiabatic (nonreversible) expansion*, or throttling, during which the working fluid is decreased in temperature and in pressure.

4 to 1   A *constant pressure heat addition* whereby heat is absorbed into the working fluid (i.e., being absorbed from the lower temperature source).

PROBLEM 7:

A standard vapor compression refrigeration cycle uses Freon-22 as the working fluid to provide three tons of cooling capacity. If the condenser operates at 140°F and the evaporator operates at 50°F, compute (a) the mass flow rate of the Freon-22, (b) the horsepower required for the compressor, and (c) the heat transferred in the condenser. Assume the compression process to be reversible and adiabatic.

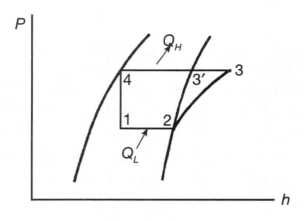

FIGURE 15
Refrigeration cycle

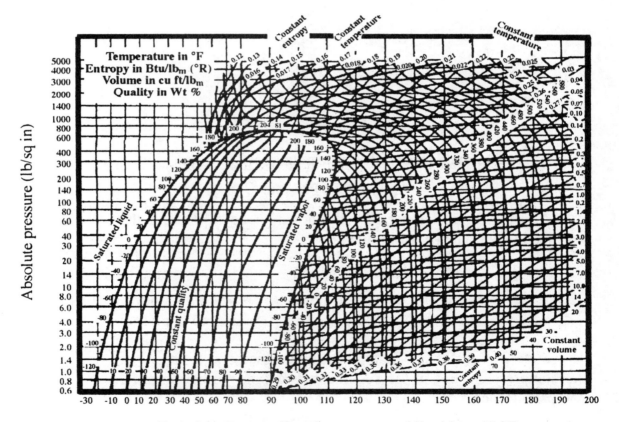

Figure 16
Pressure-enthalpy diagram for Freon-22 refrigerant

SOLUTION:

Since the process has been assumed to be reversible and adiabatic, it will also be isentropic. Assuming the throttling process to be adiabatic, then it is also isenthalpic (constant enthalpy). Furthermore, assume that the condenser and evaporator operate at constant pressure. Then this cycle can be plotted on a P-h diagram as shown in Figure 15.

The values of the various properties at the different states shown in Figure 15 are taken from the P-h diagram for Freon-22, as shown in Figure 16. The procedure is as follows:

At state 3′ the temperature is known to be 140°F, and the state is saturated vapor. Therefore, from Figure 16:

$$P_{3'} = P_3 = 350 \text{ psia.}$$

At state 4:

$$P_4 = P_{3'} = 350 \text{ psia}$$

$$T_4 = T_{3'} = 140°F$$

Hence:

$$h_4 = 52 \text{ Btu/lbm}$$

At state 1, since process 1–4 is isenthalpic:

$$h_1 = h_4 = 52 \text{ Btu/lbm}$$

At state 2 the temperature is known to be 50°F, and the state is saturated vapor. Hence, from Figure 16:

$$P_2 = 100 \text{ psia}$$

$$h_2 = 109 \text{ Btu/lbm}$$

$$s_2 = 0.218 \text{ Btu/lbm} - °R$$

State 3: Process 2–3 is an isentropic process and state three, due to the compression, lies in the superheated region. Furthermore, $P_3 = P_{3¢} = 350$ psia. Hence:

$$s_3 = s_2 = 0.218 \text{ Btu/lbm} - °R$$

$$h_2 = 109 \text{ Btu/lbm}$$

From Figure 16:

$$h_3 = 123 \text{ Btu/lbm}$$

$$T_2 = 180°F$$

Now that the values of the various properties have been obtained, we can solve the problem.

(a)   Consider the evaporator and write an energy balance around it to find the heat absorbed by the Freon-22. Neglecting potential and kinetic energies, we can write:

$$q_L = h_2 - h_1$$

$$= 109 - 52$$

$$= 57 \text{ Btu/lbm}$$

It is known, however, that the evaporator is to absorb three tons or 36,000 Btu/hr. Hence, the required mass flow rate is:

$$\dot{m} = \frac{\dot{Q}_L}{q_L}$$

$$= \frac{36,000}{57}$$

$$= 631.58 \text{ lbm/hr}$$

(b)   Consider the compressor and write an energy balance around it, neglecting potential and kinetic energies.

$$-w = h_3 - h_2$$

$$= 123 - 109$$

$$= 14 \text{ Btu/lbm}$$

or

$$w = -14 \text{ Btu/lbm}$$

The total work production is:

$$\dot{W} = \dot{m}w$$

$$= 631.58(-14)$$

$$= -8,842.12 \text{ Btu/hr}$$

However, 1 hp = 2,545 Btu/hr, and hence the compressor will need:

$$p = \frac{8,842.12}{2,545} = 3.48 \text{ hp}$$

(c)   The heat load of the condenser can be computed in two ways: either by writing an energy balance around it, or by writing the overall energy balance around the refrigerator. Here the second way is used. Hence:

$$\dot{W} = \dot{Q}_H + \dot{Q}_L$$

Solving for $\dot{Q}_H$ gives:

$$\dot{Q}_H = \dot{W} - \dot{Q}_L$$

$$= -8,842.12 - 36,000$$

$$= -44,842.12 \text{ Btu/hr}$$

The heat transferred per unit mass is:

$$\dot{Q}_H = \frac{\dot{Q}_H}{\dot{m}}$$

$$= \frac{-44,842.12}{631.58}$$

$$= -71 \text{ Btu/lbm}$$

When the refrigeration cycle is employed in an air-conditioning device, the heat absorbed into the working fluid is partially sensible heat from a temperature drop in the ambient air and partially latent heat from the condensation of moisture in the air. Psychrometric charts are used when dealing with the condition of air. The problem below is an excellent review of the use of the psychrometric chart when dealing with conditioning of the air.

PROBLEM 8:

Psychrometric charts are indispensable when calculating the mass of water removed and the refrigeration required in certain systems. Using a psychrometric chart, determine these two quantities for the following system:

Initial state:

$t_i = 80°F$

humidity = 40%

Final state:

$t_f = 50°F$

humidity = 100%

Amount of airflow:

2,000 cfm incoming air processed

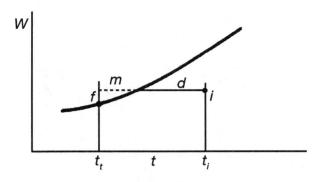

Figure 17
Schematic of refrigeration system

SOLUTION:

By using the psychrometric chart, the initial (and final) enthalpy, weight of moisture (per lb dry air), and volume are obtained. By using mass and energy balances, the mass of H_2O removed and the refrigeration required can be calculated.

Initial state properties:

$t_i = 80°F$
humidity = 40%
enthalpy = h_i = 29 Btu/lb dry air
mass of moisture = m_i = 62 grains/lb dry air
volume = V_i = 13.78 ft³/lb dry air

Final state properties:

$t_f = 50°F$
humidity = 100%
h_f = 20.4 Btu/lb dry air
m_f = 53 grains/lb dry air
V_f = 13.0 ft³/lb dry air

Therefore, the amount of water to be separated out per pound of dry air is:

$$m_{sep.} = m_i - m_f = 62 - 53$$

$$= 9 \text{ grains}$$

In conjunction with the mass balance on air and water, the energy balance yields the refrigeration requirements (per lb of dry air) as the decrease in enthalpy:

$$-Q = h_i - h_f - (m_i - m_f)h_w$$

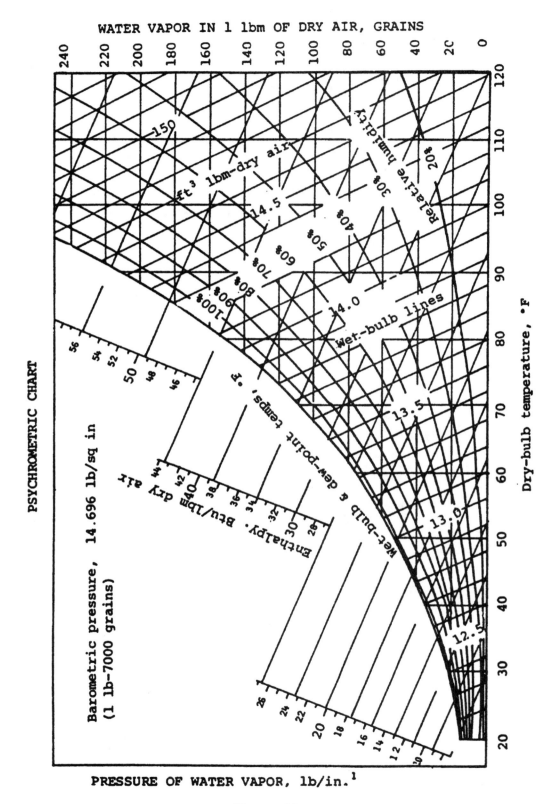

Figure 18
Psychrometric chart for air

where h_w is the enthalpy of saturated H_2O liquid at 50°F, $h_w = 18.1$ Btu. Since 1 lbm = 7,000 grains, m_i and m_f are divided by 7,000.

Therefore:

$$-Q = 29 - 20.4 - \frac{9(18.1)}{7,000}$$

$$= 8.6 \text{ Btu/lbm dry air}$$

The total moisture removed is given by:

$$M_T = \frac{2,000 \text{ cfm}}{V_i} \frac{(m_i - m_f)}{7,000}$$

$$= \frac{2,000 \text{ cfm}}{13.78 \text{ cf}} \frac{(9 \text{ grains})}{7,000 \text{ grains/lbm}} = 0.19 \text{ lbm/min}$$

and the refrigeration:

$$(-Q) \times \frac{\text{cfm}}{\text{cf}} = \frac{2,000}{13.78} \times 8.6 = 1,248 \text{ Btu/min}$$

$$= 6.24 \text{ tons}$$

THE THIRD LAW

The Third Law of thermodynamics states that for any substance in a pure state the entropy at absolute zero is equal to zero. The Third Law allows the evaluation of free energy, ΔF^o and of the equilibrium constant, K, for many chemical reactions, the values of which can be determined in no other way. These parameters are defined in terms of other parameters, which can be determined by calorimetric measurements, and the entropy, which cannot be determined by calorimetric measurements. Thus, the Third Law allows evaluation of the entropy of a chemical system, and therefore allows the evaluation of other parameters necessary for the calculations associated with chemical reactions. This application of the Third Law will be seen in the following section.

Combustion and Chemical Reactions

Combustion is the process whereby a fuel, usually composed of carbon and hydrogen, is reacted with an oxidizer, usually the oxygen in air, resulting in the release of energy. Complete combustion is a reaction in which every atom of carbon is combined with oxygen to form a molecule of carbon dioxide, and all the hydrogen atoms combine with oxygen to form water. The amount of air required for complete combustion is called the *theoretical air* (TA). The amount of air supplied over and above the theoretical air to assure complete combustion is called *excess air* (EA). Excess air also reduces the theoretical flame temperature and furnace temperature, which in turn lowers the overall efficiency of this type of heat engine system.

The useful result of combustion is the release of energy to power heat engines. The combustion process, occurring in the furnace section of the boiler, supplies heat to the water/steam working fluid of a Rankine power cycle as a steady state, constant pressure process. Applying the First Law to such a process yields the equation:

$$Q = H_2^P - H_1^R = \Delta H$$

where:

Q = quantity of heat output from the combustion reactions

H_2^P = enthalpy of the products at the temperature after combustion

H_1^R = enthalpy of the reactants at their temperature before combustion

It should be noted that if the temperature of the reactants and the products are equal, then the ΔH is the enthalpy of reaction and is equal to the heating value of the fuel.

Heating values are normally presented as either Higher Heating Values (HHV) or Lower Heating Values (LHV). The higher heating value occurs when the enthalpy of the combustion products is calculated assuming that the water is in a liquid state; while the lower heating value assumes that the water is a vapor. The difference between the two heating values is the enthalpy of evaporation of the water. Algebraically:

$$HHV = LHV + M_w \times h_e$$

where:

HHV = higher heating value

LHV = lower heating value

M_w = amount of water formed

h_e = unit enthalpy of evaporation of water

For a chemical reaction to occur, it must satisfy the Gibbs function criteria, that is, the Gibbs function of the products must be less than the

Gibbs function of the reactants. The reaction will stop when the Gibbs function reaches a minimum. Thus, we can say that a reaction reaches equilibrium when the rate-of-change of the Gibbs function with respect to temperature and pressure is equal to zero. Algebraically expressed, the Gibbs function is:

$$\Delta G = (H - T \times S)_P - (H - T \times S)_R$$

where:

ΔG = change in the Gibbs function

H = enthalpy

T = absolute temperature

S = entropy

subscripts P and R = the parameters for the products and reactants respectively

The Gibbs function requires evaluating the entropy of the reactants and the products and is accomplished by applying the Third Law. Once the Gibbs function has been determined, the equilibrium constant for the reaction can also be determined by the following equation:

$$\ln K = \Delta G(R \times T)$$

where: $\ln K$ = natural logarithm of the equilibrium constant K

ΔG = change in the Gibbs function

R = universal gas constant

T = absolute temperature

Concepts of Heat Transfer

While thermodynamics deals with the overall systems of the exchange of energy, heat transfer deals with the details of the transfer, or flow, of energy. There are three basic modes of heat transfer: conduction, convection, and radiation.

Conduction

Conduction is the transfer of heat through materials due to the molecular motion within the material. A temperature differential must exist so that the heat flows from the higher temperature to the lower. The rate of heat transfer is express by Fourier's Law:

$$Q = -k \times A \times \frac{dT}{dx}$$

where: Q = heat transfer rate

        k = thermal conductivity of the material

        A = cross-sectional area normal to the direction of heat flow

        T = temperature

        x = thickness of the material through which the heat flows

$\dfrac{dT}{dx}$ = incremental temperature gradient at any point in the material

Convection

Convection is the transfer of heat due to the motion of a fluid near the surface of an object. The convective transfer can be due to the natural convective motion of the fluid or from forced convection induced by a fan, pump, movement of the object, or by atmospheric wind. The rate of convective heat transfer is expressed by Newton's Law, valid for both natural and forced convection:

$$Q = h \times A \times (T_s - T_f)$$

where: Q = heat transfer rate

        h = convective heat transfer coefficient

        A = cross-sectional area normal to the direction of heat flow

        T_s = temperature of the surface of the object

        T_f = temperature of the fluid

The convective heat transfer coefficient can be found through the evaluation of the Nusselt number (Nu) by the formula: $h = k \times \mathrm{Nu}/x$, where k is the thermal conductivity of the fluid and x is the length of the transfer surface. The Nusselt number is itself evaluated using the Reynolds number and the Prandtl number of the flowing fluid. For more commonly encountered fluids the ranges of forced convection and natural convection have been tabulated and are readily available in standard engineering handbooks.

Radiation

Radiant heat transfer is due to thermal radiation. Radiation can occur without a transporting medium. Perfect emitters of radiant heat energy are call *black bodies*. The rate of radiation heat transfer is expressed by the Stefan-Boltzmann Law:

$$Q = \sigma \times \varepsilon \times A_1 F_{1-2} \times (T_1^4 - T_2^4)$$

where: Q = radiant heat transfer rate

σ = Stefan-Boltzmann heat transfer coefficient

ε = emissivity of the emitting body

A_1 = cross-sectional area of the emitting body

T_1 = absolute temperature of the emitting surface

T_2 = absolute temperature of the receiving surface

F_{1-2} = view of the emitting body by the receiving body

PROBLEM 9:

The temperature of a tungsten filament of a light bulb is 6,000°R. Calculate the energy emitted by the bulb in the visible wavelength spectrum from 0.4 μm to 0.7 μm, considering it as a grey body.

SOLUTION:

The given data is as follows:

$\lambda_1 = 0.4 \; \mu m$

$\lambda_2 = 0.7 \; \mu m$

$T = 6,000°R$

Therefore:

$\lambda_1 T = 0.4 \times 6,000 = 2,400 \; \mu m°R$

$\lambda_2 T = 0.7 \times 6,000 = 4,200 \; \mu m°R$

From tabulated values of λT and $E_{b(0-\lambda T)}/\sigma T^4$ it can be determined that:

For:

$\lambda_1 T = 2,400 \; \mu m°R$ $\qquad\qquad \dfrac{E_b(0-2,400)}{\sigma T^4} = 0.0053$

$$\lambda_2 T = 4{,}200 \ \mu m\,°R \qquad \frac{E_b(0 - 4{,}200)}{\sigma T^4} = 0.1269$$

Therefore, the energy emitted in the visible wavelength range is:

$$0.1269 - 0.0053 = 0.1216$$

or 12.16% of the energy is released as visible light.

λT, μm–°R	$\dfrac{E_{bh} \times 10^5}{\sigma T^5}$ (μm–°R)$^{-1}$	$\dfrac{E_{b(0-\lambda T)}}{\sigma T^4}$	λT, μm–°R	$\dfrac{E_{bh} \times 10^5}{\sigma T^5}$ lT, μm–°R	$\dfrac{E_{b(0-\lambda T)}}{\sigma T^4}$
1,000.0	0.000039	0.0000	10,400.0	5.142725	0.7183
1,200.0	0.001191	0.0000	10,600.0	4.912745	0.7284
1,400.0	0.012008	0.0000	10,800.0	4.710716	0.7380
1,600.0	0.062118	0.0000	11,000.0	4.509291	0.7472
1,800.0	0.208018	0.0003	11,200.0	4.317109	0.7561
2,000.0	0.517405	0.0010	11,400.0	4.133804	0.7645
2,200.0	1.041926	0.0025	11,600.0	3.959010	0.7726
2,400.0	1.797651	0.0053	11,800.0	3.792363	0.7803
2,600.0	2.761875	0.0098	12,000.0	3.633505	0.7878
2,800.0	3.882650	0.0164	12,200.0	3.482084	0.7949
3,000.0	5.093279	0.0254	12,400.0	3.337758	0.8017
3,200.0	6.325614	0.0368	12,600.0	3.200195	0.8082
3,400.0	7.519353	0.0507	12,800.0	3.069073	0.8145
3,600.0	8.626936	0.0668	13,000.0	2.944084	0.8205
3,800.0	9.614973	0.0851	13,200.0	2.824930	0.8263
4,000.0	10.463377	0.1052	13,400.0	2.711325	0.8318
4,200.0	11.163315	0.1269	13,600.0	2.602997	0.8371
4,400.0	11.714711	0.1498	13,800.0	2.499685	0.8422
4,600.0	12.123821	0.1736	14,000.0	2.401139	0.8471
4,800.0	12.401105	0.1982	14,200.0	2.307123	0.8518
5,000.0	12.559492	0.2232	14,400.0	2.217411	0.8564
5,200.0	12.613057	0.2483	14,600.0	2.131788	0.8607
5,400.0	12.576066	0.2735	14,800.0	2.050049	0.8649
5,600.0	12.462308	0.2986	15,000.0	1.972000	0.8689
5,800.0	12.284687	0.3234	16,000.0	1.630989	0.8869
6,000.0	12.054971	0.3477	17,000.0	1.358304	0.9018
6,200.0	11.783688	0.3715	18,000.0	1.138794	0.9142
6,400.0	11.480102	0.3948	19,000.0	0.960883	0.9247
6,600.0	11.152254	0.4174	20,000.0	0.815714	0.9335
6,800.0	10.807041	0.4394	21,000.0	0.696480	0.9411
7,000.0	10.450309	0.4607	22,000.0	0.597925	0.9475
7,200.0	10.086964	0.4812	23,000.0	0.515964	0.9531
7,400.0	9.721078	0.5010	24,000.0	0.447405	0.9579
7,600.0	9.355994	0.5201	25,000.0	0.389739	0.9621
7,800.0	8.994419	0.5384	26,000.0	0.340978	0.9657
8,000.0	8.638524	0.5561	27,000.0	0.299540	0.9689
8,200.0	8.290014	0.5730	28,000.0	0.264157	0.9717
8,400.0	7.950202	0.5892	29,000.0	0.233807	0.9742
8,600.0	7.620072	0.6048	30,000.0	0.207663	0.9764
8,800.0	7.300336	0.6197	40,000.0	0.074178	0.9891
9,000.0	6.991475	0.6340	50,000.0	0.032617	0.9941
9,200.0	6.693786	0.6477	60,000.0	0.016479	0.9965
9,400.0	6.407408	0.6608	70,000.0	0.009192	0.9977
9,600.0	6.132361	0.6733	80,000.0	0.005521	0.9984
9,800.0	5.868560	0.6853	90,000.0	0.003512	0.9989
10,000.0	5.615844	0.6068	100,000.0	0.002339	0.9991
10,200.0	5.373989	0.7078			

Table 1: Energy Radiation

FE/EIT

FE: PM General Engineering Exam

CHAPTER 6

Material Science/ Structure of Matter

CHAPTER 6

MATERIAL SCIENCE/ STRUCTURE OF MATTER

ATOMIC STRUCTURE (PERIODIC TABLE)

The Periodic Table is a delineation and arrangement of chemical elements based on their atomic weight and other atomic characteristics, such as the number of protons in their nuclei and their configuration of electrons. The Periodic Table is presented in chart form containing columns and rows. Each column represents a category, or *family*, of elements, in which the configuration of electrons in the outer shell is the same. The rows represent elements with the same number of shells of electrons, with the elements in the first column (left side) of each row containing only one electron in a given shell, and the last row (right side) containing a complete shell, usually containing eight electrons. Note that helium, the first element with a "complete" outer shell, contains only two electrons in that shell, and that hydrogen, which has only one electron, is categorized as being one electron short of a complete shell and thus, is categorized in the same column as the elements with seven electrons in the outer shell.

Elements in the same family (similar outer shell electron configuration) have the tendency to behave in the same manner chemically. This has led to the assumption that chemistry of atoms is controlled by their electrons.

The Noble Gases

The elements in the *noble gases* family have a complete outer shell of electrons. All elements in this family are either inert (that is, they do not form compounds with any other element), or have a very low reactivity (that is, they form very few compounds with other elements). They are the only elements which exist as a stable mono-molecular gas. The more familiar elements of this family are helium, neon, argon, and radon.

Alkali Metals Family

The elements of the *alkali metals* family have a single electron in their outer shell. In all reactions these elements lose the one outer shell electron to form a +1 ion. All the alkali metals are soft and malleable, and they have low melting points compared to other metals. Also, they have a bright silvery sheen and are highly reactive. The more familiar elements of the family are lithium, sodium, and potassium. When reacted with other elements, they form stable ionic crystalline molecules.

The Halogens

The elements of the *halogen* family lack only one electron in their outer shell. In reactions, they readily gain an electron to form a −1 ion. The halogens exist in their pure form as diatomic molecules. The lighter halogens, fluorine and chlorine, exist as gases at room temperature, while bromine exists as a liquid and iodine as a solid. Like the alkali metals, when reacted with other elements they form stable ionic crystalline molecules.

Hydrogen

Hydrogen is unique among the elements. A hydrogen atom has only one electron and exists as a diatomic gas. Removal of hydrogen's single electron leaves only a proton, which is a +1 ion of very small atomic dimension. This is the ion that defines an acid, the quantity of which is measured as the concentration of +1 hydrogen ions, or pH.

Other Major Families and Classifications

The elements of the *alkaline earth metals* family have two electrons in their outer shell and form +2 ions. The more familiar alkaline earth metals are beryllium, magnesium, calcium, and barium.

The *non-metals* category consists of several different families of elements. Each of the families in this category have different numbers of electrons in their outer shell. They form both positive (+) and negative (−) ions in solutions and reactions. Many have multiple ionic forms referred to as "oxidation states," that is, the fewer the electrons remaining in the outer shell, the higher the oxidation state. The more familiar elements in this category are carbon, nitrogen, oxygen, phosphorous, and sulfur.

The *transition metals* category consists of several families of metallic elements. Each of the families in this category have different numbers of electrons in their outer shell, and they always form positive ions in solutions and in reactions. Again, as with the non-metals, many have multiple ionic forms, referred to as "oxidation states"—the fewer the electrons remaining in the outer shell, the higher the oxidation state. The more familiar metals in this category include iron, nickel, copper, chromium, titanium, silver, platinum, and gold.

The *non-transition metals* category also consists of several families of metallic elements. Each of the families in this category have different numbers of electrons in their outer shell; however, they usually form positive ions in solutions and in reactions. Certain elements in this category also exist as negative ions. These species often behave like elements in the non-metals category. These elements have multiple ionic forms, referred to as "oxidation states" with the fewer the electrons remaining in the outer shell, the higher the oxidation state. The more familiar metals in this category include aluminum, zinc, cadmium, tin, mercury, and lead.

The *rare earth* elements category consists of all those naturally occurring elements with atomic numbers of 57 through 71 and 89 through 92. They have a wide variety of electron configuration and properties. The most familiar of these elements is uranium. This category also includes all the "man-made" elements with atomic numbers of 93 and above.

PROBLEM 1:

Draw the Lewis dot formulas for the formation of: (1) N_2 from two N atoms; (2) Na_2 from two Na atoms; and (3) HBr from H plus Br.

SOLUTION:

The Lewis dot formula is based on the fact that union between atoms can be attained from sharing electrons in pairs. There can be no more than eight electrons surrounding an atom (the electron octet rule) for purposes of stability. Nevertheless, there are a few exceptions to this rule. To draw Lewis structures, knowledge of the covalence (electron sharing) principle is required. For a nitrogen atom, N, there are five electrons in the outer shell and they can be represented by dots as:

$$: \overset{\bullet}{\underset{\bullet}{N}} \cdot$$

To satisfy the octet rule, N must acquire three more electrons. If it joins another N atom, they both can donate three electrons to the formation of a covalent triple bond.

Therefore:

(1) $: \overset{\bullet}{\underset{\bullet}{N}} \cdot$ + $: \overset{\bullet}{N} \cdot$ → $: N ::: N :$

Similarly, for Na_2 and HBr:

(2) $Na \cdot$ + $Na \cdot$ → $Na : Na$

(3) $H \cdot$ + $\cdot \overset{\bullet\bullet}{\underset{\bullet\bullet}{Br}}$ → $H : \overset{\bullet\bullet}{\underset{\bullet\bullet}{Br}}$

PROBLEM 2:

Draw Lewis structures with all appropriate resonance forms, for each of the following: (1) SO_2, (2) NO_2^-

SOLUTION:

There are molecules in which the arrangement of atoms is not adequately described by a single Lewis structure. Therefore, all the possible Lewis structures are used to represent them. This concept is called resonance. It does not imply that the two or more forms are different or that the molecule really exists in different forms. There is only one form of the molecule. The only differences are in how the arrangements of electrons are represented.

(1) SO_2

These structures satisfy the octet rule because each atom is surrounded by eight electrons. A bond (the straight lines) represents two electrons.

(2) NO_2-

The double-headed arrow is used to indicate that both structures are resonance forms. Note that the arrangement of the nuclei is the same in both structures differing only in the placement of the electrons.

PROPERTIES OF MATERIALS

The three basic states of materials are solids, liquids, and gases; each having its own molecular and bulk characteristics.

Solids

In the solid state, the atoms or molecules are densely packed and are generally in a fixed position relative to one another. They are held together in position by "gravitational forces" and by electromagnetic forces. Solids in which the molecules are arranged in orderly geometric patterns are called *crystalline*. Those in which the molecules are randomly arranged are called *amorphous*. Molecules with an ionic bond structure, that is, those consisting of positive and negative ions, usually form crystalline solids. Molecules with covalent bond structures, or whose atoms share electrons, form both crystalline and amorphous solids.

As the temperature of a solid is increased, the kinetic energy of the molecules increases. This increased energy tends to overcome the forces holding the molecules of a solid in place. When the temperature increases to a sufficiently high level, the forces holding the molecules in place are completely overcome. This leaves the molecules free to move with respect to one another and the material moves into the liquid state. The temperature at which this phenomenon occurs is called the *melting point*. The reverse of this phenomenon occurs when the liquid molecules lose kinetic energy to such a level that they no longer can move past each other and re-form into a solid. This process is termed *solidification*, or *freezing*.

The fixed structure of certain solids can also be broken by certain liquids. This occurs when the attraction of molecules or ions (of the solid material) to the molecules of the liquid is stronger than the forces holding the solid material together. When this phenomenon occurs, the resultant liquid is called a *solution*. This property of a solid is called *solubility*. It should be noted that solids with ionic structures tend to be soluble in liquids with ionic molecules, while solids with covalent structures tend to be soluble in liquids with covalent molecules. In general "like" dissolves "like."

Liquids

In the liquid state, the molecules are densely packed, but they are not in a fixed position relative to each other. Though they are held together by "gravitational forces," they are able to "slide" by each other and move. When the temperature increases to a sufficiently high level, the forces holding the molecules adjacent to one another are completely overcome allowing the molecules to break free of the main body of the liquid. The temperature at which this phenomena occurs is called the *boiling point*.

Individual molecules in the vicinity of the surface of the liquid and with sufficiently high kinetic energy can also break free of the liquid and enter into the gaseous phase. This process is called *evaporation*. The closer the temperature is to the boiling point, the greater the fraction of the higher potential energy molecules, resulting in a more rapid rate of evaporation. The reverse of this phenomenon occurs when molecules moving freely in the gaseous state lose kinetic energy such that they agglomerate when they collide with each other re-forming the liquid. This process is called *condensation*.

Solutions

There are certain generalizations about solutions that can be helpful in engineering work. The solubility of a given solid in a given liquid increases with temperature. The effect of pressure is very small and is usually insignificant. The addition of non-volatile solids into a liquid raises the boiling point of that liquid and lowers the temperature at which the liquid solidifies. These changes in boiling point and freezing point for commonly encountered solutions have been tabulated and are readily available in engineering handbooks. However, for solutions where a tabulation of the variation of phase change temperatures are not tabulated, they can be calculated using the Clausius-Clapeyron equation:

$$\Delta T = \frac{RT_0^2 \, / \, L_v}{N}$$

where: ΔT = increase in the temperature of the boiling point

R = universal gas constant

T_o = boiling point of the pure liquid

L_v = latent heat of evaporation of the pure liquid at its boiling point

N = ratio of the number of mols of dissolved solid to the mols of liquid. It can be expressed as: $N = (P_0{}^{sat}/P^{sat})$, the ratio of the tabulated partial pressure to the partial pressure at the conditions desired therefore, given as:

$$\Delta T = \frac{RT_0^2}{L_v}\left(\frac{P^{sat}}{P_o^{sat}}\right)$$

PROBLEM 3:

In a 7.71 molal solution of water (M.W. = 18.01) in isopropyl alcohol (M.W. = 60.11) having a density of 0.818 g/cm^3 and a mass of 100 g, calculate (1) the weight (wt) % of solute, (2) the weight (wt) % of solvent, (3) the mass of solvent, (4) the mole fractions of solvent and solute, (5) (g solute) (dm^3 solution)$^{-1}$, and (6) the molality of the solution.

SOLUTION:

$$\text{Molality is defined as } \frac{\#\text{ moles solute}}{\text{kilogram solvent}}$$

Let: $X = \#$ g of solute

$Y = \#$ g of solvent

then:

$$\frac{\dfrac{X}{18.01}}{Y\left(\dfrac{\text{kg}}{1{,}000 \text{ g}}\right)} = 7.71$$

and $X + Y = 100$

Solving the simultaneous equations gives:

$$0.005X - 0.00771Y = 0$$

$$0.00771 \, (X + Y = 100)$$

$$0.0627X = 0.771Y$$

$$X = 12.2 \text{ g}$$

$$100 - X = 87.8 \text{ g}$$

(1) $$\text{wt \% solute} = \frac{\text{g solute}}{\text{total mass}} \times 100 = 12.2\%$$

(2) $\quad$ wt % solvent $= \dfrac{\text{g solvent}}{\text{total mass}} \times 100 = 87.8\%$

(3) $\quad\quad\quad$ molality $= \dfrac{\text{moles solute}}{\text{kg solvent}}$

$$\text{\# moles of solute} = \dfrac{12.2 \text{ g}}{18.01 \text{ g/mole}} = 0.677 \text{ moles}$$

$$\text{kg solvent} = \dfrac{\text{\# moles of solute}}{\text{molality}} = \dfrac{0.677}{7.71} = 0.0878 \text{ kg}$$

$$= 87.8 \text{ g}$$

(4) mole fraction solute $= \dfrac{\text{\# moles solute}}{\text{\# moles solute} + \text{\# moles solvent}}$

$$\text{\# moles solvent} = \dfrac{87.8 \text{ g}}{60.11 \text{ g/mole}} = 1.46$$

$$\text{mole fraction solute} = \dfrac{0.677}{0.677 + 1.46} = 0.32$$

$\sum\limits_{i} x_i = 1$ where x_i = mole fraction of the ith component then:

$$1 - 0.32 = \text{mole fraction of solvent} = 0.68$$

(5) $\quad$ volume of solution $= \dfrac{100 \text{ g}}{0.818 \text{ g/cm}^3} = 122.25 \text{ cm}^3$

$$122.25 \text{ cm}^3 = 0.122 \text{ dm}^3$$

$$\dfrac{\text{g solute}}{\text{dm}^3 \text{ solution}} = \dfrac{12.2 \text{ g}}{0.122 \text{ dm}^3} = 100$$

(6) $\quad$ the molarity $= \dfrac{\text{\# moles solute}}{\text{liter solution}} = \dfrac{0.677}{0.122} = 5.5 \text{ M}$

$$= 87.56 \times 10^{-3} \text{ dm}^3 \text{ or } 87.56 \times 10^{-3} \text{ liters}$$

Therefore, (g solute) (dm^3 solution)$^{-1}$ = (13.00 g NaOH) (87.56 $\times$ 10^{-3}dm^3)$^{-1}$

$$= 148.5 \text{ g NaOH(dm}^3 \text{ solution)}^{-1}$$

Liquids in Liquids

When two liquids come in contact with each other, they can mix completely with one another, they can completely separate into layers, or one liquid can partially "dissolve" into the other. This property is called *miscibility*. The miscibility of liquids is highly dependent on the temperature and can vary from complete miscibility to complete immiscibility, depending on the concentration of each of the liquids. The boiling points and freezing points of liquid-liquid solutions are either higher or lower than the boiling point and freezing point of each of the pure liquids.

PROBLEM 4:

The vapor-liquid equilibrium data of the system chloroform-ethanol at 45°C are listed in Table 1.

x_1	y_1	P (mmHg)	P_1 (mmHg)	P_2 (mmHg)
0.1260	0.3974	249.92	99.30	150.62
0.2569	0.6060	329.62	199.60	130.02
0.4015	0.7143	391.51	279.50	112.01
0.6283	0.7954	438.89	349.00	89.89
0.8206	0.8516	455.56	388.60	66.96
0.9557	0.9319	448.49	418.00	30.49

Table 1

Assuming ideal behavior of the vapor phase, prove the thermodynamic consistency of the experimental data.

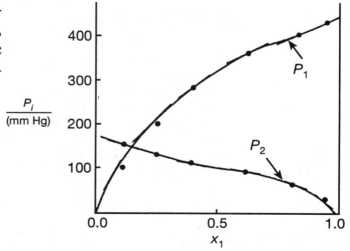

Figure 1

Variation of the partial pressure with composition: system, chloroform-ethanol at 45ºC.

SOLUTION:

The Gibbs-Duhem equation applies to this problem. When the vapor phase is assumed to be ideal (that is, $f_i = P_i$), the Gibbs-Duhem equation can be written in the form:

$$\Delta = \frac{x_1}{P_1}\frac{dP_1}{dx_1} - \frac{x_2}{P_2}\frac{dP_2}{dx_2}$$

where: P_i = partial pressure of component i

f_i = fugacity of component i

x_i = mole fraction of component i

Δ = deviation (if any)

Note that the smaller Δ is the more consistent of the experimental data. To prove the consistency of this data, the slopes

$$\frac{dP_1}{dx_1}, \frac{dP_2}{x_2},$$

P_1 and P_2, at the corresponding mole fractions must be known. The desired information can be obtained by plotting P_1 and P_2 against the mole fractions shown in Figure 1. The slopes are computed for the given values of x_1. Then the Δ values can be computed. The respective values are tabulated in the table below.

$\dfrac{dP_1}{dx_1}$	$\dfrac{dP_2}{dx_2}$	Δ
$\dfrac{mm\ Hg}{mole\ fraction}$		
792	−176	−0.016
724	−140	+0.132
416	−118	−0.033
229	− 96	+0.015
176	−153	−0.038
290	−472	−0.023

Table 2

Since the Δ values are small, the data is thermodynamically consistent.

PROBLEM 5:

Figure 2 shows the boiling point diagram for two miscible liquids. (1) Show the composition of the first and last vapor, if 50 mole % solution is boiled in an open container. (2) Find the liquid composition when half the solution is vaporized during heating in a closed system at 1 atm constant pressure. What is the temperature?

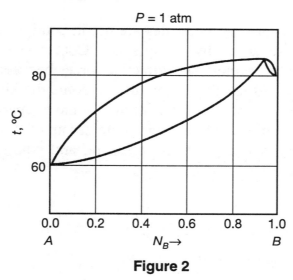

Figure 2

SOLUTION:

(1)   The composition of the liquid and vapor phases in equilibrium with each other are given by the ends of the horizontal lines called tie lines. One such line is line L of Figure 3. The composition of the first vapor corresponding to 50 mole % solution is obtained using the top curve at about $N_B = 0.1$ at a temperature of about 68°C. The last vapor composition will correspond to the maximum boiling point at T_{bmax}. Thus, $N_B = 0.95$.

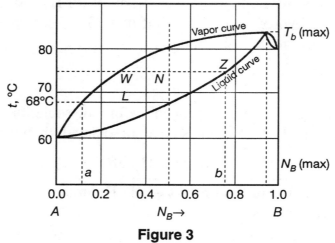

Figure 3

(2)   The temperature corresponding to half vaporization in a closed system will be such that the system composition of 50 mole % bisects the tie line at point *N*. This means that distance *WN* = distance *NZ*. This occurs at about 75°C and the liquid composition corresponding to this point is $N_B = 0.75$.

Gases

In the gaseous state the molecules are not in continuous contact with each other, but are separated by empty space. Contact is only by random collision with other molecules. The attractive forces between gaseous molecules are very low and usually unable to overcome the kinetic energy of the molecules. Thus, the molecules continue to move apart from one another until they reach the limits of their container and fill its volume. The relationship between the temperature, pressure, and volume of gases are described by the familiar *perfect gas law*:

$$PV = ZNRT$$

where: *P* = absolute pressure

   V = volume occupied by the gas

   Z = compressibility of the gas (*Z* = 1 for ideal gases, and gases at relatively low pressures)

   R = universal gas constant

   T = absolute temperature of the gas

PROBLEM 6:

Hydrogen gas will dissociate into atoms at a high enough temperature, i.e., $H_2 = 2H$. Assuming ideal gas behavior for H_2 and H, what should be the density of hydrogen at 2,000°C if it is 33% dissociated into atoms? The pressure is 1 atm.

SOLUTION:

Use as a basis 1 mol hydrogen before dissociation (which has a weight of 2 gms). After 0.33 moles have dissociated, then we have:

0.67 mole H_2 left.

Therefore, there are 0.66 moles of H. The total number of moles are $0.67 + 0.66 = 1.33$ moles.

For a mixture of gases, the density

$$\rho = \frac{PM_{average}}{RT}, \text{ where } M_{average} = \frac{\text{total weight}}{\text{total moles}} = \frac{2 \text{ gm}}{1.33 \text{ mol}}$$

Note that the units of $M_{average}$ are consistent with the units of molecular weight. This is very important.

Therefore: $\quad \rho = \dfrac{(1)(2/1.33)}{(0.0082)\,(2,273)} = 8.07 \times 10^{-2} \text{ gm/liter}$

When the molecules of a gas lose kinetic energy (i.e., drop in temperature), and they are at an appropriate density (i.e., pressure), they collide with each other and agglomerate to form a liquid. The temperature at which this phenomenom occurs is called the *condensation point*. The condensation point of a gas varies with its pressure: the higher the pressure, the higher the condensation temperature.

All gases are 100% miscible with each other. Each gas contributes to the total volume and pressure of the mixture in proportion to its presence in the mixture on a mole for mole basis. This proportion of an individual gas in a mixture of gases is usually referred to as its *partial pressure*, which corresponds directly to its molar ratio.

The solubility of gases in liquids can be described by Henry's law, which states that the quantity of a gas that can be dissolved into a liquid is directly proportional to the partial pressure of the gas in contact with the liquid. The constant of proportionality differs for each specific gas and liquid system.

PROBLEM 7:

The Henry's law constant for the solubility of air in water is found to be as follows:

$t\,°C$	atmosphere
5	4.88
15	6.07
$H \times 10^{-4}$	

Extrapolate these data to obtain the solubility at 25°C.

SOLUTION:

Henry's law is defined as:

$$P_1 = Hx_1 \tag{1}$$

where: P_1 = partial pressure

x_1 = mole fraction

H = Henry's law constant

Rearranging equation (1) yields:

$$H = \frac{P_1}{x_1}$$

$$H = P_1 x_1^{-1}$$

$$\ln H = \ln P_1 - \ln x_1 \tag{3}$$

Differentiating equation (3) with respect to T at constant P_1 gives:

$$\left(\frac{\partial \ln H}{\partial T} \right)_{P_1} = -\left(\frac{\partial \ln x_1}{\partial T} \right)_{P_1} \tag{2}$$

But by definition:

$$\left(\frac{\partial \ln x_1}{\partial T} \right)_{P_1} = -\frac{(H_1'' - H_1')}{RT^2} + \frac{\overline{H_1'} - H_1'}{RT^2}$$

$$= \frac{-H_1'' + \overline{H_1'}}{RT^2}$$

where: $H_1'' - H_1'$ = latent heat of vaporization

and $\overline{H_1'} - H_1'$ = differential heat of solution.

R = gas constant

T = temperature

From equation (2):

$$\left(\frac{\partial \ln H}{\partial T} \right)_{P_1} \text{ is also equal to } -\left(\frac{-H_1'' + \overline{H_1'}}{RT^2} \right) \tag{4}$$

If the $\left(\dfrac{\overline{H_1'} - H_1''}{R} \right)$ term in equation (4) is assumed to be a constant (because the latent heat is assumed to be constant over the temperature range), then equation (4) becomes:

$$\left(\frac{\partial \ln H}{\partial T} \right)_{P_1} = -\frac{C}{T^2} \tag{5}$$

Integrating both sides with respect to T, equation (5) becomes:

$$\ln H = \frac{C}{T} + D \tag{6}$$

where D is the integration constant.

The data give

$t°C$	$T°K$	$\dfrac{1}{T}$	$H \times 10^{-4}$	$\ln H$
5°C	278	0.003597	4.88	10.795
15°C	288	0.003472	6.07	11.014

The constants in equation (6) can be found by using the two values of $\ln H$.

That is:

$$10.795 = \frac{C}{278} + D = \frac{C + 278D}{278} \tag{7}$$

$$11.014 = \frac{C}{288} + D = \frac{C + 288D}{288} \tag{8}$$

Subtracting equation (7) from equation (8) gives:

$$(11.014 - 10.795) = \frac{C}{288} - \frac{C}{278} = 0.003472C - 0.003597C$$

$$= -0.000125C$$

$$0.219 = -0.000125C$$

Therefore, $\qquad\qquad\qquad C = -1,752.0$

Substituting this into either equation (7) or (8):

$$D = 10.795 + \frac{1,752.0}{278} = 17.097$$

Therefore, equation (6) becomes:

$$\ln H = \frac{-1,752.0}{T} + 17.097$$

At 25°C = 298°K:

$$\ln H = \frac{-1,752.0}{298} + 17.097 = -5.87919 + 17.097 = 11.218$$

or $\qquad H = e^{11.21} = 74,444.2 = 7.44 \times 10^4$

PROBLEM 8:

Henry's law constant for CO_2 gas in water is 1.25×10^6 torr and 8.57×10^4 torr in benzene. In which solvent is CO_2 more soluble?

SOLUTION:

Henry's law constant K_2 is given by:

$$K_2 = \frac{P_2}{x_2}$$

(valid in very dilute solution in the region where $x_2 \to 0$) otherwise written as:

$$K_2 = \lim_{x_2 \to 0} \frac{P_2}{x_2}$$

where: $\quad P_2 = $ partial pressure of CO_2 gas over the solution

$\qquad x_2 = $ concentration or solubility

The subscript 2 indicates that the solute which is the component at lower concentration is being considered.

Therefore, $\qquad K_{2\,(C_6H_6)}\, x_{2\,(C_6H_6)} = P_{2\,(C_6H_6)}$

and $\qquad K_{2\,(H_2O)}\, x_{2\,(H_2O)} = P_{2\,(H_2O)}$

Setting the partial pressures equal gives:

$$K_{2\,(C_6H_6)}\, x_{2\,(C_6H_6)} = K_{2\,(H_2O)}\, x_{2\,(H_2O)} \qquad (1)$$

Taking the ratio of x_2 in the solvents as given by (1):

$$\frac{x_{2\,(C_6H_6)}}{x_{2\,(H_2O)}} = \frac{K_{2\,(H_2O)}}{K_{2\,(C_6H_6)}} = \frac{1.25 \times 10^6}{8.57 \times 10^4} = 14.6$$

CO$_2$ is thus 14.6 times more soluble in benzene than in water.

PHASE DIAGRAMS

Solids, liquids, and gases of pure substances and solutions, and mixtures exist in equilibrium with each other in very specific proportions and concentrations. These vary with the temperature and pressure to which they are exposed. These relationships are often presented graphically as *phase diagrams*.

For pure substances, phase diagrams show the temperature, pressure, specific volume, and energy levels at which the substance exists as a solid, as a liquid, as a gas, or as two phases in equilibrium. Phase diagrams can have any two parameters on the X and Y axes, with the other parameters represented as families of curves. More common combinations include temperature versus pressure diagrams, temperature versus entropy diagrams, and pressure versus entropy diagrams. The format used depends on its applicability and convenience for particular applications. For example, the pressure drop of a gas passing through a turbine is ideally an isentropic process. Thus, it could be conveniently represented by a straight vertical line on a pressure versus entropy phase diagram.

Phase diagrams for commonly encountered materials are readily available in engineering manuals, or can usually be obtained from the manufacturers of less common materials.

PROBLEM 9:

The temperature-composition phase diagram for the two-component system A–B at $P = 1$ atm is given. 200 g of a mixture of A and B boiling initially at 65°C is distilled until the boiling point of the residue remaining in the still reaches 75°C.

(1) What is the composition of the residue?

(2) What is the composition of the total distillate?

(3) What is the weight of the total distillate?

SOLUTION:

The composition of the residue is obtained by using the lower (liquid) curve and that of the distillate is obtained by using the upper (vapor) curve.

(1) The mixture boils initially at 65°C. The residue at this point is

represented by the *L* composition of about 50% *A* and the distillate by the *V* composition of about 91% *A*.

Starting at the *L* curve and 65°C, trace the vertical line of this composition (about 50% *A*) until the required temperature is reached (75°C in this case). Since the lower curve gives the information about the composition of the residue, the tie-line (horizontal line) at 75° isotherm indicates that the composition of the residue is 20% *A*.

(2) The composition of the total distillate can be obtained by taking the average of the composition of the distillate (measured from the *V* curve) at 65°C and 75°C.

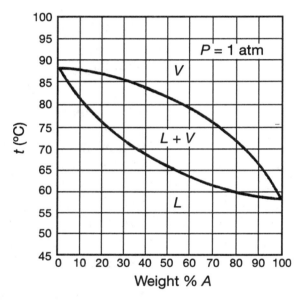

Composition of distillate at 65°C ≈ 91% *A*
Composition of distillate at 75°C ≈ 71% *A*

Figure 4

Therefore, composition of total distillate

$$= \frac{91+71}{2} = \frac{162}{2} = 81\% \; A$$

(3) This can be calculated by using the overall material balance and also the component *A* balance. This will give two unknowns and two equations.

Let $\quad w_R$ = weight of residue

$\qquad w_D$ = weight of distillate

By the overall balance:

$$w_R + w_D = 200 \qquad (1)$$

Recall that the initial mixture was at about 50%A.

Therefore, by the component A balance:

$$0.20\,w_R + 0.81\,w_D = 0.50(200) = 100 \qquad (2)$$

From equation (1), $w_R = 200 - w_D$. Substituting for w_R in equation (2):

$$0.20(200 - w_D) + 0.81\,w_D = 100$$

$$40 - .20\,w_D + .81\,w_D = 100$$

Therefore:
$$0.61\,w_D = 60$$

$$w_D = \frac{60}{0.61} = 98.36 \text{ g}$$

PROBLEM 10:

The diagram in Figure 5 shows the regions of miscibility at various temperatures for the nitrobenzene/n-hexane system. Compositions of phases in equilibrium for the two phase regions of the diagram are determined by tie lines. If 3 moles of a nitrobenzene/n-hexane mixture with a composition of 0.5 mole fraction nitrobenzene in the single phase region is brought to T^1, what would be the masses of the two phases at equilibrium? The molecular weights of nitrobenzene and n-hexane are 123.11 and 86.18, respectively.

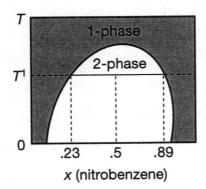

Figure 5

SOLUTION:

By material balance:

$$n_1 + n_2 = n_{N+H} \qquad (1)$$

where: n_1 = # moles of phase 1

n_2 = # moles of phase 2

n_{N+H} = # moles of nitrobenzene and hexane = 3

Also, $\dfrac{X_2^N - X_{N+H}^N}{X_{N+H}^N - X_1^N}$ = by the lever rule

(This could also be done by balancing hexane.)

X_2^N = mole fraction of nitrobenzene in phase 2

X_1^N = mole fraction of nitrobenzene in phase 1

X_{N+H}^N = mole fraction of nitrobenzene in the single phase mixture

$$\frac{n_1}{n_2} = \frac{0.89 - 0.5}{0.5 - 0.23} = \frac{0.39}{0.27} = 1.444$$

Now, there are two equations and two unknowns:

$$n_1 + n_2 = 3.00$$

$$\frac{n_1}{n_2} = 1.444$$

Upon solving them simultaneously:

$$n_1 = 1.773 \text{ moles and } n_2 = 1.227 \text{ moles.}$$

Now the mole fractions of phases 1 and 2 with respect to nitrobenzene are 0.23 and 0.89.

Phase 1 – $(0.23)(1.773)$ = # moles of nitrobenzene

$(1 - 0.23)(1.773)$ = # moles of hexane

Phase 2 – $(0.89)(1.227)$ = # moles of nitrobenzene

$(1 - 0.89)(1.227)$ = # moles of hexane

Phase 1 – $[(.23)(1.773)(123.11) + (.77)(1.773)(86.18)] = 167.86$ g

Phase 2 – $[(.89)(1.227)(123.11) + (.11)(1.227)(86.18)] = 146.07$ g

The equilibrium between the solid and liquid phase of solutions, especially those solutions with high concentration of the solute, is often described using phase diagrams. For two component systems, diagrams showing temperature versus concentration of the solute from 0 to 100% are used. The various states and species of the solid solute (i.e., solids with water of hydration attached) are delineated as the parameters. For multiple solute systems, the "triangular" diagram (with percentage of each solute shown on each leg of the triangle) is often used.

PROBLEM 11:

Discuss the changes in the three-component phase diagram shown in Figure 6, as salt *A* is added to the solution.

SOLUTION:

The line between point *a* and vertex *A* represents addition of pure *A* to the solution of composition given by point *a*. As we add *A* to the solution, the system gets richer in *A* and less rich in *B* and *C*. If enough *A* is added for the bulk concentration to reach point *b*, solid *A* becomes a second phase in equilibrium with a solution phase of composition given by point *b*. If we add more *A*, the composition does not change but the relative amounts do, indicating saturation.

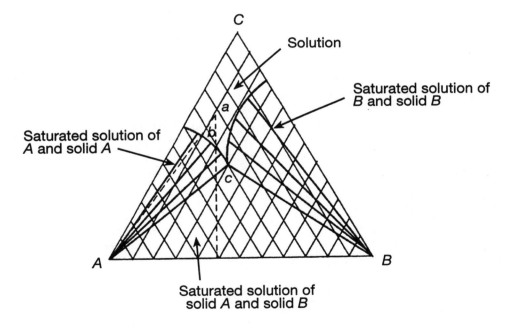

Figure 6

FE/EIT

FE: PM General Engineering Exam

CHAPTER 7

Fluid Mechanics

CHAPTER 7

FLUID MECHANICS

Fluid mechanics is the study of the inherent properties of fluids and the properties and characteristics of fluids both at rest and in motion. Fluids include materials in the liquid state and in the gaseous state. For engineering calculations, the major inherent properties of concern to fluid mechanics are the density, viscosity, and surface tension. For liquids at rest, engineering calculations are usually concerned with the force exerted against the walls of containers and submerged surfaces, and with the phenomenon of buoyancy on objects wholly or partially submerged. For fluids in motion, engineering calculations cover all aspects of compressible and incompressible flow in conduits and in open channels.

HYDROSTATICS

Hydrostatics is the study of fluids, both liquids and gases, at rest. Fluids are substances that can flow. A liquid flows to fit the shape of its container, while a gas completely fills the volume of its container. Liquids and gases also differ from one another in their physical properties including compressibility, viscosity, and density. Liquids can be considered incompressible while gases are considered compressible. The engineer is also concerned with the forces that fluids at rest exert on solid bodies and surfaces as well as with external forces on fluids at rest.

Pressure

Fluids exert a force against the walls of any container that confines them. Pressure (P) is defined as the force per unit area of the surface of the container. For a fluid at rest, this force is always exerted at right angles to the wall surface area. This is also true for any imaginary area or plane within the fluid, regardless of the plane's orientation. That is to say the force exerted by the fluid's pressure is equal in all directions.

The pressure at any depth below the surface of a liquid is equal to the pressure at the surface plus the product of the density (on a weight basis) times the depth. Due to the incompressibility of a liquid, as the pressure is increased at the surface, for example, by putting a piston at the liquid surface and applying a force, the pressure at any depth or point in the liquid will increase by the same amount. A gas is compressible and its density varies in accordance with the perfect gas law.

PROBLEM 1:

A cylinder contains a fluid at a gauge pressure of 350 kN m^{-2}. Express this pressure in terms of a head of (a) water ($\rho_{H_2O} = 1,000$ kg m^{-3}) (b) mercury (relative density 13.6).

What would be the absolute pressure in the cylinder if the atmospheric pressure is 101.3 kN m^{-2}?

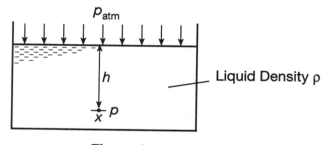

Figure 1

SOLUTION:

In a fluid of constant density, $dp/dz = -\rho g$ can be integrated immediately to give:

$$p = -\rho gz + \text{constant}$$

In a liquid, the pressure p at any depth z, measured downwards from the free surface so that $z = -h$ (see figure), will be:

$$p = \rho gh + \text{constant}$$

Since the pressure at the free surface will normally be atmospheric pressure p_{atm}:

$$p = \rho gh + p_{atm} \tag{1}$$

Pressures measured above atmospheric pressure are known as gauge pressures.

Since atmospheric pressure varies with atmospheric conditions, a perfect vacuum is taken as the absolute standard of pressure. Pressures measured above perfect vacuum are called absolute pressures:

Absolute pressure = Gauge pressure + Atmospheric pressure

Taking p_{atm} as zero, equation (1) becomes:

$$p = \rho g h \qquad (2)$$

which indicates that, if g is assumed constant, the gauge pressure at a point X can be defined by stating the vertical height h, called the head, of a column of a given fluid of mass density ρ which would be necessary to produce this pressure.

From equation (2), head, $h = \dfrac{p}{\rho h}$.

(a) Putting $p = 350 \times 10^3$ N m^{-2}, $\rho = \rho_{H_2O} = 1{,}000$ kg m^{-3}

$$\text{Equivalent head of water} = \frac{350 \times 10^3}{10^3 \times 9.81} = 35.68 \text{ m}$$

(b) For mercury $\rho_{Hg} = \sigma \rho_{H_2O} = 13.6 \times 1{,}000$ kg m^{-3}

$$\text{Equivalent head of water} = \frac{350 \times 10^3}{13.6 \times 10^3 \times 9.81} = 2.62 \text{ m}$$

Absolute pressure = Gauge pressure + Atmospheric pressure

$$= 350 + 101.3 = 451.3 \text{ kN m}^{-2}$$

"Hydrostatic Paradox"

If a number of containers are interconnected allowing a liquid to flow freely between them, the level of the liquid will stand at the same height in each of the containers. Though this sometimes seems paradoxical—thus the term, "Hydrostatic Paradox"—the pressure at any point depends only on the depth of the liquid, and not on the shape or volume of each container.

Forces Against a Dam

Water behind a dam (or any vertical wall) exerts a force against the dam that tends to slide the dam along its foundation and tries to overturn the dam about a point at its base. The line of action of this resultant force is $^1/_3$ the depth above the base, or $^2/_3$ the depth below the surface.

PROBLEM 2:

A gate 5 ft wide is hinged at point B and rests against a smooth wall at point A. Compute (1) the force on the gate due to seawater pressure; (2) the horizontal force P exerted by the wall at point A; and (3) the reactions at the hinge B. (Figure 2)

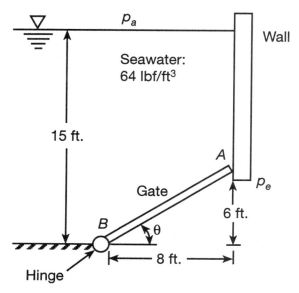

p_a

Wall

Seawater:
64 lbf/ft³

15 ft.

A

Gate

p_e

6 ft.

B

θ

8 ft.

Hinge

Figure 2

SOLUTION:

Using nomenclature based on Figure 4:

(1) By geometry the gate is 10 ft long from A to B, and its centroid is halfway between, or at elevation 3 ft above point B. The depth h_{CG} is thus $15 - 3 = 12$ ft. The gate area is $5 \times 10 = 50$ ft². Neglect p_a as acting on both sides of the gate. The hydrostatic force on the gate is

$$F = p_{CG}A = \rho g h_{CG}A = (64 \text{ lbf/ft}^3)(12 \text{ ft})(50 \text{ ft}^2) = 38{,}400 \text{ lbf}$$

(2) First we must find the center of the pressure of F. A free-body diagram of the gate is shown in Figure 3. The gate is a rectangle and hence $I_{xy} = 0$ and $I_{xx} = bL^3/12 = [(5 \text{ ft}) \times (10 \text{ ft})^3]/12 = 417$ ft⁴. The ambient pressure p_a is neglected if it acts on both sides of the plate (e.g., the other side of the plate is inside a ship or on the dry side of a gate or dam). In this case $p_{CG} = \rho g h_{CG}$, and the center of pressure becomes independent of specific weight:

$$F = \rho g h_{CG}A \Big|_{y_{CP}} = -\frac{I_{xx}\sin\theta}{h_{CG}A}\Big|_{x_{CP}} = -\frac{I_{xy}\sin\theta}{h_{CG}A} \tag{1}$$

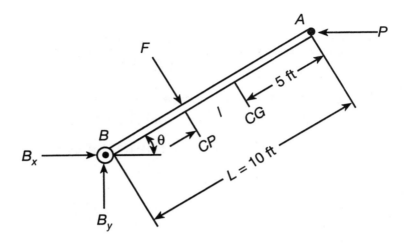

Figure 3

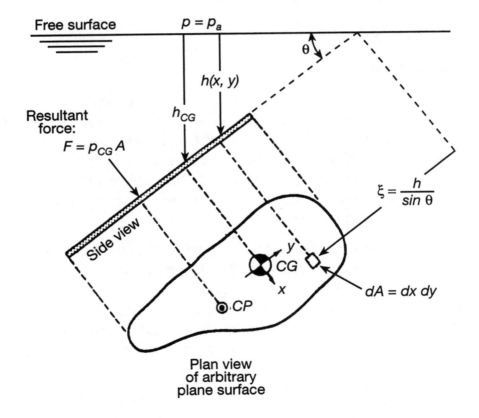

Figure 4
**Hydrostatic force and center of pressure on an arbitrary plane surface of
area *A* inclined at an angle θ below the free surface**

The distance I from the CG to the CP is given by Equation (1), since p_a is neglected.

$$I = -y_{CP} = +\frac{I_{xx} \sin \theta}{h_{CG} A} = \frac{(417 \text{ ft}^4)\left(\frac{6}{10}\right)}{(12 \text{ ft})(50 \text{ ft}^2)} = 0.417 \text{ ft}$$

The distance from point B to force F is thus $10 - I - 5 = 4.583$ ft. Summing moments counterclockwise about B gives:

$$PL \sin \theta - F(5 - I) = P(6 \text{ ft}) - (38{,}400 \text{ lbf})(4.583 \text{ ft}) = 0$$

or
$$P = 29{,}331 \text{ lbf}$$

(3) With F and P known, the reactions B_x and B_z are found by summing forces on the gate:

$$\Sigma F_x = 0 = B_x + F \sin \theta - P = B_x + 38{,}400(0.6) - 29{,}331$$

or
$$B_x = 6{,}291 \text{ lbf}$$

$$\Sigma F_z = 0 = B_z - F \cos \theta = B_z - 38{,}400(0.8)$$

or
$$B_z = 30{,}720 \text{ lbf}$$

Surface Tension

Molecules at the interface of two immiscible fluids, usually between a liquid and a gas, are subject to an imbalance of forces. The forces that hold the molecules of liquids together are far greater than the force exerted on these surface molecules by the gas to which they are exposed. This situation, where those molecules near or at the surface have a very different "force" environment than the interior molecules, gives rise to the surface effects known as surface tension (σ).

One of the most familiar effects of surface tension is the rise of liquid in a small diameter tube, a capillary. The height of the rise is dependent on the inherent surface tension of the liquid and the adhesive attraction between the liquid and the interior surface of the capillary. The liquid will rise until the adhesive force between the liquid and the capillary is equal to the force exerted by the pressure caused by the height of the liquid rise.

PROBLEM 3:

Of what diameter must a droplet of water (at 20°C) be to have the pressure within it 1.0 kPa greater than that outside?

SOLUTION:

$$\sigma_{water} = 0.0728 \; N/m$$

Basic relation:

$$p_i - p_0 = \frac{1}{R_i} + \frac{1}{R_2} \sigma$$

where:

$$R_1 = R_2 = R$$

Therefore:

$$p_i - p_0 = \sigma \frac{2}{R}$$

$$p_i - p_0 = 1.0 \times 10^3 = 0.0728 \left(\frac{2}{R} \right)$$

$$R = 0.00015 \; m$$

$$d = 0.3 \; mm$$

Viscosity

The viscosity of most liquids is relatively low, but it is sufficiently significant to be considered in engineering calculations. The viscosity of gases is very small and not usually significant in engineering calculations. Viscosity can be viewed as the internal resistance, or friction, to the flow of a fluid. Because of viscosity, a force must be applied to cause the molecules to slide past each other. Viscosity is measured as either absolute viscosity or as kinematic viscosity. Absolute viscosity (μ) is expressed in terms of (force $\times$ distance)/(area $\times$ velocity), and is usually expressed in units of "poise" or "centipoise." Kinematic viscosity (v) is expressed as the ratio of the absolute viscosity to the density (mass/volume), and is expressed in units of "stokes" or "centistokes."

PROBLEM 4:

A block weighing 100 lb and having an area of 2 ft^2 slides down an inclined plane at a constant velocity as shown in Figure 5. An oil gap between the block and the plane is 0.01 in. thick, the inclination of the plane is 30° to the horizontal, and the velocity of the block is 6 fps. Find the viscosity of the lubricating film.

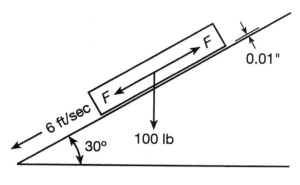

Figure 5

SOLUTION:

Consider a fluid flowing over a smooth surface so that any fluid particle has motion parallel to the surface only (see Figure 6). Such a flow is called laminar because the fluid moves in layers or "laminae."

Next to the surface, molecules of the fluid become embedded in the solid wall, and this layer of fluid is at rest relative to the wall. Further from the wall the fluid has velocity v, which increases with distance from the wall y, giving a velocity distribution as shown in Figure 6.

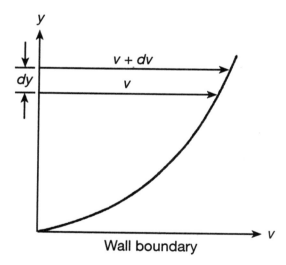

Figure 6
Laminar flow profile close to a boundary

Now consider two adjacent layers of fluid having velocities v and $v + dv$, respectively, and distance dy apart. The layer most remote from the wall has a velocity dv relative to the adjacent layer, and this causes a viscous or shearing stress to be present between the two layers. This stress is given the symbol τ (tau). The coefficient of viscosity μ (mu) is defined as the ratio:

$$\mu = \frac{\text{Shearing stress}}{\text{Rate of shearing strain}}$$

and may be compared with the modulus of rigidity of a solid.

Rate of shearing strain is given by *dv/dy*, and hence:

$$\mu = \frac{\tau}{dv / dy}$$

or

$$\tau = \mu \frac{dv}{dy}$$

μ is also called the absolute or dynamic viscosity and has units of lb-sec/ft^2 or slugs/ft-sec.

In this problem, the component of the weight acting down the plane is opposed by a viscous force exactly equal and opposite to it. Therefore:

$$F = 100 \sin 30° = 50 \text{ lb}$$

Hence:

$$\tau = \frac{F}{A} = \frac{50}{2} = 25 \text{ psf}$$

but:

$$\tau = \mu \frac{dv}{dy}$$

Therefore:

$$\int_0^{\frac{0.01}{12}} 25\,dy = \mu \int_0^6 dv$$

thus:

$$6\mu = \frac{25 \times 0.01}{12}$$

$$\mu = 0.00347 \text{ lb-sec/ft}^2$$

BUOYANCY

Buoyancy is described by "Archimedes' Principle," which states that: "A body immersed in a fluid is buoyed up with a force equal to the weight of the displaced fluid." If a body is not wholly submerged in the fluid, the buoyant force is equal to the weight of the volume of fluid displaced by the submerged portion of the body. If a body displaces its own weight before it is completely submerged, it will float. If it does not, it will sink in the fluid.

PROBLEM 5:

A 100,000 deadweight ton sunken ship is to be raised from 200 ft to the water surface by pumping air into its sealed holds. How much water is to be expelled from the ship to make it float?

SOLUTION:

We know that 10^5 tons equal 2×10^8 lb, and that 1 ft^3 of water weighs 62.4 lb. Hence:

$$2 \times 10^8 \text{ lb of water equals } 3.205 \times 10^6 \text{ ft}^3$$

which is the minimum amount of air space required.

The required air pressure to expel the water from the ship's holds is:

$$200 \text{ ft} \times 62.4 \text{ lb/ft}^3 = 12,480 \text{ lb/ft}^2$$
$$= 60,940 \text{ psi}$$

Stability of a Ship

The line of action of the upward buoyant force on a ship passes through the center of gravity of the displaced fluid and is termed the center of buoyancy. The downward force of the ship's weight passes through the center of gravity of the body. These two forces must give rise to a couple that tends to stabilize the ship otherwise the ship will be unstable and will capsize.

PROBLEM 6:

For a ship with a water-line cross-section as shown in Figure 7 and a displacement of 600 tons, determine the maximum distance *GB* that the center of gravity may lie above the center of buoyancy if the ship is to remain stable.

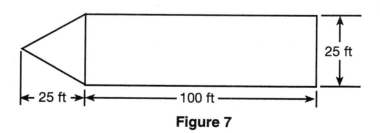

Figure 7

SOLUTION:

With reference to Figures 8 and 9, there exists the relationship:

$$MG = \frac{\bar{I}}{V} - GB \tag{1}$$

where I is the moment of inertia of the area A about the longitudinal axis O.

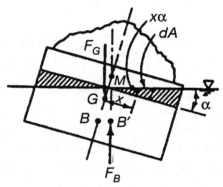

Figure 8

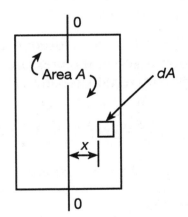

Figure 9

Clearly, the greater the distance MG, the greater the stability. Since a barge or other floating body becomes unstable as M falls below G, Equation 1 becomes a direct indicator of this condition. In particular:

$$\frac{\bar{I}}{V} > GB \quad \text{stable body}$$

$$\frac{\bar{I}}{V} < GB \quad \text{unstable body}$$

At the point of incipient instability, $GB = \bar{I}/V$, where:

$$\bar{I} = \frac{(100)(25)^3}{12} + \frac{(2)(25)(12.5)^3}{12} = 1.383 \times 10^5 \text{ ft}^4$$

and

$$V = \frac{(600 \text{ tons})(2,000 \text{ lb/ton})}{62.4 \text{ lb/ft}^3} = 1.923 \times 10^4 \text{ ft}^3$$

Finally:

$$GB = \frac{1.383 \times 10^5}{1.923 \times 10^4} = 7.19 \text{ ft}$$

Hydrodynamics

Hydrodynamics is the science of fluids in motion. In the simplest type of fluid flow called *streamline* flow, or *laminar* flow, each particle, or very small unit of fluid, follows the path of the particle which preceded it. These paths are referred to as the *streamlines*. Streamline flow usually occurs provided the velocity is sufficiently low and obstruction free. As the velocity of flow increases and/or the severity of the obstructions increase the flow becomes *turbulent*.

The fundamental equation of hydrodynamics is "Bernoulli's equation," which is a relation between the pressure, velocity, and elevations at points along its flow. The Bernoulli equation can be expressed as:

$$p_1 + \frac{1}{2}\rho v_1^2 + \rho g h_1 = p_2 + \frac{1}{2}\rho v_2^2 + \rho g h_2$$

where: p = absolute pressure (not gauge)

ρ = mass density

v = velocity

g = gravitational constant

h = elevation

PROBLEM 7:

Assume frictionless flow for the water siphon shown, and that the water exits the siphon freely at atmospheric pressure. Find (1) the velocity of the water when exiting from the siphon, and (2) the water pressure in cross-section C in the base portion of the inverted U-shaped tube.

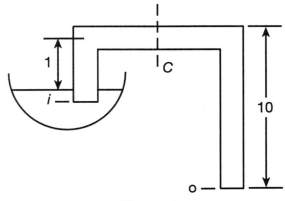

Figure 10

SOLUTION:

(1) Applying the flow (Bernoulli) equation between inlet, i, and outlet, o, of the siphon:

$$\frac{P_i}{\rho} + \frac{V_i^2}{2} + gz_i = \frac{P_o}{\rho} + \frac{V_o^2}{2} + gz_o \qquad (1)$$

The tank from which the water is to be siphoned may be assumed to have an area that exceeds by a large amount the area of the tube, and therefore V_i may be assumed to be zero.

Since atmospheric pressure prevails at the inlet, i, and the outlet, o:

$$P_i = P_o = \text{atmospheric pressure.}$$

Substituting into flow equation (1), we obtain:

$$gz_i = \frac{V_o^2}{2} + gz_o$$

from which:

$$V_o^2 = 2g(z_i - z_o)$$

and

$$V_o = \sqrt{2g(z_i - z_o)}$$

Substituting the indicated quantities:

$$V_o = \sqrt{2 \times 9.81 \times (10 - 1)} = 13.3 \text{ meters/sec}$$

(2) To find the pressure prevailing at cross-section, c, apply the Bernoulli equation between positions i and c.

$$\frac{P_i}{\rho} + \frac{V_i^2}{2} + gz_i = \frac{P_c}{\rho} + \frac{V_c^2}{2} + gz_c \qquad (2)$$

Since $V_i \approx 0$ for the reasons given previously, and $V_c = V_o$, where V_o has been calculated above, substituting in (2):

$$\frac{P_c}{\rho} = \frac{P_i}{\rho} + gz_i - gz_c - \frac{V_c^2}{2}$$

from which:

$$P_c = P_i + \rho \left\{ g(z_i - z_c) - \frac{V_c^2}{2} \right\}$$

Substituting numerical values:

$$P_c = 1.01 \times 10^5 \, \frac{N}{m^2} + 999 \, \frac{kg}{m^3} \left\{ 9.81(-1) - \frac{13.3^2}{2} \right\}$$

$$= 2,843 \, P_a - \text{absolute pressure}$$

Applications of Hydrodynamics

Three of the more frequently encountered applications of the Bernoulli equation are Torricelli's Theorem, Venturi Meter, and Pitot Tube.

Torricelli's Theorem

Torricelli's theorem relates to the discharge of a liquid from a tank and states that the velocity of such a discharge is equal to the square root of $(2 \times g \times h)$. The quantity of flow is the area of the opening times the velocity.

$$Q = A \times (2 \times g \times h)^{1/2}$$

where: Q = quantity of flow

A = area of the opening

g = gravitational constant

h = depth of the opening below the surface of the liquid

It must be noted, that as the flow "streamlines" converge as they enter the orifice, they continue to diminish for a short distance so that the area is smaller than the area of the orifice. This smaller area, known as the *vena contracta*, should be used in the Torricelli theorem.

PROBLEM 8:

An open tank containing water has an orifice located near the bottom of the tank as shown in the figure. Show that for ideal flow, the discharge velocity at the orifice is $\sqrt{2gh}$. Assume steady flow.

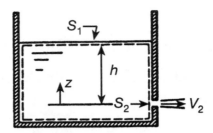

Figure 11

SOLUTION:

Consider the control volume shown in the figure. Apply the Bernoulli equation to sections S_1 and S_2.

$$\frac{p_1}{\gamma} + \frac{V_1^2}{2g_c} + \frac{gz_1}{g_c} = \frac{p_2}{\gamma} + \frac{V_2^2}{2g_c} + \frac{gz_2}{g_c} \tag{1}$$

Experiments indicate that the pressure at any section open to the atmosphere can be taken to be at atmospheric pressure. Therefore:

$$p_1 = p_2 = p_{atm}$$

Also, using the continuity equation:

$$V_1 A_1 = V_2 A_2 \tag{2}$$

and by the fact that $A_1 \gg A_2$, we can take $V_1 \ll V_2$. Thus, V_1 can be neglected. Under these circumstances, equation 1 reduces to:

$$\frac{V_2^2}{2g} = z_1 - z_2 = h$$

or

$$V_2 = \sqrt{2gh}$$

Venturi Meter

The Venturi meter consists of a constriction, or throat, in a pipeline, which has a properly designed taper at the inlet and outlet to assure streamline flow. Using Bernoulli's equation, the differential in velocity, and the resultant difference in pressure between the larger upstream cross-sectional area and the smaller cross-sectional area of the throat, the flow through the meter is computed as:

$$Q = (A_1) \times (A_2) \times \left(\frac{2 \times (P_1 - P_2)}{\rho \times (A_1^2 - A_2^2)} \right)^{1/2}$$

where:

Q = quantity of flow

A_1 and A_2 = area of the upstream conduit and the area of the throat, respectively

P_1 and P_2 = static pressure upstream of the throat and at the throat, respectively

ρ = mass density

PROBLEM 9:

A Venturi meter with a throat diameter of 4 cm is fitted into a pipeline of 10 cm diameter. The coefficient of discharge is 0.96. Calculate the flow through the meter when the reading on a mercury-water manometer connected across the upstream and throat tapping is 25 cm. If the energy loss in the downstream divergent cone of the meter is $10v_p^2/2g$ per unit weight of fluid, calculate the head loss across the meter. (v_p is the velocity in the pipeline.)

SOLUTION:

Consider the Venturi meter shown in the figure. Apply Bernoulli's equation to the entry section 1 and to the throat section 2.

$$\frac{p_1}{\gamma} + \frac{v_1^2}{2g} + z_1 = \frac{p_2}{\gamma} + \frac{v_2^2}{2g} + z_2$$

Therefore:

$$\frac{v_2^2 - v_1^2}{2g} = \frac{p_1 - p_2}{\gamma} + z_1 - z_2$$

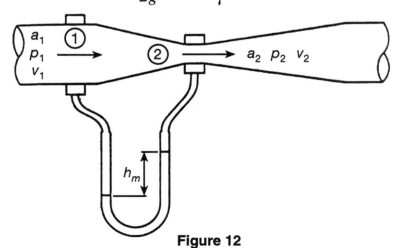

Figure 12

But by continuity $a_1v_1 = a_2v_2$, so that:

$$v_2 = \frac{a_1}{a_2}v_1$$

Therefore:

$$\left[\left(\frac{a_1}{a_2}\right)^2 - 1\right]\frac{v_1^2}{2g} = \frac{\Delta p}{\gamma} + z_1 - z_2$$

Therefore:

$$v_1 = \sqrt{\frac{2g(\Delta p/\gamma + z_1 - z_2)}{(a_1/a_2)^2 - 1}}$$

Therefore:

$$Q = a_1v_1 = a_1a_2\sqrt{\frac{2g(\Delta p/\gamma + z_1 - z_2)}{a_1^2 - a_2^2}}$$

Because small energy losses occur in the convergent section, a coefficient of discharge must be introduced into Bernoulli's equation.

Therefore:

$$Q = C_d a_1\sqrt{\frac{2g(\Delta p/\gamma + z_1 - z_2)}{(a_1/a_2)^2 - 1}}$$

$$Q = C_d a_p\sqrt{\left\{2g\,\frac{\left[\left(\frac{p_1 - p_2}{\gamma} + z_1 - z_2\right)\right]}{a_p^2 - a_t^2}\right\}}$$

$$Q = 0.96 \times \frac{\pi}{4} \times (0.10)^2\sqrt{\left\{\frac{19.62 \times 0.25 \times 12.6}{(10/4)^4 - 1}\right\}}$$

$$Q = 9.61 \times 10^{-3}\,\text{m}^3/\text{s}$$

The energy loss in the convergent cone can be calculated if the C_d value is known. The Bernoulli equation is written to include an allowance for friction loss, that is:

$$\frac{p_1}{\gamma} + \frac{v_1^2}{2g} + z_1 = \frac{p_2}{\gamma} + \frac{v_2^2}{2g} + z_2 + h_f$$

where h_f is the head loss due to friction.

Then as before:

$$Q = a_1\left(\frac{2g\,(\Delta p/\gamma + z_1 - z_2 - h_f)}{(a_1/a_2)^2 - 1}\right)^{1/2}$$

from before:

$$Q = C_d a_1 \left(\frac{2g\left(\Delta p/\gamma + z_1 - z_2\right)}{\left(a_1/a_2\right)^2 - 1} \right)^{1/2}$$

Therefore: $\quad C^2{}_d(\Delta p/\gamma + z_1 - z_2) = (\Delta p/\gamma + z_1 - z_2 - h_f)$

Therefore: $\quad h_f = (\Delta p/\gamma + z_1 - z_2)(1 - C_d^2)$

but:

$$\frac{\Delta p}{\gamma} + z_1 - z_2 = \frac{Q^2}{C_d^2 \, 2g a_1^2}\left[\left(\frac{a_1}{a_2}\right)^2 - 1\right] = \frac{1}{C_d^2}\left(\frac{v_2^2 - v_1^2}{2g}\right)$$

Therefore:

$$h_f = \left(\frac{1}{C_d^2} - 1\right)\frac{v_2^2 - v_1^2}{2g}$$

Energy loss/unit weight across the convergent cone:

$$h_f = \left(\frac{1}{C_d^2} - 1\right)\left(\frac{v_t^2 - v_p^2}{2g}\right)$$

Therefore, total energy loss across the meter:

$$h_f = \left(\frac{1}{C_d^2} - 1\right)\left(\frac{v_t^2 - v_p^2}{2g}\right) + 10\frac{v_p^2}{2g}$$

$$h_f = 1.01 \text{ m}$$

Pitot Tube

The pitot tube is a device which compares the "static" pressure at right angles to the pipe wall to the "dynamic" pressure at the center of the pipe and parallel to the wall of the pipe. This difference in pressure can be used to compute the flow through the pipe at that point. Using the Bernoulli equation, a pitot tube formula can be developed in the form of:

$$\rho_m \times g \times h_m = \tfrac{1}{2} \times \rho_f \times V^2$$

where: $\quad \rho_m$ = density of the fluid in the manometer

g = gravitational constant

h_m = differential in liquid height in the legs on the manometer

ρ_f = density of the fluid in the conduit

V = velocity of the fluid in the conduit

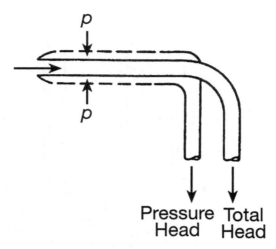

Figure 13
A pitot-static tube

Multiplication of the velocity, V, calculated with the formula shown on the previous page, times the cross-sectional area of the conduit will give the quantity of flow through the conduit.

PROBLEM 10:

A two-dimensional flow of liquid discharges from a large reservoir through the sharp-edged opening; a pitot tube at the center of the vena contracta produces the reading indicated. Calculate the velocities at points A, B, C, and D, and the flowrate.

SOLUTION:

The pitot tube reading determines the position of the energy line (and also that of the free surface in the reservoir). Since the pressures at points A, B, C, and D are all zero, the respective velocity heads are determined by the vertical distances between the points and the energy line. The velocities at A, B, C, and D are 4.66 m/s, 5.12 m/s, 4.75 m/s, and 5.03 m/s, respectively. The flowrate may be computed by integrating the product vdA over the flow cross section CD, in which $v = \sqrt{2g_n h}$:

$$q = \int_C^D vdA = \int_{h_C}^{h_D} \sqrt{2g_n h}\ dh = \sqrt{2g_n}\ \frac{2}{3}h^{3/2}\Big|_{1.15}^{1.29}$$

$$= 0.685\ m^3/s \times m$$

The limits of integration are then the vertical distances (in metres) from the energy line to points D and C, respectively. Assuming that the

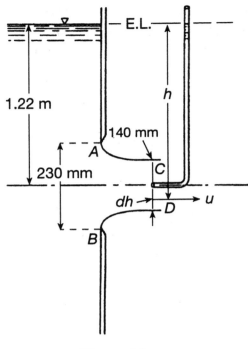

Figure 14

mean velocity at section *CD* is at the center and thus measured by the pitot tube:

$$V = \sqrt{2g_n \times 1.22} = 4.89 \text{ m/s}$$

The (approximate) flowrate, *q*, may be computed from:

$$q = 4.89 \times 0.140 = 0.685 \text{ m}^3/\text{s} \times \text{m},$$

giving the same result.

FLUID FLOW

There are three basic areas of fluid flow. These are: 1) liquid flow in pipes, 2) liquid flow in open channels, and 3) flow of compressible fluids. Flow calculations involve the determination of either the quantity of flow, the pressure drop/head loss, or the size of the conduit when the other two parameters are known.

Pipe Flow of Liquids

Calculations of flow parameters for incompressible flow in pipes is accomplished using Darcy's equation or the Fanning equation, the Reynolds Number, and a friction factor, *f*. These formulas are expressed in many forms depending on the application and information available and on whether the flow is laminar or turbulent. They are usually used to calculate the pressure drop when the quantity of flow is known and the pipe size is known or assumed.

The Darcy equation can be expressed as:

$$\Delta P = \frac{\rho f L v^2}{144 D 2 g}$$

where: ΔP = pressure differential
ρ = mass density
f = friction factor (determined from the Reynolds number)
L = length of the pipe
v = velocity
D = diameter of the pipe
g = gravitational constant

The Reynolds number can be expressed as:

$$Re = \frac{D v \rho}{\mu}$$

where: D = diameter of the pipe
v = velocity
ρ = mass density
μ = absolute viscosity

The friction factor (f) for laminar flow, which corresponds to a Reynolds number, R_e less than 2,000, is equal to: $16/Re$.

For turbulent flow, however, the relationship between the Reynolds number and the friction factor is more complex. It has been determined empirically, and has traditionally been presented in chart form, where the values of the friction factor are "read off" the chart for a calculated Reynolds number. In addition, the roughness of the internal surface of the conduit is an important factor in determining the friction factor for turbulent flow.

PROBLEM 11:

Water at 80°F flows through a horizontal, rough pipe at an average velocity of 9.30 ft/s. If the pipe diameter is 1.20 in. and the roughness ratio of the pipe is 0.02, find the pressure loss in pounds per square inch through 10 ft of pipe.

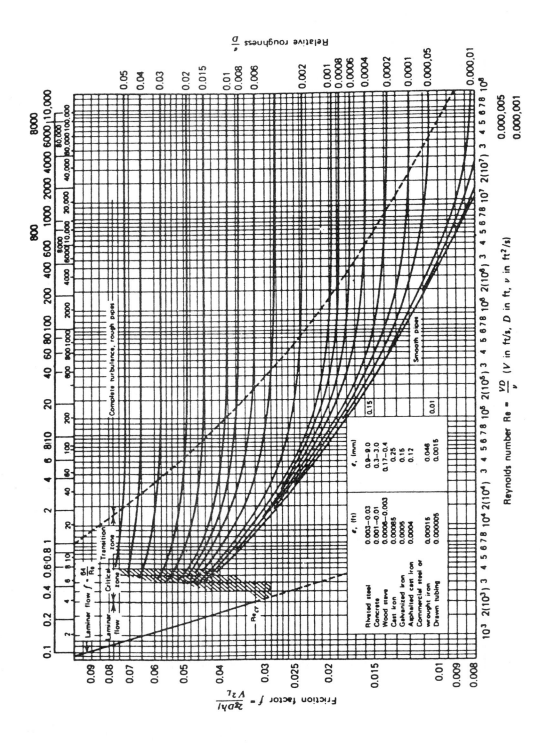

Figure 15

SOLUTION:

The pressure loss, which is a result of viscous effects, is given by the Darcy equation as:

$$H_f = f \frac{L}{D} \frac{\rho V^2}{2g_c}$$

In order to find the friction factor, f, from the figure, it is necessary to know the Reynolds number, Re. To calculate the Reynolds number, we need the kinematic viscosity, v. From the table, for water at 80°F:

$$v = 0.930 \times 10^{-5} \, \text{ft}^2/\text{s}$$

Thus:

$$\text{Re} = \frac{VD}{v} = \frac{(9.3)(0.10)}{0.930 \times 10^{-5}} = 10^5$$

From the figure, $f = 0.048$ for a roughness ratio of 0.02 and a Reynolds number of 10^5. Therefore:

$$H_f = (0.048)\left(\frac{10}{0.10}\right) \frac{62.2 \, (9.3)^2}{64.4} = 401 \, \text{lb}_f/\text{ft}^2$$

$$= 2.78 \, \text{lb}_f/\text{in.}^2$$

Flow in Open Channels

Calculation of flow in open channels can also be made using the Manning equation by substituting the Hydraulic Radius, $4 \times R_H$, for the diameter, D wherever it occurs in the Manning equation. The "Hydraulic Radius," R_H, is defined as the cross-sectional area of the stream divided by the wetted perimeter. Also the quantity, or rate of flow, is usually the parameter to be calculated, with the head loss used as the pressure drop, and the conduit dimensions known. The Chézy Formula is usually used in open channel flow calculations. It can be expressed as:

$$v = \left(\frac{2g}{f}\right)^{1/2} \times \left(\frac{R_H F}{L}\right)^{1/2}$$

where: v = average velocity of the flow

g = gravitational constant

f = Fanning friction factor (determined from the Reynolds number)

R_H = hydraulic radius

F = friction loss in the conduit

L = length of the conduit

Temperature (F)	Density ρ (lb m/ft^3)	Kinematic Viscosity $v \times 10^5$ (ft^2/s)	Surface Tension $s \times 10^2$ (lb$_f$/ft)	Vapor-Pressure Head ρ_v/g (ft)	Bulk Modulus of Elasticity $K \times 10^{-3}$ (lb$_f$/in^2)
32	62.42	1.931	0.518	0.20	293
40	62.43	1.664	0.514	0.28	294
50	62.41	1.410	0.509	0.41	305
60	62.37	1.217	0.504	0.59	311
70	62.30	1.059	0.500	0.84	320
80	62.22	0.930	0.492	1.17	322
90	62.11	0.826	0.486	1.61	323
100	62.00	0.739	0.480	2.19	327
110	61.86	0.667	0.473	2.95	331
120	61.71	0.609	0.465	3.91	333
130	61.55	0.558	0.460	5.13	334
140	61.38	0.514	0.454	6.67	330
150	61.20	0.476	0.447	8.58	328
160	61.00	0.442	0.441	10.95	326
170	60.80	0.413	0.433	13.83	322
180	60.58	0.385	0.426	17.33	313
190	60.36	0.362	0.419	21.55	313
200	60.12	0.341	0.412	26.59	308
212	59.83	0.319	0.404	33.90	300

Table 1

PROBLEM 12:

An open channel conveying water has a trapezoidal cross-section. The base width is 1.5 m and the side slopes are at 60° to the horizontal. The channel bed slope is 1 in 400 and the depth is constant at 1 meter. Calculate the discharge in cubic meters per second if the Chézy C is calculated from the Bazin relationship $C = 87/(1 + 0.2/\sqrt{m})$ where m is the hydraulic mean depth.

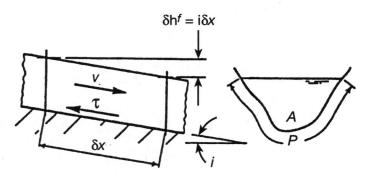

Figure 16

SOLUTION:

The energy loss due to friction per unit weight δh_f over a length δx (see figure) must be exactly balanced by conversion of potential energy. Thus:

$$\delta h_f = i\delta x$$

Therefore:

$$i = \frac{\delta h_f}{\delta_x}$$

but

$$\frac{dh_f}{dx} = \frac{fv^2}{2gm} = i$$

Therefore:

$$v = \sqrt{\frac{2g}{f}} \ \sqrt{(mi)}$$

Therefore:

$$v = C \sqrt{(mi)}$$

and

$$C = \sqrt{\frac{2g}{f}}$$

This approach links the Chézy C and the Darcy f. The flow in a channel is given by $Q = CA\sqrt{mi}$.

$$m = \frac{A}{P}$$

$$A = 1 \times \frac{3.0 + 2 \times \tan 30°}{2} = 2.077$$

$$P = 1.5 + 2 \times \sec 30° \times 1 = 3.809$$

$$m = 0.545 \text{ m}$$

$$C = \frac{87}{\left(1 + \dfrac{0.2}{\sqrt{0.545}}\right)}$$

$$C = 68.46$$

$$Q = CA\sqrt{(mi)}$$

$$= 68.46 \times 2.077\sqrt{0.545} \times \frac{1}{20}$$

$$Q = 5.25 \text{ m}^3/\text{s}$$

Flow of Compressible Fluids

In addition to the parameters considered for the flow of incompressible fluids, calculations of flow for compressible fluids require considering the relationships between pressure and volume. The flow is usually assumed to be either adiabatic or isothermal. Adiabatic flow can be assumed for relatively short lengths of pipe that are well insulated. Isothermal flow is more frequently used in calculations as it more often approximates actual conditions. It must also be remembered, that along with the pressure drop, as a compressible fluid moves down a pipe, there will be corresponding changes in both density and velocity.

The Darcy equation for incompressible fluids can be used for compressible fluids when pressure drops are less than 10% using either the upstream or downstream pressure in the calculation. For pressure drops between 10% and about 30%, the average pressure between the inlet and outlet can be used. However, for greater pressure drops, as may be encountered in long pipes, the Darcy equation cannot be used. Also the quantity, or rate of flow, is usually the parameter calculated, with a known pressure drop and conduit dimensions. There are several equations that can be used for higher pressure drops. These equations are readily available in many standard engineering textbooks.

PROBLEM 13:

Find an expression for the coefficient of compressibility at constant temperature for an ideal gas.

SOLUTION:

The coefficient of compressibility, α, is defined by:

$$\alpha = \frac{1}{V} \left(\frac{\partial V}{\partial p} \right)_T$$

For an ideal gas:

$$p = \rho RT = \frac{mRT}{V} \quad \text{or} \quad V = \frac{mRT}{p}$$

Then:

$$\left(\frac{\partial V}{\partial p} \right)_T = -\frac{mRT}{p^2}$$

$$\alpha = \frac{1}{V} \left(\frac{mRT}{p^2} \right) = \frac{1}{p}$$

PROBLEM 14:

One cubic foot of oxygen at 100°F and 15 psia is compressed adiabatically to 0.4 ft. What then, are the temperature and pressure of the gas? If the process had been isothermal, what would the temperature and pressure have been?

SOLUTION:

$$R \approx \frac{1,540}{32} = 48.1 \text{ ft./°F}$$

Using the perfect gas equation:

$$p\upsilon = RT$$

yields:

$$(15 \times 144)\upsilon_1 = 48.1 \,(460 + 100)$$

$$\upsilon_1 = 12.5 \text{ ft}^3/\text{lb} \quad \gamma_1 = \frac{1}{\upsilon_1} = 0.08 \text{ pcf}$$

To determine the pressure:

$$P_1 \, v_1{}^K = P_2 \, v_2{}^K$$

where:

$$K = 1.4$$

$$(15 \times 144) \, (12.5)^{1.4} = (P_2 \times 144) \left(\frac{12.5}{1/0.4} \right)^{1.4}$$

$$P_2 = 54.1 \text{ psia}$$

$$(54.1 \times 144) \frac{12.5}{1/0.4} = 48.1 \ (460 + T_2)$$

$$T_2 = 350°F$$

If the process had been isothermal ($T_2 = 100°F$), then:

$$Pv = \text{constant}$$

$$P_2 = \frac{15}{0.4} = 37.5 \text{ psia}$$

FE/EIT

FE: PM General Engineering Exam

CHAPTER 8

Statics

CHAPTER 8

STATICS

Statics is the part of the physical sciences that deals with the state of bodies, or objects, at rest under the action of forces. It is primarily based on Newton's first and third laws. The first law states that *when a body is at rest the **resultant of all** of the forces exerted on the body is **zero***. The third law states that *whenever a body exerts a force on another body, the second body always exerts a force on the first body. This force is **equal in magnitude, but opposite in direction**.*

When all the resultant forces on a body are equal to zero, the body is said to be in equilibrium. This applies to a body at rest as well as to a body moving at a constant velocity in a straight line. With a body oriented in a three-dimensional coordinate system, equilibrium can be expressed as that condition in which:

The sum of all the forces in the X direction is equal to 0, $\Sigma F_X = 0$

The sum of all the forces in the Y direction is equal to 0, $\Sigma F_Y = 0$

The sum of all the forces in the Z direction is equal to 0, $\Sigma F_Z = 0$

The sum of all the moments around any point is equal to 0, $\Sigma M_O = 0$

FREE-BODY DIAGRAMS AND FORCE SYSTEMS

Developing a free-body diagram showing all of the forces acting on the object is the first step for solving mechanics problems. Drawing a free-body diagram consists of diagramatically removing all other contacting and attached bodies and replacing them with vectors that represent the forces acting on the body. After the free-body diagram is completed, the forces in each direction (both those of known magnitude and those of unknown magnitude), and the moments (also both of known and unknown magnitude), are summed and equated to zero. The resultant equations can then be solved for the unknown forces and moments.

SAMPLE FREE-BODY DIAGRAMS	
Mechanism	Free-body Diagram of Isolated Body
1. Ball of weight W resting on smooth surfaces.	
2. Weight of truss assumed negligible compared with P.	
3. Weight of uniform beam AB is W.	
4. Weight of pulley is W.	
5. Weights of members are assumed negligible compared with applied loads.	

PROBLEM 1:

A telephone pole in a rural area supports a wire that carries a force of 50 lbs directed along the wire. The wire configuration is indicated in the figure shown below. Find the force on the pole from the wire.

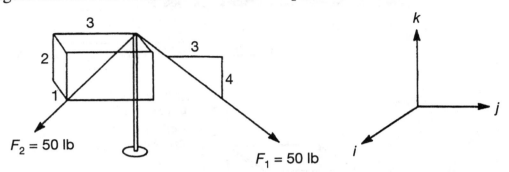

Figure 1

SOLUTION:

Forces F_1 and F_2 must be put into vector form using x, y, and z coordinates before they can be added to find the total force on the pole. We can write $\overrightarrow{F_1}$ directly as:

$$\overrightarrow{F_1} = 30\overrightarrow{j} - 40\overrightarrow{k}. \tag{1}$$

$\overrightarrow{F_2}$ has three components that can be found from vector laws as follows:

$$\overrightarrow{F_2} = (x)\overrightarrow{i} - (3x)\overrightarrow{j} - (2x)\overrightarrow{k} \tag{2}$$

$$\left|\overrightarrow{F_2}\right| = 50 = \sqrt{x^2 + 9x^2 + 4x^2}$$

$$x = 13.36$$

giving:

$$\overrightarrow{F_2} = 13.36\overrightarrow{i} - 40.08\overrightarrow{j} - 26.72\overrightarrow{k} \tag{3}$$

Adding $\overrightarrow{F_1}$ and $\overrightarrow{F_2}$ gives the force on the pole as:

$$\overrightarrow{F} = (13.36\overrightarrow{i} - 10.08\overrightarrow{j} - 66.72\overrightarrow{k})\text{ lb} \tag{4}$$

PROBLEM 2:

A winch-equipped bulldozer is trying to lift a pile of metal from a scrap pile. The bulldozer is lifting one part of the metal with the lip of its shovel and is pulling another with the winch. If the loads from the bull-dozer can be idealized as drawn in Figure 3, determine the moment of these loads about the point O.

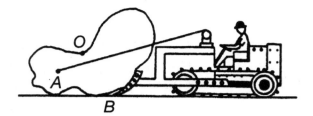

Figure 2

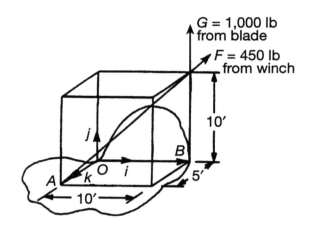

Figure 3

SOLUTION:

$$\vec{m_0} = (\vec{a} \times \vec{f}) + (\vec{b} \times \vec{G})$$

where $\vec{a}$ and $\vec{b}$ are the vectors from O to points A and B, respectively.

We choose the right-handed orthonormal basis shown for the moment vector space at O. Any position vectors can be selected to the forces, but we select ones which give convenient components with respect to a basis parallel to $i, j,$ and k.

From Figure 3 for the 1,000 lb force:

$b_1 = 10$ ft	$G_1 = 0$
$b_2 = 0$	$G_2 = 1000$ lb
$b_3 = 0$	$G_3 = 0$

For the 450 lb force:

$a_1 = 0$	$f_1 = 300$ lb
$a_2 = 0$	$f_2 = 300$ lb
$a_3 = 5$ ft	$f_3 = -150$ lb

So $m_0 = \begin{vmatrix} i & j & k \\ 10 & 0 & 0 \\ 0 & 1{,}000 & 0 \end{vmatrix} + \begin{vmatrix} i & j & k \\ 0 & 0 & 5 \\ 300 & 300 & -150 \end{vmatrix}$

$$= i(0) - j(0) + k(10{,}000 + i(-1{,}500) - j(-1{,}500) + k(0)$$

$$m_0 = (-1{,}500i + 1{,}500j + 10{,}000k)\text{ft-lb}$$

STRUCTURES

There are two basic categories of structures encountered by the engineer: (1) trusses and (2) frames and machines. A truss is a framework composed of members, such as beams or rods, joined at their ends to form a rigid structure. Frames and machines have members that are joined but have multiple forces acting on them. In general, these forces do not act in the direction of the members. The techniques for the analysis of the forces acting on each of these types of structures differ somewhat from that of the free-body diagram.

Trusses

The forces acting on a truss can be analyzed by using either the *method of joints* or the *method of sections*. The method of joints analyzes the forces acting on each of the connecting joints of the structure, treating each joint as a free body and using the results of the analysis on one joint to analyze the forces acting on an adjacent joint. With the method of joints all the forces are acting on a single point, eliminating the need to consider moments.

The method of sections analyzes the forces acting on sections of the structure, where each of the selected sections is a free body. Each of the sections must contain at least two joints. With the method of sections the summation of moments is a necessary part of the force analysis.

PROBLEM 3:

A truss, simply supported at the two ends, carries two loads 10 kN each as shown in Figure 4. Determine the force in each member of the truss by using the method of joints. In each case, state whether the member is in tension or compression.

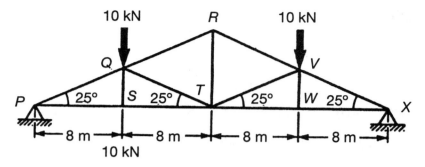

Figure 4

SOLUTION:

Since the truss and the loads are both symmetrical with respect to *RT*, only the forces on one side of the truss need to be calculated. Draw the free-body diagram for each joint and apply the principle of force equilibrium.

First consider joint *P* whose free-body diagram is shown in Figure 5. From symmetry, the external reaction at *P* is 10 kN. Setting the forces at *P* equal to zero yields:

$$+\uparrow \Sigma F_y = 0; \quad 10 \text{ kN} - F_{PQ} \sin 25° = 0 \tag{1}$$

$$F_{PQ} = 23.66 \text{ kN } C \text{ (compression)}$$

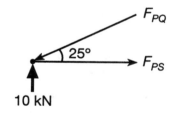

Figure 5

$$\Rightarrow \Sigma F_x = 0; \quad F_{PS} - F_{PQ} \cos 25° = 0 \tag{2}$$

$$F_{PS} = 21.44 \text{ kN } T \text{ (tension)}$$

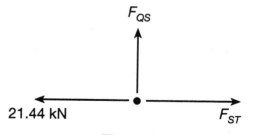

Figure 6

Now for joint *S*:

$$\overset{+}{\rightarrow}\Sigma F_x = 0;\; F_{ST} = 21.44 \text{ kN } T \tag{3}$$

$$+\uparrow \Sigma F_y = 0;\; F_{QS} = 0 \tag{4}$$

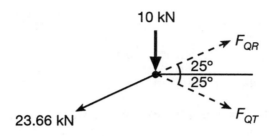

Figure 7

Looking at joint *Q*:

$$\overset{+}{\rightarrow}\Sigma F_x = 0;\; (23.66 \text{ kN} + F_{QR} + F_{QT}) \cos 25° = 0 \tag{5}$$

$$+\uparrow\Sigma F_y = 0;\; -10 \text{ kN} + (23.66 \text{ kN} + F_{QR} - F_{QT}) \sin 25° = 0 \tag{6}$$

Solving Equations 5 and 6 simultaneously results in:

$$F_{QT} = F_{QR} = -11.83 \text{ kN} = 11.83 \text{ kN } C$$

Figure 8 shows the free-body diagram for joint *T*. Due to symmetry forces F_{TW} and F_{TV} are equal and opposite to forces F_{TS} and F_{TQ}. Accordingly:

$$F_{TW} = 21.44 \text{ kN } T \quad F_{TV} = 11.83 \text{ kN } C$$

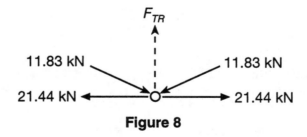

Figure 8

Summing forces in the vertical direction yields:

$$+\uparrow\Sigma F_y = 0;\; F_{TR} - 2(11.83 \text{ kN} \sin 25°) = 0$$

$$F_{TR} = 10 \text{ kN } T$$

Having found all the forces in the left-hand side of the truss, it may be stated due to symmetry that:

$$F_{RV} = 11.83 \text{ kN } C; \; F_{VW} = 0; \; F_{XY} = 23.66 \text{ kN } C; \; F_{XW} = 21.44 \text{ kN } T$$

To summarize,

$$F_{PQ} = F_{XY} = 23.66 \text{ kN Compression}$$

$$F_{PS} = F_{XW} = 21.44 \text{ kN Tension}$$

$$F_{QS} = F_{VW} = 0$$

$$F_{QT} = F_{VT} = 11.83 \text{ kN Compression}$$

$$F_{ST} = F_{WT} = 21.44 \text{ kN Tension}$$

$$F_{QR} = F_{VR} = 11.83 \text{ kN Compression}$$

$$F_{RT} = 10 \text{ kN Tension}$$

PROBLEM 4:

The truss in Figure 9 has forces acting as shown. Calculate the forces in members *NR* and *LK*

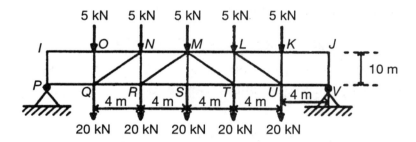

Figure 9

SOLUTION:

The free-body diagram of the whole truss and the forces acting on it is shown in Figure 10.

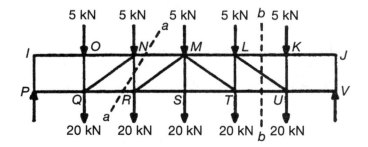

Figure 10

The equilibrium of the entire truss is considered in order to determine the reactions at P and $V + \uparrow \Sigma M_V = 0$.

$$(25 \text{ kN})(4\text{m}) + (25 \text{ kN})(8\text{m}) + (25 \text{ kN})(12\text{m}) + (25 \text{ kN})(16\text{m})$$
$$+ (25 \text{ kN})(20\text{m}) - P(24 \text{ m}) - 0$$

Therefore: $P = 62.5 \text{ kN}$

Likewise, the equation $+\Sigma M_P = 0$ yields $V = 62.5 \text{ kN}$

To calculate the force in NR, the method of sections is used. A line aa is passed through the truss dividing it into two separate parts but not intersecting more than three members. One portion of the truss shown in Figure 11 is now a free body, from which the force F_{NR} is determined.

$$+\uparrow \Sigma F_Y = 0; \ -F_{NR} - 5 \text{ kN} - 5 \text{ kN} - 20 \text{ kN} + 62.5 \text{ kN} = 0$$

$$F_{NR} = 32.5 \text{ kN Tension}$$

The section bb is used to determine the force in member LK. A free-body diagram of one portion of the truss is shown in Figure 12.

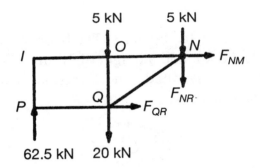

Figure 11

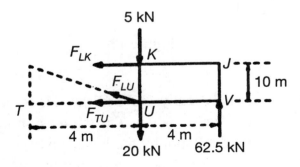

Figure 12

$$+\Sigma M_U = 0; \ (F_{LK})(10 \text{ m}) + (62.5 \text{ kN})(4 \text{ m}) = 0$$

or

$$F_{LK} = -25 \text{ kN}$$

The minus sign indicates that F_{LK} has an opposite sense to that assumed in Figure 12.

Frames and Machines

As with the analysis of forces acting on trusses, the forces acting on frames and machines are found by first creating a free-body diagram and applying the equilibrium equations. However, the members of frames and machines are acted on by multiple forces, which may not be in the direction of the member, that is, not acting along the longitudinal axis. Also, if a frame or machine-type structure includes a rigid unit, the forces of the rigid unit must be analyzed first, using the methods for analysis of trusses. Then the forces acting on the remaining sections can be analyzed.

PROBLEM 5:

A crane lifts a load of 10^4 kg mass. The boom of the crane is uniform, and has a mass of 1,000 kg. and a length of 10 m. Calculate the tension in the upper cable and the magnitude and direction of the force exerted on the boom by the lower pivot.

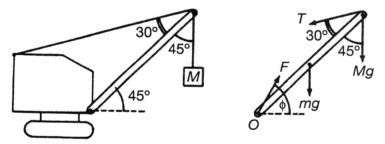

Figure 13

SOLUTION:

Isolate the boom analytically and indicate all forces on it as in the right-hand portion of the figure, where $\overrightarrow{T}$ is the tension in the upper cable, $\overrightarrow{F}$ is the force exerted on the boom by the lower pivot, m is the mass of the boom, and M is the mass of the load being lifted by the crane. The magnitude of $\overrightarrow{T}$ is unknown and both the magnitude and the direction of $\overrightarrow{F}$ are unknown. Set the net torque about point O equal to zero. If the length of the booming is S, this net torque is given by the equation.

$$\frac{S}{2} mg \sin 45° + SM g \sin 45° - ST \sin 30° = 0$$

or

$$\frac{g\,(m/2 + M)\,\sin 45°}{\sin 30°} = T$$

Substitute the values given above.

$$T = \frac{9.8(500 + 10,000)(1/\sqrt{2})}{1/2} = 1.46 \times 10^5 \, \text{N}$$

We can find F_x and F_y, the x- and y-components of $\vec{F}$ respectively, by requiring that both the x- and y-components of the net force on the boom be equal to zero.

$$\Sigma F_x = 0 \xrightarrow{+}$$

$$F_x - T \cos 15° = 0$$

$$\Sigma F_y = 0 + \uparrow$$

$$F_y - T \sin 15° - mg - Mg = 0$$

$$F_x = 1.46 \times 10^5 \, (\cos 15°)$$

$$F_y = 1.46 \times 10^5 \, (\sin 15°) + 9.8(1,000 + 10,000)$$

hence:

$$F_x = 1.41 \times 10^5 \, \text{N}$$

$$F_y = 1.46 \times 10^5 \, \text{N}$$

so that the magnitude of F is:

$$F = \sqrt{F_x^2 + F_y^2} = 2.03 \times 10^5 \, \text{N}$$

The angle ϕ which F makes with the horizontal is given by:

$$\tan \phi = \frac{F_x}{F_y} = \frac{1.46}{1.41} = 1.035$$

so that:

$$\phi = 46°$$

BEAMS

Beams are structural members that offer resistance to bending imposed by applied forces. They are usually long bars of varying cross-sectional shapes, with loads usually acting normal to the beam's longitudinal axis. Analyzing the forces acting on a beam requires first a static analysis and then an analysis of the beam's material strength. A beam that is supported in such a manner that the forces can be analyzed by the use of a static analysis alone is called a *statically determinate* beam. Beams that are supported at more points than are necessary to provide equilibrium are called *statically indeterminate* and the forces cannot be analyzed by static analysis alone.

In general, a beam acted upon by external forces is also acted upon by at least one moment, sometime referred to as a "couple." When analyzing the forces exerted on a beam, the free-body diagram depicts a section of the beam, one of the support ends of the beam, at least one of the forces acting on the beam, and an imaginary cut through a portion of the beam somewhere along its length. The forces and moments acting on the "cut" end are indicated on the free-body diagram as a function of its distance from the supported end of the beam. The forces used are the shear forces experienced tangential to the cross section and the moment is that preventing this "cut" end from "falling." With these forces and moments defined along the length of beam as a function of their position along the beam, the shear forces and bending moments at each point can be determined.

The results of this type of analysis are usually presented in a *shear force diagram* and a *bending moment diagram*. It should be noted that both the shear force diagram and the bending moment diagram have discontinuity points that correspond to the points at which the external forces are acting on the beam. Thus, for beams with multiple forces acting on it, separate free-body diagrams must be developed for sections which extend from one support end to points between each of the multiple forces.

PROBLEM 6:

Draw the shear and bending moment diagrams for the cantilever beam shown in Figure 14.

SOLUTION:

A free-body diagram of the beam with the force at C transformed to a force-couple system at B, is shown in Figure 15.

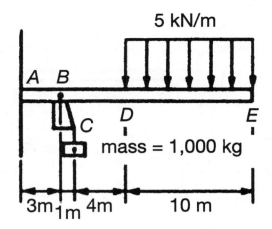

Figure 14

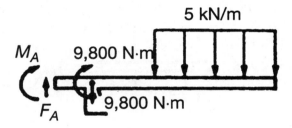

Figure 15

Assuming that the weight of the beam is negligible, it is now possible to write the equations of equilibrium.

$$+\uparrow\Sigma F_y = 0; \; F_A - 9{,}800 \text{ N} - (5 \text{ kN/m})(10 \text{ m}) = 0$$

or

$$F_A = 59.8 \text{ kN}$$

$$+\curvearrowleft\Sigma M_B = 0; \; -M_A - (59.8 \text{ kN})(3 \text{ m}) - 9.8 \text{ kN·m} - (5 \text{ kN/m})(10 \text{ m})(10 \text{ m}) = 0$$

$$M_A = -689 \text{ kN·m} = 689 \text{ kN·m} \curvearrowright$$

Sections along the beam will be analyzed to determine the shears and moments.

Referring to Figure 16:

Section 1:

$$+\uparrow\Sigma F_y = 0; \; S_1 = -59.8 \text{ kN}$$

$$+\curvearrowleft\Sigma M_A = 0; \; M_1 = 689 \text{ kN·m}$$

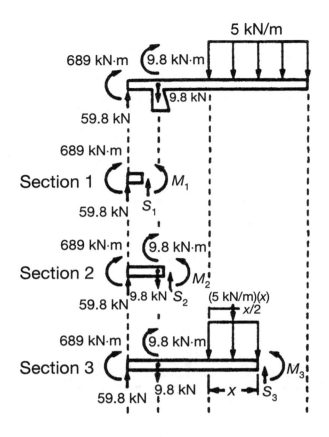

Figure 16

Section 2:

$$+\uparrow\Sigma F_y = 0;\ 59.8\ \text{kN} - 9.8\ \text{kN} + y_2 = 0$$

or

$$S_2 = -50\ \text{kN}$$

$$+\curvearrowleft\Sigma M_A = 0;\ -689\ \text{kN·m} - (9.8\ \text{kN})(3\text{m})$$

$$+ (-50\ \text{kN})(3\text{m}) - 9.8\ \text{kN·m} + M_2 = 0$$

$$M_2 = +878\ \text{kN·m}$$

Section 3:

$$+\uparrow\Sigma F_y = 0;\ 59.8\ \text{kN} - 9.8\ \text{kN} - 5x\ \text{kN} + y_3 = 0$$

or $\quad S_3 = 5x - 50\ \text{kN}$

$$+\curvearrowleft\Sigma M_B = 0;\ -689 - (59.8)(3) - 9.8 - + V_3(x + 5) + M_3 = 0$$

$$-879 - \frac{5}{2} - 25x + (5x - 50)(x + 5) + M_3 = 0$$

$$M_3 = 879 - \frac{5}{2}x^3 - 25x + 5x^2 - 50x + 25x - 250 = 2.5x^2 - 50x + 629$$

The shear and bending moment diagrams may now be constructed.

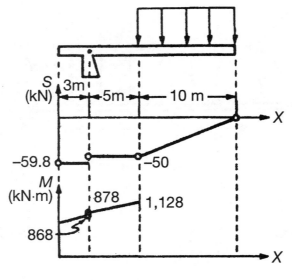

Figure 17

Beams with Distributed Loads

The shear force and bending moment diagrams for beams whose weight is not negligible or is subjected to a distributive load are different than the diagrams for beams subjected to only concentrated loads. In a free-body diagram, the distributive forces acting in the section selected are depicted as a geometric area, with the resultant force acting through the centroid of the area. The heights of the geometric area at any point along the length of the beam represent the magnitude of the distributive force at that point along the beam. The resultant shear force and bending moment diagrams of beams subjected to distributive loads are usually continuous over the length of the beams, provided there is no discontinuity in the distributive load. Similar to beams with multiple discrete forces acting on them, separate free-body diagrams must be developed for sections that extend from one support end to points between each of the discontinuities in the distributive load, if any.

For beams with both forces acting at discrete points and distributive loads, such as a beam where the weight of the beam is not negligible, the above techniques are easily combined to analyze the forces acting on the beam.

PROBLEM 7:

A distributed load, the intensity of which increases linearly from zero to a lb per unit length over a length L, acts on a beam as shown in Figure 18. Find the single rigid body force equivalent to the distributed load.

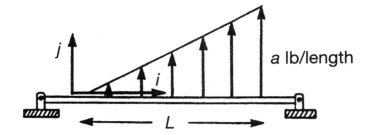

Figure 18

SOLUTION:

The single force that would be equivalent to the distributed load must satisfy the following two conditions:

(a) The single force must be equal to the resultant of the distributed load.

(b) The moment of the single force about any point must be equal to the total moment of the distributed load about the same point.

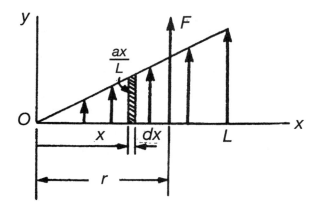

Figure 19

Figure 19 shows the chosen coordinate system with the x axis along the beam, the y axis perpendicular to it, and the origin at the left end of the distributed load. To find the resultant of the distributed load, consider an infinitesimal portion of it acting over a width dx, at distance x from the origin. By similar triangles we find that the intensity of the load at x is ax/L, acting in the y direction. The magnitude of the infinitesimal force over the width dx is $axdx/L$. Therefore, the resultant of the distributed load, which is equal to the single force F, is:

$$F = \int_0^L \frac{ax}{L}dx\,\vec{j} = \frac{a}{L}\frac{x^2}{2}\bigg|_0^L \vec{j} = \frac{aL}{2}\vec{j} \qquad (1)$$

Thus, the equivalent single force is of magnitude $aL/2$ and acts in the y direction. We consider the moments next, and choose the origin as the point about which moments are taken. Let r be the distance of the line of action of F from O. The moment of F about O is then:

$$M_0 = r\,\vec{i} \times F = r\,\vec{i} \times \frac{aL}{2}\,\vec{j} = \frac{arL}{2}\,\vec{k} \tag{2}$$

The moment of the distributed load about O is found by considering the moment of the infinitesimal portion of it and then integrating over the length L. The moment of the infinitesimal load $axdx/L$ about O is:

$$dM_0 = x\,\vec{i} \times \frac{axdx}{L}\,\vec{j} = \frac{ax^2 dx}{L}\,\vec{k}$$

Thus, the total moment of the distributed load about O is:

$$M_0 = \int_0^L \frac{ax^2}{L}\,dx\,\vec{k} = \frac{a}{L}\frac{x^3}{3}\bigg|_0^L \vec{k} = \frac{aL^2}{3}\,\vec{k} \tag{3}$$

We now equate the right-hand sides of Equations (2) and (3) and get:

$$\frac{arL}{2} = \frac{aL^2}{3}$$

or
$$r = \frac{2L}{3} \tag{4}$$

Therefore, the single equivalent force F acts at a distance $2L/3$ from the left end of the distributed load.

Flexible Cables

Flexible cables are bodies that offer negligible resistance to bending and in which all forces act along the longitudinal access of the cable. In practice, the design and analysis of cables are encountered in such things as the design of suspension bridges, power transmission lines, and telephone lines. There are two basic configurations of interest. In the first configuration, the weight of the cable is negligible compared to the load it supports, such as in most suspension bridges. In the second configuration the cable supports only its own weight such as with transmission lines. In the former configuration, the cable takes the form of a parabola, while in the latter, the cable takes the form of a catenary.

For the first case where the weight of the cable is negligible compared to the load, the tension in the cable can be defined as:

$$T = w \times \left(x^2 + \frac{L^2}{64h^2} \right)^{1/2}$$

where: T = tension in the cable

w = weight per unit length of the load

x = horizontal position along the cable

L = overall distance between the cable supports

h = vertical deflection of the cable at the point, x

For the second case where the cable is supporting only its own weight, the tension in the cable can be defined as:

$$T = T_0 \cosh\left(\frac{wx}{T_0} \right)$$

where: T = tension in the cable

w = weight per unit length of the load

x = horizontal position along the cable

T_0 = a reference tension defined by hyperbolic functions

For this second case where the cable is supporting only its own weight, the tension in the cable is defined in terms of hyperbolic trigonometric sines and cosines and is best solved using the exponential forms of the hyperbolic functions. The analysis of the forces in a cable of this type can best be explained by use of the sample problems below.

PROBLEM 8:

A chain is supported at two points on the same horizontal level and 12 ft. apart. Its slope at a point of support is $3/4$ and its density is given by the formula, for $s > 0$ where s is the length of the curve measured from the vertex, $as(1 + as)^{-1/2}$. Find the differential equation for the curve of the chain, and then in the case $a = 0$, find the curve itself.

SOLUTION:

If the burden on a cable is distributed uniformly, the differential equation for the curve of the cable is:

$$\frac{dy}{dx} = \frac{L}{P}$$

where L is the burden and P is the pull on the chain in the horizontal direction at the point (x, y).

In the given problem, the weight of the cable is distributed along the cable; hence, the nature of the burden is different. If the density of the cable is $\mu(s)$, where s is the length of the curve measured from the vertex, the load L is given by:

$$L = \int_0^s \mu(s)\, ds$$

Thus, the required differential equation is:

$$\frac{dy}{dx} = \frac{1}{P} \int_0^s \mu(s)\, ds$$

But we require a function of x on the right-hand side, not a function of s. Remembering that the differential arc-length of a curve is given by:

$$ds = \sqrt{1 + (y')^2}\, dx$$

we differentiate the differential equation to obtain:

$$dy' = \frac{\mu(s)}{P} \sqrt{1 + (y')^2}\, dx$$

in accordance with the rules for differentiation under an integral sign. From the two equations:

$$y' = \frac{1}{P} \int_0^s \mu(s)\, ds$$

$$dy' = \frac{\mu(s)}{P} \sqrt{1 + (y')^2}\, dx$$

we can sometimes eliminate s and obtain a differential equation for the curve of the chain.

Thus, in the given problem:

$$y' = \frac{1}{P} \int_0^s \frac{1}{\sqrt{1 + as}}\, ds = \frac{2}{ap} \left\{ [1 + as]^{\frac{1}{2}} \right\}_0^s$$

$$= \frac{2}{ap} \left\{ [1 + as]^{\frac{1}{2}} - 1 \right\}$$

$$dy' = \frac{\sqrt{1 + (y')^2}}{p\sqrt{1 + as}}\, dx$$

We eliminate $\sqrt{1+as}$ by noting that $\sqrt{1+as}$ is common to both equations. Then:

$$dy' = \frac{2\sqrt{1+y'^2}}{P(aPy'+2)}dx$$

Separating variables:

$$\frac{aPy'+2}{\sqrt{1+y'^2}}dy' = \frac{2}{P}dx$$

Solving: $\qquad aP\left\{\sqrt{1+y'^2}-1\right\} + 2\log\left\{y'+\sqrt{1+y'^2}\right\} = \frac{2x}{P}$

This is the differential equation describing the curve of the chain.

If $a = 0$, the density $\dfrac{1}{\sqrt{1+as}} = 1$, which means that the cable is of uniform density. The differential equation reduces to:

$$\log\left(y'+\sqrt{1+y'^2}\right) = \frac{x}{P}$$

Use the condition $y'(6) = \dfrac{3}{4}$ (the point of support is the mid-point of the distance separating the two points) to find $P = 6/\log 2$.

Then $\qquad \log\left\{y'+\sqrt{1+y'}\right\} = \dfrac{6x}{\log 2}$

may be expressed as:

$$\frac{dy}{dx} = \frac{1}{2}\left(e^{(x/6)\ \log 2} - e^{-(x/6)\ \log 2}\right)$$

Separating variables and applying the initial condition $y(0) = 0$ to the resulting integral:

$$y = \frac{3}{\log 2}\left(e^{(x/6)\ \log 2} + e^{-(x/6)\ \log 2} - 2\right)$$

or $\qquad y = \dfrac{3}{\log 2}\left(2^{x/12} - 2^{-x/12}\right)^2$

FRICTION

In a static analysis, friction is often one of the forces acting on a body. Friction is the force opposing motion when one body slides over another. It depends on the roughness of the two surfaces and the force with which the two surfaces are pushed together (normal to the surfaces). The proportionality that relates the friction forces to the force that pushes the two surfaces together is called the *coefficient of friction*. This is expressed as:

$$F_f = \mu \times N$$

where: F_f = friction force

μ = coefficient of friction

N = force normal to the surfaces, pressing them together

It must be remembered that the coefficient of friction for a body at rest on a surface is larger than for that same body moving at a constant velocity over that same surface. The engineer must be careful regarding which coefficient to use.

PROBLEM 9:

A ladder of length 10 m and mass 10 kg leans against a frictionless vertical wall at an angle of 60° from the horizontal. The coefficient of static friction between the horizontal floor and the foot of the ladder is μ_s = 0.25. A man of mass 70 kg starts up a ladder. How far along the ladder does he get before the ladder begins to slide down the wall?

SOLUTION:

The forces on the ladder are shown.

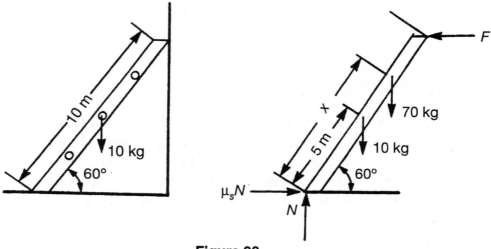

Figure 20

The horizontal force on the foot of the ladder is equal to $\mu_s N$ only at the instant before the ladder begins to slide. We wish to find the position of the man at this instant. Because the vertical wall is frictionless, it can exert a force on the ladder only perpendicular to itself as shown.

Since the net force on the ladder is zero, we find, taking vertical components:

$$N - 10 \text{ kg} - 70 \text{ kg} = 0$$

and, from horizontal components:

$$\mu_s N - F = 0$$

Let x be the distance of the man along the ladder from the foot at the instant the ladder begins to slide. Equate the torque about the foot of the ladder to zero.

$$\frac{L}{2} \times mg \cos\theta + xMg \cos\theta - FL \sin\theta = 0$$

From the first equation above:

$$N = 80 \text{ kg newtons}$$

From this and the second equation:

$$F = 0.25 \times 80 \text{ kg} = 20 \text{ kg newtons}$$

From this and the third equation:

$$\frac{1}{2} m Lg \cos\theta + xMg \cos\theta - 20gL \sin\theta = 0$$

$$x = \frac{20gL\sin\theta - \frac{1}{2}mLg\cos\theta}{Mg\cos\theta}$$

$$= \frac{200 \times 0.866 - \frac{1}{2} \times 10 \times 10 \times \frac{1}{2}}{70 \times \frac{1}{2}} = 4.2 \text{ meters}$$

WORK CONCEPTS

In physics and mechanics *work* is accomplished only when a force is exerted on a body while the same body moves in the direction of the force or of a component of the force. Work can be simply defined as the magnitude of the force applied to a body times the distance the body moves. The basic English unit of work is the *foot-pound*, which is defined as *the work done by a constant force of one pound when the body on which the force is exerted moves a distance of one foot in the same direction as the force.*

$$W = F \times (X_2 - X_1)$$

where: W = work

F = force

$(X_2 - X_1)$ = distance through which the force moves

Work done on a body by a force can be dissipated to overcome frictional losses or it can manifest itself as an increase in energy. In the case where velocity is constant, the energy increase is usually in the form of potential energy. The work done by a force on a body is equal to the increase in the energy of that body plus any frictional losses, such that:

$$F \times (X_2 - X_1) = \left(\frac{1}{2}mv_2^2 - \frac{1}{2}mv_1^2 \right) + (mgh_2 - mgh_2)$$

where: F = net of the force applied and the friction force

$(X_2 - X_1)$ = distance through which the force moves

$\left(\frac{1}{2}mv_2^2 - \frac{1}{2}mv_1^2 \right)$ = change in kinetic energy

$(mgh_2 - mgh_1)$ = change in potential energy

PROBLEM 10:

Derive an expression for the work done by the force in a spring whose free end moves from A to B, as shown.

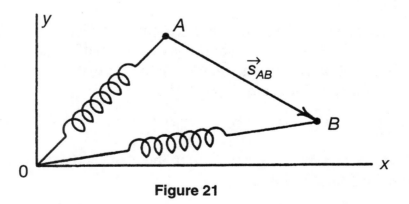

Figure 21

SOLUTION:

We consider the spring in two different deformed positions, as shown. We let the deformation of the spring at A be called s_1 and that at B (the amount of stretch from the unstretched position) be called s_2. We assume a flexible spring so that the internal force acts "along" the spring at all times.

It can be seen that, during the deformation, the force varies in magnitude and also in direction with respect to $\vec{S}_{AB}$. However, the displacement $\vec{S}_{AB}$ can be accomplished by a summation at each intermediate position of the spring of infinitesimal displacements along the spring and perpendicular to the spring, respectively. The work done by the spring force during the infinitesimal displacement perpendicular to the spring is zero. Let ds be the magnitude of an infinitesimal displacement along the spring. The work done by the spring force F during these displacements is:

$$U = \int_{s_1}^{s_2} F \, ds$$

But it is known that the force in a spring varies as the negative of the deformation; that is, if the spring is elongated, the force acts toward the center of the spring, but if the spring is compressed, the force acts away from the center of the spring. Substitution yields:

$$U = \int_{s_1}^{s_2} -ks \, ds$$

where k is the spring constant and s is the deformation. Upon performing the integration, we get:

$$U = -\frac{1}{2} k \left(s_2^2 - s_1^2 \right)$$

PROBLEM 11:

A body of mass m has an initial velocity v_0 directed up a plane that is at an inclination angle θ to the horizontal. The coefficient of sliding friction between the mass and the plane is μ. What distance d will the body slide up the plane before coming to rest?

SOLUTION:

The forces on the body, resolved in the plane and perpendicular to the plane are shown in Figure 22.

The motion is perpendicular to the normal force N and the $mg \cos \theta$ component of gravity; they do not work on the block. The other two forces, $mg \sin \theta$ and $f = \mu N = \mu \, mg \cos \theta$, are along the path of motion and do work. The amount of work is equal to their magnitudes, which are constant, times the distance d the body travels:

$$W = -mg \sin \theta \, d - \mu \, mg \cos \theta \, d$$

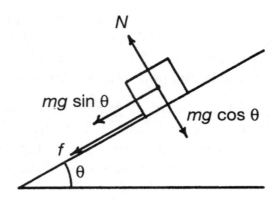

Figure 22

This quantity of work is equal to the energy loss, from the body's initial kinetic energy:

$$\Delta KE = -\frac{1}{2}mv_0^2$$

$$-\frac{1}{2}mv_0^2 = -mg\sin\theta\, d - \mu\, mg\cos\theta\, d \qquad (1)$$

$$d = \frac{v_0^2}{2g\,(\mu\cos\theta + \sin\theta)}$$

Alternatively, using the most general energy conservation law:

$$W_{nc} = \Delta E + \Delta V$$

yields equation (1) again.

$$W_{nc} = -\mu\, mg\, d\,\cos\theta$$

$$\Delta E = -\frac{1}{2}\, mv_0^2$$

and $\qquad\qquad \Delta V = mg\,\Delta h = mg\, d\sin\theta$

so that: $\qquad -\mu\, mg\, d\cos\theta = -\frac{1}{2}\, mv_0^2 + mg\, d\sin\theta$

CENTER OF GRAVITY AND THE CENTER OF MASS

The center of gravity of a body is an imaginary point within a body through which the resultant of gravitational forces on the body pass. The center of mass of a body is coincident with the center of gravity. It is more generally described as the imaginary point within a body where, when a force exerted on that body acts through that point, no movement or rotation occurs. The location of the centers of mass and gravity occur frequently in engineering calculations. The engineer should have a working understanding of this concept, and how to locate these points.

The coordinates of the centers of gravity and mass of a body are determined by first putting the body into a three-dimensional coordinate system. Each coordinate is defined as the sum of the moments of each element of "point" mass divided by the total mass of the body.

$$X = \frac{m_1 x_1 + m_2 x_2 + \ldots + m_i x_i}{m_1 + m_2 + \ldots + m_i}$$

$$Y = \frac{m_1 y_1 + m_2 y_2 + \ldots + m_i y_i}{m_1 + m_2 + \ldots + m_i}$$

$$Z = \frac{m_1 z_1 + m_2 z_2 + \ldots + m_i z_i}{m_1 + m_2 + \ldots + m_i}$$

PROBLEM 12:

Find the center of mass of a homogeneous right circular solid cone of vertical height h and base radius a.

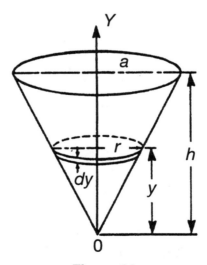

Figure 23

SOLUTION:

A well-made choice of the coordinate system exploiting the symmetry of the problem often reduces the complexity of the calculation of the center of mass. For the cone, exploiting this symmetry means that the y-axis can be placed immediately along the cone's center passing through the center of the base and the apex. Further simplification is obtained by placing the origin at the apex as shown in the figure.

Consider a horizontal thin slab of the cone whose thickness is dy, whose mean radius is r, and whose height above the origin is y. If the density or mass per unit volume of the cone is ρ, then the mass dm of the thin slab is:

$$dm = \pi r^2 \rho dy$$

The radius r of the slab is proportional to its height y, and from the figure it can be seen that:

$$\frac{r}{a} = \frac{y}{h} \quad \text{or} \quad r = \frac{ay}{h}$$

Thus:

$$dm = \frac{\pi \rho a^2 y^2}{h^2} \, dy$$

and the total mass M of the cone is:

$$M = \frac{\pi \rho a^2}{h^2} \int_0^h y^2 dy = \frac{\pi \rho a^2 h}{3}$$

The vertical distance of the center of mass from O is:

$$\bar{y} = \int_0^h \frac{y \, dm}{M} = \frac{\pi \rho a^2}{Mh^2} \int_0^h y^3 dy$$

Integrating and substituting the value for M, gives:

$$\bar{y} = \frac{3\pi a^2 h^4}{4h^2 \pi \rho a^2 h} = \frac{3h}{4}$$

or, the center of mass is three-fourths of the altitude measured from the apex.

FE/EIT

FE: PM General Engineering Exam

CHAPTER 9

Dynamics

CHAPTER 9

DYNAMICS

Dynamics is the study of bodies in motion. It has two distinct parts, kinematics and kinetics. Kinematics is the study of motion itself, that is: displacement, velocity, and acceleration without any reference to the forces acting on the body. Kinetics is the study of the relation of motion and the forces acting on a body.

KINEMATICS

Four types of motions are most frequently encountered in engineering. They are *rectilinear translation*, *curvilinear translation*, *rotation*, and *plane motion*—which is a combination of translation and rotation.

Rectilinear Translation

Rectilinear translation is the linear displacement of all points of a body an equal distance along parallel lines. An example of rectilinear motion would be the reciprocating motion of a piston in an internal combustion engine. If a point on a body moves along a straight line for a short distance, Δx, during a time increment, Δt, the average velocity, $v_{av} = \Delta x / \Delta t$. As the time increment approaches 0, the velocity approaches an instantaneous value of $v = dx/dt$. In turn, acceleration is defined as the instantaneous change of velocity with time, $a = dv/dt$. From these basic definitions, the three commonly used equations of rectilinear motion can be developed. They are:

$$x = x_o + v_o t + \frac{1}{2}at^2 \quad v = v_o + at \quad \text{and} \quad v^2 = v_o^2 + 2ax$$

where: x = distance

  v = velocity

  a = acceleration

  t = time

  o = an initial condition.

For the case of a body near the earth falling under the force of gravity, the acceleration is the force of gravity, g = 32.2 feet/sec² = 9.8 m/s². The distance is measured from the earth's surface. The above equations are modified slightly to show the reversed distance, or height, measurement as follows:

$$x = x_o - v_o t - \frac{1}{2}gt^2 \quad v = v_o^2 - gt \quad \text{and} \quad v^2 = v_o^2 - 2gx$$

PROBLEM 1:

In the two pulley systems shown in Figure 1, determine the velocity and acceleration of block 3 when blocks 1 and 2 have the velocities and acceleration shown.

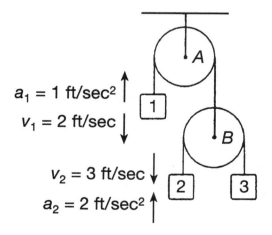

a_1 = 1 ft/sec²

v_1 = 2 ft/sec

v_2 = 3 ft/sec

a_2 = 2 ft/sec²

Figure 1

SOLUTION:

Figure 2 defines the positions relative to the fixed pulley A needed to solve this problem.

The lengths of the cord are assumed to be constant and the section of cord over the pulleys to remain constant, thus yielding the following constraint equations:

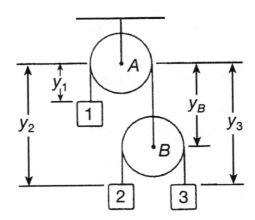

Figure 2

$$y_1 + y_B = K_1 \tag{1}$$

$$(y_2 - y_B) + (y_3 - y_B) = K_2$$

or $$y_2 + y_3 - 2y_B = K_2 \tag{2}$$

Differentiating each equation (1) and (2) twice yields:

$$\dot{y}_1 + \dot{y}_B = 0 \tag{3}$$

$$\ddot{y}_1 + \ddot{y}_B = 0 \tag{4}$$

$$\dot{y}_2 + \dot{y}_3 - 2\dot{y}_B = 0 \tag{5}$$

$$\ddot{y}_2 + \ddot{y}_3 - 2\ddot{y}_B = 0 \tag{6}$$

These equations lead directly to the desired solutions upon substitution of the information from Figure 1. If it is supposed that down is positive, then:

$$v_1 = \dot{y}_1 = -2 \text{ ft/sec} \qquad v_2 = \dot{y}_2 = 3 \text{ ft/sec}$$

$$a_1 = \ddot{y}_1 = 1 \text{ ft/sec}^2 \qquad a_2 = \ddot{y}_2 = -2 \text{ ft/sec}^2 \tag{7}$$

First solve (4) and (5) to find the motion of pulley B.

$$-2 \text{ ft/sec} + \dot{y}_B = 0$$

$$\dot{y}_B = 2 \text{ ft/sec} \tag{8}$$

$$1 \text{ ft/sec}^2 + \ddot{y}_B = 0$$

$$\ddot{y}_B = -1 \text{ ft/sec}^2 \tag{9}$$

Now using (7), (8), and (9) in Equations (5) and (6), it is possible to obtain the desired results:

$$3 \text{ ft/sec} + \dot{y}_3 - 2\,(2 \text{ ft/sec}) = 0$$
$$\dot{y}_3 = 1 \text{ ft/sec}$$
$$-2 \text{ ft/sec}^2 + \ddot{y}_3 - 2\,(-1 \text{ ft/sec}^2) = 0$$
$$\ddot{y}_3 = 0$$

Thus, block 3 is moving down with a constant velocity

$$v_3 = 1 \text{ ft/sec}$$

Curvilinear Translation

Curvilinear translation is the displacement of all points of a body an equal distance along congruent curves. The same relationships and equations apply to curvilinear translation as apply to rectilinear translation, except that the distance traveled is measured along the arc of the curve and the velocity and acceleration are in the direction of the tangent of the curve. The distance traveled, the velocity, and the acceleration all have both X and Y components. An example of curvilinear motion would be the path of a projectile resulting from the velocity imparted by the charge and by gravitational forces pulling it back to earth.

The acceleration discussed above is the *tangential acceleration*; that is the acceleration acting along the tangent of the curve. The tangential acceleration is the rate of change of the magnitude of the velocity with time. However, velocity also changes its direction with time. The rate of change of the direction of velocity with time is called the *angular acceleration*, which acts normal to the tangent of the curved path and toward its center of curvature. The angular acceleration is calculated by the following equation:

$$a_n = \frac{v^2}{r}$$

where: a = acceleration

v = velocity

r = radius of curvature

PROBLEM 2:

A projectile, fired with velocity v_0 and angle α_0 from the horizontal, is to impact at point P as shown. What is the range measured along the straight line connecting the firing point and the target?

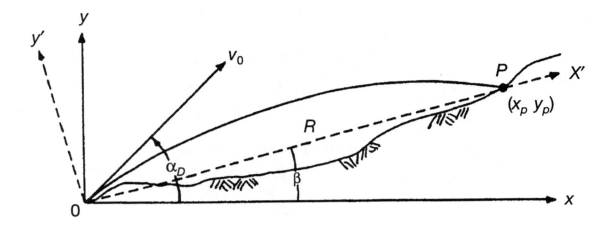

Figure 3

SOLUTION:

$$R_\beta = \frac{x_p}{\cos\beta} = \frac{2}{g\cos\beta}(v_0\cos\alpha_0)^2(\tan\alpha_0 - \tan\beta)$$

The horizontal and vertical components of the initial velocity v_0 are, respectively:

$$v_x = v_0\cos\alpha_0 \quad v_y = v_0\sin\alpha_0$$

If we let t_p be the time it takes to reach point P, the horizontal distance covered is:

$$x_p = (v_0\cos\alpha_0)t_p \tag{1}$$

Since there is no horizontal acceleration, the vertical distance covered in time t_p is:

$$y_p = (v_0\sin\alpha_0)t_p - \frac{1}{2}gt_p^2 \tag{2}$$

where $-g$ is the downward acceleration due to gravity. Equation (1) gives the elapsed time as:

$$t_p = \frac{x_p}{v_0\cos\alpha_0}$$

Substitute this along with the relationship $y_p = x_p\tan\beta$ into Equation (2) to give:

$$x_p\tan\beta = (v_0\sin\alpha_0)\frac{x_p}{v_0\cos\alpha_0} - \frac{1}{2}g\frac{x_p^2}{v_0^2\cos^2\alpha_0}$$

$$\tan\beta = \tan\alpha_0 - \frac{1}{2}\frac{gx_p}{v_0^2 \cos^2\alpha_0}$$

$$x_p = 2(v_0 \cos\alpha_0)^2 \frac{\tan\alpha_0 - \tan\beta_0}{g}$$

The range along a line from the firing point and the target is now obtained from:

$$R_\beta = \frac{x_p}{\cos\beta}$$

PROBLEM 3:

A race car is driving at a speed of 80 mph along a curved road with a radius of 2,000 ft. The brakes are applied causing constant deceleration of the car, after 8s the speed decreases to 50 mi/h. Calculate the acceleration of the car at the instant after the brakes have been applied.

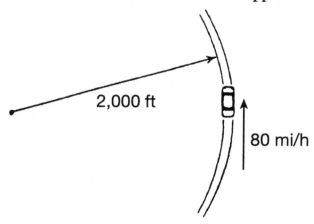

2,000 ft

80 mi/h

Figure 4

SOLUTION:

Because the car is moving on a curved road, it is essential to consider not only the acceleration that results in a decrease of speed (tangential acceleration) but also the centripetal acceleration that keeps the car moving on an arc.

Tangential Component. The standard equation for constant acceleration is:

$$a = \frac{\Delta v}{\Delta t} \tag{1}$$

However, the units, as given in the problem, are mixed. Thus, it is necessary to re-express the velocities involved:

$$80\frac{mi}{h} = \left(80\frac{mi}{h}\right)\left(\frac{5,280 \text{ ft}}{1 \text{ mi}}\right)\left(\frac{1 \text{ h}}{3,600 \text{ s}}\right) = 117 \text{ ft/s}$$

and

$$50\frac{mi}{h} = (50)(5,280)\left(\frac{1}{3,600}\right) \text{ ft/s} = 73 \text{ ft/s}$$

At this point, apply Equation (1) with Δt = braking time:

$$a_T = \frac{\Delta v}{\Delta t} = \frac{73 \text{ ft/s} - 117 \text{ ft/s}}{8 \text{ s}}$$

$$a_T = -5.50 \text{ ft/s}^2$$

Centripetal Acceleration. The standard equation for centripetal acceleration is:

$$a_C = \frac{v^2}{r} \tag{2}$$

The question asks for the acceleration immediately after the brakes have been applied, that is, when the velocity is still (approximately) 80 mph. Hence:

$$a_C = \frac{(117 \text{ ft/s})^2}{2,000 \text{ ft}} = 6.84 \text{ ft/s}^2$$

Magnitude and Direction of Acceleration. The magnitude and direction of the resultant a of the components a_C and a_T are:

$$\tan a = \frac{a_C}{a_T} = \frac{6.84 \text{ ft/s}^2}{-5.38 \text{ ft/s}^2} \qquad a = -51.8°$$

$$a = \frac{a_C}{\sin a} = \frac{a_T}{\cos a} = -8.7 \text{ ft/s}^2$$

To calculate the magnitude only:

$$a = \sqrt{a_C^2 + a_T^2} = \sqrt{(+6.84 \text{ ft/s})^2 + (-5.38 \text{ ft/s})^2}$$

$$= 8.7 \text{ ft/s}^2$$

Rotation

Rotation is the angular motion about a fixed axis. Velocity for angular motion is the angular displacement of a body around the axis and is called angular velocity (ω). If a point on a body moves around a fixed axis for a small angular displacement, $\Delta\theta$, during a time increment, Δt, the average angular velocity $\omega_{av} = \Delta\theta/\Delta t$. As the time increment approaches 0, the velocity approaches an instantaneous value of $\omega = d\theta/dt$. In turn, the angular acceleration (α) is defined as the instantaneous change of angular velocity with time, $\alpha = d\omega/dt$. From these basic definitions, the three commonly used equations of rotation can be developed. They are:

$$\theta = \theta_o + \omega_o t + \frac{1}{2}\alpha t^2 \qquad \omega = \omega_o + \alpha t \quad \text{and} \quad \omega^2 = \omega_o^2 + 2\alpha\theta$$

where: θ = angular displacement

ω = angular velocity

α = angular acceleration

t = time

While a point in a body is undergoing rotation in accordance with the above equations, that same point is experiencing translational motion around the axis point. The relationship between the angular displacement, velocity, and acceleration associated with rotation, and the translational displacement, tangential velocity, tangential acceleration, and radial acceleration associated with translation are expressed by the following equations:

$$s = r\theta \qquad v = r\omega \qquad a_t = r\alpha \qquad a_r = \frac{v^2}{r} = r\omega^2 = v\omega$$

where: s = translational displacement

r = radius of rotation (or the distance from the point in question to the axis of rotation)

θ = angular displacement

v = tangential velocity

ω = angular velocity

a_t = tangential acceleration

α = angular acceleration

a_r = radial acceleration

PROBLEM 4:

Two pulleys connected with a belt can function together in three positions as shown in the figure. Shaft A starts to move (initial angular velocity $\omega_A = 0$) with an angular acceleration $\alpha_A = 5$ rad/s. For each of the three positions of the belt, calculate the time needed for shaft B to reach 600 rpm.

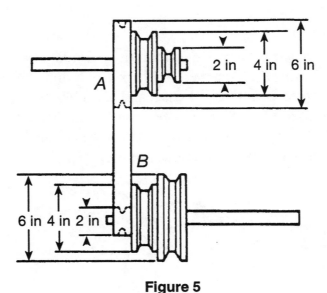

Figure 5

SOLUTION:

Use the basic relation for rotating bodies to solve this problem:

$$\omega_A = \alpha_A t$$

where ω_A = angular velocity of shaft A

α_A = angular acceleration of shaft A

t = elapsed time.

There is no initial velocity in the problem. In each case, the angular velocity of shaft B is to be 600 rev/min or:

$$\omega_B = 600\frac{rev}{min} \times 2\pi\frac{rad}{rev} \times \frac{1\ min}{60\ sec} = 62.83\frac{rad}{sec}$$

The acceleration of shaft A is given as $\alpha_A = 5$ rad/sec², while the angular velocity of shaft A can be expressed in terms of ω_B and the diameters as:

$$\omega_A D_A = \omega_B D_B \quad or \quad \omega_A = \frac{\omega_B D_B}{D_A}$$

If we substitute this into the first equation we obtain:

$$t = \frac{\omega_B D_B}{\alpha_A D_A} = \frac{62.83}{5}\frac{D_B}{D_A} = 12.57\frac{D_B}{D_A}$$

Now, in the first arrangement $D_B/D_A = {}^1/_3$ and so $t = 4.19$ sec. In the middle arrangement $D_B/D_A = 1$ and $t = 12.57$ sec. In the third arrangement $D_B/D_A = 3$ and $t = 37.7$ sec.

PROBLEM 5:

As shown, a rope is wrapped around the cylinder A and the pulley B, and another rope from B is attached to block C. Cylinder A has an angular velocity of 3 rad/sec counterclockwise and an angular acceleration of 6 rad/sec² counterclockwise. Also, the center of A has a linear velocity and an acceleration of 4 ft/sec and 6 ft/sec² downwards, respectively. Determine the linear velocity and acceleration of block C.

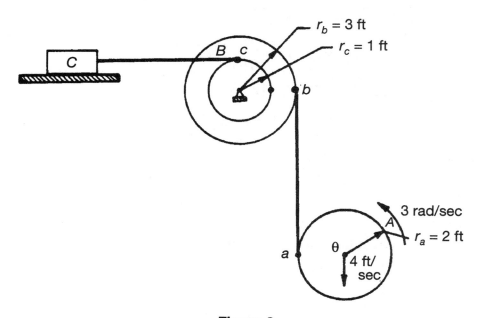

Figure 6

SOLUTION:

To solve for velocity, let a and O be points on cylinder A, and let b and c be points on cylinder B.

Since the motion of cylinder A is completely specified, begin with that cylinder and we will work our way through cylinder B to block C. The velocity of point a is first found by relating it to point O.

$$\bar{v}_a = \bar{v}_O + \bar{v}_{aO} \tag{1}$$

From the given information:

$$\bar{v}_O = 4 \text{ ft/sec} \downarrow \tag{2}$$

The velocity of a relative point to O is given by the formula:

$$v_{aO} = (aO)\omega_A$$

Distance aO is the radius of cylinder A. So:

$$v_{aO} = (2 \text{ ft}) \, 3 \text{ rad/sec}$$

$$= 6 \text{ ft/sec}$$

The direction of $\bar{v}_{aO}$ must be perpendicular to line aO and agree in sense with $\bar{\omega}_A$. Therefore:

$$\bar{v}_{aO} = 6 \text{ ft/sec} \downarrow \qquad (3)$$

Substituting (2) and (3) into (1):

$$\bar{v}_a = 4 \downarrow + 6 \downarrow$$

$$= 10 \text{ ft/sec} \downarrow$$

The ropes are assumed to be unstretchable. It is also assumed that the ropes do not slip over the cylindrical surfaces at *a, b,* or *c.* From these two assumptions, it follows that all points on the vertical rope have the same velocity as point *a.* Furthermore, it follows that point *b* has this same velocity.

Since the center of cylinder B is stationary, two simple velocity formulas can be written for points *b* and *c*:

$$v_b = r_b \, \omega_B \qquad (4)$$

$$v_c = r_c \, \omega_B \qquad (5)$$

Solving (4) and (5) for ω_B and equating, we have:

$$\frac{v_b}{r_b} = \frac{v_c}{r_c}$$

Rewriting:

$$v_c = \frac{r_c}{r_b} \, v_b$$

Substituting known values:

$$v_c = \frac{1 \text{ ft}}{3 \text{ ft}} \, (10 \text{ ft/sec})$$

$$= 3.33 \text{ ft/sec}$$

Because of the two assumptions noted above, all points on the horizontal rope will have the same velocity and the velocity of block C will be the same as point *c*:

$$\bar{v}_C = \bar{v}_c$$

$$= 3.33 \text{ ft/sec} \rightarrow$$

The direction of $\bar{v}_C$ is ascertained by noting that $\bar{\omega}_B$ is clockwise due to the downward motion of b. Thus, block C is pulled to the right.

To solve for acceleration, note that point a has two components of acceleration due to the rotation of A: one in the vertical or tangential direction and one in the normal direction along aO. The acceleration of point a can also be related to that of O as was done for velocity.

$$\vec{a_a} = \vec{a_a}^n + \vec{a_a}^t = \vec{a_O} + \vec{a_{aO}}^n + \vec{a_{aO}}^t \tag{6}$$

Equating the components of acceleration in the tangential (vertical) direction in Equation (6), we have:

$$\bar{a}_a^t = \bar{a}_O + \bar{a}_{aO}^t \tag{7}$$

From the given data:

$$\bar{a}_O = 6 \text{ ft/sec}^2 \downarrow \tag{8}$$

The tangential component of the acceleration of a relative to O is given by the formula:

$$a_{aO}^t = (aO)\ \dot{\omega}_A \tag{9}$$

From the given data:

$$a_O = 2 \text{ ft}$$

$$\bar{\omega}_A = 6 \text{ rad/sec}^2 \text{ counterclockwise}$$

Substituting these values into (9), we have:

$$a_{aO}^t = (2 \text{ ft})\ (6 \text{ rad/sec}^2)$$

$$= 12 \text{ ft/sec}^2 \downarrow \tag{10}$$

Now from (7), (8), and (10), we get:

$$\bar{a}_a^t = 6\downarrow + 12\downarrow$$

$$= 18 \text{ ft/sec}^2 \downarrow \tag{11}$$

This is the same acceleration as that of point b. Points b and c move on circular paths and the simple formulas apply:

$$a_b^t = r_b\ \dot{\omega}_B \tag{12}$$

$$a_c^t = r_c\ \dot{\omega}_B \tag{13}$$

Solving (12) and (13) for $\dot{\omega}_B$ and equating, we get:

$$\frac{a_b{}^t}{r_b} = \frac{a_c{}^t}{r_c}$$

Rewriting:

$$a_c{}^t = \frac{r_c}{r_b}\, a_b{}^t$$

Substituting known values:

$$a_c{}^t = \frac{1\text{ ft}}{3\text{ ft}}\ 18\text{ ft/sec}^2$$

$$= 6\text{ ft/sec}^2$$

The tangential component of acceleration of point c is the same as that of any point on the horizontal rope from C to c and the same as that of block C.

The direction of block C's acceleration is determined from the direction of $\bar{\omega}_B$. Referring to Equation (12), we are reminded that the direction of $\bar{\omega}_B$ must agree with the direction of $\bar{a}_b{}^t$. The latter is downward. So, $\bar{\omega}_B$ is clockwise. From this, it follows that $\bar{a}_d{}^t$ is to the right and the acceleration of the block is also:

$$\bar{a}_C = 6\text{ ft/sec}^2 \rightarrow$$

It should be noted that it is possible for the block acceleration to be to the left. This would be the case if C was moving to the right and slowing down.

ACCELERATION, MASS, AND FORCE

Kinetics is the study of the relation of motion and unbalanced forces acting on a body resulting in acceleration. This relationship can be expressed as the resultant net force on a body is equal to the time rate of change in momentum of the body:

$$F = d(mv)/dt = m \times dv/dt + v \times dm/dt$$

where: $F =$ resultant net force exerted on a body

$m =$ mass of the body

$v =$ instantaneous velocity of the body

For a body of constant mass, and recognizing the term dv/dt as equal to acceleration a, the above equation reduces to the familiar $F = ma$, or for a three-dimensional coordinate system:

$$\Sigma F_x = ma_x \qquad \Sigma F_y = ma_y \qquad \Sigma F_z = ma_z$$

PROBLEM 6:

If the pulleys have negligible mass and there is no friction, show that: (a) the acceleration of the blocks A and B are $g/7$ and $2g/7$; and (b) the tension in the string is 5.71 lb$_f$.

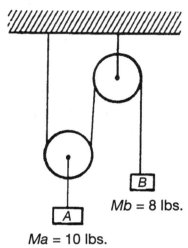

$Mb = 8$ lbs.

$Ma = 10$ lbs.

Figure 7

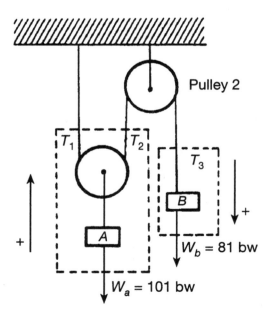

Pulley 2

$W_b = 81$ bw

$W_a = 101$ bw

Figure 8

SOLUTION:

We will apply Newton's Second Law (net $F = ma$) to the various masses to determine the accelerations. Draw regions of isolation around the weights A and B as shown and take the positive direction downward on weight B. Clearly A moves upward for positive motion of B.

First write the force equations for A and B:

$$T_1 + T_2 - W_A = m_A a_A \qquad (1)$$

$$W_B - T_3 = m_B a_B \qquad (2)$$

Since the rope with T_1 is fixed and does not stretch, each unit mass on that side of pulley 1 has zero acceleration. If each unit mass on the T_2 side undergoes an acceleration equal to a_B, then a_A must be the average of the accelerations on both sides or:

$$a_A = \frac{1}{2} a_B \qquad (3)$$

Since we have massless, frictionless pulleys, all of the tensions are equal:

$$T_1 = T_2 = T_3 = T \qquad (4)$$

Substituting (3) and (4) in (1) and (2):

$$2T - W_A = \frac{1}{2} m_A a_B \qquad (5)$$

$$W_B - T = m_B a_B \qquad (6)$$

Solving (6) for T and substituting into (5) yields after rearrangement:

$$a_B = \frac{2W_B - W_A}{2m_B + \frac{1}{2} m_A}$$

But $W = mg$, $m = w/g$, therefore:

$$a_B = \frac{2W_B - W_A}{2W_B/g + \frac{1}{2} W_A/g} = \left(\frac{2W_B - W_A}{2W_B + \frac{1}{2} W_A} \right) g$$

$$a_B = \frac{2 \times 8 - 10}{2 \times 8 + 5} g = \frac{6}{23} g \qquad (7)$$

From (3):

$$a_A = \frac{1}{2} a_B = \frac{3}{23}$$

From (6):

$$T = W_B - m_B a_B$$

$$= 8 - \frac{8}{g}\left(\frac{6}{23}g\right)$$

$$= 8 - \frac{16}{7} = 5.91 \text{ lbW}$$

MOMENTS OF INERTIA

In the analysis of forces acting on a body, an expression of the form: $I = \int y^2 da$ is used. This integral is referred to as the *moment of inertia*. It is purely a mathematical property and of itself, has no physical significance. However, it is a useful concept when analyzing a body experiencing curvilinear or rotational motion, where the expression occurs frequently.

Values for moments of inertia for common shapes rotating around normal axes have been tabulated and can be found in various engineering handbooks. Engineers sometimes encounter common shapes that are rotating or moving around a different axis. In such a case, the engineer can use the tabulated value for the moment of inertia and "correct" that value to reflect the particular axis in question. The corrected moment of inertia for an offset axis is calculated using the following relationship:

$$I_n = I_o + Ad^2$$

where: I_n = new value for the moment of inertia

I_o = tabulated value for the moment of inertia

A = area for which the moment of inertia is being calculated

d = distance from the original tabulated axis to the new axis

PROBLEM 7:

Find the moment of inertia of the channel section shown in Figure 1 with respect to the line *XX*. Find also the moment of inertia with respect to the parallel centroidal axis.

SOLUTION:

The area may be divided into triangles and rectangles as shown in the figure. The values used in the solution may be put in tabular form as shown below, where a denotes the area of any part, y_0 the distance of the centroid of the part from the line *XX*, I_0 the moment of inertia of the part

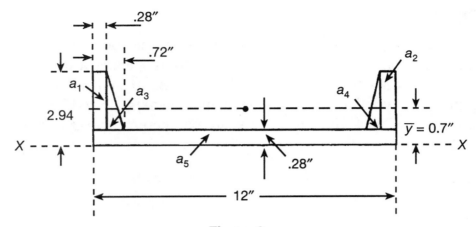

Figure 9

with respect to its own centroidal axis parallel to *XX*, and I'_x the moment of inertia of the part with respect to the axis *XX*.

Part	a	y_0	ay_0	I_0	ay_0^2	$I'_x = I_0 + ay_0^2$
a_1	0.745	1.61	1.20	0.44	1.93	2.37
a_2	0.745	1.61	1.20	0.44	1.93	2.37
a_3	0.585	1.17	0.68	0.23	0.80	1.03
a_4	0.585	1.17	0.68	0.23	0.80	1.03
a_5	3.360	0.14	0.47	0.02	0.07	0.09
	6.02 in²		4.23 in³			6.89 in⁴

Thus, the moment of inertia I_x of the area with respect to the *XX* axis is:

$$I_x = \Sigma I'_x = 6.89 \text{ in}^4$$

Further, the total area is $A = \Sigma a = 6.02$ in², and the moment of inertia of the area with respect to the *XX* axis is $\Sigma(ay_0) = 4.23$ in³. Hence, the distance $\bar{y}$ of the centroid of the area from the *XX* axis is:

$$\bar{y} = \frac{\Sigma(ay_0)}{\Sigma a} = \frac{4.23}{6.02} = 0.70 \text{ in}$$

Therefore, the moment of inertia with respect to a line through the centroid and parallel to *XX* is given by the equation:

$$I_x = I_x - Ad^2 = 6.89 - 6.02 \times (0.70)^2 = 3.94 \text{ in}^4$$

PROBLEM 8:

By using the parallel axis theorem, verify the following moment of inertia: a uniform sphere of mass M and radius r about a tangent to the sphere, $I = {}^7/_5\,Mr^2$; a uniform cylinder of mass M and radius r about a tangent to the cylinder parallel to the cylindrical axis, $I = {}^3/_2 Mr^2$; a uniform sphere attached to a rigid rod about an axis perpendicular to the rod at point A as shown in the figure:

$$I = \frac{1}{3}MD^2 + \frac{2}{5}Mr^2 + M(r+D)^2$$

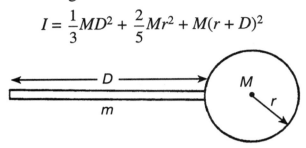

Figure 10

SOLUTION:

Parallel axis theorem states that:

$$I = I_{cm} + Mh^2$$

where I is the moment of inertia of a rigid body about an axis, I_{cm} is the moment of inertia about an axis through the center of mass and parallel to the axis of I, h is distance between these two parallel axes, and M is the mass of the body.

(a)   A uniform sphere of mass M and radius r. From tables of moments of inertia, $I_{cm} = (^2/_5)\,Mr^2$. Because $h = r$, we have:

$$I = \frac{2}{5}Mr^2 + Mr^2 = \frac{7}{5}Mr^2$$

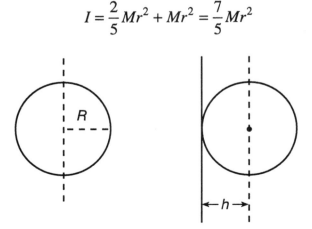

Figure 11

(b)   A uniform cylinder of mass M radius R. From tables of moments of inertia, $I_{cm} = (^1/_2)\,MR^2$. Because $h = R$, we have:

$$I = \frac{1}{2}MR^2 + MR^2 = \frac{3}{2}MR^2$$

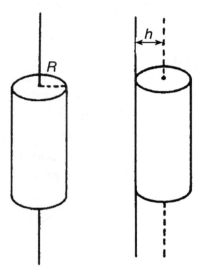

Figure 12

(c)   A uniform sphere attached to a thin rod. For a thin rod of mass m and length D, the moment of inertia about an axis passing through the center and perpendicular to the rod is given by:

$$I_{cm}^{(\text{rod})} = \frac{mD^2}{12}$$

The moment of inertia about an axis passing through one end and perpendicular to the rod is according to parallel axis theorem:

$$I^{(\text{rod})} = \frac{mD^2}{12} + m\left(\frac{D}{2}\right)^2 - \frac{1}{3}mD^2 \tag{1}$$

For the attached sphere, we have:

$$I_{cm}^{(\text{sphere})} = (^2/_5)\,Mr^2$$

$$h = r + D$$

and, therefore:

$$I^{(\text{sphere})} = \frac{2}{5}Mr^2 + M(r + D)^2 \tag{2}$$

The moment of inertia of the whole system is simply the sum of Equations (1) and (2):

$$I = I^{(\text{rod})} + I^{(\text{sphere})}$$

$$= \frac{1}{3}mD^2 + \frac{2}{5}Mr^2 + M(r+D)^2$$

WORK AND ENERGY

The principle of conservation of energy is a basic principle used in engineering calculations to analyze the quantity of work done on a body or by a body. It can be stated as: the sum of the potential energy of a body plus its kinetic energy at one point is equal to the sum of the potential energy of a body plus its kinetic energy at any other point. Algebraically:

$$\frac{1}{2}mv_1{}^2 + mgh_1 = \frac{1}{2}mv_2{}^2 + mgh_2$$

where: m = mass of the body

v = velocity

g = gravitational constant

h = height of the body above the datum

subscripts 1 and 2 refer to the initial and final positions of the body respectively.

PROBLEM 9:

A particle of mass M is attached to a string (see the figure) and constrained to move in a horizontal plane (the plane of the dashed line). The particle rotates with velocity v_0 when the length of the string is r_0. How much work is done in shortening the string to r?

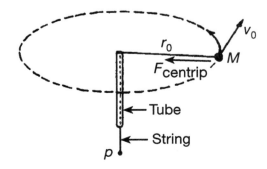

Figure 13

SOLUTION:

The string is stretched under the action of the radial centripetal force which keeps the mass M on its circular path. When we pull in the string we shorten r_0 by increasing the radial force $\vec{F}_{centrip}$ on M. As we know, a force can only produce a torque about the axis of rotation if it has a component perpendicular to the radius which locates the mass M. A purely radial force like $\vec{F}_{centrip}$ has no such component; therefore, the angular momentum must remain constant as the string is shortened.

$$Mv_0 r_0 = Mvr \tag{1}$$

The kinetic energy at r_0 is $\frac{1}{2} Mv_0^2$; at r it has been increased to:

$$\frac{1}{2} Mv^2 = \frac{1}{2} Mv_0^2 \left(\frac{r_0}{r}\right)^2$$

because $v = v_0 r_0 / r$ from above. It follows that the work W done from outside in shortening the string from r_0 to r is:

$$W = \frac{1}{2} Mv^2 - \frac{1}{2} Mv_0^2 = \frac{1}{2} Mv_0^2 \left(\left(\frac{r_0}{r}\right)^2 - 1\right) \tag{2}$$

This can also be calculated directly as the work done by $F_{centrip}$ along the distance $r_0 - r$:

$$W = \int_{r_0}^{r} \vec{F}_{centrip} \times d\vec{r} = -\int_{r_0}^{r} F_{centrip} \, dr$$

$$W = -\int_{r_0}^{r} dr \frac{Mv^2}{r}$$

$$= -\int_{r_0}^{r} dr \frac{M}{r} \frac{v_0^2 r_0^2}{r^2}$$

where we have used (1). Hence:

$$W = -Mv_0^2 r_0^2 \int_{r_0}^{r} \frac{dr}{r^3}$$

$$W = \left. \frac{Mv_0^2 r_0^2}{2r^2} \right|_{r_0}^{r} = \frac{Mv_0^2 r_0^2}{2} \left(\frac{1}{r^2} - \frac{1}{r_0^2}\right)$$

$$W = \frac{1}{2} Mv_0^2 \left(\left(\frac{r_0}{r}\right)^2 - 1\right)$$

which is (2).

We see that the angular momentum acts on the radial motion as an effective repulsive force. We have to do extra work on the particle on bringing it from large distances to small distances if we require that the angular momentum be conserved in the process.

In physics and mechanics *work* is accomplished only when a force is exerted on a body while the same body moves in the direction of the force or of a component of the force. The work W, done by a resultant force F, while a body experiences a displacement ΔX, is the product of the displacement and the component of force in the direction of the displacement.

$$W = F \times (X_2 - X_1)$$

where: $W = \text{work}$

$F = \text{force}$

$(X_2 - X_1) = \Delta X = \text{displacement}$

A body experiences an increase in energy when work is performed on it, and it experiences a decrease in energy when it does work on another body. Expressed mathematically:

$$\left(\frac{1}{2}mv_2^2 + mgh_2\right) - \left(\frac{1}{2}mv_1^2 + mgh_1\right) = F \times (X_2 - X_1)$$

Frictional losses can be taken into account by simple subtraction when determining the net total forces acting on the body using the free body diagram technique.

It should also be remembered that work and energy are not vector quantities, unlike force, velocity, and acceleration, which are vector quantities.

PROBLEM 10:

A force system is composed of a conservative spring force and a nonconservative friction force. The mass is 10 g and it rests on a horizontal surface, $\mu = 0.095$. If the mass is initially displaced 20 cm, elongating the spring ($k = 1,000$ dynes/cm, relaxed length 100 cm) and is released, determine the manner in which the total mechanical energy of the system varies with distance moved until motion ceases.

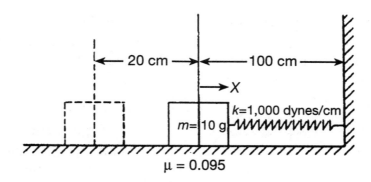

Figure 14

SOLUTION:

The mass, initially displaced to $x_0 = 20$ cm, has potential energy (PE):

$$PE = \frac{1}{2} k x_0{}^2 = \frac{1}{2} (10^3 \text{ dynes/cm}) (20 \text{ cm})^2 \tag{1}$$

$$PE = 2 \times 10^5 \text{ ergs}$$

As the mass is released, this energy is converted into kinetic energy and into work done against friction. The work done against friction is:

$$W = fs$$

where $f = mmg$, the force of friction, and s is the total distance traveled. Thus:

$$W = \mu mg \, s = (0.095) (10 \text{ g}) (980 \text{ cm/sec}^2)s \tag{2}$$

$$W = (931)s \text{ (ergs)}$$

The mechanical energy remaining is thus:

$$E = PE - W = 2 \times 10^5 - 931s \text{ (ergs)} \tag{3}$$

where s is the distance traveled in cm from the initial position.

$E = 0$ when $2 \times 10^5 = 931 \, s$, or:

$$s = \frac{2 \times 10^5}{931} = 214.8 \text{ cm before stopping}$$

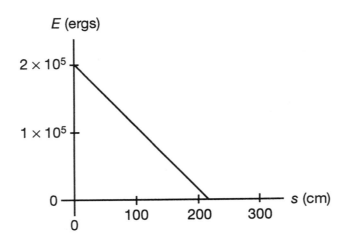

Figure 15
Mechanical energy as a function of distance travelled

MOMENTUM AND IMPULSE

Linear Momentum

Momentum is defined as the product of the mass of a body and its velocity. Impulse is defined as the force impacting on a body over the incremental time interval of the impact. Momentum and impulse are vector quantities. Momentum acts in the same direction as the velocity vector, and impulse acts in the same direction as the force vector. The concepts of momentum and impulse are used in connection with the impact or collision of one body with another.

When two bodies collide, the total momentum of the two bodies remains unchanged. That is to say that the momentum is conserved. This is commonly known as the law of the *conservation of momentum*, and it is among the more important principles in mechanics. The conservation of momentum principle applies to both the magnitude and to the direction of the momentum.

The total momentum of a body can be increased or decreased only by an external force acting on that body. When the external force is in the form of an impact, that force multiplied by the very small, but finite, period of time is the *impulse*. Thus, it can be stated that the change in momentum experienced by a body during an impact is equal to the impulse of the impact:

$$mv_2 - mv_1 = F \times (t_2 - t_1)$$

where: mv = momentum

F = force of the impact

t = time

subscripts 1 and 2 equal the initial and final state immediately before and after the impact

Bodies which experience an impact lose kinetic energy. The magnitude of the reduction in energy during a collision depends on the *elasticity* of the two bodies. Bodies which collide without the loss of kinetic energy are said to be *perfectly elastic*. For engineering calculations, the deviation from perfect elasticity is called the *coefficient of restitution*. It is defined as the negative of the ratio of the relative difference of velocity of the two bodies involved in the impact after the collision to the relative difference in velocity before the collision. Expressed algebraically:

$$E = -\frac{(v_{2a} - v_{2b})}{(v_{1a} - v_{1b})}$$

where: E = coefficient of restitution

v_2 and v_1 = velocity of each of the two bodies respectively

The subscripts a and b equal the initial and final state immediately before and after the impact.

PROBLEM 11:

Solve the ballistic pendulum problem illustrated below. Given are a bullet of known mass m_1, a block of mass m_2, and the distance the block rises after impact h. Find the velocity of the bullet, v_1.

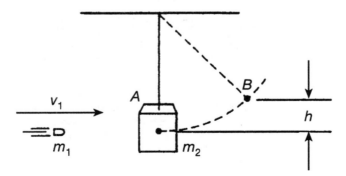

Figure 16

SOLUTION:

The ballistic pendulum problem naturally divides into two parts of analysis: The totally inelastic collision when the bullet imbeds itself into the block, and the rise of the bullet and the block together due to the momentum imparted by the collision.

The collision is inelastic so we are restricted to the always applicable conservation of momentum equation.

$$\underset{\text{before collision}}{\underline{m_1v_1 + m_2v_2}} = \underset{\text{after collision}}{\underline{m_1V_1 + m_2V_2}}$$

For the ballistic pendulum, $v_2 = 0$ and $V_1 = V_2$ since the bullet imbeds itself in the block. So:

$$m_1v_1 = (m_1 + m_2)V \tag{1}$$

Now we must determine V by consideration of the rise of the pendulum. The equation used now is the conservation of energy:

$$KE_i + PE_i = KE_f + PE_f$$

At the top of the rise, the system is not moving, so $KE_f = 0$. We set $PE_i = 0$. Therefore, we have:

$$\frac{1}{2}(m_1 + m_2)V^2 = (m_1 + m_2)\,gh \tag{2}$$

Equations (1) and (2) contain all the analyses needed for this problem. Solving for v_1 yields:

$$v_1 = \left(\frac{m_1 + m_2}{m_1}\right)\sqrt{2gh} \tag{3}$$

To put some perspective on this highly practical equation, we will provide some pertinent data: m_1 weighs 0.10 lb, m_2 weighs 25 lb, and $h = 4$ in.

$$v_1 = \frac{.1 + 25}{.1}\sqrt{2 \times 32.2 \times \left(\frac{4}{12}\right)}$$

$$= 1162.9$$

Angular Momentum

A body undergoing rotation possesses *angular momentum*. The definition of angular momentum is analogous to linear momentum. It is the product of the body's moment of inertia and its angular velocity (which corresponds to the product of mass and velocity in linear momentum). Algebraically:

$$G = I\omega$$

where: G = angular momentum

   I = moment of inertia of the body

   ω = angular velocity

Also, as the resultant force is equal to the rate-of-change of linear momentum (for a body undergoing rotation), *the resultant torque is equal to the rate-of-change of angular momentum.*

$$\tau = I \times \frac{d\omega}{dt} = I\alpha$$

where: τ = torque

   I = moment of inertia of the body

   α = angular acceleration = $d\omega/dt$

The angular impulse is also analogous to linear impulse. It is defined as the torque impacting on a body over the incremental time interval of the impact. The increase in angular momentum about any axis equals the change in angular impulse.

$$I\omega_2 - I\omega_1 = \tau \times (t_2 - t_1)$$

where: $I\omega$ = momentum

   τ = torque

   t = time

The subscripts 1 and 2 equal the initial and final states immediately before and after the impact.

PROBLEM 12:

A sphere of mass, $m = 3$ kg is attached to an elastic cord; the spring constant of the cord $K = 120$ n/m. At the position P (see Figure 18) the velocity of the sphere V_a is perpendicular to OP, $V_a = 5$ m/s and its distance from the original position O (when the cord is unstretched) is $a = 0.8$m.

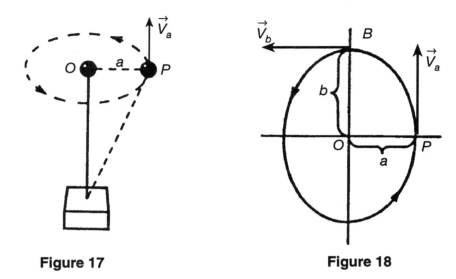

Figure 17　　　　　　　　**Figure 18**

Determine: (a) the maximum distance from the origin O attained by the sphere (b) the corresponding speed of the sphere.

SOLUTION:

Here is a system composed of a ball that is at the origin O when the elastic cord is unstretched and in position P when the cord is stretched. Since the system is conservative, one can apply to this system the conservation laws of energy and angular momentum. In this way, one may have two relations for the two quantities that must be determined: b and v_b (Figure 18).

When seen from the top, the sphere is initially at P with $a = 0.8$ m and moving with a speed $v_a = 5$ m/sec. It then travels to the point B where its speed becomes v_b and its distance $OB = b$ is an extremum which will turn out to be a maximum too. Since the energy is conserved in this process, the sum of potential energy and kinetic energy at P and B can be written as:

$$PE_a + KE_a = PE_b + KE_b$$

or

$$\frac{1}{2}ka^2 + \frac{1}{2}mv_a^2 = \frac{1}{2}kb^2 + \frac{1}{2}mv_b^2 \qquad (1)$$

Here we use the fact that the potential energy of a stretched string is $\frac{1}{2}kx^2$. Dropping the factor $\frac{1}{2}$ throughout and substituting the numerical values $k = 120$ N/m, $a = 0.8$m, $v_a = 5$ m/sec, *and* $m = 3$ kg, yields:

$$120(0.8)^2 + 3(5)^2 = 120b^2 + 3v_b^2$$

$$120(0.64) + 3(25) = 120b^2 + 3v_b^2$$

$$76.8 + 75 = 120b^2 + 3v_b^2$$

$$151.8 = 120b^2 + 3v_b^2$$

Reversing the equation and dividing by 3,

$$40^{b2} + v_b^2 = 50.6 \qquad (2)$$

We now have an equation for b and v_b. Next the conservation law of angular momentum may be used. The angular momentum of a particle of mass m, tangential velocity v, and radial distance r is given by $L = mvr$. Since the force is always radial, the torque on the particle is zero, so the angular momentum remains constant. The angular momentum at P equals that at B. That is:

$$mv_a a = mv_b b$$

Dropping m, and letting $v_a = 5$ m/sec and $a = 0.8$ m yields $5(0.8) = v_b b$ or

$$v_b = \frac{4}{b} \quad \text{or} \quad v_b^2 = \frac{16}{b^2}$$

Substituting this value of v_b^2 in Equation (2), we find:

$$40b^2 + \frac{16}{b^2} = 50.6$$

Multiplying by b^2:

$$40b^4 + 16 = 50.6b^2$$

or

$$40b^4 - 50.6b^2 + 16 = 0$$

This is a quadratic equation in b^2. Solving it by using the standard formula yields:

$$b^2 = \frac{50.6 \pm \sqrt{(50.6)^2 - 4(40)16}}{2 \times 40}$$

$$= \frac{50.6 \pm \sqrt{2,560.36 - 2560}}{80} = \frac{50.6 \pm \sqrt{0.36}}{80} = \frac{50.6 \pm 0.6}{80}$$

$$= \frac{51.2}{80} \text{ or } \frac{50}{80} = 0.64 \text{ or } 0.625$$

Thus:

$$b = \pm\sqrt{0.64} \text{ or } \pm\sqrt{0.625} = \pm 0.8 \text{ or } \pm 0.79$$

We found four values for b: $\pm\, 0.79$ and $\pm\, 0.8$ because we had a biquadratic equation in b. These four values correspond to the four extremum positions that the ball can have: p, b, R, a (Figure 18). Obviously, the answer, 0.8 m, represents the maximum distance of the sphere from the origin.

To find the velocity v_b, recall that:

$$v_b = \frac{4}{b} = \frac{4}{0.8} = 5 \text{ m/sec}$$

PROBLEM 13:

A slender rod having a weight W and a length L is rotating in a horizontal plane about a vertical axis through one end with an angular velocity of ω_0. A small weight W_1 is attached to the outer end of the rod. What will the angular velocity of the rod be immediately after the small weight breaks off?

SOLUTION:

Since no external torque acts on the rod, conservation of angular momentum applies to the entire system. The initial angular momentum is:

$$I_0\omega_0$$

$$I_0 = I_{\text{rod}} + I_{\text{small weight}}$$

so

$$I_0 = \frac{1}{3}ML^2 + mL^2$$

where $M = W/g$ is the mass of the rod and $m = W_1/g$ is the mass of the small weight. After the weight breaks off, the moment of inertia, $I = {}^1/_3\, ML^2$ is changed, so the final angular momentum of the rod is:

$$I_\omega = \left(\frac{1}{3}ML^2\right)\omega$$

However, the final angular momentum of the system is the angular momentum of the rod plus the angular momentum of the weight (see the figure following). Upon breaking off, the weight moves with linear velocity $v = w_0L$. The angular momentum of the ball is

$$\vec{r} \times m\vec{v} = Lm\vec{v} = L^2m\omega_0.$$

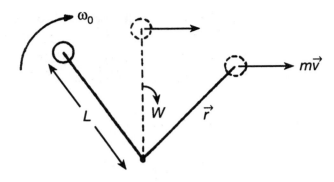

Figure 19

Thus, the result is angular momentum before = angular momentum after.

$$\left(\frac{1}{3}ML^2 + mL^2\right)\omega_0 = \left(\frac{1}{3}ML^2\right)\omega + mL^2\omega_0$$

which yields $\omega = \omega_0$; therefore, the angular velocity of the rod is unchanged.

PERIODIC MOTION

Periodic motion occurs when the force acting on a body is not constant but varies with time. Though forces may vary with time in an infinite number of ways, the engineer most frequently encounters forces that vary as sine or cosine functions. This type of periodic motion, which repeats itself at equal intervals, is also referred to as *harmonic motion* or *oscillatory motion.*

There are certain terms which are used to describe and analyze periodic motion. The time for one complete cycle of periodic motion is called the *periodic time.* The *frequency* of the periodic motion is the number of complete cycles per unit time (usually in seconds). (That is, $f = 1/T$; where f = frequency and T = time of one cycle or period.) The distance from the equilibrium or at rest position is called the *displacement.* The maximum displacement is called the *amplitude.*

The basic equations for periodic motion are usually expressed as:

$$x = A \times \cos (2\pi ft)$$

where: x = displacement

A = amplitude

f = frequency

t = time

$$v = -2\pi fA \times \sin(2\pi ft)$$

or

$$v = \pm 2\pi f \times (A^2 - x^2)^{1/2}$$

where: v = velocity

A = amplitude

f = frequency

t = time

x = displacement

$$a = -4\pi^2 f^2 A \times \cos(2\pi ft)$$

or

$$a = -4\pi^2 f^2 x$$

where: a = acceleration

A = amplitude

f = frequency

t = time

x = displacement

When analyzing bodies experiencing periodic motion, engineers also use two additional relationships, which are derived from the basic equation for acceleration of a body undergoing periodic motion: $a = -(k/m) \times x$, where k = the elastic constant. Substituting this latter equation into the above acceleration equation results in:

$$f = \left(\frac{1}{2}\pi\right) \times \left(\frac{k}{m}\right)^{1/2} \text{ and } T = 2\pi \times \left(\frac{m}{k}\right)^{1/2}$$

where: f = frequency

k = elastic constant

m = mass of the body

$T = 1/f$ = time for a complete cycle

PROBLEM 14:

Show that the period of the simple pendulum of small amplitude is given by the expression $T = 2\pi\sqrt{\dfrac{L}{g}}$. Is this equation true at the surface of

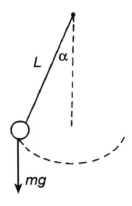

Figure 20

the moon as well as at the surface of the earth? Compare the period of the pendulum at the surface of the earth to that at the surface of the moon.

SOLUTION:

For small angles the differential equation can be shown to be:

$$\ddot{\alpha} = -\frac{g}{L}\alpha \tag{1}$$

where: α = angle of swing in radians

g = gravitational constant

L = length of string

This is the equation for simple harmonic motion, the solution for which is:

$$\alpha = D \sin(\omega t + \phi) \tag{2}$$

where D and ϕ are the amplitude and phase, respectively, and depend on the initial conditions. ω is not arbitrary but is such that:

$$\omega = \sqrt{\frac{g}{L}} \tag{3}$$

where ω is the circular frequency in radians.

Since T, the period of motion, is:

$$T = \frac{2\pi}{\omega}$$

$$\omega = \frac{2\pi}{T} \tag{4}$$

Substituting (4) in (3):

$$\frac{2\pi}{T} = \sqrt{\frac{g}{L}}$$

Inverting both sides:

$$\frac{T}{2\pi} = \sqrt{\frac{L}{g}}$$

$$T = 2\pi\sqrt{\frac{L}{g}} \tag{5}$$

In Equation (5), g is the local value of gravity. Thus, the equation would apply on the moon as long as the appropriate value of $g = g$, (g_{moon}) is used.

Evaluating Equation (5) on the earth and on the moon and taking the quotient of the two equations yields:

$$\frac{T_e}{T_m} = \frac{2\pi\sqrt{\dfrac{L}{g_e}}}{2\pi\sqrt{\dfrac{L}{g_m}}}$$

Cancelling and simplifying:

$$\frac{T_e}{T_m} = \sqrt{\frac{\dfrac{1}{g_e}}{\dfrac{1}{g_m}}} = \sqrt{\frac{g_m}{g_e}}$$

Since $g_m \cong \dfrac{1}{6}g_e$, we get:

$$\frac{T_e}{T_m} = \sqrt{\frac{\dfrac{1}{6}g_e}{g_e}}$$

$$= \sqrt{\frac{1}{6}} = 0.408$$

That is, the period of oscillation on earth is shorter or the oscillation faster (higher frequency).

Torsional vibrations (which are periodic motions) occur with rotating equipment. This type of periodic motion can be encountered when two rotors are connected on a shaft which results in an imbalance in the rotating body. The relationships involved in this type of analysis are illustrated in the following problem.

PROBLEM 15:

A disk, whose moment of inertia is I, is attached to a stepped shaft as shown. The torsional constants for the two pieces of the shaft are K_1 and K_2. Determine the torsional frequency of vibration.

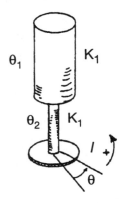

Figure 21

SOLUTION:

When the disk is in a disturbed position from equilibrium, the torque vs θ relationship will be:

$$\theta = \theta_1 + \theta_2 = \frac{T}{K_1} + \frac{T}{K_2} = T\left[\frac{K_1 + K_2}{K_1 K_2}\right]$$

The equation of motion is then obtained from:

$$\Sigma M_{AR} = I_{AR}\alpha = -\theta\left[\frac{K_1 K_2}{K_1 + K_2}\right] = I\ddot{\theta}$$

Consequently, the fundamental equation of motion is:

$$I\ddot{\theta} + \frac{K_1 K_2}{K_1 + K_2}\theta = 0$$

Now, recognizing that this falls into the basic differential equation form that is analogous to:

$$m\ddot{x} + kx = 0, \quad \omega = \sqrt{\frac{K}{m}} \text{ with } f = \frac{1}{2\pi}\omega$$

Then:

$$f = \frac{1}{2\pi}\sqrt{\frac{K_1 K_2}{I(K_1 + K_2)}} \text{ Hz (Hertz)}$$

FE/EIT

FE: PM General Engineering Exam

CHAPTER 10

Mechanics of Materials

CHAPTER 10

MECHANICS OF MATERIALS

The field of the *mechanics of materials*, sometimes referred to as *strength of materials*, concerns the physical effects on a body subjected to external forces and loads. These physical effects include the deformation, deflection, and bending of a body, as well as the ability to support the loads without breaking. It also examines how forces and moments are transferred to other bodies. Though these effects can be determined empirically for each case, basic strength information and properties of various materials have been determined experimentally and tabulated in engineering handbooks. By applying these values in mathematical analyses, the effects of external forces on bodies can be determined.

TENSION AND COMPRESSION

Stress and Strain

The intensity of a force acting on a body, that is the force per unit area, is called *stress*. Algebraically, stress is expressed as: $s = F/A$, where s equals the stress, F equals the force acting on the body, and A equals the area over which the force is distributed. Stress acting on a body that tends to "pull it apart" is called *tension*, and stress acting on a body that tends to "push it in" is called *compression*.

Stress acting perpendicular, or normal, to a cross-sectional area is called *normal stress*; stress acting in the plane of the cross-sectional area is called *shearing stress*. When the direction of the stress acts away from the area, it is called *tensile stress* and is referred to as *tension*, while stress acting toward the area is called *compressive stress*, and is referred to as *compression*.

PROBLEM 1:

Given the loaded bar shown in Figures 1 and 2, determine the normal and shear stress components for the orientation of area in each case.

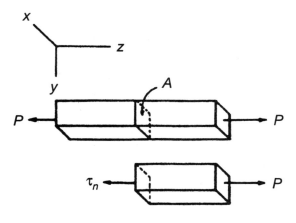

Figure 1

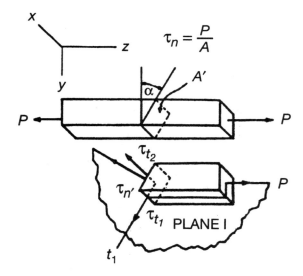

Figure 2

SOLUTION:

Shown in Figure 1 is a uniform bar subjected to a tensile force P whose line of action coincides with the centerline of the bar. A cross-section A is shown away from the applied loads. The force intensity transmitted through this section is uniform over the section. With section A normal to P, there will be only a normal stress present on A. Neglecting the force of gravity, this stress, τ_n, is given everywhere on the section as:

$$\tau_n = \frac{P}{A} \tag{1}$$

Now consider another section of area A' such as is shown in Figure 2. Here again the force intensity over the section is uniform. There is, however, a new normal stress $\tau_{n'}$, and, for directions parallel to the edges of the section, shear stresses τ_{t_1} and τ_{t_2}. Note that the force P and the stresses $\tau_{n'}$ and τ_{t_1} are coplanar (plane I). It is then apparent that τ_{t_2} lying normal to plane I must be zero from considerations of equilibrium in that direction.

Then:

$$\Sigma F_x = 0 \qquad P - \tau_{n'}A' \cos\alpha - \tau_{t_1}A' \sin\alpha = 0 \tag{2}$$

$$\Sigma F_y = 0 \qquad -\tau_{n'}A'\sin\alpha + \tau_{t_1}A'\cos\alpha = 0 \tag{3}$$

From (3) we have:

$$\tau_{n'}\sin\alpha = \tau_{t_1}\cos\alpha$$

$$\tau_{t_1} = \frac{\sin\alpha}{\cos\alpha}\tau_{n'}$$

Substituting into (2), we find:

$$P = \tau_{n'}A'\cos\alpha + \frac{\sin^2\alpha}{\cos\alpha}A'\tau_{n'}$$

But $A' \cos\alpha = A$, so that:

$$\frac{P}{A} = \tau_{n'} + \tan^2\alpha\,\tau_{n'} = (1+\tan^2\alpha)\tau_{n'}$$

$$\tau_{n'} = \frac{P}{A}\left(\frac{1}{\sec^2\alpha}\right) = \frac{P}{A}\cos^2\alpha \tag{4}$$

$$\tau_{t_1} = \frac{\sin\alpha}{\cos\alpha}\tau_{n'} = \frac{P}{A}\sin\alpha\,\cos\alpha = \frac{1}{2}\frac{P}{A}\sin 2\alpha \tag{5}$$

Notice that the normal and shear stresses vary with the orientation α of the section.

When external forces cause a deformation, deflection, or bending on a body, the body is said to be in a state of *strain*. Algebraically, strain is expressed as:

$$e = \frac{\delta}{l}$$

where: e = strain

δ = elongation of the body

l = length of the body

The work done on a body by the force causing the deformation is transformed into the *potential energy of deformation*. The ability of a body to return to its original position when a force is removed is called *elasticity*. If a body returns completely to its original position after the force is removed, it is said to be *perfectly elastic*. One that does not is *partially elastic*. Most structural material such as steel, wood, and stone exhibit perfect elasticity within certain limits of external loads.

PROBLEM 2:

Axial tensile forces are applied to a bar with uniform cross section of a square. Assuming that the volume remains constant for the elongation shown, determine the normal strains.

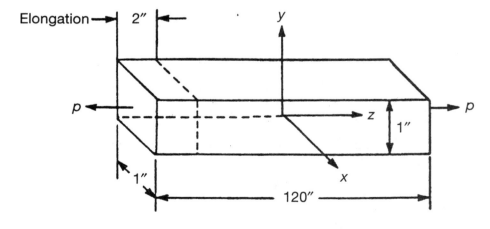

Figure 3

SOLUTION:

In this problem, the deformation is uniform and it is called uniform strain. The ratio of the elongation to original length ε is the same for corresponding sides of all elements in the bar having edges parallel to the *xyz* axes regardless of the size of the element.

$$\varepsilon_{zz} = \frac{\Delta L}{L} = \frac{2 \text{ in}}{120 \text{ in}} = 0.01667 \text{ in/in}$$

Since the total volume of the bar stays constant, then, unit volume before and after deformation is

$$v(\text{before}) = (10 \text{ ft}) (12 \text{ in/ft}) (1 \text{ in})^2 = 120 \text{ in}^3$$

$$v(\text{after}) = (120 \text{ in} + 2 \text{ in}) (1 + \delta)^2$$

where δ is the change in length of the sides of the cross section (see Figure 2). The value for δ is the same for the height and width since $\delta_x = \varepsilon x$, $\delta y = \varepsilon y$ and dimensions $x = y$ for the square cross section.

$$(120) (1)^2 = (122) (1 + \delta)^2$$

$$(1 + \delta)^2 = \frac{120}{122}$$

$$\delta = \sqrt{\frac{120}{122}} - 1$$

$$\delta = -0.00823 \text{ in}$$

$$\varepsilon_{xx} = \varepsilon_{yy} = \frac{\Delta L}{L} = \frac{-0.00823 \text{ in}}{1 \text{ in}} = -0.00823 \text{ in/in}$$

PROBLEM 3:

Linear strains ε_a, ε_b, ε_c are measured by the strain gages in a 45° rosette, as shown in Figure 4. Assuming $\varepsilon_a < \varepsilon_b < \varepsilon_c$, construct a Mohr's circle.

SOLUTION:

In drawing any Mohr's circle, the abscissa, or *x*-axis, is the normal strain, while the ordinate, *y*-axis, is the shear strain. Therefore, mark the values ε_a, ε_b, and ε_c on the *x*-axis. Draw three vertical lines *aa*, *bb*, *cc* through the values ε_a, ε_b, and ε_c. If any of the measured strains are negative, the corresponding vertical lines will lie to the left of the origin.

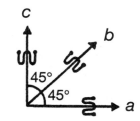

Figure 4

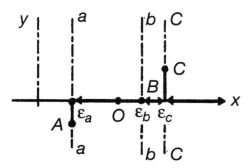

Figure 5

To locate the center of the circle, find the average value of the perpendicular normal strains ε_a and ε_c, labeled point O in Figure 5.

To construct the circle, we must find the diameter of the circle. The normal strain at 45° is:

$$\varepsilon_{45°} = \frac{\varepsilon_a + \varepsilon_c}{2} + \frac{\varepsilon_a - \varepsilon_c}{2} \cos (2 \times 45°) + \varepsilon_{ac} \sin (2 \times 45°)$$

$$= \frac{\varepsilon_a + \varepsilon_c}{2} + \varepsilon_{ac}$$

This shows that ε_b which is equal to $\varepsilon_{45°}$ has a value equal to the value at the center of the circle plus the shear strain for the perpendicular axes a and c. Therefore, the distance from O to point B is equal to the vertical distance from the x-axis at c to a point on the circle above the x-axis and is equal to the vertical distance from the x-axis at point a to a point on the circle below the x-axis, as in Figure 5.

The shear strain at point a is negative because of the sign convention, counterclockwise rotation or increase in angle is negative. Since the a and c axes are 90° apart, the angle between them in Mohr's circle is 180°.

Therefore, the line connecting them goes through the center of the circle, and line *AC* is a diameter of Mohr's circle. This circle will cut the intermediate vertical *bb* at a point *B'* such that *OB* is perpendicular to line *AC*, corresponding to a 45° angle in the rosette. (See Figure 6).

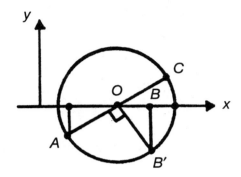

Figure 6

Hooke's Law

Stress and strain are related to each other by the *modulus of elasticity*, also known as Young's modulus, *E*. This relation is often expressed as Hooke's Law, which simply states that stress is proportional to strain, with the modulus of elasticity being the constant of proportionality. Expressed algebraically:

$$E = \frac{\text{stress}}{\text{strain}}$$

Similar to stress, strain can be either compressive or tensile. That is, the deformation can either make the dimensions of the body "smaller" (compressive strain), or make the dimensions of the body "larger" (tensile strain).

Hooke's Law is valid only up to a certain limit of stress, known as the *limit of proportionality*, or the *elastic limit*. A body does not return to its original shape when it is stressed beyond this limit.

PROBLEM 4:

A bolt is threaded through a tubular sleeve, and the nut is turned "just" tight by hand as shown in Figure 7. Using wrenches, the nut is then turned further, the bolt being put in the tension and the sleeve in compression. If the bolt has 16 threads per inch, and the nut is given an extra quarter turn (90°) by the wrenches, estimate the tensile force in the bolt if both the bolt and sleeve are of steel and the cross-sectional areas are:

Bolt area = 1.00 in^2
Sleeve area = 0.60 in^2

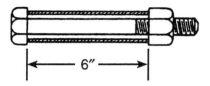

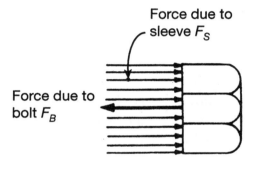

Figure 7

SOLUTION:

We will first apply equilibrium conditions to the nut. Figure 8 shows a free-body diagram.

Force due to sleeve F_S

Force due to bolt F_B

Figure 8

From $\Sigma F = 0$ we have:

$$F_s = F_B \tag{1}$$

Since there are 16 threads to the inch, one full turn produces a movement $\frac{1}{16}$ in. to the left. The quarter turn applied moves the nut

$$\frac{1}{4}\left(\frac{1}{16}\right)\text{in} = \frac{1}{64}\text{in}$$

This is the total deflection and must equal the deflection of the bolt plus the deflection of the sleeve. This is expressed mathematically as:

$$\delta_T = \delta_{\text{sleeve, compression}} + \delta_{\text{bolt, tension}} = \frac{1}{64}\text{ in} \tag{2}$$

For simple extension or compression in one dimension, we have:

$$\delta = \frac{FL}{AE} \quad \text{or} \quad F = \frac{AE\delta}{L} \tag{3}$$

From (3) and (1) we have:

$$F_B = \frac{A_B E_B \delta_B}{L_B} = \frac{A_s E_s \delta_s}{L_s} = F_s \tag{4}$$

where B subscripts refer to the bolt, and s subscripts refer to the sleeve.

Substituting values into (4) we obtain:

$$\frac{(1 \text{ in}^2)(E_B)(\delta_B)}{6 \text{ in}} = \frac{(0.6 \text{ in}^2)(E_s)(\delta_s)}{6 \text{ in}}$$

Since the bolt and sleeve are both steel, $E_B = E_s$ and cancel out. Therefore:

$$\delta_B = 0.6\delta_s \tag{5}$$

From (2):

$$\delta_s + 0.6\delta_s = \frac{1}{64} \text{ in} = 1.6\delta_s$$

$$\delta_s = 0.0097656 \text{ in}$$

From (5):

$$\delta_B = 0.00586 \text{ in}$$

We can now use (3) to solve for F:

$$F = F_B = \frac{(1 \text{ in}^2)(30 \times 10^6 \text{ psi})(0.00586 \text{ in})}{6 \text{ in}}$$

$$F_B = 29,300 \text{ lb}$$

When the stress experienced by a body exceeds its limit of proportionality, the relationship between stress and strain can no longer be described by Hooke's Law. Such relationships are usually presented graphically by a tensile test diagram in which the elongation is presented along the X axis, and the stress necessary to produce that elongation is presented on the Y axis. Each material has its own unique, empirically determined diagram that shows the proportional region of elongation and stress; the *yield* point, where deviation from Hooke's Law occurs; and the *ultimate strength* point where the material fails.

Working Stress and Thermal Stress

The range of stress in which a material can be used is referred to as the *safe stress* or *working stress*. It is usually the yield stress divided by a safety factor, or the ultimate strength divided by a safety factor. For engineering materials such as steel where a permanent set, or deformation, is not acceptable, the yield point is used to determine working stress. For brittle materials the ultimate strength is used to determine working stress.

$$s_w = \frac{s_{yp}}{n} \text{ or } s_w = \frac{s_{ult}}{n}$$

where: s_w = working stress

s_{yp} = yield point stress

s_{ult} = ultimate strength stress

n = safety factor, greater than 1

When the temperature of a bar is raised from T_0 to T_1, the length of the bar will increase in proportion to the temperature increase. This thermal expansion is expressed as:

$$\delta_t = \alpha L \times (T_1 - T_o)$$

where: δ_t = temperature coefficient of expansion for the particular material

α = change in unit length per degree temperature rise

L = length of the bar

$(T_1 - T_0)$ = temperature increase

When a body or bar is prevented from expanding because its ends are secured, then a stress will occur within the bar such that the compression strain will be equal to the thermal expansion strain. Expressed algebraically:

$$s = E\alpha \times (T_1 - T_o)$$

where: s = stress in the bar

E = Young's modulus (as defined above)

α = change in unit length per degree temperature rise

$(T_1 - T_o)$ = temperature increase

PROBLEM 5:

A rod held between two walls is heated from 30° to 200°F. What is the stress in the rod if $\alpha = 10 \times 10^{-6}/°F$ and the walls move apart a distance of 0.001 ft? Take $E = 20 \times 10^6$ psi.

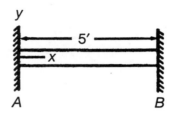

Figure 9

SOLUTION:

Neglecting the weight of the member, we have a one-dimensional problem. Using the one-dimensional, temperature-dependent Hooke's Law:

$$\varepsilon_{xx} = \frac{1}{E}(\tau_{xx}) + \alpha\Delta T$$

$$\varepsilon_{xx} = \frac{\Delta L}{L} = \frac{.001 \text{ ft}}{5 \text{ ft}}$$

$$\Delta T = 200°F - 30°F = 170°F$$

Therefore:
$$\frac{0.001}{5} = \frac{1}{20 \times 10^6 \text{ psi}}(\tau_{xx}) + \frac{10 \times 10^{-6}}{°F}(+170°F)$$

Computing, we obtain:

$$\tau_{xx} = -30{,}000 \text{ psi}$$

Notice that large compressive stresses can be created by a temperature increase.

PROBLEM 6:

In the diagram are shown a steel rod and an aluminum sleeve held between two immovable supports A and B. If the temperature is raised from 60° to 100°F, what is the thermal stress in the materials and what is the force developed on the supports? Take α to be $6.5 \times 10^{-6}/°F$ for the steel rod and $12 \times 10^{-6}/°F$ for the aluminum sleeve. E for the rod is 30×10^6 and for the sleeve is 10×10^6 psi.

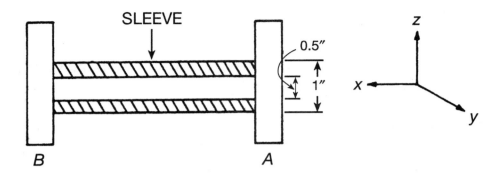

SOLUTION:

Since the supports are immovable, there can be no strain in the *x*-direction. Thus:

$$e_{xx} = 0$$

Using the one-dimensional, temperature-dependent Hooke's Law:

$$\varepsilon_{xx} = \frac{1}{E}(\tau_{xx}) + \alpha \Delta T = 0$$

where α is the coefficient of linear expansion:

$$-\frac{1}{E}(\tau_{xx}) = \alpha \Delta T$$

or

$$\tau_{xx} = -E\alpha \Delta T$$

But:

$$\tau_{xx} = \frac{Fx}{A}$$

So:

$$F_x = -AE\alpha T \qquad (1)$$

Substituting in (1) for each material:

For the steel rod:

$$F_{x_{\text{ROD}}} = -\left[\frac{\pi \left(\frac{1}{2}\text{in}\right)^2}{4} \, (30 \times 10^6 \text{ psi}) \left(6.5 \times \frac{10^{-6}}{\degree\text{F}} \right) (+40\degree\text{F}) \right]$$

$$F_{x_{\text{ROD}}} = -1{,}531.5 \text{ lb}$$

For the aluminum sleeve:

$$F_{x_{\text{SLEEVE}}} = -\left[\frac{\pi \left(1 \text{ in}^2 - \frac{1}{2} \text{ in}^2\right)}{4} (10 \times 10^6 \text{ psi}) \left(12 \times \frac{10^{-6}}{°\text{F}}\right) (+40°\text{F}) \right]$$

$$F_{x_{\text{SLEEVE}}} = -2{,}827.4 \text{ lb}$$

$$F_{x_{\text{TOTAL}}} = F_{x_{\text{SLEEVE}}} + F_{x_{\text{ROD}}} = (-2{,}827.4) + (-1{,}531.5)$$

$$= -4{,}359 \text{ lb}$$

The negative sign indicates compression of the members, so the force developed on the supports acts upward on the top support and downward on the lower support. The force in each case is 4,359 lb.

Hoop Stress

Hoop stress is the term applied to the tensile stress experienced in the relatively thin walls of cylindrical or spherical containers, such as cans, drums, and tanks, when they are subjected to an internal pressure or static head.

When a force in the form of a uniformly distributed pressure acts on the inside of a cylindrical surface a tensile stress, or *hoop stress*, is set up in the cylindrical wall. This stress is defined as:

$$s_t = \frac{pr}{L}$$

where: s_t = tensile stress

             p = pressure acting on the cylindrical surface

             r = radius of the cylindrical surface

             L = length of the cylinder

For the design of cylindrical drums or tanks, the longitudinal stress in the cylindrical surface is one-half the hoop stress.

When a force, in the form of a uniformly distributed pressure, acts on the inside of a spherical surface, a tensile stress, or *hoop stress*, is set up in the spherical wall. This stress is defined as:

$$s_t = \frac{pr}{2t}$$

where: s_t = tensile stress

p = pressure acting on the spherical surface

r = radius of the spherical surface

t = wall thickness of the sphere

PROBLEM 7:

Based on Figure 10 calculate (a) the maximum normal stress in the Horton sphere of diameter 60 ft and wall thickness of 1.13 in with welded joints by a gas at a pressure of 75 psi and t, and (b) the force transmitted by the internal pressure to a 10 in length of the vertical meridian joint of the shell.

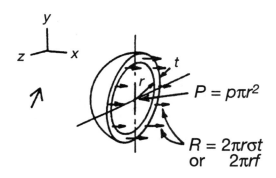

$$P = p\pi r^2$$

$$R = 2\pi r\sigma t \quad \text{or} \quad 2\pi r f$$

Figure 10

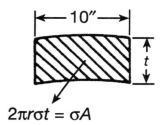

$$2\pi r\sigma t = \sigma A$$

Figure 11

SOLUTION:

(a) Applying the formula for a pressure vessel:

$$\frac{\sigma_\varphi}{r_1} + \frac{\sigma_\theta}{r_2} = \frac{p}{t}$$

For a sphere $\sigma_\varphi = \sigma_\theta = \sigma$, $r_1 = r_2 = r$ by symmetry. So:

$$\frac{2\sigma}{r} = \frac{p}{t} \Rightarrow \sigma_{max} = \frac{pr}{2t}$$

$$\sigma_{max} = \frac{75(30)(12)}{2(1.13)} = 11,946.9 \text{ psi}$$

(b) Force resisted by the joints from internal pressure:

$$F = \sigma A \qquad A = (t)\,(10)$$

$$F = \sigma\,(t)\,(10)$$

$$F = 11,946.9\,(1.13)\,(10) = 135,000 \text{ lbs}$$

BEAM DEFLECTION AND BENDING

The deflections of beams under concentrated loads, uniform loads, varying loads, and bending moments can be determined analytically using a double integration technique. For most situations encountered by engineers, the deflections caused by such loads and moments have been parametrically determined and tabulated. Some of the more basic beam loading configurations are delineated below:

CANTILEVERS		
LOAD	Slope at Free End, θ	Maximum Deflection, D
1. Concentrated Load at Free End	$\theta = PL^2/2EI$	$D = PL^3/3EI$
2. Concentrated Load at Any End	$\theta = Pa^2/2EI$	$D = (Pa^2/6EI) \times (3L - a)$
3. Uniform Load	$\theta = WL^3/6EI$	$D = WL^4/8EI$
4. Uniformly Varying Load	$\theta = wL^3/24EI$	$D = wL^4/8EI$
5. Couple Only Applied at Free End	$\theta = ML/EI$	$D = ML^2/2EI$

where: P = concentrated load, or force

L = length of the beam

E = Young's modulus for the beam material

I = moment of inertia for the beam cross section

W = weight per unit length of the uniform load

w = maximum load for a uniformly varying load

M = applied moment

BEAMS FREELY SUPPORTED AT BOTH ENDS		
LOAD	Slope at End, θ	Maximum Deflection, D
1. Concentrated Load at Center	$\theta = PL^2/16EI$	$D = PL^3/48EI$
2. Concentrated Load at Any Point, "a" from one end; "b" from other; and $a > b$	At "a" End: $\theta_a = Pb(L^2 - b^2)/6EI$ At "b" End: $\theta_b = Pab(2L-b)/6EI$	At center: $D = Pb(3L^2 - 4b^2)/48EI$
3. Uniformly Distributed Load	$\theta_a = Wx(L^3 - 2lx^2 + x^3)/24EI$	$D = 5WL/384EI$
4. Couple Only at One End Moment at $x = L$	$\theta_a = Mx(L - x)(2L - x)/6LEI$	At center: $D = ML^2/16EI$

where: P = concentrated load, or force

L = length of the beam

E = Young's modulus for the beam material

I = moment of inertia for the beam cross section

W = weight per unit length of the uniform load

M = applied moment

x = distance from one end of the beam

These basic formulas for the deflections and "end slope" of beams can be superimposed upon each other to solve problems involving more complicated configurations of supports and loads. These include such configurations as statically indeterminate beams supported with a hinged but immovable end, with a hinged but moveable end, or with both ends fixed, (i.e., with a slope of 0° at both ends).

PROBLEM 8:

For the beam loaded and supported as shown in Figure 12, determine the maximum deflection between the supports in terms of *P*, *L*, *E*, and *I*.

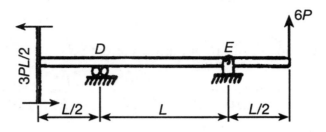

Figure 12

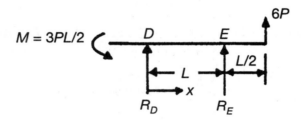

Figure 13

SOLUTION:

This problem will be solved using the moment curvature equation,

$$EI\frac{d^2y}{dx^2} = M_x$$

In order to write the expression for the moment, the reaction forces at the supports are needed (see Figure 13). The reactions are found by moment equilibrium.

$$\Sigma M_D = 0 = \frac{3PL}{2} + R_E L + 6P\left(\frac{3L}{2}\right)$$

$$R_E = -\frac{3P}{2} - \frac{18P}{2} = -\frac{21P}{2}$$

$$\Sigma M_E = 0 = \frac{3PL}{2} - R_D L + \frac{6PL}{2}$$

$$R_D = \frac{9P}{2}$$

The moment at x is then:

$$\Sigma M = 0 = \frac{3PL}{2} - \frac{9Px}{2} + M_x$$

$$M_x = \frac{9Px}{2} - \frac{3PL}{2}$$

Substituting into the curvature equation yields:

$$EI\frac{d^2y}{dx^2} = M_x = \frac{9Px}{2} - \frac{3PL}{2}$$

Integrating twice gives the deflection:

$$EIy = \frac{9Px^3}{12} - \frac{3PLx^2}{4} + C_1x + C_2$$

Since the deflection at D is zero, C_2 is zero. At $x = L$, thus, y is also zero. Substituting:

$$0 = \frac{9PL^3}{12} - \frac{3PL^3}{4} + C_1L$$

$$C_1 = PL^2(-9 + 3(3))12 = 0$$

The deflection equation is thus:

$$EIy = \frac{3Px^3}{4} - \frac{3PLx^2}{4}$$

Setting the first derivative equal to zero locates the point of maximum deflection:

$$EI\frac{dy}{dx} = \frac{9Px^2}{4} - \frac{3PLx}{2} = 0$$

$$\frac{9Px^2}{4} = \frac{3PLx}{2}$$

$$x = \frac{2L}{3}$$

The maximum deflection occurs at the point $x = 2L/3$. Substituting this value into the deflection equation will give the maximum deflection.

$$EIy = \frac{3P(2L/3)^3}{4} - \frac{3PL(2L/3)^2}{4}$$

$$EIy = \frac{2PL^3}{9} - \frac{3PL^3}{9}$$

$$EIy = -\frac{PL^3}{9}$$

The maximum deflection between the supports is thus $PL^3/9\ EI$ downwards.

PROBLEM 9:

For the continuous beam in Figure 14 the bending moment at the second support is $-wL^2/6$ and the vertical shear just to the right of the second support is $+7wL/12$. Determine the equation of the elastic curve for the portion of the beam between the second and third supports.

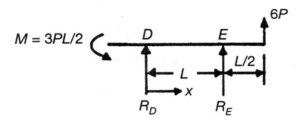

Figure 14

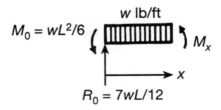

Figure 15

SOLUTION:

This problem will be solved by integration of the curvature equation. The moment equation can be written using the information given in the statement of the problem (see Figure 15).

Figure 15 is a free-body diagram of that part of the beam that extends from the second support to some point x which is between the second support and the third support. The moment equation is found by moment equilibrium about point x.

$$\Sigma M = 0 = \left(\frac{wL^2}{6}\right) - \left(\frac{7wLx}{12}\right) + \left(\frac{wx^2}{2}\right) + M_x$$

$$M_x = -\left(\frac{wx^2}{2}\right) + \left(\frac{7wLx}{12}\right) - \left(\frac{wL^2}{6}\right)$$

This expression for the moment is substituted into the curvature equation:

$$EI\frac{d^2y}{dx^2} = M_x = \frac{-wx^2}{2} + \frac{7wLx}{12} - \frac{wL^2}{6}$$

Integrating twice results in the deflection curve equation:

$$EIy = -\left(\frac{wx^4}{24}\right) + \left(\frac{7wLx^3}{72}\right) - \left(\frac{wL^2x^2}{12}\right) + C_1x + C_2$$

The deflection at the origin is zero; therefore, $C_2 = 0$. At $x = L$, y is also zero. Substituting:

$$0 = -\left(\frac{wL^4}{24}\right) + \left(\frac{7wL^4}{72}\right) - \left(\frac{wL^4}{12}\right) + C_1L$$

$$C_1 = \frac{wL^3(3 - 7 + 6)}{72} = \frac{wL^3}{36}$$

Thus, the equation of the elastic curve for the portion of the beam between the second and third supports is:

$$EIy = -\left(\frac{wx^4}{24}\right) + \left(\frac{7wLx^3}{72}\right) - \left(\frac{wL^2x^2}{12}\right) + \left(\frac{wL^3x}{36}\right)$$

Beams composed of two different materials are sometimes encountered in engineering situations. For example, consider a wooden beam which has been reinforced with a steel plate bolted to its lower side. The modulus of elasticity of the wooden portion of this composite beam is much lower than that of the steel plate. For calculation purposes, the wooden portion is "replaced" by an equivalent narrow steel plate. The required width of this surrogate steel plate would be:

$$W_1 = W_0 \times \left(\frac{E^w}{E^s} \right)$$

where: W_1 = equivalent width of the "replacement" steel

W_0 = original width of the wooden portion of the composite beam

E^w and E^s = elastic modulus of the wood and steel, respectively

With this substitution, the problem becomes that of the bending of a T-section beam and is readily solved as a single material beam using the techniques discussed above.

PROBLEM 10:

Consider a composite beam of the cross-sectional dimensions shown in Figure 16(a). the upper 6 in-by-10-in (full-sized) part is wood, $E_w = 1.5 \times 10^6$ psi; the bottom $\frac{1}{2}$ in-by-6 in strap is steel, $E_s = 30 \times 10^6$ psi. If this beam is subjected to a bending moment of 20,000 ft-lb around a horizontal axis, what are the maximum stresses in the steel and wood?

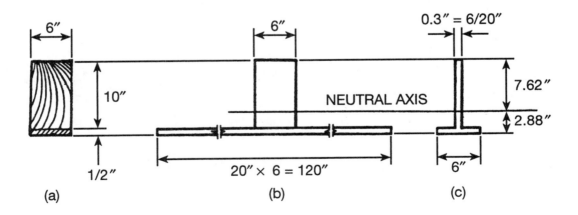

Figure 16

SOLUTION:

The ratio of the elastic moduli $E_s/E_w = 20$. Hence, using a transformed section of wood, the width of the bottom strip is $6(20) = 120$ in. The transformed area is shown in Figure 16(b). Its centroid and moment of inertia around the centroidal axis are the centroid, $\bar{y}$, measured down from the top edge:

$$\bar{y} = \frac{\Sigma A_y}{\Sigma A}$$

$$\bar{y} = \frac{6(10)5 + (0.5)120(10.25)}{6(10) + (0.5)120} = 7.62 \text{ in from the top}$$

The equivalent moment of inertia about the centroidal axis is the moment of inertia about the centroidal axis of each area, plus the parallel axis theorem term to transfer the moment of inertia to the centroid of the whole cross section:

$$I = \Sigma(I_0 + Ad^2)$$

$$I_{zz} = \frac{6(10)^3}{12} + (6)10(2.62)^2 + \frac{120(0.5)^3}{12} + (0.5)120(2.63)^2$$

$$= 1{,}328 \text{ in}^4$$

The maximum stress in the wood is:

$$(\sigma_w)_{max} = \frac{Mc}{I} = \frac{(20{,}000)12(7.62)}{1{,}328} = 1{,}377 \text{ psi}$$

The maximum stress in the steel is:

$$(\sigma_s)_{max} = n\sigma_w = 20\frac{(20{,}000)12(2.88)}{1{,}328} = 10{,}410 \text{ psi}$$

ALTERNATE SOLUTION:

A transformed area in terms of steel may be used instead. Then the equivalent width of wood is $b/n = 6/20$, or 0.3 in. This transformed area is shown in Fig. 16(c).

$$\bar{y} = \frac{(0.3)10(5.5) + 6(0.5)(0.25)}{(0.3)10 + 6(0.5)} = 2.88 \text{ in from the bottom}$$

$$I_{zz} = \frac{(0.3)10^3}{12} + (0.3)10(2.62)^2 + \frac{6(0.5)^3}{12} + (0.5)6(2.63)^2$$

$$= 66.4 \text{ in}^4$$

$$(\sigma_s)_{max} = \frac{(20,000)12(2.88)}{66.4} = 10,410 \text{ psi}$$

$$(\sigma_w)_{max} = \frac{\sigma_s}{n}\left(\frac{1}{20}\right)\frac{(20,000)12(7.62)}{66.4} = 1,377 \text{ psi}$$

The stress in a material stiffer than the material of the transformed section is greater, since to cause the same unit strain, a higher stress is required.

BEAM SHEARING STRESSES AND STRAINS

Types of Beams and Beam Loadings

Beams are usually classified by the manner in which they are supported and loaded. These categories are:

Simple beams: Beams that have both ends freely supported with the concentrated load applied perpendicular to the beam. If the concentrated load has a horizontal component, then one of the ends must be an immovable hinged support.

Beams in pure bending: A beam is in pure bending when it is acted upon only by bending moments. There are no shearing forces acting on a beam loaded only with bending moments.

Cantilever beams: A cantilevered beam is one firmly supported at only one end, in which the end is usually in a wall. The force system at this supported end is the same as a moment being applied to the beam.

Beams with overhanging ends: A beam is said to have an overhanging end if it is simply supported at two points, at least one of which is not at the end and at least one, or part of, the load is applied to the overhanging portion of the beam.

Statically indeterminate beams: When the magnitude of the supporting forces acting on a beam cannot be determined by static analysis, such as a beam where both ends are built into a wall, is said to be statically indeterminate.

Varying types of loadings: Beams can also be described by the types of loadings, such as concentrated loads, end moments, horizontal axial or transverse loads, and nonuniform distributed loads.

Shearing Forces and Bending Moments

Whenever a beam experiences bending, stresses are induced into the beam. The sum of all the vertical forces on any section of the beam, including one supported end through a distance X along the beam (where X is less than the total length L), is called the *shearing force* at that cross section of the beam.

The sum of all the moments of all external forces on any section of the beam, including one supported end through a distance X along the beam (where X is less than the total length L), is called the *bending moment* at that cross section of the beam.

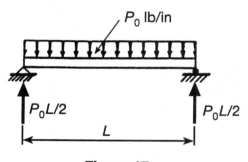

Figure 17
Applied vertical force

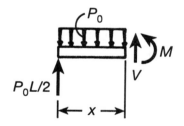

Figure 18
Applied vertical force and subsequent bending momentum (*m*)

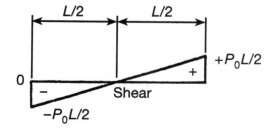

Figure 19
Graph of shearing force along beam

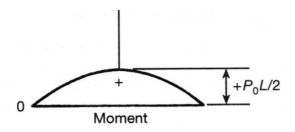

Figure 20
Graph of bending moment along the beam

Shearing and bending moment diagrams are developed to show the differences in magnitude of the shear and moments at all points along the length of the beam. The curves, which are the graphic representation of forces and moments for beams, have discontinuities coincident with each concentrated point load. Thus, for beams with multiple loads, individual curves must be developed for each section of the beam between loads, and between loads and supports. For beams with only uniformly distributed loads, no discontinuity will occur in the forces. Thus, curves can be determined only once.

Observation of the shear and bending moment equations, or of the graphic curves described by these equations, shows that the shear diagram merely represents the slope of the bending moment curve. In calculus terms, the rate of change of bending moment with respect to the length of the beam is equal to the shear.

$$S = \frac{dM}{dx}$$

where: S = shear

dM/dx = derivative of the bending moment M, with respect to the distance x

To illustrate, the bending moment for a uniformly loaded beam has been determined to be:

$$M = \frac{WLx}{2} - \frac{Wx^2}{2}$$

where: M = applied moment

W = weight per unit length of the uniform load

L = length of the beam

x = distance from one end of the beam

The shear force, S, for the same uniformly loaded beam has been determined to be:

$$S = \frac{WL}{2} - \frac{Wx}{2} = \frac{dM}{dx}$$

PROBLEM 11:

Find the maximum tensile and compressive bending stresses in the symmetrical T beam of Figure 21 under the action of a constant bending moment M_b.

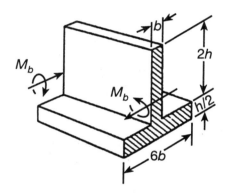

Figure 21

SOLUTION:

Since we have the relation $\sigma = M_b y/I$ available, our task in this problem centers around the location of the neutral surface and the evaluation of I_{yy}. As a first step we must locate the z-axis in the centroid of the cross section. In Figure 22, on the following page, consider the beam to be made up of rectangle 1 of dimensions b by $2h$ and rectangle 2 of dimensions $6h$ by $h/2$, and let $\bar{y}$ represent the distance from the base to the centroid of the cross section. Then:

$$\bar{y} = \frac{\sum_i \bar{y}_i A_i}{\sum_i A_i} = \frac{3/2h(2bh) + (h/4)(3bh)}{2bh + 3bh} = \frac{3}{4}h \qquad (1)$$

where: $A_i \equiv$ area of the ith rectangle

$\bar{y}_i \equiv$ distance of the centroid of the ith rectangle to a chosen surface

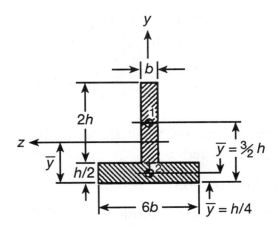

Figure 22

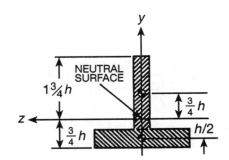

Figure 23

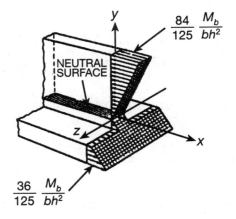

Figure 24

In this case, use the outer surface of the flange. The location of the axes in the cross section is shown in Figure 23. Now calculate the moment of inertia for rectangle 1 by using the parallel-axis theorem, i.e.:

$$I_{yy_1} = I_{yy} + Ah^2$$

where: $I_{yy} \equiv$ moment of inertia about the centroidal axis of the section being considered

$A \equiv$ area of the section

$h \equiv$ distance from the centroidal axis of the section to the axis about which we desire to find the moment of inertia

$$(I_{yy})_1 = \frac{b(2h)^3}{12} + 2bh\left(\frac{3}{4}h\right)^2 = \frac{43}{24}bh^3 \tag{2}$$

Similarly, for rectangle 2 we obtain:

$$(I_{yy})_2 = \frac{6b(h/2)^3}{12} + 3bh\left(\frac{h}{2}\right)^2 = \frac{13}{16}bh^3 \tag{3}$$

Then, for the entire cross section:

$$I_{yy} = (I_{yy})_1 + (I_{yy})_2 = \frac{43}{24}bh^3 + \frac{13}{16}bh^3 = \frac{125}{48}bh^3 \tag{4}$$

Now, substituting (4) in the expression relating stress and moment together with $y = -\frac{3}{4}h$, we find the maximum tensile bending stress:

$$\sigma_x = -\frac{M_b(-3/4\,h)}{125/48\,bh^3} = \frac{36}{125}\frac{M_b}{bh^2} \tag{5}$$

The maximum compressive bending stress occurs at $y = +1\frac{3}{4}h$:

$$\sigma_x = -\frac{M_b(7/4\,h)}{125/48\,bh^3} = -\frac{84}{125}\frac{M_b}{bh^2}h \tag{6}$$

The stress distribution in the beam is illustrated in Figure 24. We see that the maximum compressive stress is approximately 2.3 times greater than the maximum tensile stress.

PROBLEM 12:

Determine the maximum shear stress in the web of a beam having the T-shaped cross section shown in Figure 25 if $b = 4$ in, $t = 1$ in, $h = 8$ in, $h_1 = 7$ in, and $V = 10,000$ lb.

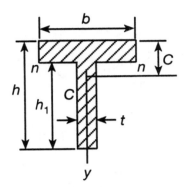

Figure 25

SOLUTION:

The maximum shear stress in the web of a beam occurs at the neutral axis and is given by the formula:

$$\tau = \frac{VQ}{Ib}$$

To find this stress we must first find the location of the neutral axis, given with respect to the top of the section by:

$$C = \frac{\Sigma yA}{\Sigma A}$$

where y is the distance from the top of the section to the centroid of the area. Considering the T section to be an 8 in web with two 1.5 in flanges, we have:

$$C = \frac{2(1.5)(1)(0.5) + 8(1)(4)}{2(1.5)(1) + 8(1)} = 3.05 \text{ in}$$

The moment of inertia I of the cross section about the neutral axis can be found by first obtaining the moment of inertia about axis *nn* and then using the parallel axis theorem.

Again considering an 8 in web with no 1.5 in flange on either side we calculate:

$$I = \frac{1(8)^3}{12} + (1)(8)(4-3.05)^2 + \frac{(3)(1)^3}{12} + (3)(1)(3.05-0.5)^2$$

$$= 69.64 \text{ in}^4$$

The maximum shear stress occurs at the neutral axis; the first moment Q of the area below the neutral axis is:

$$Q = \frac{(8-3.05)^2}{2} = 12.3 \text{ in}^3$$

Now substituting into the shear formula, we get:

$$\tau = \frac{VQ}{It} = \frac{10,000(12.3)}{69.7(1)} = 1,765 \text{ psi}$$

which is the maximum shear stress.

Moving Loads

Beams or girders experiencing moving concentrated loads is an important practical problem. For such beams or girders, the maximum shearing force and the maximum bending moment that occur under each of the concentrated loads need to be determined by the engineer. The largest of the loads and moments will govern the design of the beam or girder.

Parametric equations for the moment at any point M, as a function of the distance x, from one end of the beam or girder are developed for each position between each pair of concentrated loads similar to nonmoving concentrated loads. These equations are then differentiated with respect to x and equated to zero. The solution for x is the point of maximum moment. It has been found that the solution to these equations have a common characteristic which can be stated as follows: *The bending moment under a particular moving concentrated load is a maximum when the mid-point between that load and the resultant of all loads on the beam or girder is coincident with the center of the beam or girder.*

Using this observation, the point of maximum moments can be determined by locating the resultant of all the concentrated loads relative to each load and adjusting the position until the mid-point is coincident to the center of the span. The moment at that point is then determined.

PROBLEM 13:

Determine the maximum bending moment and the maximum shearing force set up by a truck with axle loads A, B, and C, as shown in Figure 26(a) when passing over a freely supported span, 22 ft long.

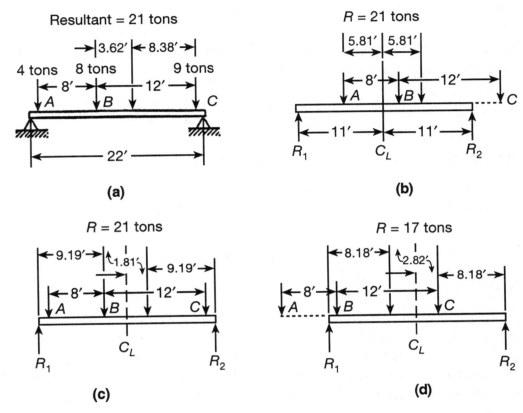

Figure 26

SOLUTION:

Determine the maximum bending moment when all three axle loads are on the span. The resultant of loads A, B, and C is 21 tons located to the right of B a distance:

$$\bar{x} = \frac{9 \times 12 - 4 \times 8}{21} = 3.62 \text{ ft}$$

The bending moment may be a maximum under A when the bisector of distance (11.62 ft) between A and the resultant of A, B, and C coincides with the center of span. This requirement, however, moves wheel C off the span (Figure 26b), which is contrary to our assumption.

The bending moment may be a maximum under B when the loads are placed as shown in Figure 26(c) in accordance with the rule for location of maximum bending moment. All three wheels are on the span, which agrees with the assumption made. The reaction R_1 may most easily be determined by equating the moments of R_1 and of the resultant R about the right end of the beam; $22R_1 = 9.19(21)$ and hence $R_1 = 8.78$ tons. The bending moment at B is obtained by summing the moments with respect to B of all forces to the left of B; $M_B = 8.78(9.19) - 4(8) = 48.7$ ft tons.

The condition for the bending moment to be a maximum under C puts wheel A off the span, which is contrary to our assumption that all three loads are on the span; but this circumstance indicates the likelihood of a maximum bending moment under C when calculated for loads B and C only on the span.

When axle loads B and C are on the span, the resultant of B and $C = 17$ tons, located at $(9/17)12 = 6.35$ ft to the right of B or 5.65 ft to the left of C.

The bending moment may be a maximum under C when the loads are placed as shown in Figure 26(d). A is off the span, which is compatible with the assumption made. Here $R_2 = (8.18/22)17 = 6.32$ tons and $M_C = (6.32)(8.18) = 51.7$ ft tons.

The bending moment may be a maximum under B. Investigation shows that this may occur with loads B and C only on the span and $M_B = 47.2$ ft tons.

When axle loads A and B are on the span, the procedure is the same as above. One finds $M_A = 37.9$ ft tons and $M_B = 51.0$ ft tons.

When axle load C is at the center of the span, both A and B are coming off, which gives $M_C = Pl/4 = 49.5$ ft tons.

The greatest bending moment is therefore $M_C = 51.7$ ft tons for the case where only B and C are on the span.

Determination of the maximum shearing force.—The maximum reaction for any group of loads on a span, and thus the maximum shearing force, occurs either when the left-hand load is over the left-hand support or when the right-hand load is over the right-hand support. Of these two choices, the one where the resultant of the group of loads is nearer to the respective support will give the greater reaction.

Consider first the group A, B, and C. Referring to Figure 26(a), the end load C is nearer the resultant than the end load A so the maximum reaction for this group occurs when C is at R_2; then $22R_2 = (22 - 8.38)$ (21) and $R_2 = 13$ tons.

Other groups must also be considered. The resultant of loads B and C has been found to be 17 tons, 6.35 ft from B and 5.65 ft from C. Although load C is nearer the resultant, it is found that with C over R_2, load A is on the span contrary to our assumption. With load B just to the right of R_1, $22R_1 = (22 - 6.35)$ (17) and $R_1 = 12.1$ tons.

The group A and B need not be considered because the total resultant load of 12 tons is less than the reaction $R_2 = 13$ tons found above. Load C alone, acting just to the right of R_1, produces a reaction $R_1 = 9$ tons.

Hence, the greatest reaction, and thus the maximum shearing force, is that of 13 tons found in the first case.

FE/EIT

FE: PM General Engineering Exam

CHAPTER 11

Electrical Circuits

CHAPTER 11

ELECTRICAL CIRCUITS

Electricity is the flow of an electrical charge along a path and is called electric *current*. Although the subject of electricity is usually divided into two categories, direct current and alternating current, the categories share certain basic principles. The medium through which the current flows is called the *conductor*.

The basic unit of electrical charge is the *coulomb* and the basic unit of current is the *ampere*, which can be defined as the net charge of one coulomb crossing a cross-sectional area of a conductor in a time interval of one second. Similar to the flow of fluids or of heat, electric current is proportional to the difference in potential level, or *voltage*. It is inversely proportional to the resistance to that flow inherent in the conductor. This relationship is expressed by the familiar formula known as Ohm's Law:

$$V = I \times R$$

where: V = voltage differential, or drop, across an element, in volts

I = electric current, in amperes

R = resistance to electric current of an element, in ohms

In metallic conductors, the net movement of electric charge is due to the displacement of electrons. By convention, the flow of electric current is opposite to the direction of the movements of the electrons.

DIRECT CURRENT (DC) CIRCUITS

Direct current (DC) is defined as a current that is constant due to a steady, unidirectional flow of electrical charge. The voltage (V or v), or the *potential* difference between two points is a measure of the work required to move a unit charge from one point to another. The *volt* is equal to an energy level of one joule per coulomb. The flow of the current through a conductor generates heat because of the internal resistance. This is expressed by:

$$W = RI^2t$$

where: W = work performed

R = resistance (the coefficient of proportionally between W and I^2t)

I = current

t = time that the current flows

The electric flow in DC circuits can be supplied by an independent voltage source, by an independent current source, or by dependent voltage and current sources. An independent voltage source supplies the same level of voltage regardless of the amount of current drawn. An independent current source supplies the same level of current (amperes) regardless of the level of voltage. The source current quantity of a dependent source is determined by a voltage or current source at some other location in the electrical system under consideration.

Resistance (R) is the measure of the tendency of a material to impede the flow of electrical charges through it. Resistance is "low" in a good conductor and "high" in poor conductors (the latter known as insulators). The unit of resistance, the ohm, is defined as a drop of one volt per ampere. Conductance (G) is the reciprocal of resistance, and can be viewed as the ratio of current to voltage.

For resistances connected in *series* with each other, the resultant effective *resistance* is the sum of the individual *resistances*. For resistances connected in *parallel* with each other, the resultant effective *conductance* is the sum of the individual *conductances*.

Another configuration of resistive elements is known as a Wheatstone Bridge. It is a device used to determine an unknown resistance.

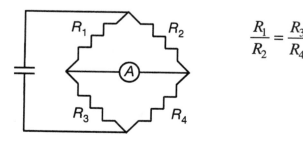

$$\frac{R_1}{R_2} = \frac{R_3}{R_4}$$

Figure 1
Wheatstone Bridge

It consists of two parallel electrical paths, each path containing two resistive elements in series. The voltage differential is measured from the point between the two resistors on one path to the point between the two resistors on the other path. When the voltage differential is equal to zero, the bridge is "balanced." By adjusting the resistance of one of the elements in a path, an unknown resistance in the comparable position on the other path can be determined.

Kirchhoff's Current Law (KCL) and Kirchhoff's Voltage Law (KVL) apply to all circuits. The KCL states that the algebraic sum of all currents entering a node, or any point in a circuit, equals the algebraic sum of all currents leaving that node. The KVL states that the algebraic sum of all voltages around a closed loop is zero.

DC circuits are analyzed by the application of the two Kirchhoff's laws and Ohm's Law. The two common DC circuit analysis techniques are the "nodal analysis" (which utilizes Kirchhoff's Current Law), and the "mesh analysis" (which utilizes Kirchhoff's Voltage Law).

PROBLEM 1:

Analyze the following circuit using Kirchhoff's laws. Find the magnitude of I_2, the current in the upper 2 Ω resistor.

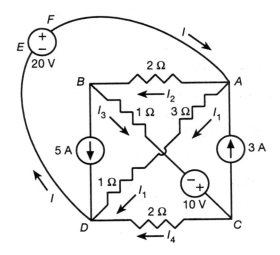

Figure 2

SOLUTION:

The circuit contains two constant voltage sources and two constant current sources. It has four junctions where three or more wires join, labelled A, B, C, and D, as shown. To begin, we label the unknown currents, I, I_1, I_2, I_3, and I_4, as indicated in Figure 2.

This problem has five unknowns (the five unknown currents) and, therefore, requires five independent equations. Three independent equations are obtained by applying Kirchhoff's Current Sum rule at any three of the four junctions. For convenience we ignore units and choose junctions A, B, and C.

$$\text{at } A, I + 3 = I_2 + 5; \tag{1}$$

$$\text{at } B, I_2 = I_3 + 5; \tag{2}$$

$$\text{at } C, I_3 = I_4 + 3. \tag{3}$$

The two additional independent equations required for the solution are obtained by applying Kirchhoff's Voltage Sum rule about closed loops in the circuit. As it is difficult to represent the potential drops across the constant current sources, we choose the loops $ADEF$ and $ABCDEF$:

$$\text{loop } ADEF, 20 = 3I_1 + I_1 \tag{4}$$

$$\text{loop } ABCDEF, 20 = 2I_2 + I_3 - 10 + 2I_4 \tag{5}$$

From (4), by inspection $I_1 = 5$ amperes. Multiplying (2) by minus two gives:

$$-2I_2 + 2I_3 = -10$$

and, rewriting (5):

$$2I_2 + I_3 + 2I_4 = 30$$

The sum of these two equations is:

$$3I_3 + 2I_4 = 20 \tag{6}$$

Multiplying (3) by two gives:

$$2I_3 - 2I_4 = 6$$

which, when summed with (6), results in:

$$5I_3 = 26$$

or, $I_3 = {}^{26}/_5$ amperes.
Substituting this result gives:

$$3\left(\frac{26}{5}\right) + 2I_4 - 20$$

or $I_4 = {}^{11}/_{15}$ amperes.

The remaining two currents are found by substituting these results, first into (2) and then into (1):

$$I_2 = \left(\frac{26}{5}\right) + 5$$

$$I = I_2 + 2$$

Therefore, the current in the upper 2Ω resistor has the magnitude $I_2 = 10.2$ amperes, and flows in the direction of the arrow shown in the figure. The total current flowing in the circuit is $I = 12.2$ ampere.

Also useful in DC circuit analysis is the Thevenin Equivalent circuit concept. A Thevenin equivalent circuit consist of a voltage source in series with a resistor. This equivalent circuit is used to represent a two-terminal network of a more complex arrangement of resistances, which may contain both independent and dependent current and voltage sources.

CAPACITANCE AND INDUCTANCE

A parallel plate capacitor consists of two plates of a conducting material separated by a layer of dielectric material. The quantity of charge which a capacitor is capable of holding is measured as "capacitance," which is defined as the ratio of charge (coulombs) per unit volt across the plates and by the equation:

$$C = K \varepsilon_o \left(\frac{A}{d}\right)$$

where: C = capacitance, farads

K = relative dielectric constant for the "filler" material

$\varepsilon_o = 8.854$ pF/m

A = area of the parallel plates

d = distance, or spacing between the plates

PROBLEM 2:

Consider a capacitor with capacitance $C = 10^{-6}$ farad. Assume that initial voltage across this capacitor is $v_c(0) = 1$ volt. Find the voltage $v_c(t)$ at time $t \geq 0$ on this capacitor if the current through it is $i_c(t) = \cos(10^6 t)$.

SOLUTION:

We use the definition:

$$i = C \frac{dv}{dt}$$

solving for v:

$$\frac{1}{C} \int_{-\infty}^{t} i(t) \, dt = v(t)$$

If we have an initial voltage at time t_0, $-\infty < t_0 < t$, we may state that:

$$\frac{1}{C} \int_{-\infty}^{t_0} i(t)dt + \frac{1}{C} \int_{t_0}^{t} i(t)dt = v(t)$$

$$v(t_0) + \frac{1}{C} \int_{t_0}^{t} i(t)dt = v(t) \qquad (1)$$

In this problem we are given $v(t_0) = v_c(o) = 1$ volt, $C = 10^{-6}$ farad, and $i_c(t) = \cos(10^6 t)$. We are asked to find $v_c(t)$ at time $t \geq 0$.

Substituting the above conditions into Equation (1):

$$v_c(t) = 1 + \frac{1}{10^{-6}} \int_0^t \cos(10^6 t)dt$$

$$v_c(t) = 1 + \frac{1}{10^6 \times 10^{-6}} \left[\sin(10^6 t) \right]_0^t$$

$$v_c(t) = 1 + \sin(10^6 t)$$

An inductor consists of an iron core wrapped with a number of coils of a conductor through which a current may flow and establishes a magnetic field within and without the iron core. Inductance (L) is defined as:

$$L = \mu N^2 \frac{A}{l}$$

where: L = inductance, in henrys

μ = permeability of the core material

N = number of turns of coil

A = cross-sectional area of the core

l = mean length of the core

If a magnetic flux produced by the current in one coil links with the flux produced by a second coil, and if this flux changes due to changes in current, then the change in the current in one coil induces a back voltage in the second coil. In such cases, it is said that a *mutual inductance* exists between the two coils. A commonly encountered mutual inductance device is the iron core transformer. For a transformer, there is a *primary coil*, or *winding*, and a secondary coil, or winding. The relationship between these two coils is expressed by the following relationship:

$$\left(\frac{V_p}{V_s}\right) = \left(\frac{N_p}{N_s}\right)$$

where: V_p = voltage drop across the primary coil

V_s = voltage drop across the secondary coil

N_p = number of turns in the primary coil

N_s = number of turns in the secondary coil

When the secondary voltage is greater than the primary voltage, the device is called a "step up" transformer. Conversely, when the secondary voltage is less than the primary voltage, the device is called a "step-down" transformer.

Circuits that contain both resistance elements and inductive elements and/or capacitance elements exhibit *transients*. That is, the current flow around a loop will change from the initial flow when the circuit is first powered. For such circuits with resistive and inductive elements (RL circuits), the voltages and current flows are described by the following equations:

$$V_R + V_L = R \times i + L \times \left(\frac{di}{dt}\right) = 0$$

where: V_R = voltage drop across the resistive element

V_L = voltage drop across the inductive element

R = magnitude of the resistance in ohms

i = current flow in amperes

L = inductance in henrys

$\left(\dfrac{di}{dt}\right)$ = instantaneous rate of change of the current with time and:

$$i = I_o \, e^{(-Rt/L)}$$

where: i = current flow as a function of time t

I_o = current flow at time $t = 0$

R = magnitude of the resistance in ohms

t = time

L = inductance of the coil

It should be noted that the ratio of L/R is referred to as the time constant τ.

PROBLEM 3:

A 30-mH inductor is in series with a 400 Ω resistor. If the energy stored in the coil at $t = 0$ is 0.96 μJ, find the magnitude of the current at (a) $t = 0$; (b) $t = 100$ μs; and (c) $t = 300$ μs.

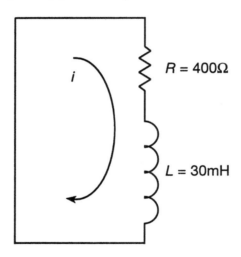

$R = 400\Omega$

$L = 30\text{mH}$

Inductor and resistor

SOLUTION:

(a)   Find the initial current ($i(0)$) by making use of the energy relationship for an inductor:

$$W = \frac{1}{2} L i^2$$

Since we are given W and asked to find i:

$$i = \sqrt{\frac{2W}{L}}$$

$$i = \sqrt{\frac{2(0.96 \times 10^{-6})}{0.03}}$$

$$i = \sqrt{\frac{1.92 \times 10^{-6}}{3 \times 10^{-2}}} = \sqrt{64 \times 10^{-6}}$$

$$i = 8 \times 10^{-3} = 8\text{mA}$$

(b)   After $t = 0$ the current through the inductor is governed by the response of the series *RL* circuit.

$$i(t) = I_0 e^{\frac{-Rt}{L}}$$

To find i at 100 μs:

$$i(100 \ \mu s) = (0.008) \ \exp \left[\frac{-400 \ (100 \times 10)^{-6}}{0.03} \right]$$

$$i(100 \ \mu s) = (0.008) \ (2.64) = 2.11\text{mA}$$

(c)   To find i at 300 μs:

$$i(300 \ \mu s) = (0.008) \ \exp \left[\frac{-400 \ (300 \times 10^{-6})}{0.03} \right]$$

$$i(300 \ \mu s) = (0v(t)e^{-4} = (0.008) \ (0.018) = 0.15\text{mA}$$

A source-free *RC* circuit is shown.

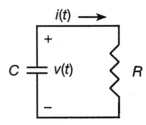

Figure 3
Source-free *RC* circuit

The following equation is produced by summing the current through the resistor and capacitor:

$$C\frac{dv}{dt} + \frac{v}{R} = 0$$

The voltage $v(t)$ is:

$$v(t) = v(0)e^{\frac{-t}{RC}} = V_0 e^{\frac{-t}{RC}}$$

where V_0 is the voltage at time $t =$ zero, and the time constant τ is:

$$\tau = RC$$

as shown in Figure 3. The current $i(t)$ may be expressed as follows, where I_0 is the current at time $t =$ zero.

$$i(t) = i(0)\, e^{\frac{-t}{RC}} = I_0\, e^{\frac{-t}{RC}}$$

For circuits with resistive and capacitance elements, the voltages and current flows are described by the following equations:

$$V = V_o\, e^{(-t/RC)}$$

where: $V =$ voltage drop across the capacitance element
        $V_o =$ voltage drop across the capacitance element, at $t = 0$
        $R =$ magnitude of the resistance in ohms
        $C =$ magnitude of the capacitance in farads
        $t =$ time

and:

$$i = I_o\, e^{(-t/RC)}$$

where: $i =$ current flow as a function of time t
        $I_o =$ current flow at time, $t = 0$
        $R =$ magnitude of the resistance in ohms
        $C =$ capacitance of the capacitor in farads
        $t =$ time

For circuits that contain resistive elements with both inductance and capacitance elements in parallel, Kirchhoff's current law produces the following second-order homogeneous differential equation:

$$C \times \left(\frac{d^2V}{dt^2}\right) + \left(\frac{1}{R}\right) \times \left(\frac{dV}{dt}\right) + \frac{V}{L} = 0$$

For circuits that contain resistive elements with both inductance and capacitance elements in series, Kirchhoff's current law produces the following second-order differential equation:

$$L \times \left(\frac{d^2 V_c}{dt^2} \right) + R \times C \times \left(\frac{dV_c}{dt} \right) + \frac{i}{C} = 0$$

PROBLEM 4:

Use Kirchhoff's current law to write an integrodifferential equation for $v(t)$ for the circuit shown.

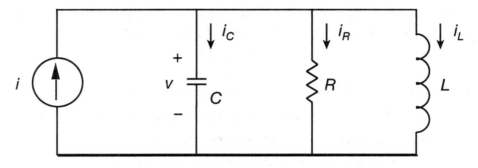

Figure 4 Parallel and series circuit

SOLUTION:

Kirchhoff's current law applied to the upper node of the circuit yields the equation:

$$i = i_C + i_R + i_L$$

The currents for each element i_C, i_R, and i_L can be expressed in terms of the same voltage v:

$$i_C = C \frac{dv}{dt}$$

$$i_R = \frac{1}{R} v$$

$$i_L = \frac{1}{L} \int_{-\infty}^{t} v \, dt$$

Substituting these terms into the KVL equation, yields the required integrodifferential equation:

$$i = C \frac{dv}{dt} + \frac{1}{R} v + \frac{1}{L} \int_{-\infty}^{t} v \, dt$$

PROBLEM 5:

Find the voltage across an inductor, shown in the figure, whose inductance is given by:

$$L(t) = te^{-1} + 1$$

and the current through it is given by:

$$i(t) = \sin \omega t$$

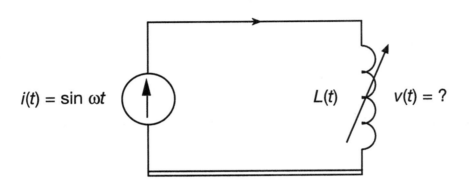

Figure 5
Simple inductor

SOLUTION:

The voltage across an inductor is defined as $d\phi/dt$ and $\phi = L\,i(t)$. In this problem L is a time-varying inductance $L(t)$:

$$\phi(t) = L(t)\,i(t) = (te^{-t} + 1)\,(\sin \omega t)$$

the voltage becomes:

$$v(t) = \frac{d}{dt}[(te^{-t} + 1)(\sin \omega t)]$$

$$v(t) = (1 + te^{-t})\,(\omega \cos \omega t) + (\sin \omega t)\,(e^{-t} - te^{-t})$$

$$v(t) = (\omega \cos \omega t)\,(1 + te^{-t}) + (1 - t)\,e^{-t} \sin \omega t$$

PROBLEM 6:

Consider the capacitor shown in Figure 6. The capacitance $C(t)$ is given by:

$$C(t) = C_0 (1 + 0.5 \sin t)$$

The voltage across this capacitor is given by:

$$v(t) = 2 \sin \omega t$$

Find the current through the capacitor.

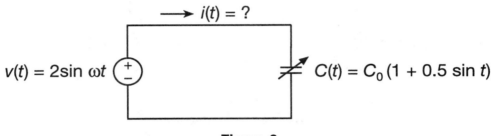

Figure 6
Simple capacitor

SOLUTION:

We can find the charge on the capacitor $q(t)$ by using the definition $q(t) = C v(t)$. In this problem C is a time varying function $C(t)$:

$$q(t) = C(t)v(t)$$

$$q(t) = C_0 (1 + 0.5 \sin t) (2 \sin \omega t)$$

Since $i(t) = dq/dt$ we have:

$$i(t) = \frac{d}{dt}\left[C_0(1 + 0.5\sin t)(2\sin \omega t)\right]$$

$$= (2 \sin \omega t)(0.5C_0 \cos t) + C_0 (1 + 0.5 \sin t)(2\omega \cos \omega t)$$

$$i(t) = C_0 \sin \omega t \cos t + 2 \omega C_0 \cos \omega t (1 + 0.5 \sin t)$$

PROBLEM 7:

Find R, L, and C for the networks shown on the following page.

SOLUTION:

(a)   First, combine the parallel resistances, the two 3-Ω resistors and the two 4-Ω resistors (i.e. the single 4-Ω resistor and the two 2-Ω resistors in series).

From that comes:

$$(1.5 + 2)\ \Omega || 2\Omega$$

$$R = \frac{3.5(2)}{5.5} = 1.272\Omega$$

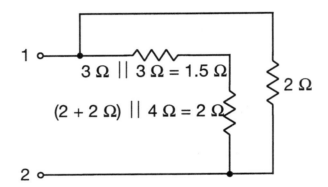

Figure 7
Combined parallel resistors

(b)   Capacitors combine the conductances so that:

$$C = \frac{1}{\dfrac{1}{C_1} + \dfrac{1}{C_1} + \dfrac{1}{C_1}} = \frac{1}{\dfrac{3}{C_1}}$$

$$C = \frac{C_1}{3} F$$

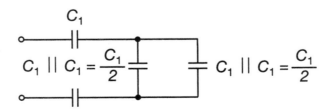

Figure 8
Combined capacitors

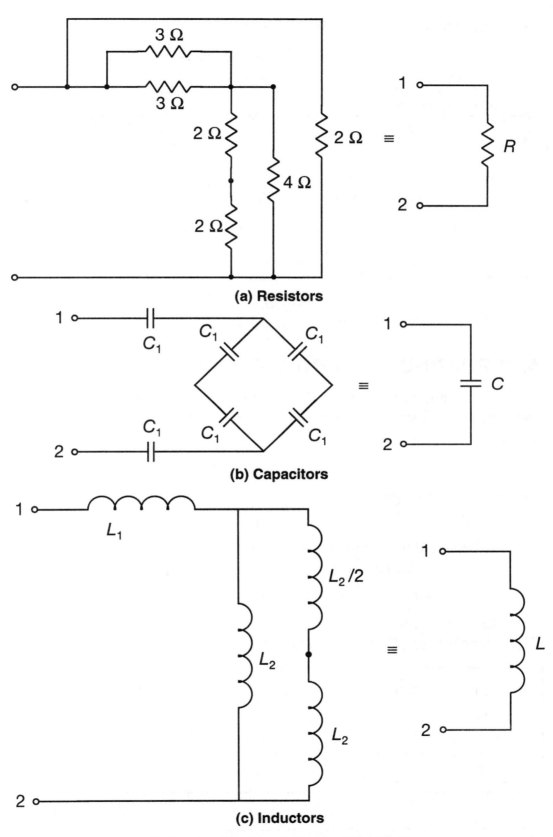

(a) Resistors

(b) Capacitors

(c) Inductors

Component networks and equivalents

(c)   Since inductors combine like resistances:

$$L = (L_1 + 0.6L_2)H$$

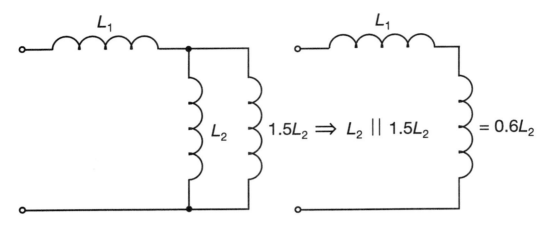

Figure 9
Combined inductors

ALTERNATING CURRENT (AC) CIRCUITS

Alternating current (AC) is electrical current that varies in magnitude and direction approximating a sinusoid. It can be described by the formula:

$$V = V_m \times \cos(\omega t + \theta)$$

where V = voltage at any time t

V_m = maximum value of voltage

ω = angular frequency and equals $2\pi f$

f = frequency in cycles per second, or hertz

θ = phase angle in degrees or radians

The voltages across and currents through resistance (R), inductance (L), or capacitance (C) have been tabulated:

Element	Voltage		$I = I_m \sin\omega t$	$I = I_m \cos\omega t$
R	V_R	$=$	$RI_m\sin\omega t$	$RI_m\cos\omega t$
L	V_L	$=$	$\omega L I_m\cos\omega t$	$\omega L I_m(-\sin\omega t)$
C	V_C	$=$	$(I_m/\omega C) \times (-\cos\omega t)$	$(I_m/\omega C) \times \sin\omega t$

Element	Voltage	$V = V_m \sin\omega t$	$V = V_m \cos\omega t$
R	$I_R \quad =$	$(V_m/R)\sin\omega t$	$(V_m/R)\cos\omega t$
L	$I_L \quad =$	$(V_m/\omega L) \times (-\cos\omega t)$	$(V_m/\omega L) \times \sin\omega t$
C	$I_C \quad =$	$\omega C V_m \cos\omega t$	$\omega C V_m (-\sin\omega t)$

Analyzing AC circuits involves transformations from the time domain to the frequency domain and the use of "RMS" (root mean square) voltage instead of using maximum voltage. The following problems illustrate the application of the familiar DC theorems to AC circuits:

PROBLEM 8:

Procedures similar to DC analysis and theorems are used for AC analysis except that they are in terms of phasor voltage and current (*V* and *I*) and impedance (*Z*) or admittance (*Y*). The following examples illustrate the application of familiar theorems to AC circuits. In the case of source conversions, the general format is as shown.

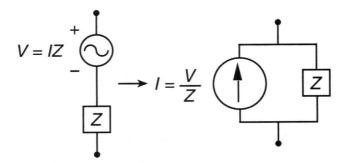

Figure 10
Source conversions

The rms, or effective, value of current and voltage are:

$$I_{\text{eff}} = I_{\text{rms}} = \sqrt{\frac{1}{T} \int_0^T [i(t)]^2 \, dt}$$

and

$$V_{\text{eff}} = V_{\text{rms}} = \sqrt{\frac{1}{T} \int_0^T [v(t)]^2 \, dt}$$

(1) Effective value of $a \sin \omega t$ and $a \cos \omega t = \dfrac{a}{\sqrt{2}}\omega$.

(2) I_{eff} for sinusoidal current $i(t)$ equals $I_m \cos(\omega t - \theta)$ with $T = \dfrac{2\pi}{\omega} = \dfrac{I_m}{\sqrt{2}}$

$= 0.707 I_m$.

The effective value of $a \sin (\omega t)$ and $a \cos (\omega t)$ is:

$$\frac{a}{\sqrt{2}}$$

Therefore, for a sinusoidal current as follows:

$$i(t) = I_m \cos (\omega t - \theta)$$

The effective current, I_{eff} is:

$$I_{\text{eff}} = \frac{I_m}{\sqrt{2}} = 0.707 I_m$$

where the period T is:

$$T = \frac{2\pi}{\omega}$$

The power P, absorbed by an element in an AC electrical circuit, can be described as:

For a resistive element: $P = i^2 R = V^2/R$

For an inductive element: $P = Li \times (di/dt)$

For a capacitive element: $P = CV \times (dV/dt)$

For a sinusoidal steady state: $P = \frac{1}{2} V_m I_m \cos\theta$ (average power)

For a sinusoidal steady state: $P = V_{\text{rms}} I_{\text{rms}} \cos\theta$ (apparent power)

where: $P = $ power

$i = $ current

$R = $ resistance

$V = $ voltage

$L = $ inductance

$C = $ capacitance

subscript "*m*" = average of the voltage and current

subscript "*rms*" = the "root mean square" of the voltage and current

$\theta = $ phase angle

The power factor (*pf*) is defined as the ratio of the average power to the apparent power and is equal to $\cos\theta$. The angle θ is referred to as the *pf* angle. Power factor corrections are used to reduce electric utility charges by changing the *pf* angle without changing real power. The power factor can be corrected by adding inductance to a capacitive circuit or by adding capacitance to an inductive circuit. The capacitance in farads needed to correct the power factor is found by the application of the formula:

$$C = \frac{V_{rms}I_{rms}\sin\theta}{2\pi f V^2}$$

where: f = the frequency

PROBLEM 9:

A circuit draws $4A$ at $25V_m$, and dissipates $50W$. Find: (a) apparent power; (b) reactive power; (c) power factor and phase angle; (d) impedance in both polar and rectangular forms.

SOLUTION:

(a)   The apparent power is:

$$|S| = V_{eff}I_{eff} = (4)\,(25) = 100VA$$

(b)   Since:

$$\vec{S} = P + jQ$$

and

$$|S| = \sqrt{P^2 + Q^2} = 100VA$$

we can find Q because we are given P (dissipated power) = $50W$.

Hence:

$$Q = \sqrt{|S|^2 - P^2}$$
$$Q = \sqrt{100^2 - 50^2} = \sqrt{7,500} = 86.6VA$$

(c)   The power factor is defined as the ratio of dissipated power to apparent power.

Hence:

$$pf = \frac{P}{|S|} = \frac{50}{100} = 0.5$$

The phase angle is the $\cos^{-1}pf$, thus $\phi = \cos^{-1}0.5 = 60°$.

(d)   The magnitude of the impedance can be found from:

$$|z| = \frac{V_{eff}}{I_{eff}} = \frac{25}{4} = 6.25\Omega$$

We can therefore write z in polar form:

$$\vec{z} = |z|\angle\phi$$

$$\vec{z} = 6.25\angle60°$$

In rectangular form we must write:

$$\vec{z} = 3.125 \pm j5.41\Omega$$

Since we are not given any information to determine the polarity of the phase angle (that is, whether V lags or leads I), the j term could be either plus or minus.

PROBLEM 10:

Calculate the magnitude of a line current in the circuit shown

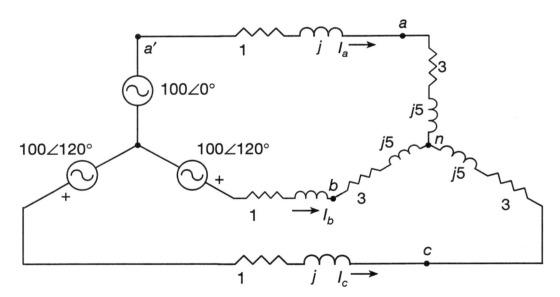

Figure 11 Line current

SOLUTION:

The circuit is balanced because the load for each phase is the same, the magnitude of the source for each phase is the same, and the angle for each phase is displaced by 120°. Since the circuit is balanced, the magnitude of the line current in each phase is the same.

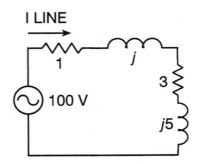

Figure 12 Simplified circuit

The total impedance of one phase is $1 + j + 3 + j5 = 4 + j6\,\Omega$. The magnitude of the line current is:

$$|I_{\text{line}}| = \left|\frac{100}{4+j6}\right| = \frac{100}{\sqrt{4^2+6^2}} = \frac{100}{7.21} = 13.85A$$

ELECTRIC AND MAGNETIC FIELDS

The magnitude of an electric field force F, is expressed in Coulomb's Law as follows:

$$\frac{k \times (Q_1 \times Q_2)}{d^2}$$

where: Q_1 and Q_2 = point charges on either object, in coulombs

d = distance between the two charges

k = constant of proportionality, which is a function of the free space media

An electric field is a force field that exists whenever an electric force acts on an electric charge. To help visualize an electric field, lines of equal force are drawn schematically in the area of interest. A positive charge placed in the field will experience a force on it in the direction of the lines of force. Magnetism is defined in terms of the electrical force exerted on a charge moving at a velocity V. Magnetism is defined by the formula:

$$B = \frac{F}{(QV\sin\theta)}$$

where: B = magnitude of the magnetic field

F = electromagnetic force

Q = magnitude of the charge

V = velocity of the charge

θ = angle between the lines of force, F, and the path of the charge, Q

A magnetic force is generated by the motion of an electrical charge in a conducting media. For example, a wire moving through a magnetic field will cause movement of electrical charges, which is electrical current. This phenomenon is called electromagnetic induction and is the principle of operation of transformers, electric generators, and electric motors.

Faraday's Law introduces the concept of magnetic flux Φ, which is the product of the magnetic field B, and the area of the conductor A, perpendicular to the magnetic field. Faraday's Law then says that the electromotive force generated F_{emf}, is equal to the rate of change of flux through the magnetic field.

$$F_{emf} = -\frac{\Delta\Phi}{\Delta t}$$

(The negative sign is by convention to indicate the direction of current flow.)

If a coil of N turns is used in place of a single coil, the electromotive force would be:

$$(F_{emf})_N = -N \times \left(\frac{\Delta\Phi}{\Delta t}\right)$$

PROBLEM 11:

The current through an inductor with inductance $L = 10^{-3}$ henry is given as:

$$i_L(t) = 0.1 \sin 10^6 t$$

Find the voltage $V_L(t)$ across this inductor.

SOLUTION:

We apply the definition for voltage across an inductor:

$$V_L(t) = L\frac{di_L(t)}{dt}$$

$$V_L(t) = L\frac{d}{dt}(0.1 \sin 10^6 t)$$

$$V_L(t) = 10^{-3}10^6\,(.1)\cos 10^6 t$$

$$V_L(t) = 100\cos 10^6 t$$

PROBLEM 12:

Find the voltage across an inductor, shown in Figure 13 whose inductance is given by:

$$L(t) = te^{-t} + 1$$

and the current through it is given by:

$$i(t) = \sin \omega t$$

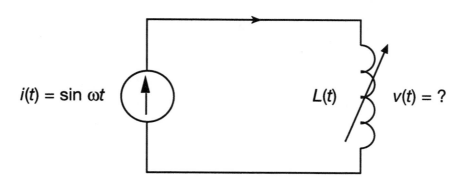

Figure 13

SOLUTION:

The voltage across an inductor is defined as $V(t) = d\Phi/dt$ and $\phi f = L\,i(t)$. In this problem L is a time-varying inductance $L(t)$. Thus:

$$\phi(t) = L(t)\,i(t) = (te^{-t} + 1)(\sin \omega t)$$

The voltage becomes:

$$V(t) = \frac{d}{dt}\Big[(te^{-t} + 1)(\sin \omega t)\Big]$$

$$V(t) = (1 + te^{-t})\,(\omega \cos \omega t) + (\sin \omega t)(e^{-t} - te^{-t})$$

$$V(t) = \omega \cos \omega\,(1 + te^{-t}) + e^{-t}\sin \omega t\,(1 - t)$$

FE/EIT

FE: PM General Engineering Exam

CHAPTER 12

Computers

CHAPTER 12

COMPUTERS

FLOWCHARTS

The first step in preparing a computer program is developing a logic diagram, also referred to as a flowchart, of the desired steps (algorithms) to be performed by the program. There are three basic symbols used to represent algorithms: 1) the oval symbol is used as a beginning or termination box, 2) the rectangular box is used as a command or processing box, and 3) the diamond box is used as a decision box. In addition, the parallelogram box is used to represent input and outputs.

There are three fundamental logic structures used to describe algorithms with flowcharts:

1. Simple sequencing

2. Decision making

3. Repetition or looping

1. **Simple Sequencing:**

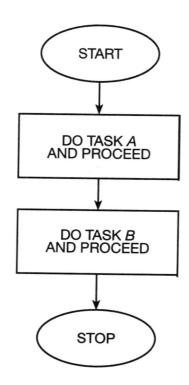

2. **Decision Making:**

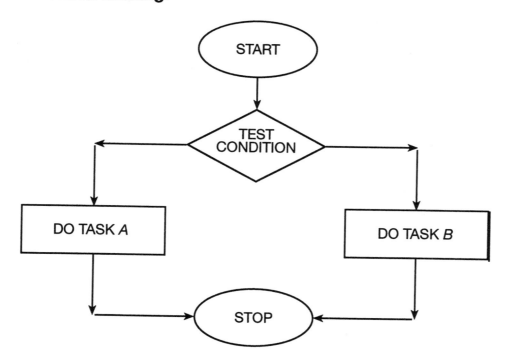

3. Repetition or Looping:

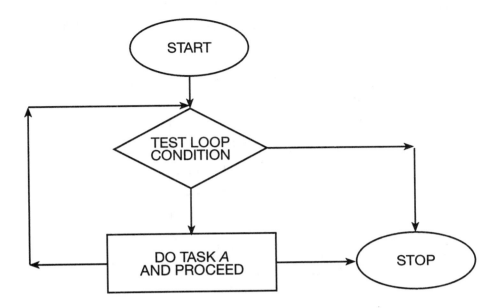

The decision boxes (diamonds) can have several forms. They can:

1. Indicate the variable being tested with a question mark inside the diamond, with the possible results shown on the appropriate arrows/lines outside the diamond (for example, "= 1").

2. Compare a variable with another constant (>, <, =, etc.) inside the diamond, with the possible results shown on the appropriate arrows/lines outside the diamond (for example, "TRUE").

3. With more than two outcomes possible, present variables with a colon between them inside the diamond, with the possible results shown on the appropriate arrows/lines outside the diamond (for example, "= 0," "= 1," "> 1").

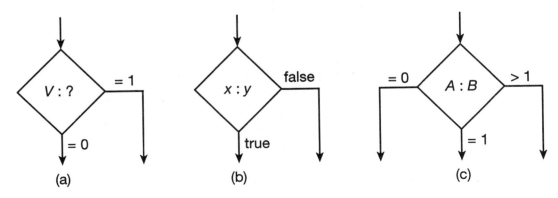

Figure 1
Decision Box Forms

The process boxes generally contain one or more assignment statements. However, using equal signs in these statements is usually avoided and arrows are often used to assign values to variables within the process boxes.

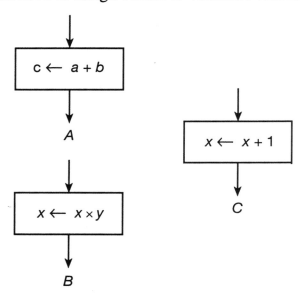

Figure 2
Examples of process boxes

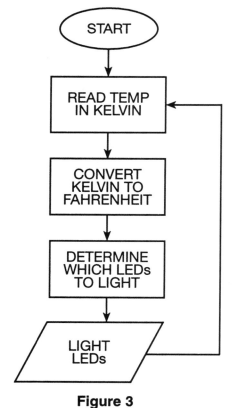

Figure 3
High-level flowchart for embedded heat sensor system

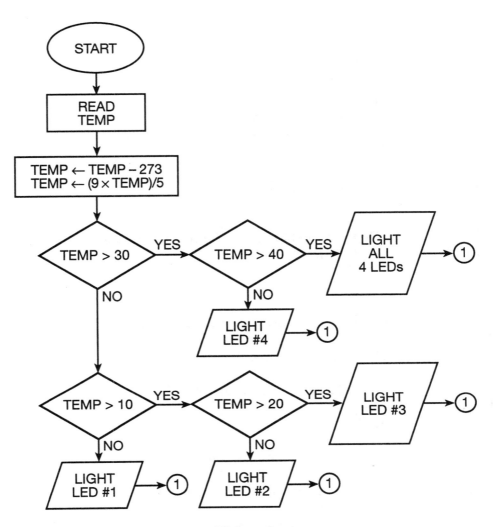

Figure 4
Flowchart of Algorithm for Embedded System with Heat Sensor and LEDs

PSEUDOCODE

Pseudocode is a combination of a computer programming language and English. Pascal and block-structured Pascal-like languages are used the most often in pseudocode. As an example, look at the following sample Pascal program. The line numbers are not part of the Pascal program, but are shown for purposes of identification.

The brackets to the left of the example mark the "blocks" of the program "DoubleForMonth." The blocks of Pascal programs are made up of three parts:

1. The header, which consists of the program statement by CONSTANT, TYPE, and VARIABLE declarations. Lines 1 through 11 in the example.

```
1       PROGRAM DoubleForMonth:
2
3           CONST
4                   Size = 30;
5           TYPE
6                   Dollars = REAL;
7                   Thirty = ARRAY (1. .Size) OF Dollars:
8           VAR
9                   Month : Thirty;
10                  FirstDay : Dollars;
11                  Cntr : INTEGER;
12
13      PROCEDURE ComputeMonth (InitialAmount : Dollars;
14              VAR ThirtyDays : Thirty);
15      VAR
16                  Day : INTEGER;
17
18      FUNCTION Double (DollarAmount : Dollars) : Dollars;
19
20          BEGIN (* Begin Double *)
21
22                  Double := Dollar Amount * 2;
23
24          END; (* End Double *)
25
26          BEGIN (* Begin ComputeMonth *)
27
28                  ThirtyDays (1) ; = InitialAmount;
29                  FOR Day := 1 TO Size – 1 DO
30                          ThirtyDays [Day+1] := Double (ThirtyDays [Day])
31
32          END; (* End ComputeMonth *)
33
34          BEGIN (* DoubleForMonth *)
35
36                  READLN ('Enter Initial Amount $', Firstday; 12:2)
37                  ComputeMonth (FirstDay, Month);
38                  Cntr := 1;
39                  WHILE Cntr < Size DO
40                          BEGIN (* Begin While *)
41                                  WRITELN ('Day', Cntr, "$', Month [Cntr];1
42                                  Cntr := Cntr + 1
43                          END (* End While *)
44
45          END. (* EndDoubleForMonth *)
```

Figure 5
Example of a Pascal program

2. Declaration of subprograms. Lines 13 through 32 in the example.

3. The body of statements to be executed. Lines 34 through 45 in the example.

There are two types of subprograms in Pascal—procedures and functions. Lines 13 through 32 consist of a procedure declaration for the procedure "ComputeMonth" and has three parts:

1. The header, consisting of the procedure statement and a variable procedure: Lines 18 through 32 in the example.

2. Declaration of subprograms: Lines 18 through 24.

3. The body of statements to be executed: Lines 26 through 32.

The second type of subprogram is the function. Lines 18 through 24 in the example. The function provides a declaration for the function "Double" and has three main parts:

1. The header: Line 15 in the example.

2. Declaration of subprograms within this block. (There are none in this example program.)

3. The body of statements to be executed: Lines 20 through 24 in the example.

An unlimited number of subprograms may be declared in a program or subprogram, and they may be nested to any level. Each block contains a header, which includes the program or subprogram statement and constant, type, and variable declarations.

This example program represented in pseudocode would look like the following:

```
type
    dollars = dollars and cents
    thirty = array [days of month] of dollars
var
    initial_amount : dollars
    month : thirty
begin
    read initial_amount
    COMPUTE_MONTH – double initial_amount repeatedly for each day of
            month
    write the entire array month
end
```

Pseudocode of algorithm

As can be seen from this pseudocode example, there are no program or subprogram statements; the types are defined with English combined with Pascal reserved words. Certain details of read and write statements are also omitted. There is considerable variance from one pseudocode representation to another. However, it is most important that step-by-step descriptions of the algorithms are represented.

The Concept of a Well-Structured Program

A pseudocode algorithm should be well-structured, so that it is easily understood. It is also important that there is one point of entry and one point of exit for each program module (a module is a group of statements that perform a specific task). An actual program implemented from a well-structured algorithm—whether shown as a pseudocode or flowchart—is much more likely to be well-structured. To illustrate, the following flowchart shows an algorithm which violated the one entry–one exit rule.

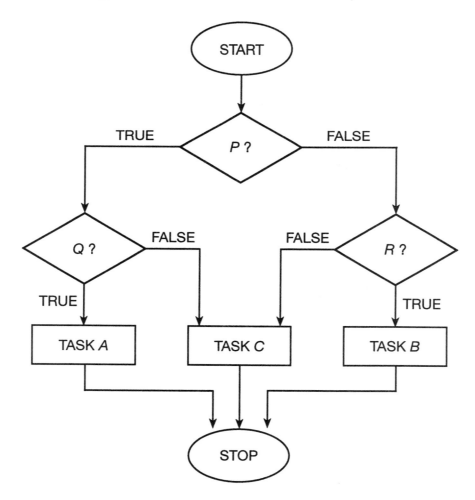

Figure 5 Violation of one entry-one exit rule

This problem of the violation of the one entry–one exit rule is easily solved by pseudocode:

```
if P and Q then:
        TASK-A
else if not P and R then:
        TASK-B
else    TASK-C
```

Solution to one entry–one exit problem

Stepwise Refinement as a design Tool

When a program is designed, the process usually starts with a diagram, called a structure chart, which shows the high-level general structure of the program. In the next step the main program modules are represented with a high-level pseudocode representation that omit a lot of detail by giving a general description in English. The design phase begins with the program details being filled in with pseudocode or flowcharts. Then the detailed design is converted into actual computer code. This process is called stepwise refinement.

DATA STORAGE AND TRANSMISSION

The most basic unit of data storage is the bit, or binary bit, which has a value of 0 or 1.

- A byte is a group of 8 bits.

- A word is 1, 2, 4, or 8 bytes (depending on the computer's CPU, central processing unit).

- A kilobyte is 2^{10} or 1,024 bytes.

- A megabyte is 2^{20} or 1,048,576 bytes.

- A gigabyte is 2^{30} or 1,073,741,824 bytes.

- Data is stored in several ways: registers, RAM (Random Access Memory), ROM (Read Only Memory), and peripheral devices such as disks and tapes.

Data Storage

Registers

Registers are the fastest memory devices and generally hold one word of data. A word is the amount of data that can be read from or written to the memory unit in one memory cycle. Memory cycles can be further divided into clock cycles, with a memory cycle taking three or four clock cycles.

Though registers are part of the central processing unit (CPU), they can have other uses. The interface between a computer and a peripheral device has what is called a command register. CPUs communicate with peripheral devices by storing a command in the command register or by receiving a response from reading a response register.

Registers are formed with the combination of devices called "gates" and "flip-flops." A gate is an electronic device that has two inputs, each of which can be either a "0" or a "1," and one output, which can be either a "0" or a "1." A flip-flop is a device that stores a single binary digit.

Random Access Memory

The main memory of a computer is made up of random access memory (RAM). All data stored in RAM is lost when the power is turned off. RAM also has other applications such as serving as interfaces with certain peripheral devices such as printers. In computers, RAM is organized into words with each word being the size of the registers in the CPU. RAM operates in conjunction with devices called "decoders" and with devices called "logic gates." Decoders are devices that are used to address words in RAM. Logic gates are devices that process two or more inputs to give certain outputs based on the logic of the device such as OR, AND, NAND, NOR.

Read Only Memory

A Read Only Memory (ROM) cell is much simpler than a RAM cell. The biggest advantage of ROM is that data stored in it is not lost when power is turned off. The data is stored on disk drives that have been formatted with electromagnetic tracks. The tracks on disks are subdivided into sectors, and then into clusters. Data stored on disks is not lost when power is turned off. Disks can be read-only or can be "written-to" by the computer.

Data Transfer

In a computer system, it is desirable to transfer data between two registers, which requires a data path between the registers. This transfer of data is greatly simplified by a "bus system" utilizing a device called a "multiplexer." A multiplexer is a digital function that receives information from a large number of input lines and transmits the information in a single output line. A group of wires that transmits binary information between registers is called a "bus."

Data Transmission

Data transmission involves using standards and protocols. Although these terms are sometimes used interchangeably, they have different meanings. Standards are procedures or systems that have been sanctioned by an official standards organization such as ANSI. A protocol defines in detail precisely the form data must take before it is transmitted, the transmission rate, and how the data will be verified. For example, if a computer is to be connected to a modem by means of an RS-232 interface—an EIA recommended standard—then the computer designer needs only to be concerned that the input to the interface conform with the RS-232 standard, and to the unique requirements (or protocol) of the modem. Thus, a protocol allows the engineer to think of what is on the other side of the interface as a black box that will respond properly if it receives the correct inputs. Standard protocols allow the transmission of data anywhere—between two computers sitting on the same desk or through worldwide networks.

Digital computers process characters such as numbers, letters of the alphabet, and certain other special characters. Errors can occur when data is transmitted. Most handling of alphanumeric characters is done using the American Standard Code for Information Interchange, known as ASCII. ASCII uses the rightmost seven bits of each byte to represent 128 characters. The leftmost, or most significant bit of each byte, is called the "parity bit" and is used for error detection.

Although ASCII does not define transmission rate, and it is generally referred to as a standard or a character code, it is actually a coding protocol. This is because it includes special characters that were especially designed for data transmission and also because it provides a means for different types of computers to interface with one another.

The "parity bit" indicates whether the number of 1's in the first seven bits is odd or even. An error is detected by the receiving device by matching the number of 1's with the parity bit information. Parity checking is an effective error-checking method when the error rate is low enough so that there is almost never more than one incorrect bit in each byte.

One of the best known communications standards is the RS-232 interface. It allows the interconnection of computers and communications equipment from different manufacturers. The RS-232 with a DB-25 connector is used for communication between computers and peripherals. Since the RS-232 is a digital interface, the voltage level of the pins is either a logic 0 or a logic 1. The voltage levels for the RS-232/DB-25 connector are:

> −15 to −5V Mark, logic 1
> −5 to −3V Noise margin
> −3 to +3V Transition region
> +3 to +5V Noise margin
> +5 to +15 Space, logic 0

The circuit functions of the pins used for control purposes, and for actual data transmission are:

Pin 4 RTS, Request to Send. The transmitter signals that it is ready to send data.

Pin 5 CTS, Clear to Send. The receiver signals that it is ready to accept data.

Pin 6 DSR, Data Set Ready. For use with modems. Means the modem is connected to the telephone line.

Pin 8 DCD, Data Carrier Detect. For use with modems. Means the modem has found a modem on the other end of the telephone line.

Pin 20 DTR, Data Terminal Ready. The transmitter signals that it is powered up.

Pin 2 TD, Transmitted Data. The transmitter transmits data on this pin.

Pin 3 RD, Received Data. The receiver receives data on this pin.

Cables

Coaxial cable, also called shielded cable, is the medium of choice for cable television and for most computer network installations. It is very good for data transmission, offering a large bandwidth, high immunity from electrical interference, and a low error rate.

Twisted pairs are also used for certain networks. Twisted pairs do provide some immunity from outside interference and to signal degradation. The twisted pairs are more flexible than coaxial cables, and they are less expensive to install.

Fiber-optic cables are much more difficult to connect than coaxial cables or twisted pairs, and they require special technical expertise and equipment to handle. Fiber-optic cables, however, easily support data rates far greater (in the 100 megabits per second to gigabits per second range) than that supported by coaxial cable or twisted pairs.

Telephone lines have actually been used for data transmission between computers since the early 1960s. However, in the last ten years revolutionary progress has been made in telephone line transmissions with the installation of digital switches and fiber-optic trunk lines.

Nearly all telephone lines are connected to central offices with twisted pairs, which use an analog signal meant to transmit voice signals. Modems can be connected to telephone lines and, thus, are able to transmit digital data over the telephone lines to other computers elsewhere on the telephone network. Modems use different modulation techniques to accomplish this, which include amplitude modulation, frequency modulation, and phase shift keying. There is a modulation method called quadrature amplitude modulation (QAM), which combines two amplitude levels with four phases for eight possible values for each signal change.

SPREADSHEETS

A spreadsheet is, basically, a two-dimensional display of data. It contains horizontal rows and vertical columns of information, the intersection of which is called cells. When a spreadsheet program is run, a "worksheet" appears on the monitor screen with gridlines that outline individual cells. The columns are usually designated with letters (A, B, C, etc.) at the top of the worksheet, and the rows are designated with numbers (1, 2, 3, etc.) at the left of the worksheet.

Worksheets also may include: 1) a menu bar which allows the user to invoke various command groups such as Edit, Formula, Help, etc.; 2) a tool bar which allows the use of Icons (actually shortcut means for invoking certain commands) or such tools as scrolling; and 3) a formula bar which displays the contents of individual cells.

Entries are made into individual cells by typing. There are three kinds of entries that can be made in spreadsheet cells: *labels*, *values*, and *formulas*. Labels are text, or word strings, used for the purpose of describing data. Values are numerical data. Formulas are equations that may include mathematical operators, references to other cells, functions such as trigonometric, logarithmic, or logic functions, and special spreadsheet functions such as sum and average. When a function is entered into a cell, the cell shows the value that results from the function.

Functions can be entered into a cell by typing each of the characters, or by invoking the formula command and selecting the desired function. The user then needs only to enter the arguments into the function template as required for that particular function.

Spreadsheets give the user the ability to design their own display. The contents of each cell can be formatted as to size, style, and alignment within the cell. Columns can be widened to accommodate larger labels or values. Spreadsheets also give the user flexibility to make changes such as adding or deleting rows and columns.

The *address* of a cell is usually the letter which identifies the column and the number which identifies the row. Rectangular ranges of cells can also be identified by identifying the address of the cell in the uppermost left-hand corner of the range and the address of the cell in the lowermost right-hand corner of the range. Once a range has been identified, it can be moved, copied, erased, formatted, named, or used for application of certain functions, and so forth.

In addition to the three most common types of entries: labels, values and formulas—*macros* can also be added into spreadsheets. Macros used in spreadsheets are similar to those used in word processors in that they save a series of keystrokes or commands, which can be later invoked. When invoked they will automatically be executed. In some spreadsheet applications, the macros are entered into cells away from the main worksheet area.

FE/EIT

FE: PM General Engineering Exam

CHAPTER 13

Engineering Economics

CHAPTER 13

ENGINEERING ECONOMICS

Engineering economics provides the framework for the preparation of economic feasibility studies. Accurate, meaningful analyses must be based on realistic and accurate engineering information, including detailed design of the proposed project or facility, and an accurate definition of all operating materials requirements, labor requirements, utility requirements, maintenance requirements, and support requirements. With all the necessary engineering information in-hand, the meaningful economic evaluation of a project can proceed. The latter requires that the engineer understand certain economic concepts.

TIME VALUE OF MONEY

The cost of borrowed money is called *interest*. Simple interest is defined as the interest rate times the principle for the specified period of time. Thus:

$$I = i \times n \times P$$

where: I = total interest earned

i = interest rate for the specified time period

P = amount of money for which the interest is calculated

n = number of unit time periods

Simple interest is rarely used alone in economic analyses. It is, however, used for short periods of time, for short-term borrowing and investment, and for the first step in developing the long-term interest costs of money. Note that dollars are used in the calculations and that the interest, expressed as a percent, must be converted to decimal form (by dividing by 100).

Compound interest means that the interest which has accrued during a unit time interest period is also subject to the interest rate for the next unit time period. Thus:

$$F_n = P \times (1 + i)^n$$

where: F_n = total interest

i = interest rate for the interest period

P = amount of money for which the interest is calculated

n = number of unit time periods over which the interest is calculated

Compounding can be calculated for any period such as a year, a quarter, semiannually, monthly, or daily. The effective interest rate for a longer period of time, when the interest is compounding at shorter intervals, is expressed as:

$$i_e = \left(1 + \frac{r}{k}\right)^k - 1$$

where: i_e = effective interest rate

r = interest rate for the unit time period

k = number of times of compounding during the unit time period

As defined above, the future worth F_n, of an amount of money P, is that amount of money times the compound interest factor $(1 + i)^n$. This relationship can be rearranged to determine the present value of money to be received or paid out at some future time, at a given interest rate. Thus:

$$P = \frac{F_n}{(1+i)^n}$$

For example, $1,469 to be received in five years with an available interest rate of 8% has a present value of $1,000. Put another way, $1,000 invested now would have to earn an additional $469 in five years, with an 8% available interest rate, to "break even."

PROBLEM 1:

What amount of money would have to be invested to have $4,000 at the end of three years at a 10% compound interest rate?

SOLUTION:

$$P = \frac{F}{(I+i)^n} = \frac{4,000}{(1+0.10)^3} = \$3,005$$

PROBLEM 2:

Five hundred thousand dollars is borrowed at a nominal rate of 8%, compounded quarterly. If no payments are made in the first three years, how much will be owed? How much would the amount be if interest was compounded annually? Daily?

SOLUTION:

For quarterly compounding, first find the effective interest rate:

$$\left(1+\frac{0.08}{4}\right)^4 - 1 = 8.24\%$$

$$F = \$500,000\left(\frac{F}{P},\ 8.24\%,\ 12\right)$$

$$= \$636,064$$

Compounded annually:

$$F = \$500,000\left(\frac{F}{P},\ 8\%,\ 3\right)$$

$$= \$629,856$$

Compounded daily:

$$F = \$500,000\left(\frac{F}{P},\ \frac{8}{365\%},\ 1,095\right)$$

$$= \$635,608$$

INFLATION

Inflation is usually expressed as a percentage compounded annually. For a constant inflation rate, the cost of a commodity would increase in relation to its present cost by the following equation:

$$F_c = P_c \times (1 + f)^n$$

where: F_c = future cost of the commodity, in dollars

      f = annual interest rate, %/100

      P_c = present cost of the commodity, in dollars

      n = number of unit time periods over which the interest is calculated

Also the future worth of money decreases due to inflation in relation to the present value. The resultant "devaluation" is given by the following equation for a constant inflation rate:

$$F = \frac{P}{(1 + f)^n}$$

where: F = future worth of the money, in dollars

      f = annual interest rate, %/100

      P = present value of the money, in dollars

      n = number of unit time periods over which the interest is calculated

However, if an amount P is invested at an annual interest rate of i, the future worth F at a constant annual inflation rate of f would be given by the following equation:

$$F = P \times \left[\frac{(1 + i)}{(1 + f)} \right]^n$$

Using the same example as earlier—for an inflation rate of $f = 6\%$, when \$1,000 is invested for a period of five years, at an 8% interest rate, the future worth is only \$1,098 compared to the \$1,469 returned when inflation is not considered.

PROBLEM 3:

If the inflation rate is 8%, and you invest $20,000 at an 11% simple interest rate, will you have retained your buying power at the end of (a) 5 years? (b) 10 years?

SOLUTION:

(a) The principal will grow to:

$$F = \$20,000[1 + 5(0.11)] = \$31,000$$

To see if the buying power is the same, the future amount must be discounted for inflation, so that $1.00 in the future can be converted to an equivalent amount today.

$$F_I = \frac{P_I}{(1+r)^n}$$

where F_I is the future worth, measured in today's dollars P_I, and where r is equal to the rate of inflation. Notice that discounting for inflation is the reverse of compound interest problems.

$$F_I = \frac{31,000}{(1+0.08)^5}$$

$$F_I = \$21,098$$

Buying power is retained, plus a little extra.

(b) $$F = \$20,000[1 + (10 \times 0.11)]$$

$$= \$42,000$$

$$F_I = \frac{42,000}{(1+0.08)^{10}}$$

$$F_I = \$19,454 < \$20,000$$

With an increase in time, buying power diminishes because of the compounding nature of inflation.

TAXES

The taxes paid on any interest earned during a tax period must be subtracted from that earned interest before compounding. Consequently, the future worth F after one year accounting for taxes is:

$$F = P + (1 - t) \times i \times P, \text{ or } F = P \times [1 + (1 - t) \times i]$$

where: t = tax rate.

If the inflation proceeds at a rate f during that same year, the above equation can be written:

$$F = P \times \frac{[1 + (1 - t) \times i]}{[1 + f]}$$

Again, using the same earlier example, for a tax rate of 20% and an inflation rate of f = 6%, when \$1,000 is invested for a period of five years at an 8% interest rate, the future worth is only \$1,019 compared to the \$1,469 when neither inflation nor taxes are considered.

CASH FLOW

The cash flow for a period of time, such as a month, quarter, or year, is the difference between all of the funds received and all of the funds disbursed. A cash flow projection will show what is expected to take place over the life of a project. Such projections are often presented as a diagram, with the horizontal axis representing the time periods and the vertical axis representing the annual amount of cash flow or the cumulative cash flow. For a typical project, the projection will show a negative cash flow during the earlier years, rising to a positive cash flow in later years. The *break-even point* is defined as the years when the cumulative cash flow equals zero. The *break-even capacity* of the project is the production rate at which all the costs, excluding depreciation, are equal to the sales realized. A break-even analysis is one of the tools often used in analyzing the viability of a project.

INTEREST FACTORS

There are several interest factors, or parameters, that are routinely used in economic engineering calculations. These include present value, P, future worth, F, and other parameters. The formulas defining these factors and parameters require a constant interest rate i, over a series of uniform time intervals or periods (n). The values for many of these factors and parameters have been tabulated and are available in appropriate financial handbooks.

Some important factors include:

Single-Payment, Compound-Amount Factor, F/P:

$$F/P = (1 + i)^n$$

This factor can be multiplied by the present value, P, to determine the future worth, F. There is a standard notation that is sometimes used to denote this factor: (F/P, $i\%$, n).

Single-Payment, Present-Worth Factor, P/F:

$$P/F = (1 + i)^{-n}$$

This factor is the reciprocal of the previous factor. This parameter is also called a *discount factor*. It can be multiplied by the future worth, F, to determine the present value, P.

Uniform-Series, Compound-Amount Factor, F/A:

$$F/A = \frac{\left[(1+i)^n - 1\right]}{i}$$

This factor gives the future worth F of a series of uniform annual payments or receipts A that are made of a period of n years at an interest rate of i.

Uniform-Series, Sinking-Fund Factor, A/F:

$$A/F = \frac{i}{\left[(1+i)^n - 1\right]}$$

This factor is the reciprocal of the previous factor. This parameter provides a means to calculate the uniform payment A required to have a total amount of F accumulated at the end of n years at an interest rate of i.

Uniform-Series, Capital-Recovery Factor, A/P:

$$A/P = \frac{i}{\left[1 - (1+i)^{-n}\right]}$$

This factor gives the uniform amount of money A that depletes an amount of total present value P dollars over a period of n years at an interest rate of i.

Uniform-Series, Present-Worth Factor, P/A:

$$P/A = \frac{\left[1-(1+i)^{-n}\right]}{i}$$

This factor is the reciprocal of the previous parameter, and it is used to compute the principal needed to assure a uniform series of payments A, over a period of n years at an interest rate of i.

Gradient Series Factor, A/G:

$$A/G = \left(\frac{1}{i}\right) - \left\{\frac{n}{\left[\left[(1+i)^n - 1\right]\right]}\right\}$$

This factor is used to convert a series of increasing amounts into a series of uniform payments (A). The increasing series consists of an initial series amount of A_o, with each succeeding year increased by an amount, G. After n years the series amount would be: $[A_o + (n - 1) \times G]$, and the total amount accumulated would be F.

METHODS FOR PROJECT ANALYSIS

The present worth and annual worth methods are two commonly used methods for the evaluation of project viability. These methods assume that all engineering and technical information has been already generated, and economic parameters, such as initial investment, cash flow, and minimum acceptable rate of return (*MARR*), have been set.

Present-Worth Method

The present-worth method converts project cash flow into an equivalent present value for a given minimum acceptable rate of return. The present worth (*PW*) is defined by the formula:

$$PW = \sum_{j=1}^{n} CF_j \left(\frac{P}{F}\right)$$

where: PW = present worth

CF = annual cash flow

n = total number of years

(P/F) = single-payment, present-worth factor evaluated for the interest rate i, and the year j, for each cash flow

PROBLEM 4:

Consider the following series of payments and profits from ABC Pipes Inc.'s plan to institute a new product line of pipe fittings.

$150,000	initial cost for new equipment
$22,000	yearly after-tax cash flow
$40,000	maintenance of equipment in year 10
$30,000	salvage value of equipment in 20 years

SOLUTION:

To find the present worth of this project at a 10% *MARR*, the equation gives:

$$PW = \$150,000 + \$22,000\left(\frac{P}{A}, 10\%, 20\right) - \$40,000\left(\frac{P}{F}, 10\%, 10\right)$$

$$+ \$30,000\left(\frac{P}{F}, 10\%, 20\right)$$

$$= \$9,238$$

The present worth is greater than zero, and this project would be acceptable to a corporation requiring a 10% rate of return.

Annual-Worth Method

The annual-worth method converts uneven project cash flow into uniform project cash flow. The results are similar to that of the previously described present-worth method. The annual worth (also referred to as a Equivalent Uniform Annual Series, *EUAS*) is determined by first determining the present worth (*PW*), and then converting the *PW* to a uniform annual cash flow using the following formula:

$$EUAS = PW\left(\frac{A}{P}\right), \text{ where } \left(\frac{A}{P}\right) \text{ is the uniform-series, capital-recovery}$$

factor defined earlier.

PROBLEM 5:

A company needs additional warehouse space for product as a result of plant expansion. The options include constructing a prefabricated steel building, a tilt-up concrete building, or renting space. The steel building has a cost of $150,000 and a service life of 25 years with annual maintenance and property taxes of $6,000 per year. The concrete building has a cost of $200,000 and a service life of 50 years with annual maintenance and property taxes of $4,000. Both buildings have no realizable salvage value, and the company uses a 15% minimum attractive rate of return. The company can rent suitable space for $32,000 per year. Basing the decision for additional warehouse space on the Equivalent Uniform Annual Cost, should the company construct the steel building, construct the concrete building, or rent warehouse space?

SOLUTION:

The Equivalent Uniform Annual Cost (*EUAC*) for the building is given by:

$$EUAC = -P\left(\frac{A}{P}, i\%, n\right) - [\text{maintenance and taxes}]$$

where $\left(\frac{A}{P}, i\%, n\right)$ is the uniform series capital-recovery factor and P is the cost of the building.

Steel Building:

$$EUAC = -150,000\left(\frac{A}{P}, 15\%, 25\right) - 6,000$$

$$EUAC = -150,000\,(0.15470) - 6,000 = -\$29,205$$

Concrete Building:

$$EUAC = -200,000\left(\frac{A}{P}, 15\%, 50\right) - 4,000$$

$$EUAC = -200,000(0.15014) - 4,000 = -\$34,028$$

Comparing the above annual rates with renting at $32,000 per year, the best decision is to build the steel building for $29,205 Equivalent Uniform Annual Cost.

PROFITABILITY ANALYSIS

The two standard methods used by private companies to measure the profitability of a project are the net present value (*NPV*) and the rate of return (*ROR*). The net present value is the sum of all the cash flows discounted to the present value. The rate of return is the interest rate used in the present value calculation which will give a net present value of zero. The rate of return is sometimes called the discounted cash flow rate of return (*DCFRR*) or the internal rate of return (*IRR*).

Net Present Value

The net present value (*NPV*) is evaluated using the net annual cash flows CF_j in the following formula:

$$NPV = -CF_0 + \sum_{j=1}^{n} CF_j (1+i)^{-j}$$

where: CF_0 = initial capital investment

i = interest rate specified for the project

n = number of years specified for the project

PROBLEM 6:

A straight-run fuel oil stream in a refinery can be converted to a high octane fuel for blending into premium gasoline using hydrocracking. A proposal has been made to add a 15,000 bbl/day unit at a capital cost of $71.0 million. The annual net profit in million dollars is given below for the estimated life of the hydrocracking unit. The net present value is to be evaluated for interest rates of 15% and 25%, and the profitability compared. These results are shown in the following table.

SOLUTION:

Computing the net present value gives:

$$NPV(15\%) = -71.0 + 80.84 = 9.64$$

$$NPV(25\%) = -71.0 + 66.66 = -4.34$$

The investment is marginally attractive with a positive net present value if funds are available at 15%, but the project is not considered with a negative net present value for funds available at 25%.

End of Year n	Annual Net Profit, F	$\frac{P}{F}(15\%)(1.15)^{-n}$	Present Value	$\frac{P}{F}(25\%)(1.25)^{-n}$	Present Value
1	32.0	0.8695	27.83	0.8000	25.60
2	28.0	0.7561	21.17	0.6400	17.92
3	22.0	0.6575	14.47	0.5120	11.26
4	17.0	0.5718	9.72	0.4091	6.96
5	15.0	0.4972	7.46	0.3277	4.92
Total	114.0		80.65		66.66

Table 1. Annual Net Profit for Estimated Life of Hydrocracking Unit

Rate of Return

The rate of return (ROR) or internal rate of return (IRR) is the interest rate or discount rate at which the net present value is equal to zero. Thus:

$$CF_0 = +\sum_{j=1}^{n} CF_j (1+i)^{-j}$$

where: CF_0 = initial capital investment

i = interest rate specified for the project

n = number of years specified for the project

PROBLEM 7:

A division of a company has been allocated $100,000 to invest at the start of the next fiscal year in cost-reduction projects. Three projects are under consideration and are summarized below.

The minimum attractive rate of return for the company is 20% for projects with this economic life. Would the recommendation based on the rate of return for these projects be (A) invest in A only, (B) invest in B only, (C) invest in A and B, (D) invest in C only, or (E) seek other alternatives?

SOLUTION:

Alternatives are evaluated for investing $100,000 by comparing the rate of return for the projects with the minimum attractive rate of return of

Project	Investment Required	Estimated Economic Life (years)	Net Annual Cash Flow
A	$50,000	9	$16,600
B	$50,000	8	$15,000
C	$100,000	6	$30,000

Table 2. Sample Cost = Reduction Projects

20%. The rate of return (i) is the interest rate where the net present value is zero. For a uniform net annual cash flow (A), the equation for the net present value (NPV) is:

$$NPV = CF_0 = A\left(\frac{P}{A}, i\%, n\right)$$

where CF_0 is the capital investment and $\left(\frac{P}{A}, i\%, n\right) = \dfrac{\left[1-(1+i)^{-n}\right]}{i}$ is the uniform series capital recovery factor.

For Project A:

$$0 = -50,000 + 16,600\left(\frac{P}{A}, i\%, 9\right) \text{ or } \left(\frac{P}{A}, i\%, 9\right) = 3.012$$

In addition to using tabulations of $\left(\frac{P}{A}, i\%, 9\right)$ factors in standard texts gives $i = 30.0\%$.

For Project B:

$$0 = -50,000 + 15,000\left(\frac{P}{A}, i\%, 8\right) \text{ or } \left(\frac{P}{A}, i\%, 8\right) = 3.3333$$

Using standard tables of compound interest factors, gives $i = 25.0\%$.

For Project C:

$$0 = -100,000 + 30,000\left(\frac{P}{A}, i\%, 6\right) \text{ or } \left(\frac{P}{A}, i\%, 6\right) = 3.33$$

Using standard tables of compound interest factors, gives $i = 20.0\%$.

Summary:

Project	Rate of Return
A	30.0%
B	25.0%
C	20.0%

The investment decision is to select Projects *A* and *B* because their rate of return is greater than the minimum attractive rate of return; and all of the available capital is used.

It should be noted that the rate of return method is best when comparing independent alternatives. It is probably one of the most popular tools used in capital budgeting. Net present value is widely used to choose among dependent alternatives. A thorough economic analysis will use more than one method, and it will try to include as much information as can be made available.

Equivalence

The concept of "equivalence" means that the present value of two or more projects are equal or "equivalent." The projects in question may have very different initial capital costs and very different cash flows, but with equal present value the projects are considered equivalent. As examples:

a) A uniform annual payment of $655.56 for 20 years at an interest rate of 8% is equivalent to, that is, has the same present value of, a single payment of $30,000 in 20 years.

b) A single payment today of $30,000 would be equivalent to an annual payment of $3,055.57 over 20 years at an 8% interest (discount) rate, that is, has the same present value as $30,000 today.

PROBLEM 8:

Manufacturers of motors for small household equipment wonder if they should close one of their two plants (Plant *A*) and expand operations at Plant *B*. It seems there is not enough business to keep both plants running at capacity, yet expansion of Plant *B* would have to occur for it to handle double the usual load. Net income has been a steady $800,000 at Plant *A*, and $840,000 at Plant *B*. Due to savings in overhead costs, it is thought that, with the same level of business, net income from an upgraded Plant *B* alone would equal $1,780,000. Salvage value of Plant *A* and sale of the land is estimated at $120,000. The investment to expand Plant *B* would cost $1.1 million, and it would take three years before the level of production could be increased.

(a) If the company has a required *MARR* of 11%, and operations are thought to be steady for the next 15 years, how desirable would this course of action be, if disassembly of Plant *A* were to begin immediately and the total cost of upgrading was incurred at time zero?

(b) If disassembling Plant *A* was to occur at the end of year three, when the expansion is completed?

(c) If the disbursement for upgrading was spread evenly over the first three years of construction?

SOLUTION:

(a) The first task is to separate all factors unique to the proposed course of action. If disassembling the plant were to occur immediately, that is, at time zero, a cost of $980,000 would be incurred, which is the expenditure for upgrading minus the income from sale and salvage of Plant *A*. The first three years of the project would incur a loss of $800,000 from Plant *A* with no changes in income from Plant *B*. The next 15 years would see a positive cash flow of $140,000, which is the change in income caused by the project.

The internal rate of return is a negative 4.65%, and the return on investment is –2,198,866, clearly unacceptable.

(b) If disassembling is delayed until the third year, the cost in year zero is $1.1 million, no income change occurs in years one and two, with a positive cash flow in year three from sale of land and Plant *A*. Income of $140,000 is then constant for 15 years. Delaying the plant disassembly is clearly the more practical choice, yet return on investment at 7.4%, still does not meet the requirement of the company. Net present value is –$276,150.

(c) If the disbursements for upgrading were spread evenly over the three years, instead of a lump sum at time zero, then at the close of years one and two, –$366,667 is incurred, –$246,667 at year three ($366,667 – $120,000), and $140,000 for the 15 years thereafter. This makes the investment more attractive at a return on investment of 9.6%, but this is still not sufficient to meet an *MARR* of 11%. The new present value is – $72,180.

TAXES AND DEPRECIATION

It is important to distinguish between *before tax* cash flows and *after tax* flows (BTCF and ATCF). Although project decisions are best made using after tax cash flows, before tax cash flows are often used in preliminary stages of project analysis. Tax analysis requires an understanding of the concept of depreciation, which, in turn, requires an understanding of the terms *fixed capital, working capital*, and *capital goods.*

Capital goods are those accumulated in order to produce other goods. Fixed capital is that capital which cannot be readily converted into another type of asset (such as the buildings and machinery used to produce the goods). Working capital is the investment that puts a project, or plant, into production. Total capital is the sum of the fixed and working capital, but does *not* include operating expenses. Depreciation for any given year depends upon the *fixed* capital only.

Though the depreciable base of a project consists of fixed capital only, the value of land is not included. The IRS has guidelines for the write-off life of assets, and has three methods of computing depreciation: straight line (steady linear loss over a period of time), accelerated (more depreciation in earlier years), and decelerated (more depreciation in the latter years).

Straight-Line Method

With straight-line depreciation, the annual depreciation of fixed capital is constant over the depreciation period. The depreciation charge for any year r can be computed by the following formula:

$$D_r = \frac{(P-S)}{n}$$

where: D_r = depreciation in year, r
  P = original cost
  S = salvage value
  n = total number of years over which the depreciation is taken

For this case the book value (BV) at the end of the rth year would be:

$$BV_r = P - r \times D_r$$

For example, the original cost of a piece of equipment is \$20,000, the depreciation period is 12 years, and the salvage value is equal to zero. The depreciation for year 1 is: $D_1 = (20,000 - 0)/12 = \$1,667$; the book value is: $BV_1 = 20,000 - (1 \times 1,667) = \$18,333$.

Sum-of-Years-Digits Method

The sum-of-years (SY) depreciation is an accelerated depreciation method whereby about 75% of the cost is in the first half of the project life. The depreciation charge for any year r can be computed by the following formulas:

- Calculate the sum-of-years, n: $SY = n \times (n + 1)/2$
- Calculate a "unit of depreciation," C: $C = (P - S)/SY$
- Calculate the depreciation D for any year, r: $D_r = (n + 1 - r) \times C$

Using the same information as in the straight-line depreciation method:

- $SY = 12 \times (12 + 1)/2 = 78$ (sum of the 12 years)
- $C = (20,000 - 0)/78 = \$256$ (the "unit depreciation")

Now the depreciation for each year can be calculated:

- $D_1 = (12 + 1 - 1) \times 256 = 12 \times 256 = \$3,072$ for year 1
- $D_2 = (12 + 1 - 2) \times 256 = 11 \times 256 = \$2,816$ for year 2

The book value for the project at any year, can be calculated by substituting the value of the sum-of-the-digits depreciation for that year into the same book value formula as for straight-line depreciation.

Double-Rate Declining Balance Method

The double-rate declining balance depreciation is an accelerated depreciation method at double the straight-line depreciation rate for the remaining depreciable balance. The depreciation charge for any year, r, can be computed by the following formulas:

- Calculate the double-declining factor, f: $f = 2/n$
- Then calculate the book value, BV_r: $BV_r = P \times (1 - f)^r$
- Calculate the depreciation, D, for year, r: $D_r = (BV_{r-1} - BV_r)$; or $D_r = f \times (BV_{r-1})$

Using the same information as in the straight-line depreciation method:

- $f = 2.0/12 = 0.167$
- $BV_1 = 20,000 \times (1 - 0.167)^1 = \$16,660$ for year 1

- $D_1 = (20,000 - 16,660) = \$3,340$ for year 1
- $BV_2 = 20,000 \times (1 - 0.167)^2 = \$13,889$ for year 2
- $D_2 = (16,000 - 13,889) = \$3,111$ for year 2

Other Methods

The *Sinking Fund* method depreciates equipment with an imaginary sinking fund that is equivalent to the company making a series of equal annual payments to a fund which will equal the cost of replacing the equipment at the end of its useful life. This method is used only with equipment that has to be replaced with equipment which costs at least as much as the original. This is a decelerated depreciation method with larger annual depreciation values taken in the later years.

Often it is more convenient to group assets bought in the same year for depreciation purposes into a *group account*. A *classified account* groups items according to use, and a *composite account* includes items which have diverse uses and lives. All of the methods discussed work. They are selected for use by consideration of a company's overall economic situation.

SENSITIVITY AND RISK ANALYSIS

A "sensitive" project is one whose desirability is highly affected by the small change in one or more certain variables. A project is "insensitive" to certain variables if wide variations in the value of that variable does not alter the conclusions of the project evaluation. The variables which are sources of risk and which could lead to project sensitivity, include everything that is estimated such as: disbursements, receipts, project service time, salvage value, tax rate, cost of raw materials, cost of energy, and revenues from products.

Risk analysis is linked to sensitivity analysis and attempts to quantify the risks, uncertainties, and variability associated with a project. A simple risk assessment for economic decision analysis involves the following steps:

- Determine the range of possible outcomes that would effect the profitability of the project (e.g., the range in product selling price).
- Evaluate the profit over the range of possible outcomes.

- Estimate the probability of occurrence of each of the possible outcomes (e.g., the probability that the price will be at the lowest value when the plant is constructed and begins operation).

- Evaluate the weighted average of the profit by computing the sum of the profits times the probabilities.

This weighted average profit is an estimate of the expected value of the profit from the project.

As an example, if it was determined that the supply of seafood is directly related to weather conditions, the probability that a seafood processing plant will be used to capacity in any one year could be predicted using weather data from past years and what the effect of seafood harvests will be. With this information, for this example it is predicted that the probability of the plant being used at 75% capacity in a given year is 30%, the probability for a full capacity year is 45%, and the probability of usage at 125% of capacity is 25%. The following table shows the calculations that give the expected value of the annual worth:

% Capacity	Annual Worth	Probability	Expected Value
75%	$22,314	0.30	$6,694.20
100%	$124,045	0.45	$55,820.25
125%	$212,151	0.25	$53,037.75
		Expected Value = $115,552.75	

Table 3. Calculation of Expected Worth

Note that the sum of the probabilities is equal to one. This must always be the case.

FE/EIT

FE: PM General Engineering Exam

Practice Test 1

FUNDAMENTALS OF ENGINEERING EXAMINATION

TEST 1

(Answer sheets appear in the back of this book.)

TIME: 4 Hours
            60 Questions

DIRECTIONS: For each of the following questions and incomplete statements, choose the best answer from the four answer choices. You must answer all questions.

1. Water runs into a conical tank shown below at a constant rate of 2 m³ per minute. How fast is the water level rising when the water is 6 m deep?

    (A) 5.849 m/minute

    (B) 2.0 m/minute

    (C) 0.071 m/minute

    (D) 0.42 m/minute

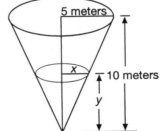

2. Determine the limit for the following:

$$\lim_{x \to 1} \frac{x^2 + x - 2}{(x-1)^2}$$

    (A) 0   (C) $\dfrac{1}{3}$

    (B) 1   (D) ∞

Questions 3 and 4 refer to the following:

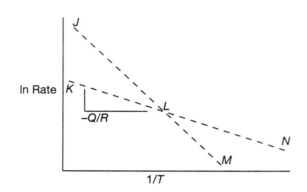

This graph describes two reaction mechanisms in a system by the lines K-N and J-M. The natural log of the rate of reaction is shown as a function of inverse absolute temperature. The slope is $-Q/R$, where R is the gas constant and Q is the activation energy for a mechanism to occur.

3. Which of the following equations describes the behavior of either of these mechanisms? Express rate of reaction as a function of the activation energy, temperature, gas constant R, and a constant, A.

    (A) Rate $= Ae^{(-QT/R)}$ (C) Rate $= Ae^{(-Q/RT)}$

    (B) Rate $= A + e^{(-Q/RT)}$ (D) Rate $= Ae^{(Q/RT)}$

4. Which of the following curves will approximate the actual rate of this reaction in the system as a function of $1/T$ in the above figure?

    (A) K-L-N   (C) K-L-M

    (B) J-L-M   (D) J-L-N

5. A car traveling at 60 kph locks its wheels and skids 150 m before stopping. Assuming constant deceleration, how long (in seconds) will it take for the car to come to a standstill?

    (A) 12.2 sec   (C) 18.0 sec

    (B) 10.5 sec   (D) 4.20 sec

6. Find the reaction at point A for the figure below.

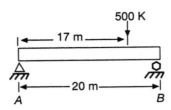

(A) 736 N-m   (C) 1,670 N-m

(B) 1,178 N-m   (D) 2,454 N-m

7. The Griffith equation relates σ (stress) required to extend a crack of length c to the material constants E (elastic modulus) and γ (fracture energy):

$$\sigma = \sqrt{\frac{2E\gamma}{\pi c}}$$

The stress intensity factor, K_{Ic}, is given by the equation:

$$K_{Ic} = \sigma_f \sqrt{\pi c_c}$$

where σ_f is the fracture strength and C_c is the critical crack length for fracture. What changes will increase the fracture strength?

(A) Increase the fracture energy, and decrease the average crack size.

(B) Decrease the fracture energy, and decrease the average crack size.

(C) Increase the fracture energy, and decrease the peak crack size.

(D) Decrease the fracture energy, and decrease the peak crack size.

8. At what annual rate of return, compounded monthly, will an investment be worth 175% of its original value in three years?

(A) 1.57%   (C) 20.5%

(B) 18.8%   (D) 25.0%

9. The third law of thermodynamics dictates that a substance at absolute zero has zero entropy if

   (A) it is a pure element.

   (B) it is in internal equilibrium.

   (C) it is a single crystal.

   (D) it consists of a single phase.

10. Determine the ratio of the final to initial energy stored in the circuit shown below. The two capacitors C_1 and C_2 are charged to the same potential difference, but with opposite polarity.

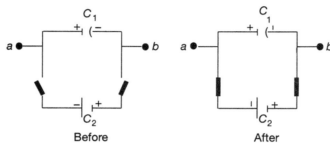

(A) $(C_1 + C_2)^2$

(C) $\left(\dfrac{C_1}{C_2}\right)^2$

(B) $\dfrac{1}{2}\left(\dfrac{C_1}{C_2}\right)$

(D) $\left[\dfrac{(C_1 - C_2)}{(C_1 + C_2)}\right]^2$

11. A computer operates in the binary number system. Convert the binary number 1011 to base 10.

   (A) 3   (C) 11

   (B) 10   (D) 12

12. Given a pressure of 80 kPa and flow velocity of 5 m/s, at point 1 (diameter = 0.5 m) of the pipe system given in the figure below, find the pressure at point 2 (diameter = 0.35m).

   (A) 20.3 kPa

   (B) 40.5 kPa

   (C) 76.0 kPa

   (D) 120.0 kPa

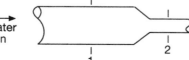

13. A computer operates in the binary number system. Convert the decimal number 45 to a binary number.

    (A) 10101

    (B) 101101

    (C) 11000

    (D) 111001

14. A 30 g bullet traveling at 850 m/s strikes a 5 kg wagon (initially at rest) and after impact they move together. Determine the momentum, in N-sec, of the bullet and wagon immediately after the impact.

    (A) 12.7 N-sec

    (B) 25.5 N-sec

    (C) 2.6 N-sec

    (D) 5.2 N-sec

15. For the figure below, determine the tension of cord A-D for equilibrium of the 5 kg mass.

    (A) 41.0 N

    (B) 58.5 N

    (C) 64.0 N

    (D) 76.3 N

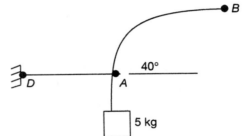

16. What is the probability of rolling either 7 or 11 with one roll of a pair of dice?

    (A) 5%

    (B) 7%

    (C) 10%

    (D) 22%

17. A centrifugal pump with an 8 cm diameter impeller delivers 40 liters per second of 15°C water at a total head of 110 m when operating at 1,750 rpm. Find the impeller diameter of a geometrically similar pump that delivers 65 liters per second when operating at 3,500 rpm.

    (A) 4.44 cm

    (B) 5.40 cm

    (C) 7.21 cm

    (D) 7.46 cm

18. Find the total head of the 3,500 rpm pump in the previous problem, if $D = 10$ cm, when it is delivering 65 liters per second.

(A) 0 m

(C) 1,237 m

(B) 687 m

(D) 1,584 m

19. Determine the DC current for the circuit shown below.

(A) $-\dfrac{2}{3}$ amps

(B) $-\dfrac{1}{3}$ amps

(C) $\dfrac{1}{3}$ amps

(D) 1 amps

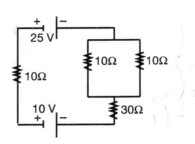

20. A block shown in the figure below has a mass of 20 kg. Determine the force P so that the block is on the verge of moving up the plane. The coefficient of static friction is $\mu = 0.3$.

(A) 133.3 N

(B) 149.1 N

(C) 159.6 N

(D) 169.9 N

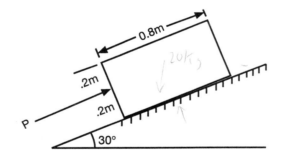

21. Which one of the following is the slope-intercept form of a straight line passing through (1.9, 5.4) and (9.6, 11.1)?

(A) $y = 3.99x + 0.74$

(C) $y = 0.74x + 3.99$

(B) $y = 0.74x - 6.81$

(D) $y = 1.35x + 7.96$

22. Find the value of $\dfrac{7!}{(3! \; 0!)}$

(A) 0

(C) 4.6

(B) 2.3

(D) 840

23. A rope is wrapped around a wheel that is initially at rest as shown in the figure below. If a force is applied to the cord and gives it an acceleration of $a = (4t)$ m/s², determine the angular velocity (in radians/second) of the wheel.

(A) $2\pi t$

(B) $10t^2$

(C) $5t$

(D) $20t^2$

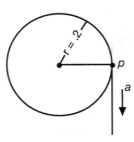

24. Determine the banking angle of a circular track so that the wheels of a car will not have to depend on friction to prevent sliding. The car travels at a constant speed of 35 m/sec. The radius of the track is 200 m.

(A) 10°

(B) 16°

(C) 32°

(D) 64°

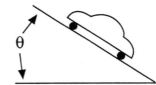

25. Find the centroidal moment of inertia about an axis parallel to the x axis for the object in the figure below.

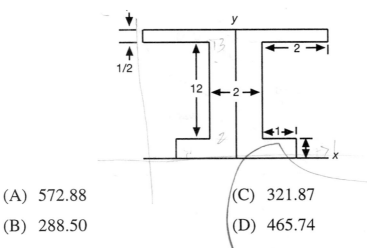

(A) 572.88

(C) 321.87

(B) 288.50

(D) 465.74

26. Evaluate K for the following FORTRAN expression:
$K = (7.0 + 2.0) \times 3.0/2.0 + 4.0 - 6.0 \times\times 2.0$

(A) −18

(C) 5.5

(B) −18.5

(D) 5

27. Once the thermodynamic conditions are right for the following phase transformations to take place, which one of them can commence with *no* kinetic barrier to overcome?

    (A) Liquid → Solid

    (B) Liquid → Gas

    (C) Solid (α phase) → Solid (β phase) (reconstructive transformation)

    (D) Solid → Liquid

28. In the United States, who can be held legally responsible for an accident involving a manufacturing process which was flawed in some way?

    (A) The company's owners or board of directors

    (B) The manager or supervisor of the process or workers

    (C) The person responsible for designing the process

    (D) All of the above.

29. Gibb's phase rule states that the number of phases in equilibrium plus the number of degrees of freedom equals the number of components plus two. In the following single component phase diagram use Gibb's phase rule to determine how many degrees of freedom there are at points *W*, *X*, *Y*, and *Z*.

	W	X	Y	Z
(A)	2	2	2	0
(B)	2	1	1	0
(C)	2	1	2	0
(D)	3	2	2	1

30. Strain hardening in metals can be attributed to

    (A) increased inhomogeneity leading to higher stress fields.

    (B) increased tangling of dislocations.

    (C) linking of voids and necking.

    (D) All of these.

31. After much debate, a dilapidated industrial area in swampy land has been chosen for conversion to low-income housing by the local government. Your company, a local engineering firm, has been asked to be involved in the redevelopment. Your company's main concern in deciding whether to be involved with this project should be:

    (A) Is this land environmentally sensitive?

    (B) Does our company have a conflict of interest with the local government?

    (C) Are low-income individuals being discriminated against by the local government?

    (D) Is this land safe for residential habitation?

32. Two supports on level ground are 100 m apart and support a transmission line weighing 2 N/m. If the mid point sag is 10 m, what is the maximum tension in the line?

    (A) 198.0 N   (C) 253.2 N

    (B) 200.0 N   (D) 273.2 N

33. Locate the centroid (distance on the x axis from the y axis) on the object shown in the figure below.

    (A) 1.33

    (B) 1.52

    (C) 1.67

    (D) 2.00

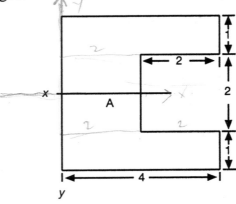

34. For a proposed project, the declining balance method (33% deprecia-
    tion rate) is used to determine the amount which will be depreciated
    each year from a piece of equipment which will cost $50,000 at the
    beginning of the project. At the end of which year will it become
    beneficial to switch to the straight line method for depreciation of the
    remainder of the equipment's value?

    (A) Year 2

    (B) Year 3

    (C) Year 4

    (D) Never, the declining balance method is always preferred over
        straight line.

35. Which of the following is the least important factor in densification
    of crystalline grains and grain growth?

    (A) Temperature   (C) Surface energy

    (B) Firing time   (D) Impurities

36. A handbook table shows you that for the equation

    $$ABC_2(s) \leftrightarrow AB(g) + 2C(g)$$

the equilibrium constant is 16×10^{-8} at room temperature. The units for the
equilibrium constant are said to be "in the appropriate units." What are the
equilibrium pressures for the two gases at room temperature?

    (A) $p_{AB} = 4.0 \times 10^{-4}$ atm, $p_C = 4.0 \times 10^{-4}$ atm

    (B) $p_{AB} = 4.0 \times 10^{-3}$ atm, $p_C = 8.0 \times 10^{-3}$ atm

    (C) $p_{AB} = 3.42 \times 10^{-3}$ atm, $p_C = 6.84 \times 10^{-3}$ atm

    (D) The starting amount of solid must be known to calculate the gas
        pressures.

37. Solve the following simultaneous linear equations for x and y:

    $$2x + 3y = 12 \ (1)$$
    $$5x + 4y = 9 \ (2)$$

    (A) $(0, 6)$ (C) $(3, 6)$

    (B) $(-3, 6)$ (D) $(9, -7.5)$

38. Water flows through the pipe system shown below. The diameter at point 1 is 0.5 m and at point 2 is 0.35 m. The velocity at point 1 is 5 m/s and the density of the water is 9.80 kN/m³. Find the velocity at point 2.

(A) 1.2 m/s

(B) 12.5 m/s

(C) 2.4 m/s

(D) 10.2 m/s

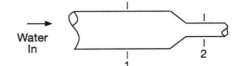

39. Find the resistance between points *a* and *b* for the combination resistance shown below.

(A) 1.33 Ω

(B) 2.52 Ω

(C) 3.62 Ω

(D) 5.46 Ω

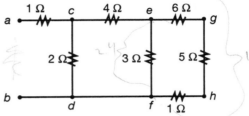

40. Adding a second phase of material in particulate or fiber form with a higher elastic modulus to a brittle solid matrix material will make the overall composite

(A) more brittle than the matrix material alone.

(B) tougher than the matrix material alone.

(C) weaker than the matrix material alone.

(D) more sensitive to thermal shock.

41. Solve the following first order linear differential equation:

$$\frac{dy}{dx} + y = e^x$$

(A) $y = e^x + C$

(C) $y = \frac{1}{2}e^x + Ce^{-x}$

(B) $y = \frac{1}{2}e^x + Ce^x$

(D) $y = e^x + Ce^{-x}$

42. A cache is five times faster than the main memory. The cache can be used 90% of the time. How much speed do we gain by using the cache?

    (A) 0.93
    (B) 1.5

    (C) 2.2
    (D) 3.6

43. Find the current I_3 in the circuit shown below:

    (A) −3 amps
    (B) −1 amp
    (C) 1 amp
    (D) 3 amps

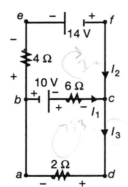

44. Determine the limit for the following:

    $$\lim_{x \to 0}\left(\frac{\sin 3x}{2x}\right)$$

    (A) 0

    (B) 1

    (C) $\dfrac{2}{3}$

    (D) $\dfrac{3}{2}$

45. Calculate the total power dissipated across the three resistors shown below:

    (A) 11 W
    (B) 18 W
    (C) 106 W
    (D) 198 W

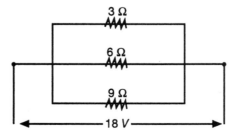

46. When working with a hazardous substance, which of the following should be provided to a worker?

    (A) The chemical name

    (B) A material safety data sheet (MSDS)

    (C) The chemical formula

    (D) All of the above.

Questions 47 – 50 are based on the following:

The vapor pressure p (in atmospheres) of zinc is given by the equations:

$$\ln p \text{ (solid)} = -\frac{15,780}{T} - 0.755 \ln T + 19.25$$

and:

$$\ln p \text{ (liquid)} = -\frac{15,250}{T} - 1.255 \ln T + 21.79$$

where T is absolute temperature in K.

The Clausius-Clapeyron equation correlates the change in enthalpy (ΔH) and pressure for a solid or liquid in equilibrium with vapor:

$$\frac{d \ln p}{dT} = \frac{\Delta H_{L(\text{or } S) \to V}}{RT^2}$$

where the gas constant $R = 8.3144$ J/(mol × K).

47. What is the temperature at the triple point of zinc?

    (A) 712°C   (C) 439°C

    (B) 985°C   (D) –130°C

48. What is the heat of vaporization of boiling zinc at 5.0×10^{-4} atm?

    (A) 3.00 J/mol   (C) 132 kJ/mol

    (B) 119 kJ/mol   (D) 32.9 MJ/mol

49. At what temperature will solid zinc evaporate if the pressure is 10^{-8} atm?

    (A) $-139°C$ (C) $478°C$

    (B) $205°C$ (D) $751°C$

50. What would happen to zinc vapor at $430°C$ and 3×10^{-4} atm?

    (A) It would remain a vapor.

    (B) It would form a solid.

    (C) The solid and vapor phases would be in equilibrium.

    (D) The solid and liquid phases would be in equilibrium.

51. Find the current in the single loop circuit shown below:

    (A) $\dfrac{1}{3}$ amp

    (B) $\dfrac{1}{2}$ amp

    (C) 1 amp

    (D) 3 amps

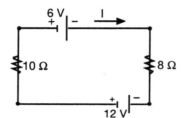

52. Find the equation of a circle through points $A(1, 0)$, $B(0, 1)$, and $C(2, 2)$.

    (A) $3x^2 + 3y^2 = 0$

    (B) $x^2 + y^2 - 2x = 0$

    (C) $3x^2 + 3y^2 - 7x - 7y + 4 = 0$

    (D) $3x^2 + 3y^2 - 2x - 2y + 4 = 0$

53. Stress is applied to an annealed single crystal of pure copper, starting at zero, and increasing linearly until the crystal has extended to 110% of its original length. The stress is then released. Which of the following occurs?

    (A) Plastic deformation will start immediately and continue until the stress is relieved. The crystal will remain at its fully extended length when stress is released.

    (B) Elastic deformation will occur first, followed by plastic deformation. When stress is relieved, the crystal will elastically return to its original length.

(C) Elastic deformation will occur first, followed by plastic deformation. When stress is relieved, the crystal will elastically return to a length slightly below 110%.

(D) Plastic deformation will start immediately and continue until the stress is relieved. The crystal will then elastically return to a length slightly below 110%.

54. The slope of a line perpendicular to the line through (4, –1) and (2, 3) is

(A) –3.

(C) $-\dfrac{1}{2}$.

(B) –2.

(D) $\dfrac{1}{2}$.

55. When a rubber band is extended, the behavior exhibited is described as

(A) plastic flow.

(C) elastomeric strain.

(B) elastic strain.

(D) viscous flow.

56. All glasses have the characteristic of being

(A) brittle.

(C) poor electrical conductors.

(B) transparent.

(D) amorphous.

57. Find the equation of a line tangent to the curve $y = 3x^2 - x$ at $x = 0$:

(A) $y = -x + 3x^2$

(C) $y = -x$

(B) $y = x$

(D) $y = x + 3x^2$

58. Find the determinate of the following matrix:

$$\begin{vmatrix} 2 & -1 & 2 \\ 1 & 3 & -1 \\ 1 & 2 & 3 \end{vmatrix}$$

(A) 24

(C) 21

(B) 12

(D) 22

59. In solid materials, the energy of the electrons at a certain level occupy a range of values. Bands of energy of different orbitals may overlap so that the "band gap" between levels is zero. This most frequently occurs in

   (A) semiconductors.

   (B) ionic solids.

   (C) metal alloys.

   (D) covalent solids.

60. A machine three years old which cost $35,000 and can currently be sold for $10,000 is being considered for replacement by a higher capacity machine which will cost $45,000 and increase profits by an estimated $5,000 per year. Both pieces would last for seven more years, with the current one having a salvage value of $500 and the new one $6,000. The old machine costs $3,500/year to maintain, and the new one would cost $1,000/year to maintain. Installation of the new equipment and removal of the old would cost $5,000. Based on an interest rate of 10% compounded annually, should the new machine be purchased? On an annual basis, how much would be saved or lost by buying the new machine?

Factors for 10% interest rate compounded over n periods

n	F given P	P given F	F given A	A given F	P given A	A given P
1	1.1000	0.9091	1.0000	1.0000	0.9091	1.1000
2	1.2100	0.8265	2.1000	0.4762	1.7355	0.5762
3	1.3310	0.7513	3.3100	0.3021	2.4869	0.4021
4	1.4640	0.6830	4.6410	0.2155	3.1699	0.3155
5	1.6110	0.6209	6.1050	0.1638	3.7908	0.2638
6	1.7720	0.5645	7.7160	0.1296	4.3553	0.2296
7	1.9490	0.5132	9.4870	0.1054	4.8684	0.2054

P = Present value, F = Future value, A = Annuity (Annual amount for n years)

   (A) Yes, $136/year would be saved.

   (B) Yes, $4,244/year would be saved.

   (C) No, $136/year would be lost.

   (D) No, $4,244/year would be lost.

FUNDAMENTALS OF ENGINEERING

TEST 1

ANSWER KEY

1.	(C)	16.	(D)	31.	(D)	46.	(B)
2.	(D)	17.	(D)	32.	(D)	47.	(C)
3.	(C)	18.	(B)	33.	(C)	48.	(B)
4.	(D)	19.	(B)	34.	(B)	49.	(B)
5.	(C)	20.	(B)	35.	(B)	50.	(B)
6.	(A)	21.	(C)	36.	(C)	51.	(A)
7.	(C)	22.	(D)	37.	(B)	52.	(C)
8.	(B)	23.	(B)	38.	(D)	53.	(C)
9.	(B)	24.	(C)	39.	(B)	54.	(D)
10.	(D)	25.	(A)	40.	(B)	55.	(C)
11.	(C)	26.	(A)	41.	(C)	56.	(D)
12.	(B)	27.	(D)	42.	(D)	57.	(C)
13.	(B)	28.	(D)	43.	(B)	58.	(A)
14.	(B)	29.	(B)	44.	(D)	59.	(C)
15.	(B)	30.	(B)	45.	(D)	60.	(C)

DETAILED EXPLANATIONS
OF ANSWERS

TEST 1

1. **(C)**

    Using the following variables:

    v = the volume (m³) of water in the tank at time t (minutes)

    x = the radius (m) of water in the tank at time t

    y = the depth (m) of water in the tank at time t

Using the general relationship:

$$\frac{dv}{dt} = \frac{dy}{dt} A$$

The dimensions of the tank remain constant along with the rate that the tank fills as:

$$\frac{dv}{dt} = 2 \text{ m}^3/\text{minute}$$

The relationship between the volume of water v and depth y is expressed by the equation:

$$v = \frac{1}{3}\pi x^2 y$$

Eliminate x by using the geometric operation of similar triangles:

$$\frac{x}{y} = \frac{5}{10}; x = \frac{1}{2} y$$

Therefore:

$$v = \frac{1}{12}\pi y^3$$

Differentiating with respect to t:

$$\frac{dv}{dt} = \frac{1}{4}\pi y^2$$

Hence:

$$\frac{dy}{dt} = \frac{4}{\pi y^2}\frac{dv}{dt}$$

And when $dv/dt = 2$ and $y = 6$, the solution gives:

$$\frac{dy}{dt} = \frac{4 \times 2}{\pi \times 36} = 0.071 \text{ m/minute}$$

Answer choice (C) is correct; the other choices are not the correct value of dy/dt at $y = 6$.

2. **(D)**
    To determine the limit as x approaches 1, factor the numerator as follows:

$$\lim_{x\to 1}\frac{x^2 + x - 2}{(x-1)^2} = \lim_{x\to 1}\frac{(x-1)(x+2)}{(x-1)(x-1)} = \frac{3}{0} = \lim_{x\to 1}\frac{(x+2)}{(x-1)}$$

Recognizing that the given function is not defined at $x = 1$, but that it is defined for all other values of x and, therefore, that the limit of the function as x approaches 1 exists, to evaluate the limit, by factoring the function to obtain:

$$\lim_{x\to 1}\frac{(x-1)(x+2)}{(x-1)(x-1)} = \lim_{x\to 1}\frac{(x+2)}{(x-1)}$$

for all values of x except $x = 1$.

Then by examination, as $x \to 1$, $x + 2 \to 3$, and $x - 1 \to 0$ (or very small). Therefore:

$$\lim_{x\to 1}\frac{(x+2)}{(x-1)} = \infty$$

Answer choice (D) is correct; the other choices do not give the correct limit.

3.   **(C)**

The correct expression for the behavior, known as Arrhenius behavior, is Rate $= Ae^{(-Q/RT)}$.

This can be found from the graph by substituting for the standard equation for a linear graph: $y = mx + b$, where m is the slope and b is the y-axis intercept.

This gives:

$$ln \text{ (Rate)} = \left(-\frac{Q}{R}\right)\left(\frac{1}{T}\right) + A' \text{ [a constant]}.$$

Taking e to the power of both sides gives:

$$\text{Rate} = e^{(-Q/RT + A')} = e^{(A')} e^{(-Q/RT)} = A \ e^{(-Q/RT)}.$$

This equation appears correct since, as is shown on the graph, as the required activation energy increases the rate decreases, and as the temperature increases the rate increases.

A is a theoretical rate which would occur at an infinitely high temperature. (A) is incorrect since e is raised to the power T and not $1/T$. In (B) the constant is added rather than multiplied, and in (D) e is raised to a positive rather than negative power.

4.   **(D)**

More than one reaction mechanism is possible in this system, and their curves intersect. Therefore, at different temperatures, different mechanisms may determine the reaction rate. The dominant reaction at any temperature, i.e., the fastest, will determine the reaction rate. The mechanism with the steeper negative slope will dominate at high temperatures, and the one with the higher negative slope will dominate at lower temperatures. The correct answer is J-L-N. Answer choices (A), (B), and (C) are incorrect since they follow paths with slower mechanisms in part or in whole.

5.   **(C)**

First convert 60 kph to m/sec:

$$\frac{60 \text{ km/hour } (1,000 \text{ m/km})}{3,600 \text{ sec/hour}} = 16.67 \text{ m/sec}$$

For this problem of uniformly accelerated motion, the basic equations of motion ($v = ds/dt$ and $a = dv/dt$) are integrated and combined to obtain an expression for time as a function of position and velocity.

From $v = \dfrac{ds}{dt}$ and $\dfrac{dv}{dt} = a$

where: $v = $ velocity
          $s = $ position
          $t = $ time
          $a = $ acceleration

we integrate and combine to obtain:

$$t = \frac{2s}{v + v_0}$$

then solve:

$$t = \frac{2.150}{16.67 + 0} = 17.6 \text{ sec.}$$

$$t = 18.0 \text{ sec}$$

6.   **(A)**
      Draw the free-body diagram for the system.

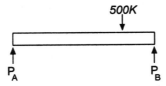

Sum the forces in the x and y directions:

$$+ \rightarrow \Sigma F_x = 0 \tag{1}$$

$$+ \uparrow \Sigma F_y = 0; \; P_A + P_B - 500 \text{ kg } (9.81 \text{ m/sec}^2) = 0 \tag{2}$$

Choose the left end of the system as the reference point for the moment arm and sum the moments:

$$\uparrow + \Sigma M_{\text{left}} = 0; \; 4{,}905(17) - P_B(20) = 0 \tag{3}$$

$$P_B = 4{,}169$$

Substitute back into Equation (2) to find:

$$P_A = 4{,}905 - 4{,}169$$

$$P_A = 736 \text{ N–}m$$

Answer choice (A) is correct; the other choices do not give the correct reaction, as calculated in the solution.

7.   **(C)**

From the equations, it can be seen that the K_{Ic} is equal to $\sqrt{2E\gamma}$. Therefore, increasing the fracture energy would increase the stress intensity factor. (This would require changing the material itself.) Answer choices (B) and (D) are therefore incorrect.

The equation:

$$\sigma = \sqrt{\frac{2E\gamma}{\pi c}}$$

shows that the longest crack will determine the strength of the material. Therefore, the peak crack length, not the average crack size, should be decreased, making (A) incorrect.

8.   **(B)**

Compounded monthly, there are 36 time periods over which an annual rate of return of $x/12$ is compounded. The starting amount is not needed since only a percent increase is necessary. The total each time period $(1 + x/12)$ is compounded 36 times. The equation to be solved would be:

$$(1 + \frac{x}{12})^{36} = 1.75$$

Therefore, $x = \left(\sqrt[36]{1.75} - 1\right)(12) = 0.188 = 18.8\%$.

Other choices, including (A) and (C), are found by various calculation errors. For example, using simple interest (no compounding), choice (D) would be found, 25.0%.

9.   **(B)**

Complete internal equilibrium must exist if entropy is to be taken as zero. (A) A pure element may still have entropy due to vacancies, different isotopes, or by being in a glassy phase. A compound can be in internal equilibrium if the multiple types of atoms are arranged in an absolutely ordered structure. (C) Even a crystal with no grain boundaries may have vacancies, dislocations, impurities, or, if a compound, a randomness in the positions of the different types of atoms. (D) A single phase is not always the equilibrium condition for a substance. Depending on composition, pressure, electric, or magnetic fields, etc., there may be multiple phases which could exist.

10. **(D)**

Before the switches are closed, the total energy stored is:

$$\text{Initial Energy} = \frac{1}{2} C_1 V_o^2 + \frac{1}{2} C_2 V_o^2 = \frac{1}{2} (C_1 + C_2) V_o^2$$

After the switches are closed, the total energy stored is:

$$\text{Final Energy} = \frac{1}{2} C_1 V^2 + \frac{1}{2} C_2 V^2 = \frac{1}{2} (C_1 + C_2) V^2$$

$$= \frac{1}{12} (C_1 - C_2) \left[\frac{(C_1 - C_2)}{(C_1 + C_2)} \right] V_0^2$$

$$= \left[\frac{(C_1 - C_2)}{(C_1 + C_2)} \right]^2 (\text{Initial Energy})$$

Therefore, the ratio of final to initial energy stored is:

$$\frac{\text{Final Energy}}{\text{Initial Energy}} = \left[\frac{(C_1 - C_2)}{(C_1 + C_2)} \right]^2$$

Answer choice (D) is correct; the other choices do not give the correct ratio of final to initial energy stored.

11. **(C)**

A binary number can be converted to a base 10 number by performing the following calculations:

$$A_n 2^n + \ldots + A_2 2^2 + A_1 2^1 + A_0 2^0$$

Therefore,

$$(1)2^3 + (0)2^2 + (1)2^1 + (1)2^0 = 11$$

Answer choice (C) is correct; the other choices do not give the correct base 10 number, as shown in the solution.

12. **(B)**

Use the Bernoulli equation:

$$\frac{p}{\rho} + \frac{v^2}{2g} + z = c$$

and the continuity equation:

$$Q = VA$$

first using continuity:

$$v_2 = \frac{0.5^2 \frac{\mu}{4}}{0.35^2 \frac{\mu}{4}}(0.5)$$

$$v_2 = 10.2 \frac{\mu}{5}$$

then from conservation of energy principles to obtain:

$$\frac{P_1}{\rho} + \frac{V_1^2}{2g} = \frac{P_2}{\rho} + \frac{V_2^2}{2g}$$

Solve for the given data and using the gravity constant of $g = 9.81$ m/s:

$$P_2 = P_1 + \left[\left(\frac{5^2}{2 \times 9.81} \right) - \left(\frac{10.2^2}{2 \times 9.81} \right) \right] 9.80$$

$$P_2 = 40.5 \text{ kPa}$$

Answer choice (B) is correct; the other choices do not give the correct pressure at point 2 as shown in the solution.

13. **(B)**

A binary number can be converted to a base 10 number by performing the following calculations:

$$A_n 2^n + \ldots + A_2 2^2 + A_1 2^1 + A_0 2^0$$

Therefore:

$$(1)2^5 + (0)2^4 + (1)2^3 + (1)2^2 + (0)2^1 + (1)2^0 = 45$$

Answer choice (B) is correct; the other choices do not give the correct base 10 number.

14. **(B)**

Use the conservation of momentum equation (where $p = mv$):

$$m_1 v_1 + m_2 v_2 = m_1 v_1' + m_2 v_2'$$

Since $v_1' = v_2'$, simplify equation to obtain $v'(v' = v' = v_2')$ and convert terms to the same units (e.g., grams to kilograms):

$$v' = \frac{m_1 v_1 + m_2 v_2}{m_1 + m_2}$$

$$v' = \frac{\left(30 \text{ g}/\left(10^3 \text{ g/kg}\right)\right)850 + 5}{\left(30/10^3\right) + 5}$$

$$v' = 5.07 \text{ m/s}$$

Solve for momentum, p:

$$p = mv'$$

$$p = \left(\left(\frac{30}{10^3}\right) + 5\right)5.07 \text{ m/s}$$

$$p = 25.5 \text{ N-sec}$$

Answer choice (B) is correct; the other choices do not give the momentum, as calculated in the solution.

15. **(B)**
Draw the free-body diagram, acting on point A, as follows:

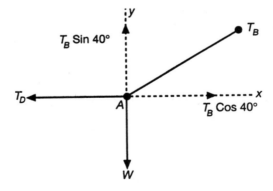

Determine the weight of the mass by multiplying it by the gravity constant:

$$w = 5 \text{ kg } (9.81 \text{ m/sec}^2) = 49.05 \text{ N}$$

Sum the forces in the x and y direction:

$$+ \rightarrow \Sigma F_x = 0; \ T_B \cos 40° - T_D = 0$$

$$+ \uparrow \Sigma F_y = 0; \ T_B \sin 40° - 49.05 = 0$$

Solving two simultaneous equations:

$$T_B = 76.3 \text{ N}$$

$$T_D = 58.5 \text{ N}$$

Answer choice (B) is correct; the other choices do not give the correct tension, as shown in the solution.

16. **(D)**

There are 36 possibilities in one roll of a pair of dice. There are eight possibilities of making either 7 or 11:

1–6	6–1
2–5	5–2
3–4	4–3
6–5	5–6

Therefore, the probability of making either 7 or 11 on one roll of the dice is:

$$\frac{8}{36} = 0.22 = 22\%$$

Answer choice (D) is correct; the other choices do not give the correct probability.

17. **(D)**

Use the similarity parameter (capacity coefficient) $C_0 = Q/nD^3$ where:

Q = discharge quantity

n = speed

D = diameter of impeller

Note that this means:

1) For centrifugal pumps with a fixed diameter of the impeller, Q is proportional to n.

2) For centrifugal pumps with a fixed speed but variable diameter, Q is proportional to D^3.

Setting the capacity coefficient of each pump equal to each other ($C_1 = C_2$) we obtain:

$$\frac{Q_1}{n_1 D_1^3} = \frac{Q_2}{n_2 D_2^3}$$

$$D_2 = D_1^3 \sqrt{\left(\frac{Q_2}{Q_1}\right)\left(\frac{n_1}{n_2}\right)}$$

Solving for the given variables:

$$D_2 = 0.8^3 \sqrt{\left(\frac{65}{40}\right)\left(\frac{1,750}{3,500}\right)}$$

$$D_2 = 7.46 \text{ cm}$$

Answer choice (D) is correct; the other choices do not give the correct impeller diameter, as shown in the solution.

18. **(B)**
 Use the similarity parameter (head coefficient) $C_H = \Delta H/(D^2 n^2/g))$ where:

ΔH = pump head

D = impeller diameter

n = pump speed

g = gravity constant

Note that this means:

1) For centrifugal pumps with a fixed diameter of the impeller, H is proportional to n^2.

2) For centrifugal pumps with a fixed speed but variable diameter, H is proportional to D^2.

Setting the head coefficients equal to each other, we obtain:

$$\frac{\Delta H_1}{\dfrac{D_1^2 n_1^2}{g}} = \frac{\Delta H_2}{\dfrac{D_2^2 n_2^2}{g}} \text{ or:}$$

$$H_2 = H_1 \left(\frac{n_2}{n_1} \right)^2 \left(\frac{D_2}{D_1} \right)^2$$

Solving for the given variables

$$H_2 = 110 \left(\frac{3500}{1750} \right)^2 \left(\frac{10}{8} \right)^2$$

$$H_2 = 687.5 \text{ m}$$

Answer choice (B) is correct; the other choices do not give the correct total head for the 3,500 rpm pump.

19. **(B)**

First, find the equivalent resistance (R_{eq}) of the parallel resistors:

$$\frac{1}{R_{eq}} = \frac{1}{10} + \frac{1}{10} = \frac{2}{10}, \text{ yielding}$$

Using Kirchhoff's second rule where I = current:

$$\Sigma \Delta V = 0$$

$$25 + I(5 + 30) - 10 + I(10) = 0$$

Solve for I:

$$I = \frac{-15}{45} = \frac{-1}{3} \text{ amp}$$

Answer choice (B) is correct; the other choices do not give the correct DC current for the given circuit, as shown in the solution.

20. **(B)**

Draw the free-body diagram:

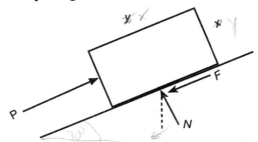

Determine the weight of the object by multiplying the mass by gravity constant:

$$w = 20 \text{ kg} \times 9.81 \text{ m/sec}^2 = 196.2 \text{ N}$$

Determine the force of friction:

$$F = \mu N = 0.3 \text{ N}$$

Summing the forces and moments we get:

$$\Sigma F_x = 0; \; P - 0.3 \text{ N} - 196.2 \sin 30°$$

$$\Sigma F_y = 0; \; N - 196.2 \cos 30°$$

Solving the simultaneous equations:

$$N = 169.9 \text{ N}$$

$$P = 149.1 \text{ N}$$

Answer choice (B) is correct; the other choices do not give the correct force, as calculated in the solution.

21. **(C)**

The equation of a straight line through an origin of a two-dimensional Cartesian coordinate system (x, y) can be written as $y = mx + b$, where M is the slope (rise over run) and b is the point of y-axis interception. The slope must be determined as:

$$m = \frac{y_1 - y_2}{x_1 - x_2} = \frac{11.1 - 5.4}{9.6 - 1.9} = \frac{5.7}{7.7} = 0.74$$

Using the first point, the slope point form is $(y - 5.4) = 0.74(x - 1.9)$.

Putting the slope and one point into the slope-intercept form $(y = mx + b)$ we get:

$$5.4 = (0.74)1.9 + b$$

Solving for b gives:

$$b = 3.99$$

This results in the slope-intercept form of a line through the given points:

$$y = 0.74x + 3.99$$

Answer choice (C) is correct; the other choices do not give the equation of a line through the points given.

22. **(D)**

By factoring:

$$\frac{(7)(6)(5)(4)(3)(2)(1)}{(3)(2)(1)(1)} = 840$$

Answer choice (D) is correct; the other choices do not give the correct value of the expression.

23. **(B)**

The acceleration of the rope tangent to point p is represented by:

$$a = \alpha r \text{ (where } \alpha = \text{angular velocity and } r = \text{radius)}$$

Therefore:

$$\alpha = 20t \text{ rad/sec}^2$$

The wheel's angular velocity can then be determined by using the formula:

$$\alpha = \frac{dw}{dt}$$

Integrating, with the initial conditions of $w = 0$ at $t_o = 0$, we get:

$$\alpha = \frac{dw}{dt} = 20t$$

$$\int_0^w dw = \int_0^t 20t \, dt$$

$$w = 10t^2 \text{ rad/sec}$$

Answer choice (B) is correct; the other choices do not give the correct angular velocity for the problem.

24. **(C)**
   Drawing a free-body diagram:

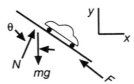

Using the *x-y* axis of the free-body diagram, write the equations of motion where $a_x = v^2/\rho$ and the friction force is zero:

$$\Sigma F_y = ma_y; \ N \cos \theta - mg = 0 \tag{1}$$

$$\Sigma F_x = ma_x; \ N \sin \theta - \frac{mv^2}{\rho} = 0 \tag{2}$$

Eliminating *N* and *m* and dividing Equation (1) into Equation (2):

$$\tan\theta = \frac{v^2}{g\rho} = \frac{(35)^2}{9.81(200)}$$

$$\theta = \tan^{-1}(0.624) = 32°$$

Answer choice (C) is correct; the other choices do not give the correct angle for the given conditions.

25. **(A)**
   Divide the object into three areas:

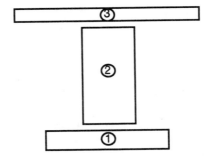

Determine the area and $\bar{y}$ for each area:

$$A_1 = (4)(1) = 4$$

$$\bar{y}_1 = \frac{1}{2}$$

$$A_2 = (2)(12) = 24$$

$$\bar{y}_2 = 1 + 6 = 7$$

$$A_3 = (6)\left(\frac{1}{2}\right) = 3$$

$$\bar{y}_3 = 13.25$$

Determine the composite y using the following equation:

$$\bar{y}_{composite} = \frac{\Sigma(A)(\bar{y})}{\Sigma A} = \frac{(4)(0.5) + (24)(7) + (3)(13.25)}{4 + 24 + 3} = 6.77$$

Determine the centroidal moment of inertia and distance from composite y for each part, where the moment of inertia for a rectangle is $I = bh^3/12$:

$$I_{c1} = \frac{bh^3}{12} = \frac{4(1)^3}{12} = 0.333$$

$$d_1 = 6.77 - 0.5 = 6.27$$

$$I_{c2} = \frac{(2)(12)^3}{12} = 288$$

$$d_2 = 0.23$$

$$I_{c3} = \frac{(6)(1/2)^3}{12} = 0.0625$$

$$d_3 = 6.48$$

Using the parallel axis theorem ($I = I_c + Ad^2$):

$$I_{total} = 0.333 + 4(6.27)^2 + 288 + 24(0.23)^2 + 0.0625 + 3(6.48)^2$$

$$= 572.88$$

Answer choice (A) is correct; the other choices do not give the correct centroidal moment of inertia, as calculated in the solution.

26. **(A)**

The expression within the parentheses is evaluated first.

$$K = \frac{9.0 \times 3.0}{2.0} + 4.0 - 6.0 \times\times 2.0$$

The exponentiation is performed next.

$$K = \frac{9.0 \times 3.0}{2.0} + 4.0 - 36.0$$

The multiplication and division is performed next.

$$K = 13.5 + 4.0 - 36.0$$

Finally, addition and subtraction are performed.

$$K = -18.5$$

However, K is an integer value, so the real number -18.5 is truncated and converted to the integer -18.

Answer choice (A) is correct; the other choices do not give the correct value of K.

27. **(D)**

Although it is thermodynamically favorable for all four processes to occur, forming a solid [(A), (C)] or a gas (B) requires nucleation of a crystal or bubble. This can occur homogeneously (due to fluctuations in position of atoms) or heterogeneously (such as at an impurity or at a container wall). Going from one solid phase to another (B) will also require nucleation. In fact, the kinetic barriers for solid-to-solid transitions are usually very high. (Sometimes the transformation is *displacive* rather than *reconstructive,* which does not require nucleation, but these would have designations such as α and α'.) Melting, the formation of a liquid from a solid, requires no nucleation, so the best answer is (D).

28. **(D)**

Any of these people [(A), (B), or (C)] may be held responsible, so the best answer is (D). A company as an entity, and hence its board of directors, may be sued if anyone in that company acted negligently. Furthermore, anyone, including a process designer or supervisor, who acted negligently may be legally responsible.

29. **(B)**

The Gibb's phase rule can be written as:

phases + degrees of freedom = # components + 2, or

$$P + F = C + 2.$$

Since $C = 1$, the degrees of freedom $= 3 - P$.

At W, there is only one phase, so $F = 2$, meaning the pressure and temperature can be changed independently in this region. At X, two phases are in equilibrium, the solid and gas, so $F = 1$. This means that although the pressure or the temperature can be changed along this line, only one can be changed independently. At Y, the two solids are different phases, and both are in equilibrium at Y, so $F = 1$. At Z, the two solid phases and the liquid are all in equilibrium together, so $F = 0$; it is a point of fixed temperature and pressure.

30. **(B)**

Although any of these, including (A) and (C), may lead to failure, only choice (B) increases hardness, so it is the best answer, making (D) incorrect also. As the material is strained, dislocations are created and move through the material, and become tangled at surfaces, grain boundaries, impurities, etc. During strain hardening, or "work" hardening, strains are applied in many directions, so dislocations are created and move in different directions, increasing the likelihood of tangling. As the dislocations tangle with each other, this flow mechanism becomes defeated, and it becomes more and more difficult for plastic deformation to occur.

31. **(D)**

All of these are of some concern. Protecting the environment is always important to consider (A). Acting in a professional manner is important, so, conflict of interest must be avoided (B), and the rights of all people in our society are to be respected (C). However, the safety of human life is always of paramount importance, so (D) is the best answer.

32. **(D)**

$$w = 2 \text{ N/m} \qquad y = 10\text{m}$$

Using the equations of a catenary, we solve for c by trial and error:

$$y = c \left[\cos h(a/c) - 1 \right]$$

$$c = 126.6 \text{ m}$$

Using the equation, $H = wc$, we solve for the horizontal midpoint tension:

$$H = 253.2 \text{ N}$$

Using the equation, $T = ws$ (where $s = c + y$), we solve for the endpoint tension:

$$T = 2(126.6 + 10) = 273.2 \text{ N}$$

Therefore, the maximum tension in the line is 273.2 N.

Answer choice (D) is correct; the other choices do not give the correct maximum tension for the line, as shown in the solution.

33. **(C)**
    Divide the object into three parts:

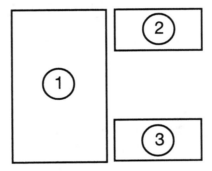

Determine the area and $\bar{x}$ for each part:

$$A_1 = 2(4) = 8$$

$$\bar{x}_1 = 1$$

$$A_2 = A_3 = 1(2) = 2$$

$$\bar{x}_2 = \bar{x}_3 = 3$$

To find the composite $\bar{x}$, we use the following equation:

$$\bar{x}_{composite} = \frac{\Sigma(A)(\bar{x})}{\Sigma A} = \frac{(8)(1) + (2)(3) + (2)(3)}{8 + 2 + 2} = 1.67$$

Answer choice (C) is correct; the other choices do not give the correct distance on the x axis from the y axis, as calculated in the solution.

34. **(B)**

The chart below details the analysis. Column one shows the balance at the end of each year based on the declining balance method. Column two shows the amount depreciated each year by the declining balance method. The amount depreciated is 33% of the value at the end of the previous year. The straight line depreciation amount (column 3) is the previous year's value divided by the number of remaining years (five the end of year 1 and one at the end of year 5). At the end of the third year, this amount (column 3) is larger than the amount found by the declining balance method (column 2), so year 3 is the year the switch to straight line depreciation occurs. Thereafter, the same amount ($7,482) will be depreciated each year, until the end of the equipment's life, at which time its undepreciated value will be zero. Answer choice (D) is therefore wrong since it is better to switch to straight line at one point, and since the year is 3, answer choices (A) and (C) are also wrong. The actual amounts that would be used in the final cost analysis are in bold.

	1	2	3	4
year	declining balance value at end of year	declining balance depreciation amount	straight line depreciation (on column1 value)	value at end of year (after switch to straight line)
0	**50,000**	0	0	
1	**33,500**	**16,500**	10,000	
2	**22,445**	**11,055**	8,375	
3	15,038	7,407	**7,482**	**14,963**
4	10,076	4,963		**7,482**
5	6,751	3,325		**0**

35. **(B)**

Temperature (A) is extremely important in densification and grain growth. The transport rates of atoms are exponentially dependent on temperature. The surface energy (C) is the driving force for densification. Impurities (D) have a strong effect on densification, most often increasing the rate (especially if a liquid phase is present) and sometimes decreasing grain growth rate. Firing time (B) is the least important factor. The other factors [(A), (C), (D)] will determine the feasibility of a process, and the final state of the material will come into place in a relatively short time. If the desired process is not achieved in an adequate time, the necessary firing time will need to be extended by geometrically increasing factors. It is therefore desirable to change the other conditions to achieve the result in the desired time. The best answer is therefore firing time (B).

36. **(C)**
     The numerator of the equilibrium constant contains the concentration of the products of the reaction (either concentration in liquid solution or partial pressures of gases), and the denominator contains the concentrations of the reactants. Solids and liquids have constant concentrations (amount per volume) and so are not used in the determination of K. The equilibrium constant would therefore be given by $p_{AB} \times p_C^2$. The units of the equilibrium constant are therefore atm³. At equilibrium there would be twice as much C gas as AB gas. These can be called $2x$ and x. Using the equilibrium equation, $p_{AB} \times p_C^2 = 16 \times 10^{-8}$ atm³ we then see $(x)(2x)^2 = 16 \times 10^{-8}$ atm³. So, $x = 3.42 \times 10^{-3}$ atm. The pressures of the AB at equilibrium is therefore $x = 3.42 \times 10^{-3}$ atm and of the C is $2x = 6.84 \times 10^{-3}$ atm. By failing to use appropriate powers or factors, answer choices (A) and (B) may be obtained. The above analysis shows that the actual starting amount is not necessary to determine the answer, so (D) is incorrect.

37. **(B)**
     The solution requires expressing one variable in terms of the other.

From equation (1), solve for $x = 6 - 1.5y$

By substituting $(6 - 1.5y)$ into equation (2) wherever x appears:

$$5(6 - 1.5y) + 4y = 8$$

Solving for y:

$$y = 6$$

Solving for x in equation (1), we get $2x + (18) = 12$ or $x = -3$; therefore, our answer is $(-3, 6)$.

Answer choice (B) is correct; the other choices are not solutions to the simultaneous equations.

38. **(D)**
     Using the continuity equation $Q = VA$, where ρ is constant and:

ρ = density of water

A = area of pipe

V = velocity of water flow

Q = flow rate

Applying the conservation of mass yields the following equation:

$$V_2 A_2 = A_1 V_1$$

or:

$$V_2 = \frac{A_1}{A_2} V_1$$

Solving for V_2:

$$V_2 = \frac{[0.5^2(\pi/4)]}{[0.35^2(\pi/4)]} \times 5 \text{ m/s}$$

$$V_2 = 10.2 \text{ m/s}$$

Answer choice (D) is correct; the other choices do not give the correct velocity, as shown in the solution.

39. **(B)**

To determine the resistance between points a and b, find the equivalent resistance for each part of the circuit. First find the equivalent resistance of the series resistors between e and f:

$R_{eq} = 6 + 5 + 1 = 12 \; \Omega$, yielding (see diagram):

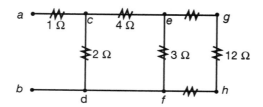

Next find the equivalent resistance of the parallel resistors in loop $eghf$:

$$\frac{1}{R_{eq}} = \frac{1}{12} + \frac{1}{3} = \frac{5}{12} \Omega, \text{ yielding (see diagram):}$$

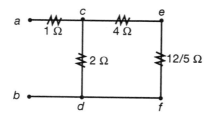

Now find the equivalent resistance of the series resistors between c and d:

$$R_{eq} = 4 + \frac{12}{5} = \frac{32\ \Omega}{5}, \text{ yielding:}$$

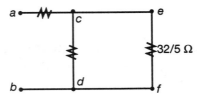

Find the equivalent resistance of the parallel resistors in loop *cefd*:

$$\frac{1}{R_{eq}} = \frac{1}{2} + \frac{5}{32} = \frac{21}{32}\Omega, \text{ yielding:}$$

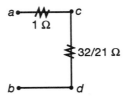

Finally, find the series resistance between a and b:

$$R_{eq} = 1 + \frac{32}{21} = \frac{53}{21}\Omega \text{ or } 2.52\ \Omega$$

Answer choice (B) is correct; the other choices do not give the correct resistance, as shown in the solution.

40. **(B)**
Second phases of higher modulus material is often added to make materials tougher. Failure mechanisms such as cracking (common in ceramics), flowing (common in polymers), and plastic deformation (such as in metals) are complicated by the second phase. Although in some cases the material may be weaker, this is not true in many cases, thus (C) is not the best answer. However, toughness will almost always increase. The reduced in effect of the failure mechanisms allow the composite to absorb more energy before failure, even if the actual strength of the material is not as high. The brittleness (A) and thermal shock resistance (D) usually improve when the second phase is included.

41. **(C)**
Recognizing that the differential equation is of the standard form:

$$\frac{dy}{dx} + Py = Q$$

or $\quad dy + Py\,dx = Q\,dx$

we note that $P = 1$ and determine the integrating factor, R, that would make the left side of the equation an "exact" differential. To do this we use the integrating factor function:

$$R = e\int P\,dx$$

In the problem, $R = e^x$, because $P = 1$.

Therefore, the problem becomes:

$$e^x dy + ye^x dx = e^{2x} dx$$

or

$$d(ye^x) = e^{2x} dx$$

solving,

$$ye^x = \frac{1}{2}e^{2x} + C$$

$$y = \frac{1}{2}e^x + Ce^{-x}$$

Answer choice (C) is correct; the other choices do not give a correct solution to the given equation.

42. **(D)**
Amdahl's Law defines the "Speed Up Ratio" that can be gained by a particular feature as:

Simplifying:

$$\text{Speed Up} = \frac{\text{execution time for the entire task without enhancement}}{\text{execution time for entire task using enhancement when possible}}$$

$$\text{Speed Up} = \frac{1}{(1 - \% \text{ of time cache can be used}) + \dfrac{\% \text{ of time cache can be used}}{\text{speed up using cache}}}$$

Therefore:

$$\text{Speed Up} = \frac{1}{(1-0.9) + \dfrac{0.9}{5}} = 3.6$$

Hence, the Speed Up produced by the cache is about 3.6 times.

Answer choice (D) is correct; the other choices do not give the correct speed up as shown in the solution.

43. **(B)**

First, apply Kirchhoff's first rule ($\Sigma I = 0$) to junction c:

$$I_1 + I_2 = I_3 \qquad (1)$$

Next, using Kirchhoff's second rule ($\Sigma \Delta V = 0$), analyze each loop:

Loop *abcd* : $\quad 10 - (6)I_1 - (2)I_3 = 0 \qquad (2)$

Loop *befc* : $\quad -14 - 10 + (6)I_3 - (4)I_2 = 0 \qquad (3)$

This gives three equations and three unknowns. By solving for I_1, I_2 and I_3 find that:

$$I_1 = 2 \text{ amps}$$

$$I_2 = -3 \text{ amps}$$

$$I_3 = -1 \text{ amp}$$

Answer choice (B) is correct; the other choices do not give the correct current for the circuit shown, as calculated in the solution.

44. **(D)**

Because the:

$$\lim_{x \to 0} \frac{\sin 3x}{2x} = \frac{0}{0}$$

the limit is indeterminate and l'Hôpital's Rule is used.

l'Hôpital's Rule states:

$$\frac{\lim f(x)}{\lim g(x)} = \frac{\lim f'(x)}{\lim g'(x)}, \text{ provided } g'(x) \text{ does not equal zero}$$

Therefore:

$$\lim_{x \to 0} \frac{\sin 3x}{2x} = \lim_{x \to 0} \frac{3 \cos 3x}{2} = \frac{3}{2}$$

Answer choice (D) is correct; the other choices do not give the value of the limit.

45. **(D)**

Find the equivalent resistance (R_{eq}) for the three resistors, knowing that resistors in a parallel arrangement are summed as reciprocals.

$$\frac{1}{R_{eq}} = \frac{1}{3} + \frac{1}{6} + \frac{1}{9}$$

$$R_{eq} = \frac{18}{11}\ \Omega$$

Using:

$$P = \frac{V^2}{R_{eq}}$$

where:

P = total power

V = voltage

calculate the total power dissipated:

$$P = \frac{V^2}{R_{eq}} = \frac{18^2}{(18/11)} = 198\ \text{W}$$

Answer choice (D) is correct; the other choices do not give the correct power dissipated.

46. **(B)**

A worker does not necessarily need to know the chemical name or composition of the material he or she is using (A), but should have access to the material safety data sheet (mSDS) (B). This sheet provides information describing the hazards of the materials, the potential effects of exposure, how to avoid exposure, and what to do if exposed. The chemical name and formula (C) are of no help to unskilled workers, except for purposes of identification. Commonly in plants though, materials are referred to by names other than the chemical name or formula. (D) is incorrect since (A) and (C) are incorrect, however, the mSDS will also contain the chemical name and composition.

47. **(C)**

At the triple point the solid, liquid, and vapor phases are in equilibrium. Therefore, the vapor pressure of the solid and liquid are equal. Setting both of the vapor pressure equations equal to each other:

$$-15,780/T - 0.755 \ln T + 19.25 = -\frac{15,250}{T} - 1.255 \ln T + 21.79$$

$$-\frac{530}{T} = -0.5 \ln T + 2.54$$

$$T = -\frac{530}{(-0.5 \ln T + 2.54)}$$

and solving for T, the answer is 712°K, which is 439°C, choice (C). Failure to convert to Celsius would leave 712°, choice (A). Converting by adding 273° Celsius rather than subtracting would result in choice (B). The equation can be solved by an iterative feedback process on a calculator. Also, since the correct answer is among the four choices, converting to degrees K and putting them into the equation will also reveal the correct response. If the vapor pressure of liquid were set to zero and solved, choice (D) would result.

48. **(B)**

Boiling zinc is on the liquid/vapor equilibrium line, so the temperature under these conditions can be found using the equation for vapor pressure of the liquid.

$$\ln p_l = \ln(5.0 \times 10^{-4}) = -\frac{15,250}{T} - 1.255 \ln T + 21.79$$

Solving for T gives 721.7°K. Now, using the Clausius-Clapeyron equation and taking the first derivative of the equation for $\ln p$:

$$\frac{d \ln p_l}{dT} = 15,250 T^{-2} - \frac{1.255}{T} = \frac{\Delta H_{L \to V}}{RT^2}$$

$$\Delta H_{L \to V} = RT^2 \left(15,250 T^{-2} - \frac{1.255}{T} \right)$$

which gives $\Delta H = 119$ kJ/mol. Choices (A) or (D) result from equating p/T or $\ln p/T$ to $\Delta H/RT^2$. Choice (C) results from an improper integration $(15,250T^{-2} + 1.255/T)$.

49. **(B)**

Solid zinc evaporating would occur at the solid/vapor equilibrium line. Therefore, the pressure temperature relationship is described by the vapor pressure of solids equation.

$$\ln p_s = \ln(10^{-8}) = -\frac{15,780}{T} - 0.755 \ln T + 19.25$$

Using an iterative feedback process on a calculator, or by plugging the possible answers into the equation, it can be found that the temperature is 478°K or 205°C, choice (B). By not converting or converting in the wrong direction to Celsius, choices (C) and (D) result. If p is used instead of $\ln p$, choice (A) will result.

50. **(B)**

Using the vapor pressure equations for liquid and solid zinc in equilibrium with vapor, it can be found that the equilibrium vapor pressure of the solid at 430°C (703°K) is equal to 2.89 atm, and of the liquid is 2.95 atm. Since the solid vapor pressure is lower, the temperature/pressure condition indicated must be below the triple point temperature, and the liquid phase cannot exist, as is shown in the phase diagram:

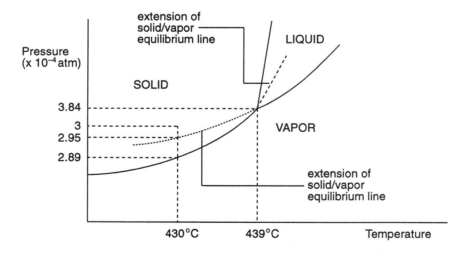

Therefore, answer choice (D) is wrong. Also, since 3×10^{-4} atm is at a higher vapor pressure than the solid/vapor equilibrium pressure, answer choices (C) and (A) are wrong. Since liquid zinc cannot exist at this temperature the equilibrium phase would be the solid, and so the vapor in question would precipitate as a solid, and the correct answer is (B).

51. **(A)**

Apply Kirchhoff's second rule by going around the circuit in the direction of the current:

$$\Sigma \Delta V = 0;\ E_1 - IR_1 - E_2 - IR_2 = 0$$

where:

I = current

R = resistance

E = voltage

Solve for I using the variables given:

$$I = \frac{E_1 - E_2}{R_1 - R_2} = \frac{12 - 6}{8 + 10} = \frac{1}{3}\ \text{amp}$$

Answer choice (A) is correct; the other choices do not give the correct current for the circuit shown, as calculated in the solution.

52. **(C)**

A table can be developed by substituting x and y into the general equation of a circle ($x^2 + y^2 + C_1 x + C_2 y + C_3 = 0$), hence:

Point	x^2	$+ y^2$	$+ C_1 x$	$+ C_2 y$	$+ C_3$	$= 0$
A(1, 0)	1		$+ C_1$		$+ C_3$	$= 0$
B(0, 1)		1		$+ C_2$	$+ C_3$	$= 0$
C(2, 2)	4	$+ 4$	$+ 2C_1 x$	$+ 2C_2$	$+ C_3$	$= 0$

There are now three equations and three unknowns (C_1, C_2, C_3). Therefore, through subtraction and substitution:

$$x^2 + y^2 - \frac{7}{3}x - \frac{7}{3}y + \frac{4}{3} = 0$$

Simplifying:

$$3x^2 + 3y^2 - 7x - 7y + 4 = 0$$

Answer choice (C) is correct; the other choices are not equations of a circle through the given points.

53. **(C)**

No matter how much a solid is prone to yielding, it will always exhibit some elastic deformation before plastically deforming, making (A) and (D) incorrect. Before much stress is applied, the copper will start to deform plastically. After the stress is relieved, some, but only a small amount of, elastic recovery will occur, making choice (B) incorrect. The recovery will actually be less than the original elastic deformation since the copper will be much harder now due to the deformation which occurred.

54. **(D)**

The slope of a line through $(4, -1)$ and $(2, 3)$ is:

$$m = \frac{y_2 - y_1}{x_2 - x_1} = \frac{3 - (-1)}{2 - 4} = \frac{4}{-2} = -2$$

The slope of a line perpendicular to a given line is equal to the negative inverse of the slope of the given line; therefore, the answer is:

$$-\frac{1}{m} = -\frac{1}{-2} = \frac{1}{2}$$

Answer choice (D) is correct, the other choices do not give the correct slope of a line perpendicular to the given line.

55. **(C)**

(A) Plastic flow refers to permanent deformation in a solid when it is strained, such as in a metal stretched beyond its yield point. A rubber band recovers its shape when relieved of stress. (B) Elastic strain refers to bonds between atoms being stretched, such as in an ionic or ceramic material, or a metal before its yield point. The atomic bonds in a rubber band are not being stretched, but straightened to line up with the direction of stress. This is elastomeric behavior (C). Viscous flow (D) refers to permanent deformation in liquid flow.

56. **(D)**

Although most materials commonly referred to as "glass" are ceramic, and therefore brittle, most polymers are also glassy, and are often made to be soft. Glass metals are also not brittle (A). Polymeric and ceramic glasses can both be made opaque, while metallic glass can transmit no light whatsoever (B). Glass metals like all metals are good electrical conductors (C). The only characteristics all glasses share are that they have no long range atomic structure (amorphous) and exhibit the "glass transition," so the answer is (D).

57. **(C)**

The equation of a line tangent to a curve is given by the derivative of the curve.

Differentiating $y = 3x^2 - x$ obtains:

$$\frac{dy}{dx} = 6x - 1$$

at $x = 0$, $y = 0$, $\frac{dy}{dx} = -1$.

Therefore, the slope is -1, substituting into the point slope equation of a line:

$$\frac{y - 0}{x - 0} = -1$$

Simplifying:

$$y = -x$$

Answer choice (C) is correct; the other choices do not give the equation of a line tangent to the given curve.

58. **(A)**

Using the general form $\begin{vmatrix} a & b \\ c & d \end{vmatrix} = ad - bc$:

$$\begin{vmatrix} 2 & -1 & 2 \\ 1 & 3 & -1 \\ 1 & 2 & 3 \end{vmatrix} = 2\begin{vmatrix} 3 & -1 \\ 2 & 3 \end{vmatrix} - (-1)\begin{vmatrix} 1 & -1 \\ 1 & 3 \end{vmatrix} + 2\begin{vmatrix} 1 & 3 \\ 1 & 2 \end{vmatrix}$$

Simplifying:

$$2(11) + 1(4) + 2(-1) = 24$$

Answer choice (A) is correct; the other choices do not give the correct value of the matrix.

59. **(C)**

Semiconductors have small band gaps, which allow electrons to jump from one level to another relatively easily, but the bands do not overlap, making choice (A) incorrect. Band gaps in ionic or covalently bonded solids, (B) and (D), generally have large band gaps. Metals (C) usually have overlapping band gaps.

60. **(C)**

The present, future, and annual costs of keeping the current machine and buying a new machine must be listed (as below). The new machine would presently cost $45,000, plus $5,000 to install, minus $10,000 for selling the old one, for a total cost of $40,000. Annually, the new machine would cost $1,000, but make $5,000 in profits, for a total yearly cost of –$4,000/year. The future cost at seven years is the salvage value of the systems (negative). The overall annual cost over seven years is then determined by adding the regular annual cost to the annual costs of the present and future values. This is done by multiplying them by the appropriate factors from the interest factor table: 0.2054 for annual cost given the present value, and 0.1054 for annual cost given the future value. For example, for the new machine option: $40,000 × 0.2054 – $4,000 – $6,000 × 0.1054 = $3,584. Since this is more expensive per year than the old system ($3,447), you would be losing $136 per year. Using the wrong factors or confusing the signs will result in the incorrect answers [(A), (B), or (D)].

P	A	F(7)	A (P, A, F)
0	$3,500	–$500	$3,447.3
$40,000	–$4000	–$6,000	$3,583.6
		Total:	$136.3

FE/EIT

FE: PM General Engineering Exam

Practice Test 2

FUNDAMENTALS OF ENGINEERING EXAMINATION

TEST 2

(Answer sheets appear in the back of this book.)

TIME: 4 Hours
            60 Questions

DIRECTIONS: For each of the following questions, choose the best answer from the four answer choices.

1.   Sound is measured on a logarithmic intensity-level scale called the decibel scale which defines the intensity level β in decibels (dB) of a sound intensity I by $\beta = \log I/I_O$, where I_O, the reference intensity, is 10^{-12} W/m^2. The intensity level of an industrial machine operating at location "A" is measured as 100 dB at location "B." If two identical machines are operating at location "A," what is the intensity level at location "B"?

(A) 103 dB   (C) 150 dB

(B) 130 dB   (D) 200 dB

2.   The point of inflection, if any, of $f(x) = x^3 - 3x^2 + 4$ is

(A) $(-1, 0)$.   (C) $(1, 2)$.

(B) $(0, 4)$.   (D) None.

3. The following sequence of statements does not comprise a FOR-TRAN program to compute and print the length of a square's side when its area is input because

    30 READ   AREA
    10 LENGTH = AREA**.5
    20 PRINT, LENGTH
    40 END

    (A) the line numbers are not in numerical order.

    (B) line 30 contains too many blank spaces.

    (C) the variable name LENGTH is invalid for real variables.

    (D) the sequence does not contain a STOP statement.

4. The sinusoidal current leaving a junction into which flow the following three currents is

    $$i_1 = 10\sqrt{2}\sin\omega t,$$

    $$i_2 = 15\sqrt{2}\sin(\omega t + 60°),$$

    $$i_3 = 20\sqrt{2}\sin(\omega t + 120°)$$

    (A) $15.0\sin(\omega t - 60.0°)$.   (C) $35.5\sin(\omega t + 105.2°)$.

    (B) $26.9\sin(\omega t + 134.2°)$.   (D) $44.1\sin(\omega t + 76.2°)$.

5. The magnitude of the bending moment five meters from the left support in the simply supported beam having a weight density of 100 N/meter is

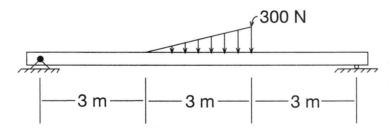

    (A) 616 Nm.   (C) 1,934 Nm.

    (B) 1,867 Nm.   (D) 1,991 Nm.

6. The magnitude of the piston velocity for the arrangement shown when the constant crankshaft velocity is 3,000 rpm clockwise is

   (A) 27 m/s.

   (B) 31 m/s.

   (C) 34 m/s.

   (D) 44 m/s.

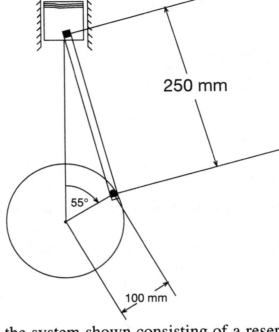

7. The operating point for the system shown consisting of a reservoir, a pump, a total of 400 meters of 300 mm inner diameter pipe having a Darcy friction factor of .02, and an open storage tank, when the pump has the operating characteristics shown by the given pump curve is

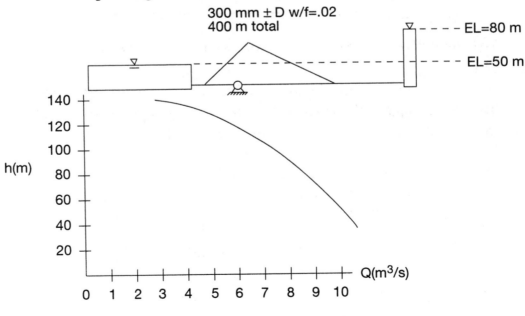

   (A) 5.5 m³/s.   (C) 6.5 m³/s.

   (B) 6.0 m³/s.   (D) 7.0 m³/s.

8. The derivative with respect to x of $y = (6 - x^6)^6$ is

   (A) $-36x(6 - x^5)^6$.

   (B) $(6 - x^6)^5 - 36x^5$.

   (C) $36x^5 - (6 - x^6)^5$.

   (D) $-36x^5(6 - x^6)^5$.

9. If widgets are sold at a profit of $10 per widgit when sold in batches of 100 or less, and at a per widget profit that is reduced by five cents times the number of widgets above 100 for batches of greater than 100, the batch size that yields the greatest profit per batch is

   (A) 100.

   (B) 101.

   (C) 150.

   (D) 300.

10. The resistance of the variable load resistor R when the maximum power is dissipated in the circuit shown is
    (Use Thevenin's theorem and the maximum power transfer theorem.)

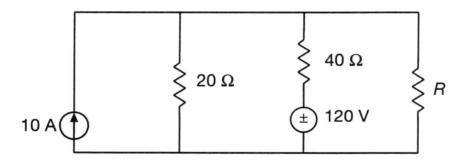

   (A) 13 ohm.

   (B) 26 ohm.

   (C) 52 ohm.

   (D) 173 ohm.

11. The displacement from time $= 0$ to 10 of a particle in rectilinear motion with initial ($t = 0$) speed of 20 m/s and acceleration as shown is
    (Solve by constructing acceleration and velocity curves from the data on the following page.)

   (A) 200 m.

   (B) 230 m.

   (C) 245 m.

   (D) 250 m.

time (sec)	acceleration (m/s²)
0 – 1	0
1 – 3	+5
3 – 4	–10
4 – 5	0
5 – 6	+15
6 – 9	–5
9 –10	0

12. The area between the curve $y = 5x - x^2$ and the x-axis in square units is

(A) 0.

(C) $\dfrac{250}{6}$.

(B) $\dfrac{125}{6}$.

(D) $\dfrac{625}{6}$.

13. Given a coefficient of friction between the block and the incline surface $\mu = .2$, the minimum spring constant k necessary to prevent the spring from compressing more than one meter (C–B) when impacted by the 20 kilogram block released from a distance of three meters along the incline (B–A), as shown, is

(A) 256 N/m.

(B) 493 N/m.

(C) 589 N/m.

(D) 768 N/m.

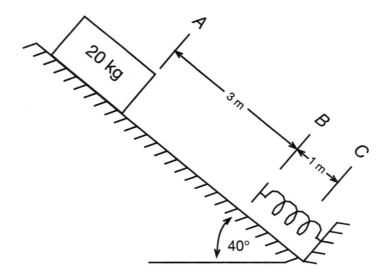

14. The solution to the following system of linear equations is

$$x + y + 3z = -75$$

$$4x + 6y - z = 600$$

$$3x - 2y + 4z = 150$$

(A) 140, –5, –70   (C) –50, –100, 25

(B) 5, 10, –30   (D) –100, –50, 25

15. The tension in each of the members *CD* and *DE* of the symmetrically loaded plane truss shown is

(A) 175 N.

(B) 225 N.

(C) 325 N.

(D) 375 N.

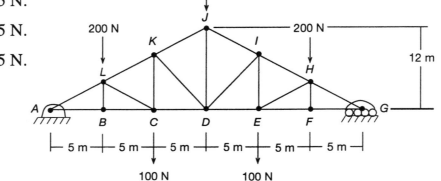

16. The discharge rate of water from a horizontally mounted venturi meter, for which the venturi coefficient of discharge is .85, when the pressures are 30 kPa and 70 kPa, as shown, is

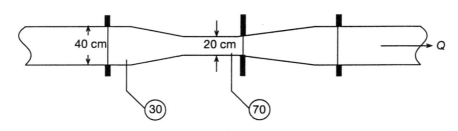

(A) 0.213 m³/s.   (C) 0.985 m³/s.

(B) 0.772 m³/s.   (D) 1.20 m³/s.

17. In order to produce a magnetic flux of 1.0 mWb, the current necessary in a 100 turn coil wound around a toroid of ferromagnetic material having a relative permeability of 500 with a uniform circular cross section and mean inner and outer diameters of 20 cm and 25 cm, respectively, assuming constant permeability and reluctance, is

$$(\mu_{air} = 4\pi \times 10^{-7} \text{ rational MKS})$$

(A) 7.29 ampere.

(C) 71.9 ampere.

(B) 22.9 ampere.

(D) 2.3×10^3 ampere.

18. The sum of tensions in the three guy wires securing a balloon that exerts a vertical buoyant force of 20 kilonewtons, where the point coordinates are $A = (-10, 0, -5)$, $B = (8, 0, 7)$, $C = (10, 0, 0)$, $D = (0, 6, 0)$, as shown, is

(A) 20.0 kN.

(B) 24.9 kN.

(C) 40.6 kN.

(D) 46.1 kN.

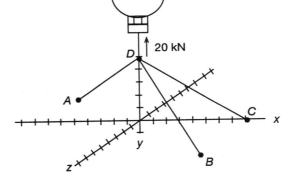

19. Neglecting minor losses, the total flow rate for the parallel-pipe system consisting of the 20 cm diameter pipe shown, where the head loss for each pipe is 20 m, and the pipe lengths and Darcy friction factors are as indicated, is

(A) 0.49 m³/s.

(B) 1.46 m³/s.

(C) 2.00 m³/s.

(D) 2.92 m³/s.

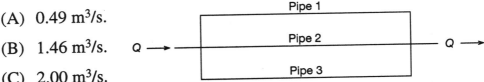

$$I_1 = 220 \text{ m} \qquad f_1 = .025$$

$$I_2 = 200 \text{ m} \qquad f_2 = .030$$

$$I_3 = 220 \text{ m} \qquad f_3 = .020$$

20. Two linear distances to a leaning building are measured from the same point as 30.0 meters and 33.0 meters with an angle of 30° between the measurements. The building's angle of inclination in degrees with respect to horizontal ground at its foundation is

(A) 83.

(C) 88.

(B) 85.

(D) 92.

21. The magnitude of the force acting on an electron 20 cm from a negative 1.5×10^{-10} coulomb point charge in a vacuum is

(A) -4.0×10^{-23} N.

(C) 5.4×10^{-18} N.

(B) -2.0×10^{-21} N.

(D) 3.4×10^{-17} N.

22. Ignoring minor losses, the power that must be supplied to a pump that is 70 percent efficient to force 1.0 m³/s of water from a lake with a surface elevation of 100 m to a reservoir with a surface elevation of 200 m through a total of 2,000 m of 50 cm diameter pipe is (Assume a Moody pipe roughness $\varepsilon = .05$ mm and kinetic viscosity $\nu = 1 \times 10^{-6}$ m²/s.)

(A) 0.61×10^3 kN.

(C) 1.45×10^3 kN.

(B) 1.02×10^3 kN.

(D) 2.32×10^3 kN.

23. The minimum coefficient of friction between the linear member of negligible mass and the ten kilogram block necessary to prevent rotation of the member about the right support is

(A) $\dfrac{1}{3}$.

(B) $\dfrac{2}{3}$.

(C) $\sqrt{1/2}$.

(D) $2\sqrt{1/2}$.

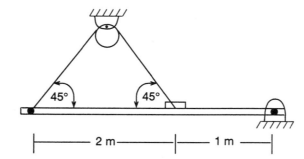

24. The distance between the points of intersection of the circle $x^2 + y^2 = 10$ and the line $3x - y = 0$ is

(A) $\sqrt{10}$.

(C) $\sqrt{32}$.

(B) 10.

(D) $\sqrt{40}$.

25. The magnitude of the bending moment about a line that intersects the points (0, 4, 0) and (2, 6, 1) made by forces of 200 kilonewtons directed along the x axis and 200 kilonewtons directed along the z axis from the point of application (5, 2, 3) in a three-dimensional orthogonal coordinate system (x, y, z) is

(A) 200 Nm.

(C) 400 Nm.

(B) 300 Nm.

(D) 600 Nm.

26. The magnitude of the area moment of inertia along either axis of the pipe section is

(A) .049 m⁴.

(B) .145 m⁴.

(C) .500 m⁴.

(D) 1.45 m⁴.

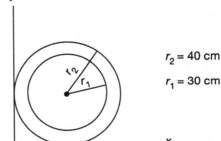

r_2 = 40 cm

r_1 = 30 cm

27. Water flows at a rate of 0.1m/s through the horizontally mounted 60 degree reducing bend shown in which the entrance pressure at the 200mm inner diameter entrance is four atmospheres. Neglecting the weight of water in the bend and friction effects, the magnitude of the force acting on the water is

(A) 7.15 kN.

(B) 11.4 kN.

(C) 13.5 kN.

(D) 18.7 kN.

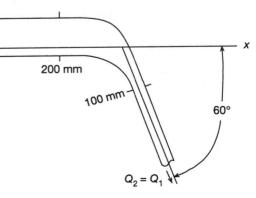

$Q_1 = 0.1$

200 mm

100 mm

60°

$Q_2 = Q_1$

28. The solution to the equation $2x^4 = 7x^2 - 3$ is

    (A) $\frac{1}{2}, -\frac{1}{2}.$

    (C) $\sqrt{3}, \sqrt{\frac{1}{2}}.$

    (B) $3, \frac{1}{2}.$

    (D) $3, -3.$

29. The variance of the numbers 52, 86, 99, 101, 43, 48, 49, 88, 76, 43, and 49 is

    (A) 49.5.

    (C) 495.

    (B) 66.7.

    (D) 667.

30. The output voltage from the ideal operational amplifier circuit shown is

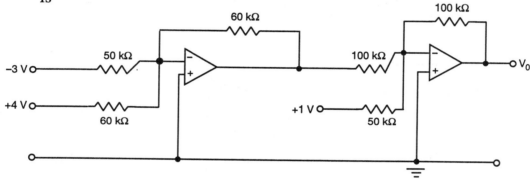

    (A) –2.4 volt.

    (C) –1.6 volt.

    (B) 2.4 volt.

    (D) 1.6 volt.

31. If the population of a nation increases at a rate proportional to the population, and the populations in the years 1900 and 2000 are 50 million and 300 million, respectively, the population in the year 2100 is

    (A) 500 million.

    (C) 800 million.

    (B) 750 million.

    (D) 1800 million.

32. A FORTRAN FORMAT statement used in conjunction with READ and WRITE statements to accommodate input and output consisting of sets of four real constants, each with either a positive or negative sign containing up to ten digits with up to eight digits to the right of the decimal point is

    (A) 100   FORMAT(4C10.8)

    (B) 50   FORMAT(4F12.8)

    (C) 200   FORMAT(4I10.8)

    (D) 100   FORMAT(4F10.8)

33. Current response in a reverse bias p-n semiconductor diode is essentially constant until the breakdown voltage is applied, at which point the voltage/current response curve slope becomes essentially infinite. The phenomenon that causes this infinite response is

    (A) Zener breakdown voltage.

    (B) covalent bond disruption.

    (C) excess recombining electron current.

    (D) excess recombining hole current.

34. A FORTRAN algebraic expression corresponding to the following algebraic equation is

$$x = \frac{2(a+b)^2/c - 4.5a/\sqrt{b+c}}{(a-b)^{\frac{1}{5}}}$$

    (A) $x = (2.\times(A+B)\times\times2/C-4.5\times A/(B+C)\times\times0.5)/(A-B)\times\times0.2$

    (B) $x = (2.\times(A+B)\times\times2/C)-(4.5\times A/(B+C)\times\times0.5)/(A-B)\times\times0.2$

    (C) $x = (2.\times(A+B)\times\times2/C-4.5\times A/(B+C)\times\times0.5)(A-B)\times\times-0.2$

    (D) None of the above.

35. Neglecting air effects, the initial speed necessary for a balloon traveling only in the x direction, such that a dart released from the balloon at coordinates $x = 0$ meters, $y = 50$ meters will strike a target on the ground at coordinates $x = 100$ meters, $y = 0$ meters, is

    (A) 15 m/s.

    (B) 23 m/s.

    (C) 31 m/s.

    (D) 35 m/s.

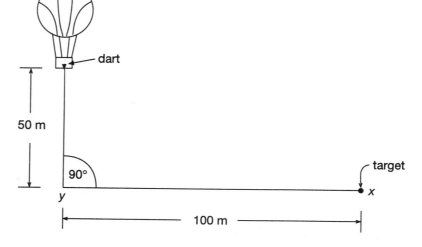

36. The antiderivative of $-\dfrac{40dx}{(6+8x)^6}$ is

    (A) $(6 + 8x)^{-5} + C.$

    (C) $\dfrac{1}{8}(6 + 8x)^{-5} + C.$

    (B) $\dfrac{1}{5}(6 + 8x)^{-5} + C.$

    (D) $\dfrac{1}{40}(6 + 8x)^{-5} + C.$

37. Which of the following is usually increased by the incremental addition of a second metal element into a pure elemental metal?

    (A) Hardness

    (C) Electrical conductivity

    (B) Thermal conductivity

    (D) Melting point

38. One thousand cubic feet of propane (as a gas) is burned using ten percent excess air of the same temperature. Assuming that all combustion products cool to the starting temperature after burning, what will the volumes of carbon dioxide, water vapor, nitrogen, and oxygen be? (Assume air is 21% oxygen and 79% nitrogen.)

	CARBON DIOXIDE	WATER VAPOR	NITROGEN	OXYGEN
(A)	3,000 ft^3	4,000	20,691	0
(B)	3,000 ft^3	4,000	20,691	500
(C)	3,000 ft^3	4,000	13,810	500
(D)	1,000 ft^3	1,000	3,762	100

39. Which one of the following is the most important to include on a package containing material with a potential for a serious safety problem if handled or opened incorrectly?

(A) A symbol describing the danger

(B) The danger described in English and Spanish

(C) A toll-free number to contact

(D) A material safety data sheet (MSDS)

40. In an adiabatic enclosure during an irreversible process, the entropy of a system will

(A) not change.

(B) decrease.

(C) increase.

(D) either increase or decrease, depending on whether work is done on or by the system.

Use the table below for Problems 41 and 42.

Factors for 10% interest rate compounded over *n* periods

n	F given P	P given F	F given A	A given F	P given A	A given P
1	1.1000	0.9091	1.0000	1.0000	0.9091	1.1000
2	1.2100	0.8265	2.1000	0.4762	1.7355	0.5762
3	1.3310	0.7513	3.3100	0.3021	2.4869	0.4021
4	1.4640	0.6830	4.6410	0.2155	3.1699	0.3155
5	1.6110	0.6209	6.1050	0.1638	3.7908	0.2638

P = Present value, F = Future value, A = Annuity (Annual amount for *n* years)

41. A proposed five-year project will cost $15,000 initially, and $3,500 per year for years one to five. At year five, there will be a salvage value of $5,000. Using a ten percent interest rate, compounded annually, calculate the overall annual cost for this project.

    (A) $3,500
    (B) $5,032

    (C) $5,500
    (D) $6,638

42. For the previous problem, what would the annual cost be if you first convert the costs to constant dollars using a five percent inflation rate?

    (A) $6,210
    (B) $6,361

    (C) $6,531
    (D) $6,904

Use the figure below for Problems 43 and 44.

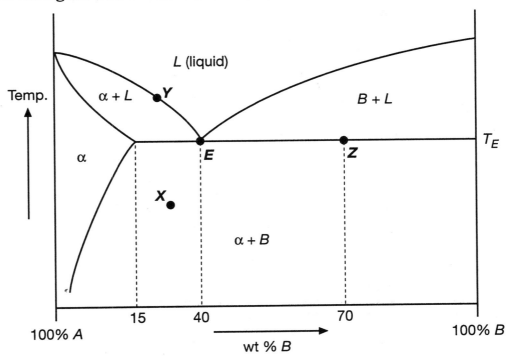

This binary phase diagram shows regions of equilibrium in the *A-B* system. The phase α is an alloy of *A*. *B* is the same phase which exists at 100% pure *B*. Only negligible amounts of *A* will alloy with *B* near the 100% *B* composition.

43. In the above binary diagram, how many phases are in equilibrium at the points *E* (the eutectic point), *X* (in the $\alpha + B$ region), *Y* (along the liquidus line), and *Z* (along the solidus line)?

	E	X	Y	Z
(A)	2	2	1	2
(B)	4	3	2	3
(C)	4	1	2	2
(D)	3	2	2	3

44. What fraction of the total material are α and *B* just below the eutectic at 70% (below point *Z*)?

	α	*B*
(A)	0.700	0.300
(B)	0.647	0.353
(C)	0.353	0.647
(D)	0.500	0.500

45. Which of the following can increase the degradation rate of metal by chemical corrosion?

    (A) Presence of an electric field

    (B) Cyclic stress

    (C) Temperature cycling

    (D) All of the above.

46. Which of the following people should receive credit as an author of a journal publication?

    (A) Technicians, researchers, staff members, etc. who have performed the experiments or assisted with equipment operation

    (B) People who have made significant intellectual contributions to the text of the article

    (C) Anyone who performed data analysis on the experimental results

    (D) Any of the above people

47. 1,520 liters of ammonium hydroxide solution with a concentration of 0.026 M must be neutralized. How much hydrochloric acid solution with a concentration of 0.05 M would be needed to perform the neutralization?

    (A) 395 liters   (C) 1,580 liters

    (B) 790 liters   (D) 2,923 liters

48. Engineering strain, ε_E, equals the final length minus the initial length divided by initial length, or $(\ell_f - \ell_o)/\ell_o$. The true strain is given by $\varepsilon_T = \ln(\ell_f/\ell_o)$. If a process is to apply ε_T of 0.85% on a cylinder of material with an elastic modulus 62 GPa, what is the engineering stress required?

(A) 529 MPa

(C) 83.1 MPa

(B) 527 MPa

(D) 52.7 MPa

49. The following figure shows the free energy, G, in a mixture of two components, A and B, at equilibrium. In the composition region between 100% A and X, one phase (α) exists. In the region between Y and 100% B, one phase (β) exists. Between the compositions X and Y, both α and β exist. Free energy curves are shown for both G_β and G_α. Which one of the following curves describes the equilibrium (minimum) free energy of the system from 100% A to 100% B?

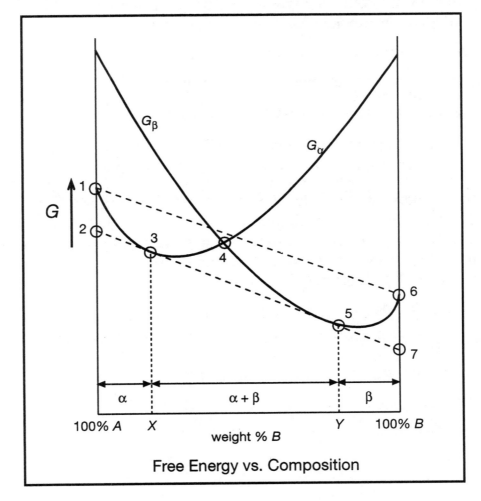

Free Energy vs. Composition

(A) 1–3–4–5–6

(C) 2–3–5–7

(B) 1–3–5–6

(D) 1–6

50. For reaction in an aqueous solution:

$$W^{2-}_{(aq)} + 2X_{(s)} \leftrightarrow \frac{1}{2}Y_{(g)} + Z^-_{(aq)} + H_2O_{(l)}$$

the equilibrium constant, K, would be given by

(A) $\dfrac{[Y]^{1/2} + [Z^-]}{[W^{2-}]}$.

(C) $\dfrac{[W^{2-}][X]^2}{[Y]^{1/2}[Z^-][H_2O]}$.

(B) $\dfrac{[Y]^{1/2}[Z^-]}{[W^{2-}]}$.

(D) $\dfrac{[Y]^{1/2}[Z^-][H_2O]}{[W^{2-}]}$.

51. Which of the following types of polymeric materials would be most difficult to incorporate into a remelting process?

(A) Amorphous polymer with side chains

(B) Amorphous polymer with no side chains

(C) Crystalline polymer with no side chains

(D) Amorphous cross-linked polymer

52. A container of ideal gas is at 200 atm pressure, has a volume of 50 liters, and is at 300K. The system is heated irreversibly to 400K at constant pressure (volume increases) and does 20,000 Joules work. Calculate the change in entropy for the system and for the surroundings. Gas constant, $R = 0.0821$ (liter·atm)/(K·mole) = 8.3144 J/(K·mole). Heat capacity for ideal gas: $c_p = 2.5R$, $c_v = 1.5R$.

	SYSTEM	SURROUNDINGS
(A)	2,428 J/K	1,316 J/K
(B)	23.97 J/K	1,316 J/K
(C)	2,428 J/K	1,216 J/K
(D)	23.97 J/K	1,216 J/K

53. Which one of the following would not constitute negligence in the performance of your duties as an engineer in a process which you designed and are responsible for maintaining?

(A) Damage to property of an outside company due to lack of application of minimum skill commonly expected by a person of your profession

(B) Injury to a person due to lack of application of minimum skill commonly expected by a person of your profession

(C) Damage to property of an outside company resultant from an occurrence which could not be foreseen by a person of your skill

(D) Damage to your company's property due to a willful breech of duty on your part

Use the figure below for Problems 54 and 55.

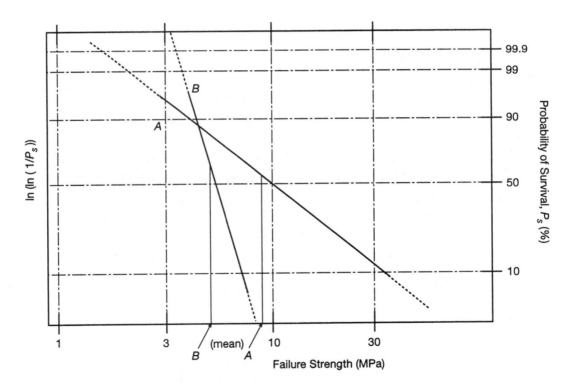

Two sets of failure data were analyzed using Weibull statistics. The plot above shows the results for the samples processed under condition A and condition B. The Weibull modulus and 95% confidence intervals for the two conditions are A: 9.6 ± 0.30, B: 7.4 ± 0.09. Process B is more expensive than process A.

54. Which conditions should be used if less than one in ten failures is allowable at 3 MPa? At 1 MPa?

	3 MPa	1 MPa
(A)	Either *A* or *B*	Either *A* or *B*
(B)	*B*	Either *A* or *B*
(C)	*B*	*A*
(D)	*A*	*A*

55. For the previous problem, which processing conditions should be used if less than one in a thousand failures are acceptable?

	3 MPa	1 MPa
(A)	*A*	*A*
(B)	*B*	*A*
(C)	Neither can be used.	*A*

(D) Cannot determine based on this analysis.

56. You are considering a project for which the major piece of equipment is already owned by your company from a previous project. The start-up costs, including some new, small pieces of equipment, are insignificant compared to the price of the major piece mentioned. Which of the following will have the most significant effect on the IRR (internal rate of return)?

(A) Estimated useful life of the major piece

(B) Break even point

(C) Original purchase price of the major piece

(D) Future value of other pieces of equipment purchased

57. In the figure at the top of the following page, a liquid with 50% *B* is cooled slowly until T_E, and then quenched to room temperature. Another batch of 40% *B* is cooled through the same heating cycle. What will the microstructures of these two batches be at room temperature? (*B* = black, α = white. Black and white striped areas represent layers of *B* and α.)

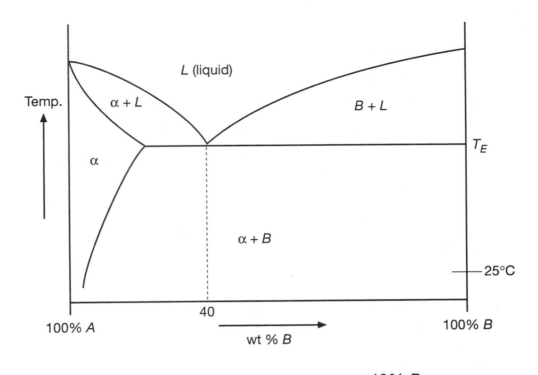

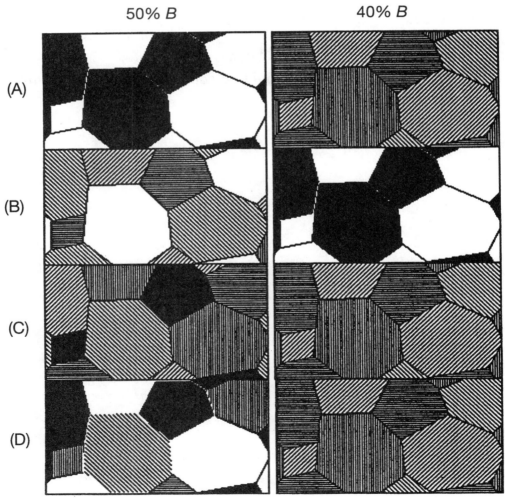

50% *B*   40% *B*

(A)

(B)

(C)

(D)

58. If an electron in an inner shell is knocked out by a high-energy electron or photon, an electron from a higher shell will take its place. This change in energy level will be accompanied by

    (A) the release of a photon of a characteristic wavelength.

    (B) the release of an electron of characteristic energy.

    (C) the release of either an electron or photon of characteristic energy or wavelength.

    (D) the release of an electron of characteristic energy or a photon of wavelength which depends on the characteristics of the particle which ejected the inner-shell electron originally.

59. For which one of the following would the results of a thermodynamic calculation concerning a chemical reaction be most applicable in predicting what will occur experimentally?

    (A) A hydrocarbon burning

    (B) A metal being cooled from a melt

    (C) A ceramic body being fired

    (D) The calculated results should be equally appropriate for any of the above experiments.

60. In which of the following cases is loading of a metal most likely to cause severe damage? (The figure is shown to clarify the choices, not to illustrate each situation.)

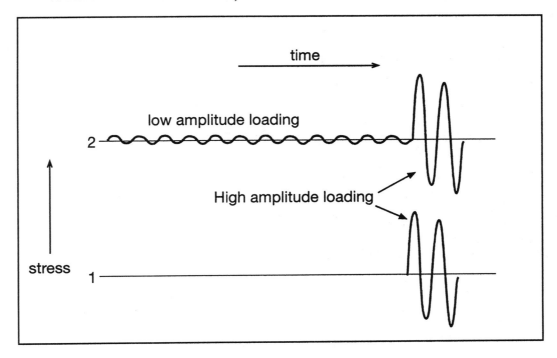

(A) Small amplitude cycling for an extended period with average stress level 2 followed by high amplitude loading at average stress level 1 for an extended period

(B) Large amplitude cycling for a short period with average stress level 2 followed by low amplitude loading at average stress level 2 for an extended period

(C) Small amplitude cycling for an extended period with average stress level 2 followed by high amplitude loading at average stress level 2 for a short period

(D) Both (B) and (C) will be equally likely to cause severe damage.

FUNDAMENTALS OF ENGINEERING

TEST 2

ANSWER KEY

1.	(A)	16.	(A)	31.	(D)	46.	(B)
2.	(C)	17.	(B)	32.	(B)	47.	(B)
3.	(C)	18.	(C)	33.	(B)	48.	(A)
4.	(D)	19.	(B)	34.	(A)	49.	(B)
5.	(B)	20.	(B)	35.	(C)	50.	(B)
6.	(B)	21.	(C)	36.	(A)	51.	(D)
7.	(C)	22.	(D)	37.	(A)	52.	(A)
8.	(D)	23.	(A)	38.	(B)	53.	(C)
9.	(C)	24.	(D)	39.	(A)	54.	(D)
10.	(A)	25.	(C)	40.	(C)	55.	(B)
11.	(C)	26.	(A)	41.	(D)	56.	(A)
12.	(B)	27.	(C)	42.	(B)	57.	(C)
13.	(D)	28.	(C)	43.	(D)	58.	(C)
14.	(A)	29.	(C)	44.	(C)	59.	(A)
15.	(D)	30.	(C)	45.	(D)	60.	(B)

DETAILED EXPLANATIONS
OF ANSWERS

TEST 2

1. **(A)**
The solution is found by first calculating the intensity with one machine in operation followed by calculating the intensity level with an intensity that is doubled for two machines operating.

First the intensity is determined for one machine operating with an intensity level of 100 dB.

$$100 \text{ dB} = 10 \log\left(\frac{I}{I_0}\right)$$

$$100 \text{ dB} = 10 \log\left(\frac{I}{10^{-12}}\right)$$

$$100 \text{ dB} = 10 \left(\log I - \log 10^{-12}\right)$$

$$\log I = -2$$

$$I = 10^{-2}$$

Now, the intensity level for two identical machines is calculated by the same formula.

$$\beta = 10 \log\left(\frac{2I}{I_0}\right)$$

$$\beta = 10 \log(2)\frac{10^{-2}}{10^{12}}$$

$$\beta = 103 \text{ dB}$$

The correct answer is (A). The other choices are not correct because they do not give the correct intensity.

2.   **(C)**

Points of inflection are those points where $f'' = 0$, and f is concave upward on one side of the point and concave downward on the other side of the point. Therefore, in addition to locating the point(s) where $f'' = 0$, the solution also requires evaluation of the function on either side of the point(s) as follows:

First the points where $f''(x) = 0$ are located by differentiating.

$$f(x) = x^3 - 3x^2 + 4$$

$$f'(x) = 3x^2 - 6x$$

$$f''(x) = 6x - 6 = 6(x - 1)$$

The points where $f''(x) = 0$ are determined by setting $f''(x) = 0$.

$$0 = 6(x - 1)$$

$$1 = x$$

Therefore, by solving $f(x)$ at $x = 1$ the point $(1, 2)$ is established as a possible inflection point. Now $f(x)$ is evaluated on either side of the possible inflection point. This step may be accomplished in a number of ways, which include using the first derivative test to establish the slope of the function in the region of interest or graphing the function to visually establish the shape of the function in the region of interest. The solution presented here is accomplished using a third method, the second derivative test. A graph of the function is also provided.

Because $f''(x) = 6(x - 1)$ is 0 at $x = 1$, it is negative for all $x < 1$, and is positive for all $x > 1$. Therefore, $(1, 2)$ is an inflection point. The function is graphed below.

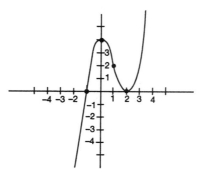

The correct answer is (C). The other choices are not correct because they do not give the correct inflection point.

3. **(C)**

Variable names beginning with *I*, *J*, *K*, *L*, *M*, or *N* are defined as integer variables. A variable name beginning with letters other than these must be used to define a real variable. In this example, because the square's side is defined as an integer variable, its values will be truncated during calculation.

Answer choice (A) is incorrect because FORTRAN program statements need not be numbered in order; program statements are executed in the order they are written. Answer choice (B) is incorrect because blank spaces may be included wherever desired in a FORTRAN statement. Answer choice (D) is incorrect because a STOP statement is not required with an END statement; the END statement accomplishes computation and program cessation.

4. **(D)**

The solution is easily accomplished using the phasor method.

First, the current functions are converted to phasor representation including converting maximum (max) currents to effective (rms) currents by

$$I_{rms} = I_{max} / \sqrt{2}.$$

The phasor representations are:

$$\bar{I}_1 = 10 \angle 0°$$

$$\bar{I}_2 = 15 \angle 60°$$

$$\bar{I}_3 = 10 \angle 120°$$

Expression of these phasors as complex numbers gives:

$$\bar{I}_1 = 10 + 0j = 10$$

$$\bar{I}_2 = 15(\cos 60° + j \sin 60°) = 7.5 + 13j$$

$$\bar{I}_3 = 20(\cos 120° + j \sin 120°) = -10 + 17.3j$$

Adding the complex numbers gives:

$$\bar{I} = 7.5 + 30.3j$$

Next, calculate the phasor resultant magnitude ($\bar{I}$) and phase lag (θ).

$$\bar{I} = \sqrt{7.5^2 + 30.3^2}$$

$$\bar{I} = 31.2$$

$$\theta = \sin^{-1}(\text{opp/hyp})$$

$$\theta = \sin^{-1}(30.3/31.2)$$

$$\theta = 76.2°$$

The resulting phasor representation is:

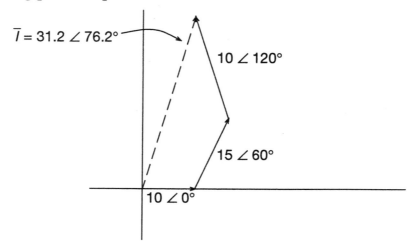

Finally, converting the phasor representation to the time varying format gives:

$$i = \sqrt{2}\,(31.2)\,\sin(\omega t + 76.2°)$$

$$i = 44.1\,\sin(\omega t + 76.2°)$$

The correct answer is (D). The other choices are not correct because they do not give the correct expression for the time variation of current.

5. **(B)**

The solution is obtained using the equations of equilibrium, with equivalent loads, at the location in question, five meters from the left support.

First, the reaction at the left support *A* is determined by rotational equilibrium.

Free-Body Diagram:

$$\Sigma M_B = R_A(9) - 900(4.5) - 450(4) = 0$$

$$R_A = 650 \text{ N}$$

Next, the moment at the specified location is determined by "cutting" the beam and applying equilibrium, including equivalent forces for the distributed loads, to determine the bending moment. A free-body diagram incorporating the equivalent loads and their points of application is shown.

Free-Body Diagram:

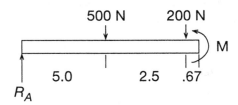

$$M = 650 \ N(5m) - 500 \ N(2.5m) - 200 \ N(.67m)$$

$$M = 1,867 \ Nm$$

The correct answer is (B). The other choices are not correct because they do not give the correct moment magnitude.

6. **(B)**

The solution of this problem of general plane motion for two rigid bodies connected at a point with angular motion can be obtained by relating the vector velocity components.

Initially, it is necessary to convert 3,000 rpm = 314.2 rad/sec, and calculate ϕ in the diagram below from the law of sines, $\phi = 19.13°$.

Here, the vector polygon method will be used. The vector equation for the velocities of points B and C is

$$v_B = v_C + v_{BC}$$

The direction of each vector is known: v_C is directed along the line AC, v_B is perpendicular to the line AB, and v_{BC} is perpendicular to the line BC. One line through point B is perpendicular to to the line AB, another one is perpendicular to BC.

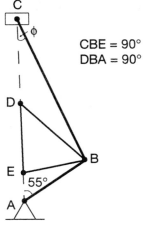

CBE = 90°
DBA = 90°

It is necessary to find the angles of triangle *BDE*. From the right triangle *DBA* we have the angle *EDB* as equal to 35. From right triangle *CBE* we have the angle *DEB* is equal 70.9. So the angle *DBE* is equal to 180-35-70.9 = 74.1. Since the lengths of the sides of the triangle are proportional to the magnitudes of the velocities, we can write (again, from the law of the sines)

$$v_C = v_B \times \frac{\sin DEB}{\sin DBE}, \text{ so}$$

$$v_C = v_B \times \frac{\sin 70.9}{\sin 74.1} = .98 \times v_B$$

On another side v_B is the velocity of rotation the end of AB, so $v_C = \omega_{AB} \times L_{AB}$, and we have: $v_C = .98 \times 314 \times .1 = 30.8 \text{m/sec}$.

The correct answer is (B). The other choices are not correct because they do not give the correct piston speed.

7. **(C)**
The solution is obtained by writing the system equation in terms of flow rate Q and finding the point of intersection of the system equation and pump curve.

First, the system equation is established from the energy equation.

$$0 + 0 + 50 + h_p = 0 + 0 + 80 + f\left(\frac{L}{d}\right)\left(\frac{V^2}{2g}\right)$$

Using continuity to solve in terms of Q gives:

$$h_p = 30 + 2.14Q^2$$

Now this system curve is plotted with the pump curve and the point of intersection is read. This is accomplished by first tabulating values of Qv·h_p then plotting the curve.

Q (m/s)	h_p (m)	Q (m/s)	h_p (m)
0	30	5	84
1	32	6	107
2	38	7	134
3	49	8	167
4	64		

Then the curve is plotted and the intersection is read.

From the curve below $Q_{intersect} = 6.5\ m^3/s$.

The correct answer is (C). The other choices are not correct because they do not give the correct operating point (flow rate).

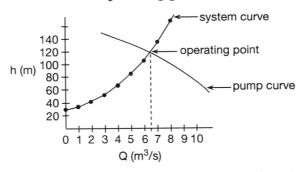

8. **(D)**

The solution is easily obtained using the chain rule for differentiation for a function of the form u^n.

Letting $u = 6 - x^6$, the problem becomes:

$$\frac{dy}{dx} = 6u^5 \times \frac{du}{dx}$$

Differentiating gives:

$$\frac{dy}{dx} = 6(6 - x^6)^5 \times -6x^5$$

$$\frac{dy}{dx} = -36x^5(6 - x^6)^5$$

The correct answer is (D). The other choices are not correct because they do not give the correct derivative of the function.

9. **(C)**

This solution requires defining an equation in terms of the variable, profit, to be maximized.

First, profit, P, is defined in terms of the number of widgets, x, supplied.

$$P = 10x \qquad\qquad x \le 100$$

$$P = x[10 - .05(x - 100)] \qquad\qquad x > 100\ \text{or}$$

$$P = 15x - .05x^2 \qquad\qquad x > 100$$

Next, the maxima of these functions are determined.

First, the ranges of the functions are noted.

$$P = 10x \qquad\qquad [0, 100]$$

$$P = 15x - .05x^2 \qquad [100, 300] \text{ (because for } x > 300, P \text{ is negative)}$$

The points 0 and 100 are used in the ranges for continuity.

Second, the critical numbers for the functions are determined; these are values where $F'(x) = 0$ or does not exist.

$$\text{for } P = 10x \qquad\qquad f' = 10$$

$$\text{for } P = 15x - .05x^2 \qquad f' = 15 - .1x$$

Setting $f'(x) = 0$ gives $x = 150$. Therefore, $x = 150$ is a critical number.

Third, the critical number and endpoints are tested to determine whether they are extrema. Using the first derivative test, it is determined that $x = 150$ is a maximum.

$$\text{for } x < 150 \qquad\qquad f' \text{ is positive}$$

$$\text{for } x > 150 \qquad\qquad f' \text{ is negative}$$

Now comparing the endpoint values to the value at $x = 150$, it is determined that the function assumes its maximum value at $x = 150$.

$$P(100) = 1{,}000$$

$$P(300) = 0$$

$$P(150) = 1{,}125$$

The correct answer is (C). The other choices are not correct because they do not give the correct batch size at which profit is maximized.

10. **(A)**

The solution is obtained by use of the maximum power transfer theorem which states that maximum power is dissipated when the resistance is equal to the Thevenin resistance, and by use of Thevenin's theorem which allows solution of linear resistive networks by representing them as an equivalent voltage source with resistance in series.

First, a Thevenin equivalent voltage for the circuit is determined by removing the resistor, thus creating an open circuit consisting of a simple voltage source with series resistor. In the circuit given, this includes converting the voltage source and 40 ohm resistor to an equivalent current source with parallel resistor. The open circuit is then used to calculate the open circuit or Thevenin voltage V_{oc}.

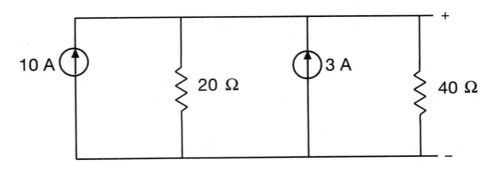

$$V_{oc} = 10 + \frac{3}{\left(\dfrac{1}{20} + \dfrac{1}{40}\right)}$$

$$V_{oc} = 173.33 \text{ volt}$$

Second, the Thevenin short-circuit current I_{sc} is calculated by creating a short circuit (i.e., by setting $V = 0$).

$$I_{sc} = I_1 + I_2 + 0\left(\frac{1}{\left(\dfrac{1}{20} + \dfrac{1}{40}\right)}\right)$$

$$I_{sc} = 13 \text{ ampere}$$

Finally, the Thevenin resistance is calculated as:

$$R_0 = V_{oc}/I_{sc}$$

Solving,

$$R_0 = \frac{173.33}{13}$$

$$R_0 = 13.3 \text{ ohm}$$

The correct answer is (A). The other choices are not correct because they do not give the correct current at which the maximum power is dissipated.

11. **(C)**

This solution is obtained, as suggested, by use of acceleration and velocity curves where acceleration = dv/dt and displacement is the sum of the areas above and below the v–t curve.

The a–t and v–t curves:

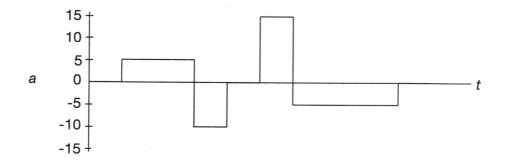

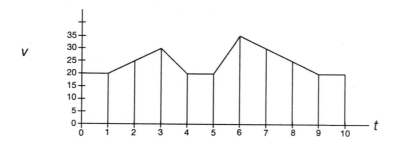

The area enclosed by the v–t curve from 0 to 10 seconds is 245 m.

The correct answer is (C). The other choices are not correct because they do not give the correct displacement.

12. **(B)**

The solution requires finding the intersection of the curve and the x-axis and integrating the function between these points to calculate the area between them.

First, the intersection is determined as the points where $y = 0$.

$$5x - x^2 = 0$$

$$x = 0, 5$$

Then the area is calculated as the definite integral between the points of intersection.

$$A = \int_0^5 5x - x^2 dx$$

$$A = \left[\frac{5x^2}{2} - \frac{x^3}{3} \right]_0^5$$

$$A = \left[\frac{125}{2} - \frac{125}{3} - (0) \right]$$

$$A = \frac{125}{6} \text{ square units}$$

The correct answer is (B). The other choices are not correct because they do not give the correct area between the curve and the x-axis.

13. **(D)**

This solution is obtained by considering the balance of energy in going from point A to point C. It can be written such that

$$P_A - A_{AC} = P_C$$

Here P_A is the change of the potential energy of the body in going from point A to point C, A_{AC} is the work of the friction force in going from point A to point C, and P_C is the potential energy of the spring.

The amount of P_A is the product of the body weight on the change of its vertical coordinate. So $P_A = mg \sin\alpha(L_1 + L_2)$, where α is the slope, L_1 is the distance between A and B, and L_2 is the distance between B and C.

A_{AC} can be calculated with the formula

$$A_{AC} = F_f (L_1 + L_2),$$

where F_f is a friction force. It is clear that $F_f = mg\mu\cos\alpha$.

The amount of P_C can be found using spring constant k: $P_C = .5kL_2^2$. Using $P_A - A_{AC} = P_C$ and solving it in regard of k we will have:

$$k = 2mg(L_1 + L_2)(\sin\alpha - \mu\cos\alpha) / L_2^2 = 768N/m$$

The correct answer is (D). The other choices are not correct because they do not give the correct minimum spring constant k.

14. **(A)**

The solution is obtained by using linear algebra and matrix theory including Cramer's Rule by creating a matrix of the equations and calculating determinants of x, y, and z, as the quotient of matrices having the system matrix as the denominator. This requires finding:

$$x = \frac{\det x}{\det \text{system}}, \; y = \frac{\det y}{\det \text{system}}, \text{ and } z = \frac{\det z}{\det \text{system}}$$

First, the system matrix and its determinant are established.

$$\begin{vmatrix} 1 & 1 & 3 \\ 4 & 6 & -1 \\ 3 & -2 & 4 \end{vmatrix} = 1\begin{vmatrix} 6 & -1 \\ -2 & 4 \end{vmatrix} - 1\begin{vmatrix} 4 & -1 \\ 3 & 4 \end{vmatrix} + 3\begin{vmatrix} 4 & 6 \\ 3 & -2 \end{vmatrix} = -75$$

Now the values of x, y, and z are determined as the quotients of their matrices and the system matrix by employing Cramer's Rule which allows substitution of the appropriate row or column in a system matrix to determine the variables. Also, noting that the right-hand sides of the three equations contain a multiple of 75 enables simplification by reducing each value in the substitution column by this multiple prior to forming the matrices; this multiple will be factored back into the solution after the matrices have been determined, in accordance with the rules of linear algebra.

Thus, the determinant for x is:

$$x = \frac{\begin{vmatrix} -1 & 1 & 3 \\ 8 & 6 & -1 \\ 2 & -2 & 4 \end{vmatrix}(75)}{-75} = 140$$

Similarly, the determinants of y and z are determined.

$$y = \frac{\begin{vmatrix} 1 & -1 & 3 \\ 4 & 8 & -1 \\ 3 & 2 & 4 \end{vmatrix}(75)}{-75} = -5$$

$$z = \frac{\begin{vmatrix} 1 & 1 & -1 \\ 4 & 6 & -1 \\ 3 & -2 & 2 \end{vmatrix}(75)}{-75} = -70$$

Hence, the solution to the system of equations is:

$$x = 140, \; y = -5, \; z = -70$$

The correct answer is (A). The other choices are not correct because they do not give the correct solution to the system of equations.

15. **(D)**

Finding the solution by the method of sections is most expedient.

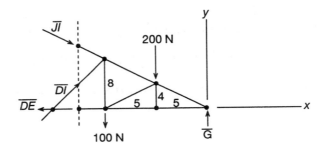

First, the truss is "cut" to expose a section including the load desired, in this case either *CD* or *DE* which are the same by symmetry. Because the truss and its loading are symmetric, either side may be selected for analysis. A free-body diagram for a cut exposing the force *DE* is shown.

The reaction at the right support *G* is calculated from the entire truss.

$$G = \frac{1}{2} (3 \times 200 \text{ N} + 2 \times 100 \text{ N})$$

$$G = 400\text{N}$$

Next using the equation of rotational equilibrium, the sum of moments about the point containing the unknown force *DE* is taken. Point *I* is selected.

$$\Sigma M_I = -8DE - (5)200 + 10G = 0$$

Combining and solving for *DE*

$$DE = 375 \text{ N (T)}$$

The correct answer is (D). The other choices are not correct because they do not give the correct tension in the members *CD* and *DE*.

16. **(A)**

This solution is obtained directly by use of the venturi equation.

$$Q = \left(\frac{C_v A_2}{\sqrt{1 - \left(\dfrac{A_2}{A_1} \right)^2}} \right) \times \sqrt{2g(h_1 - h_2)}$$

where:

Q = discharge rate

C_v = venturi coefficient of discharge

A = area of flow at location of pressure measurement

h = pressure head at location of pressure measurement

Solving:

$$Q = \left(\frac{(.85)(.0314)}{\sqrt{1 - \left(\dfrac{.0314}{.126} \right)^2}} \right) \times \sqrt{19.62(3.06)}$$

$Q = 0.213$ m³/s

The correct answer is (A). The other choices are not correct because they do not give the correct flow rate.

17. **(B)**

The current is determined using the basic equation of magnetic circuits

$F = NI$

where:

F = magnetic force (AT)

N = number of turns (T)

I = current (A)

and:

$$\Phi = F/R = \text{magnetic flux (Wb)}$$

$$R = I/\mu A = \text{reluctance (AT/Wb)}$$

$$I = \text{mean path length (m)}$$

$$\mu = \text{permeability } (4\pi \times 10^{-7} \text{ in rationalized MKS})$$

$$A = \text{cross sectional area (m}^2)$$

Combining and solving for I after determining I and A,

$$I = \frac{\Phi I}{\mu A N}$$

$$I = \frac{\left(1 \times 10^{-3} \text{Wb}\right)(.2257\pi m)}{\left(4\pi \times 10^{-7} \times 500\right)\left(4.9 \times 10^{-4} m^2\right)(100T)}$$

$$I = 22.9 \text{ ampere}$$

The correct answer is (B). The other choices are not correct because they do not give the correct current to produce the required flux.

18. **(C)**
The solution requires determining the tension in each guy wire in terms of the directed unit vectors then summing the tensions.

First, the unit vectors are established and the tensions are resolved into components.

Free-Body Diagram:

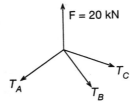

Then, for T_A:

$$n_A = \frac{-10i - 6j - 5k}{\sqrt{10^2 + 6^2 + 5^2}}$$

$$n_A = -0.788i - 0.473j - 0.394k$$

Similarly, for T_B and T_C :

$$n_B = 0.655i - 0.491j + 0.573k$$

$$n_C = 0.857i - 0.545j + 0k$$

Next, the equilibrium equations for each direction are used to solve for the tensions in each wire.

$$\Sigma F_x = -0.788T_A + 0.655T_B + 0.857T_C = 0$$

$$\Sigma F_y = -0.473T_A - 0.491T_B + 0.545T_C + 20 \text{ kN} = 0$$

$$\Sigma F_z = -0.394T_A + 0.573T_B + 0T_C = 0$$

Simultaneous solution of these equilibrium equations by any method will give the tension in each wire.

$$T_A = 19.5 \text{ kN}$$

$$T_B = 13.4 \text{ kN}$$

$$T_C = 7.69 \text{ kN}$$

The sum of the tensions is 40.6 kN.

The correct answer is (C). The other choices are not correct because they do not give the correct sum of the tensions in the wires.

19. **(B)**

The solution for a parallel-pipe system is made by use of continuity and loss relationships.

For this system:

$$Q = Q_1 + Q_2 + Q_3$$

$$h_f = h_{f1} + h_{f2} + h_{f3}$$

Note that for a typical real-world problem, friction factors may not be given and that this necessitates an iterative solution to establish velocities and appropriate friction factors/losses.

Here, friction factors are given so we proceed directly to the Darcy equation for the losses.

$$20 \text{ m} = (V_1^2/2g)(L/d)f = (V_2^2/2g)(L/d)f = (V_3^2/2g)(L/d)f$$

$$20 \text{ m} = (V_1^2/19.62)(220/.2).025$$

$$= (V_2{}^2/19.62)(200/.2).030$$

$$= (V_3{}^2/19.62)(220/.2).020$$

Solving gives:

$$V_1 = 3.78 \text{ m/s} \quad V_2 = 3.62 \text{ m/s} \quad V_3 = 4.23 \text{ m/s}$$

And from continuity:

$$Q = (V_1 + V_1 + V_1)A$$

$$Q = 1.46 \text{ m}^3/\text{s}$$

The correct answer is (B). The other choices are not correct because they do not give the correct total flow rate.

20. **(B)**

This solution is obtained by using the law of cosines and the law of sines.

From a sketch of the problem it is seen that two sides and an included angle are given. This information is used to determine the third side of the triangle using the law of cosines.

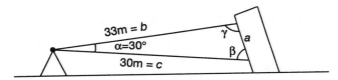

Defining variables as indicated in the sketch, the law of cosines gives:

$$a^2 = b^2 + c^2 - 2bc \cos\alpha$$

$$a^2 = 33^2 + 30^2 - 2(33)(30)\cos\alpha$$

$$a = 16.56 \text{ meters}$$

Now the angle of inclination is determined by using the law of sines.

$$\frac{a}{\sin a} = \frac{b}{\sin\beta}$$

$$\frac{16.56}{\sin 30} = \frac{33.0}{\sin\beta}$$

$$= 85.12° = \beta$$

The correct answer is (B). The other choices are not correct because they do not give the correct angle.

21. **(C)**

The force on an electron at a distance from another charge is determined by Coulomb's Law, which gives the fundamental formula for the force acting on two charged particles.

$$F = \frac{kQ_1Q_2}{r^2}$$

where:

F = force acting on the particle (N)

Q_1 = particle charge (C)

Q_2 = particle charge (C)

r = distance between the particles (m)

k = proportionality constant ($k = 1/4\pi\epsilon$)

($k_{vacuum} = 9 \times 10^9 N$) ($\epsilon$ = permitivity (F/m))

Solving:

$$F = \frac{(9 \times 10^9)(-1.5 \times 10^{-10})(-1.602 \times 10^{-19})}{.2^2}$$

$$F = 5.4 \times 10^{-18} N$$

The correct answer is (C). The other choices are not correct because they do not give the correct force on the electron.

22. **(D)**

This solution is obtained using the energy equation and the Moody diagram to determine friction loss.

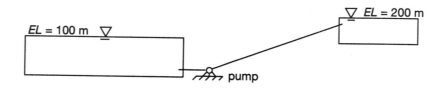

First the energy equation for the system is written.

$$\frac{p_2}{\Gamma} + \frac{V_2}{2g} + z_2 + h_f = \frac{p_1}{\Gamma} + \frac{V_1}{2g} + z_1 + h_p$$

$$h_p = 200 - 100 + h_f$$

Now h_f is calculated using the Darcy equation in conjunction with the Moody diagram.

$$h_f = f\,(L/d)\,(v^2/2g)$$

where continuity is used to determine $V = 5.09$ m/s.

Next, the Reynolds number is determined:

$$R_e = \frac{Vd}{v}$$

$$R_e = \frac{(5.09)(.5)}{1 \times 10^{-6}} = 2.55 \times 10^6$$

Now using the Moody diagram at $R_e = 2.55 \times 10^6$ and $\varepsilon/d = .0001$ gives a friction factor $f = 0.0125$.

Now,

$$h_f = (.0125)\left(\frac{2,000}{.5}\right)\left(\frac{5.09^2}{19.62}\right) = 66 \text{ m}$$

and,

$$h_p = 200 - 100 + 66 = 166 \text{ m}$$

Finally, power is calculated.

$$W = \frac{Q\Gamma h}{\eta}$$

$$W = \frac{(1.0)(9,800)(166)}{0.7}$$

$$W = 2.32 \times 10^3 \text{ kW}$$

The correct answer is (D). The other choices are not correct because they do not give the correct power to the pump.

23. **(A)**

The solution is independent of the mass, as will be shown, and is obtained using the equations of force and rotational equilibrium. Two free-body diagrams are needed as shown.

Free-Body Diagram:

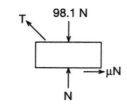

Free-Body Diagram:

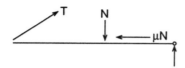

First, force equilibrium:

$$\Sigma F_x = T\sin45° - \mu N = 0$$

$$T\sin45° = \mu N$$

Then rotational equilibrium about the hinged support:

$$\Sigma M_o = (3)T\cos45° - (1)N = 0$$

$$3T\cos45° = N$$

Note here that the value of the normal force N (98.1 N) could be inserted into the equations; however, it is unnecessary because it will factor out.

Finally, combining and solving for μ:

$$\mu = \frac{T\sin45°}{N}$$

$$\mu = \frac{T\sin45°}{3T\cos45°}$$

$$\mu = \frac{1}{3}$$

The correct answer is (A). The other choices are not correct because they do not give the correct minimum coefficient of friction.

24. **(D)**

This solution requires solving the two equations $x^2 + y^2 = 10$ and $3x - y = 0$ simultaneously to obtain the points of intersection followed by calculating the distance between these points.

First, the two equations are solved simultaneously in any of several possible ways. Here, the linear equation is solved first for y.

$$3x - y = 0$$

$$y = 3x$$

Then this value of y is substituted into the equation of the circle to solve for x.

$$x^2 + y^2 = 10$$

$$x^2 + (3x)^2 = 10$$

$$10x^2 = 10$$

$$x = \pm\sqrt{1}$$

$$x = +1, -1$$

Then substituting the values of x into the linear equation, the corresponding values of y are obtained.

For $x = 1$, $y = 3$

For $x = -1$, $y = -3$

Therefore, the equations intersect at the two points $(1, 3)$ and $(-1, -3)$.

Now, the distance between these points is determined using the distance formula:

$$|P_1P_2| = \sqrt{|x_2 - x_1|^2 + |y_2 - y_1|^2}$$

$$|P_1P_2| = \sqrt{40}$$

The correct answer is (D). The other choices are not correct because they do not give the correct distance between the points of intersection.

25. **(C)**

The solution is easily obtained recognizing that a determinant can be used to solve the mixed vector multiplication.

Here, $M = n \times (r \times F)$,

where:

M = moment

n = unit vector of the line

r = distance from the origin to the point of application

F = force

Or in determinant form:

$$M = \begin{vmatrix} n_x & n_y & n_z \\ r_x & r_y & r_z \\ F_x & F_y & F_z \end{vmatrix}$$

First, the unit vectors for the line are calculated.

$$n = \frac{1}{I\left(I_x i + I_y j + I_z k\right)}$$

$$n = \frac{2}{3}i + \frac{2}{3}j + \frac{1}{3}k$$

Now the distance r is calculated from any point on the line and the force vector. For this problem selecting the point $(0, 4, 0)$ and the point of application simplifies calculation.

$$r = (x_2 - x_1)i + (y_2 - y_1)j + (z_2 - z_1)k$$
$$r = 5i - 2j + 3k$$

Now solving the determinant:

$$M = \begin{vmatrix} 2/3 & 2/3 & 1/3 \\ 5 & -2 & 3 \\ 200 & 0 & 200 \end{vmatrix} = -400$$

The correct answer is (C). The other choices are not correct because they do not give the correct magnitude of the bending moment.

26. **(A)**
This solution is obtained by inspection and reference to formulas provided in the NCEES engineering examination booklet. It could also be obtained by establishing the appropriate formula through integrating the expressions for the area moments over the distances given, r_1 and r_2.

Using the appropriate formula for the given shape:

$$I_x = I_y = 5\pi\frac{r_2^4}{4} - \pi r_2^2 r_1^2 - \pi\frac{r_1^4}{4}$$

$$I_x = I_y = 5\pi\frac{(.4)^4}{4} - \pi(.4)^2(.3)^2 - \pi\frac{(.3)^4}{4}$$

$$I_x = I_y = .049 \text{ m}^4$$

The correct answer is (A). The other choices are not correct because they do not give the correct magnitude of area moment of inertia.

27. **(C)**
The solution is obtained using the momentum equation, and continuity and Bernoulli equations.

Sketch:

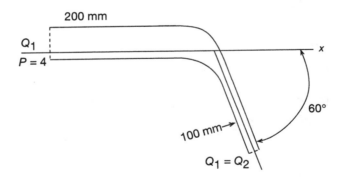

The momentum equation in the x and z directions gives:

$$\Sigma F_x = \Sigma V\rho V_x \times A$$

$$\Sigma F_z = \Sigma V\rho V_z \times A$$

In this case:

$$\Sigma F_x = p_2 A_2 \cos 60 - p_1 A_1 + \rho Q(V_2 \cos 60 - V_1)$$

$$\Sigma F_z = -p_2 A_2 \sin 60 + \rho Q V_2 \sin 60$$

Determine V_1 and V_2 from continuity.

$$V_1 = \frac{Q_1}{A_1} \qquad V_2 = \frac{Q_2}{A_2}$$

$$V_1 = \frac{0.1}{.013} = 3.18 \text{ m/s}$$

$$V_2 = \frac{0.1}{.018} = 5.56 \text{ m/s}$$

Now determine p_2 from the Bernoulli equation.

$$\frac{p_2}{\Gamma} + \frac{V_2}{2g} + z_2 = \frac{p_1}{\Gamma} + \frac{V_1}{2g} + z_1$$

$$p_2 = 494{,}600 \text{ N/m}^2$$

Now determine the force using the momentum equation.

$$\Sigma F_x = (494{,}600)(.018)\cos 60 - (505{,}000)(.0314)$$
$$+ \rho(.1)(5.56\cos 60 - 3.18)$$
$$\Sigma F_z = -(494600)(.018)\sin 60 + \rho(.1)(5.56)\sin 60$$
$$F_x = -11{,}446 \text{ N}$$
$$F_y = -7{,}228 \text{ N}$$

The resultant force is 13,537 N.

The correct answer is (C). The other choices are not correct because they do not give the correct magnitude of force on the bend.

28. **(C)**

This solution requires recognizing that the equation $2x^4 = 7x^2 - 3$ is a quadratic where x is squared.

First, rewrite the equation with the terms equal to zero.

$$2x^4 - 7x^2 + 3 = 0$$

Then let a variable (v) equal x^2.

$$2v^2 - 7v + 3 = 0$$

Now solve by any quadratic method. Here the quadratic formula is used.

$$v = \frac{-b \pm \sqrt{b^2 - 4ac}}{2a}$$

$$v = \frac{7 \pm \sqrt{49 - 24}}{4}$$

$$v = 3, 1/2$$

Now substitute x^2 back in for v ($x = \sqrt{v}$) to obtain:

$$v = \sqrt{3}, \ \sqrt{\frac{1}{2}}$$

As a check, the values of x can be substituted into the original equation.

The correct answer is (C). The other choices are not correct because they do not give the correct solution to the equation.

29.   **(C)**
Variance, s^2, is defined as:

$$\sigma^2 = \sum \frac{(x - \bar{x})^2}{n}$$

Therefore:

$$\sigma^2 = \sum \frac{(x - 66.7)^2}{11}$$

$$\sigma^2 = \frac{5488}{11} = 495$$

The correct answer is (C). The other choices are not correct because they do not give the correct variance of the numbers.

30. **(C)**

The output voltage from the simple operational amplifier is calculated using the formula for gain in an inverting op-amp:

$$G_O = \frac{-R_F}{R_1} = \frac{V_0}{V_S}$$

or

$$V_O = -\left(\frac{R_F}{R}\right)V_S$$

Defining the circuit components as shown, the solution is obtained.

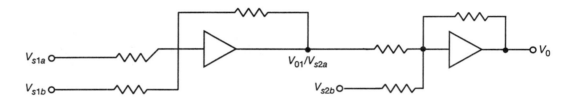

Substituting and solving first for V_{01}:

$$V_{01} = -\left[\left(\frac{60}{50}\right)(-3) + \left(\frac{60}{60}\right)(4)\right]$$

$$V_{01} = -0.4$$

Then using this value to solve for V_0

$$V_0 = -\left[\left(\frac{100}{100}\right)(-0.4) + \left(\frac{100}{50}\right)(1)\right]$$

$$V_0 = -1.6 \text{ volt}$$

The correct answer is (C). The other choices are not correct because they do not give the correct output voltage for the given amplifer circuit.

31. **(D)**

The solution requires writing and solving a simple differential rate equation.

First, letting P = population, the rate of increase is:

$$\frac{dP}{dt} = kP$$

Then writing the differential equation in the integral form gives:

$$\int \frac{dP}{P} = k \int dt$$

Antidifferentiating and introducing a constant, $\ln C$, gives:

$$\ln P + \ln C = kt$$

$$\ln PC = kt$$

$$PC = e^{kt}$$

Now to determine C the value of P at $t = 0$ is substituted into $PC = e^{kt}$:

$$50C = 1$$

$$C = 1/50; \; P = 50e^{kt}$$

Now the value of k is determined by substituting the boundary conditions into the equation.

At $t = 100$, $P = 300$.

$$300 = 50e^{100k}$$

$$6 = e^{100k}$$

Solving:

$$k = \frac{1}{100} \ln 6$$

$$k = \frac{1}{100} (1.792)$$

$$k = .0179$$

So at the year 2100 ($t = 200$):

$$P = 50e^{200(.0179)}$$

$$P = 1.794 \times 10^9$$

The correct answer is (D). The other choices are not correct because they do not give the correct population in the year 2100.

32. **(B)**

In addition to the requirement that they be numbered, FORTRAN FORMAT statements for real constants must consist of FORMAT and five terms within parenthesis (aFw.d):

- a is an integer indicating the number of real constants (record length) to be read.

- F indicates the format type, in this case a real constant.

- w is an integer representing the number of characters in each constant (field length) including signs, blanks, and decimal points.

- d is an integer representing the number of digits to the right of the decimal point.

Answer choice (A) is incorrect because the letter C does not designate a real constant format, the w term should be 12, and there is no C format designation. Answer choice (C) is incorrect because the I format designation indicates an integer constant. Answer choice (D) is incorrect because the w term should be 12.

33. **(B)**

The diode current-to-voltage response is exponential to forward bias and is essentially constant to reverse bias until the breakdown or Zener voltage is applied; at this point covalent bonds in the p and n materials are almost completely disrupted releasing many electrons that increase conductance.

Answer choice (A) is not correct because the term Zener breakdown voltage is the name given to the point at which the breakdown (disruption) occurs in the negative portion of the current/voltage curve. Answer choice (C) is not correct because recombining electron current refers to the movement of electrons from the voltage source into the n region during recombination of excess electrons with holes (to preserve charge neutrality) due to forward bias. Answer choice (D) is not correct because recombining hole current refers to the movement of holes from the voltage source into the p region during recombination of excess holes with electrons (to preserve charge neutrality) due to forward bias.

34. **(A)**

The given algebraic equation is converted to a FORTRAN algebraic expression in accordance with the hierarchical rules of FORTRAN operations as follows:

  (i)   Operations within parentheses are performed first.

  (ii) Exponentiation is performed next.

  (iii) Multiplication and division are performed next.

  (iv) Addition and subtraction are performed next.

Answer choice (B) is incorrect because the additional set of parentheses causes the second part of the numerator and the denominator to be evaluated before subtracting the result from the first part of the numerator. Answer choice (C) is incorrect because the operation of multiplication for the numerator term of the algebraic equation is not designated; operations cannot be implicit. Answer choice (D) is incorrect as explained for (B) and (C).

35. **(C)**

The solution is obtained by using the equations of motion where the acceleration in the x direction is constant and the time for vertical travel under the influence of gravity determines the time of travel in the x direction.

First, vertical motion gives:

$$y = y_0 + v_0 t + \frac{1}{2} a t^2$$

$$0 = 50 - 0 - \frac{1}{2}(9.81)t^2$$

$$t = 3.19 \text{ sec.}$$

Then horizontal motion gives:

$$x = x_0 + v_0 t + \frac{1}{2} a t^2$$

$$100 = 0 + v_0(3.19) + 0$$

Finally solving for v_0:

$$v_0 = 31.35 \text{ m/s}$$

The correct answer is (C). The other choices are not correct because they do not give the correct initial speed.

36. **(A)**

The solution is facilitated by recognizing the equation as of the general form $u^n(du/dx)$, where:

$$u = 6 + 8x \text{ and } n = -6$$

First, the integral is written in the form:

$$\int -40\,(6 + 8x)^{-6}\,dx$$

Next $du = 8dx$ is obtained by multiplying the integral by the constant $-\dfrac{1}{5}$ to give:

$$\int -5(6 + 8x)^{-6}\left(-\frac{1}{5}\right)(-40dx)$$

Finally, the integral of the form $u^n\,(du/dx)$ is solved.

$$\int = \frac{-5(6+8x)^{-5}}{-5} + C$$

$$\int = (6 + 8x)^{-5} + C$$

The correct answer is (A). The other choices are not correct because they do not give the correct antiderivative.

37. **(A)**

Mechanisms of yielding in pure metals are impeded by different atoms, so hardness increases. On the other hand, thermal and electrical conduction in pure metals is also impeded by different atoms, so these properties [(B), (C)] decrease. The melting point (D) may either decrease or increase, depending on the elements in question, so the best answer is (A).

38. **(B)**

First, write the equation for combustion:

$$C_3H_8 + 5O_2 \rightarrow 3CO_2 + 4H_2O$$

To burn 1,000 cubic feet of propane, 5,000 cubic feet of oxygen would be needed, which requires 5,000/0.21 = 23,810 cubic feet of air. Including ten percent excess air, this would be 26,191 cubic feet. After combustion, there would be 3,000 cubic feet of carbon dioxide, 4,000 cubic feet of water vapor, and the excess material from the air. The 26,191 cubic feet of air originally contained 26,191 × 0.21 = 5,500 cubic feet of oxygen, of which 5,000 was needed for combustion. The remaining 500 cubic feet of oxygen is excess. The remainder of the air (26,191–5,500 = 20,691 cubic feet) is nitrogen, which remains after the combustion. Using an improperly balanced equation or different quantities of combustion gases will result in the incorrect responses, (A), (C), and (D).

39. **(A)**

Although all of these would be good to have on the box, it is most important to have a symbol which can be understood by anyone. It should not be assumed that everyone can read in English, Spanish, or any language (B). Toll-free numbers (C) and MSDSs (D) are good and necessary resources, but they do not warn of immediate or possible danger. Universal symbols (A) should be used such as those for flammable, corrosive, this end up, do not stack, poison, etc.

40. **(C)**

In an adiabatic system heat cannot enter or leave. Therefore, entropy cannot decrease [(B) or (D)], as this would be against the second law of thermodynamics; it can only be created. In a reversible process, entropy would not change (A), but since this is an irreversible process, entropy will increase (C).

41. **(D)**

The overall annual cost can be found by adding the annual equivalents of the present and future values to the regular annual cost of $3,500. The annual cost of the initial layout of $15,000 is found by multiplying by the factor 0.2638 in the "A given P" column. The salvage value of $5,000 is converted to the annual equivalent using the factor 0.1638. The total is then $3,500 + $15,000 × 0.2638 – $5,000 × 0.1638 = $6,638. Other quantities [(A), (B), (C)] may result from using other numbers from the table, or by using an oversimplified method.

42. **(B)**

Converting to constant dollars can be done by multiplying the cost each year by $(0.95)^n$ where n is the year. The constant dollars are then as in the following table:

Actual $	15,000	3,500	3,500	3,500	3,500	3,500	–5,000
Year	0	1	2	3	4	5	5
Constant $	15,000	3,325	3,159	3,001	2,851	2,708	–3,869
P given F factor	—	0.9091	0.8265	0.7513	0.6830	0.6209	0.6209
Present value	15,000	3,023	2,611	2,255	1,947	1,682	–2,402

Also shown in the table are the factors from the ten percent interest factor table for finding the present value given the future value for each number of years. The total of the last row of numbers is $24,114, which is the present value for the project in constant dollars. The annual cost given the present cost (multiplying by 0.2638) is equal to $6,361. The other choices [(A), (C), (D)] would result from using incorrect values from the table, or by leaving out steps in this process.

43. **(D)**

A phase is a part of the material with distinct borders and composition. A phase is not restricted to solid, liquid and gas. The alpha and B phases are distinct from each other in the microstructure. The liquid in the "L" region and that in the $(\alpha + L)$ or $(B + L)$ region are the same phase. At the eutectic the α, B, and L phases all exist in equilibrium. At Y, along the liquidus line, the α and liquid are in equilibrium. At X the α and B solid phases are in equilibrium, and at Z along the solidus the α and B solid phases are in equilibrium with the liquid also. The correct answer is therefore E: 3, X: 2, Y: 2, and Z: 3. The other answer choices [(A), (B), and (C)] are therefore incorrect.

44. **(C)**

Just below the solidus line is a two phase region $(\alpha + B)$. In a two phase region, the fraction of each phase can be determined by drawing tie lines to the left, up to the α region, and to the right, up to the 100% B composition. The distance of the line opposite to the composition in question divided by the total length of the line is equal to the fraction.

Therefore, the closer you are to the B composition, the smaller the line segment to the right would be, and hence a smaller fraction of the α composition. In this case, the fraction of α would be 30/85, and the frac-

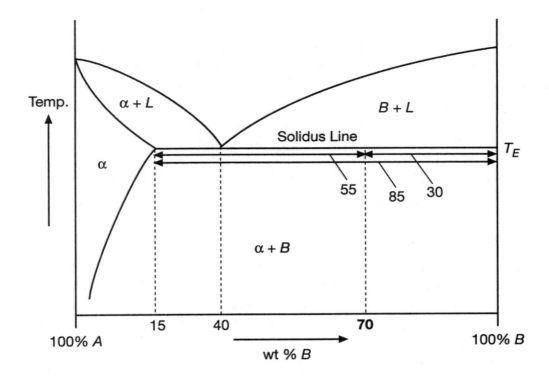

tion of *B* would be 55/85, or 0.353 and 0.647, respectively. Therefore, answer (C) is correct and choices (A), (B), and (D) are incorrect.

45. **(D)**

All of these can alter the chemistry of the system. Electric fields (A) can cause the chemistry of the system to change. For example, oxidation may occur more quickly. Stress (B) increases the reactivity of the chemical bonds. Also, work hardening leads to cracking, vacancies, and dislocations, which offer more reaction sites. Altering the temperature (C) can change the chemistry of the surface as well as increasing rates of reaction. More than one corrosion mechanism may even be taking place since different ones may be dominant at different temperatures. The best answer is therefore (D), all of the above.

46. **(B)**

Only people who have made significant contributions to the creation of the actual article should be listed as authors. Although others [(A),(C)] such as project supervisors, technicians, secretaries, etc. were necessary to perform the work, they did not write the article and should not be given credit for having done so. Their contributions may however be noted in an acknowledgment. The article is an intellectual work and thus only the contributors to it as such should be authors. Since (A) and (C) are incorrect, (D) is also incorrect.

47. **(B)**

Ammonium hydroxide, NH_4OH has one mole of hydroxide ions per mole, which is to be neutralized by H^+ ions from the hydrochloric acid. At 0.026M, the moles of OH^- would be:

$$1,520 \text{ liters} \times \frac{0.026 \text{ mole } NH_4OH}{\text{liter}} \times \frac{1 \text{ mole } OH^-}{\text{mole } NH_4OH} = 39.52 \text{ mole } OH^-$$

This must be neutralized with 39.52 mole H^+ from the HCl. The amount of 0.05M HCl which must be used is:

$$39.52 \text{ mole } H^+ \times \frac{1 \text{ mole HCl}}{1 \text{ mole } H^+} \times \frac{1 \text{ liter}}{0.05 \text{ mole HCl}} = 790.4 \text{ liters}$$

If the wrong number of ions per mole is used (twice as many for one or the other), other choices [(A), (C), and (D)] would result.

48. **(A)**

From the given equation, the engineering strain is:

$$\varepsilon_E = \frac{\ell_f - \ell_0}{\ell_0} = \frac{\ell_f}{\ell_0} - 1 = \left[e^{\ln(\ell_f/\ell_0)} \right] - 1$$

and since $\ln(\ell_f/\ell_0) = \varepsilon_T$, then,

$$\left[e^{\ln(\ell_f/\ell_0)} \right] - 1 = e^{\varepsilon_T} - 1 = e^{(0.0085)} - 1 = 0.8536\%$$

The engineering stress is equal to the engineering strain times the elastic modulus, which is 529 MPa. If random lengths are used for the initial or final lengths, then calculating the other quantity to plug into the engineering strain equation directly will result in incorrect answers [(B), (C), and (D)]. This cannot be done because the strain changes continuously during stressing, and the two quantities must be related logarithmically or exponentially.

49. **(B)**

The minimum free energy of the system depends on the phases which exist at any given composition. In the α region, the minimum point is along the G_α curve (1–3). Similarly in the β region, the free energy of the system is from 5–6. In the ($\alpha + \beta$) region both phases exist, so the free energy of the physical mixture of the two phases, given by the tangential line of the two curves, represents the free energy of the system (3–5). So, from 100% A to 100% B, the free energy is described by line 1–3–5–6. The other responses [(A), (C), and (D)] are incorrect since they follow different paths.

50. **(B)**

In an aqueous solution the numerator of the equilibrium constant contains the concentration of the products of the reaction ($[y]^{1/2}$ and $[Z^-]$), and the denominator contains the concentrations of the reactants ($[W^{2-}]$). Solids and liquids have constant concentrations (amount per volume) and so are not used in the determination of K, making (C) an incorrect response. This also applies to liquid water in an aqueous solution, making both (C) and (D) incorrect. The aqueous concentrations and partial pressures are to be multiplied, not added, making (A) incorrect.

51. **(D)**

The other responses [(A), (B), and (C)] are types of polymers which melt when moderately heated. Even when there are side chains, or if crystallized, the chains will eventually become separated since they are bonded with weak Van der Waals bonds. The crystalline polymer (C) would require a higher temperature and the side linked polymer (B) would be more viscous, also requiring a higher temperature, but both would melt. Cross-linked polymers have the same type of bonds between chains as within the chains, i.e., covalent bonds. In order to break the cross-linked bonds holding the chains together, a temperature would be required which would break up the chains also, thereby decomposing the entire material. This choice (D) is therefore the most difficult to incorporate into a remelting process.

52. **(A)**

Substituting into the equation $PV = nRT$,

$$(200 \text{ atm})(50 \text{ } \ell) = n\left(0.0821\frac{\ell \times \text{atm}}{\text{K} \times \text{mol}}\right)(300 \text{ K}),$$

you can find that there are 406 moles in the system. With the same expression you can find that after the expansion there are 66.6 liters of gas. Now from the second law of thermodynamics,

$$dS = \frac{\delta q_{\text{reversible}}}{T},$$

so at constant pressure:

$$dS = \frac{\left(nc_p dT\right)}{T}, \text{ so } \Delta S = \int\left(\frac{nc_p dT}{T}\right),$$

which starting at T_1 and finishing at T_2,

$$\Delta S = n\, c_p\, \ln(T_2/T_1) = 406 \text{ mol} \times 2.5R \times \ln(400K/300K) = 2{,}428 \text{ J/K},$$

making (B) and (D) incorrect. Note that R in units of J/(K × mole) were used here, where previously it was used in l × atm/(K × mol). Now, the total heat flow, q, can be found from the first law:

$$\Delta U = q - w.$$

Since:

$$\Delta U = n\, c_v\, \Delta T, \text{ then:}$$

$$q = n\, c_v\, (400K - 300K) + w = 406 \text{ mol} \times 1.5R \times 100K + 20{,}000 \text{ J}$$

$$= 526{,}347 \text{ J}$$

Now,

$$\Delta S_{\text{surroundings}} = \frac{q}{T}, = \frac{526{,}347J}{400K} = 1{,}316 \text{ J/K},$$

making (C) also incorrect, and leaving (A) as the correct choice.

53. **(C)**

Negligence occurs when damage to persons or property occurs due to acts on your part [(A) and (B)]. Negligence only applies if you did not apply knowledge which someone of your profession would be expected to know. If an incident occurred due to an occurrence which you would not be expected to predict, you would not have acted negligently. Therefore, the correct answer is (C). You can be held liable to damage to your own company's property if you acted negligently (D).

54. **(D)**

Although the mean strength of B is higher, and it has a higher Weibull modulus, there is less scatter. The critical factors here are probability of survival and cost. If one in ten must survive, the 90% probability of survival line should be examined. At 3 MPa either A or B may survive. At 1 MPa, again, either A or B may be used. Since process A is cheaper, it should be used in both cases, making the best answer (D), and the other choices [(A), (B), and (C)] incorrect.

55. **(B)**

For 3 MPa, condition *A* does not lie within the 99.9% confidence interval, which is what is required for 1 in 1,000 maximum failure, so *B* must be used, which does fall within the interval, making choice (A) incorrect. For 1 MPa, both are within the interval, so *A*, the less expensive alternative, is used, making choice (B) the best and choice (C) invalid. Choice (D) is also not valid: Weibull statistics are commonly used in this way to determine survival rates of materials. Furthermore, the confidence intervals on the Weibull moduli are very small, so the lines can be extended to at least the 99.9% levels for this decision.

56. **(A)**

(A) This is an important factor since it may limit the lifetime of the project. If a new piece of this equipment must be purchased at a later date, the long-term IRR would be severely diminished. (B) Although the time before a monetary break even occurs is often considered, it does not affect the IRR. (C) Original purchase price is a sunk cost. It should have absolutely no bearing on any decisions. (D) Future value of equipment is usually not significant. Since the start-up costs are not significant compared to the purchase price, they will be of little value at the end of the project. The best answer is (A).

57. **(C)**

During the first part of the cooling process of the 50% *B* liquid, grains of *B* will form while in the (*B* + liquid) region. When the eutectic temperature is reached, the mix is cooled rapidly, and the *B* grains will remain intact. The remainder of the liquid will form α and *B* phases simultaneously when brought below the eutectic. The quenching will result in a lamellar structure of the two phases, which is fine alternating planes of α and *B*, as seen in the figure. The lamellar structure as well as the *B* grains which had formed in the (*B* + *L*) region will both be in the final microstructure, as seen in choice (C) only, making choices (A), (B), and (D) incorrect. The liquid with 40% *B* will not go through the (*B* + *L*) region, and will remain entirely liquid until the quenching occurs. The final microstructure of this composition will consist of lamellae only, as seen in choice (C).

58. **(C)**

When an electron falls from a higher to lower shell, it is going to a lower energy level, and so the atom must release energy, either as a photon or an electron (known as an Auger electron). Therefore, choice (C) is best since it accounts for either possibility, and (A) and (B) each only account for one possibility. Since the old and new energy levels (orbitals) are at discrete and defined energy levels, the energy of the released particle is restricted to finite numbers, which are characteristic of the type of atom in question. This is commonly used to identify the atoms which are present in a material of unknown composition. Once the inner-shell electron is ejected from the atom, the energy of the initial photon or electron is not relevant to the characteristic energy or wavelength, making choice (D) incorrect.

59. **(A)**

Thermodynamic calculations predict the properties a system will have at equilibrium. However, kinetics will determine how quickly a system will go towards equilibrium. Metals cooling (B) and especially a ceramic being fired (C) have high activation energies in the solid state, and may not reach equilibrium during a process. A burning hydrocarbon reacts quickly, and will most likely reach the equilibrium state during the process, so the best answer is (A). Choice (D) is incorrect since (A) is a better choice than (B) and (C).

60. **(B)**

In case (A) , even though it is for an extended period, the magnitude of the high amplitude stress is lower than that of the extended period high stress of low amplitude, so it cannot do any further damage to the metal. In the other cases, the high amplitude stress for a short period is more likely to create flaws than the low amplitude stress at extended periods. In case (B), however, the high amplitude precedes the low amplitude period, where in (C) it follows. In (C) any flaws created during high amplitude stress will not have the opportunity to grow further. In (B) they are created first, so during the low amplitude stress they can grow by work hardening, possibly leading to failure. Therefore, (B) is the worst case scenario and the best answer. Choice (D) is incorrect since (B) is a better choice than (C).

FE/EIT

FE: PM General Engineering Exam

Answer Sheets

FUNDAMENTALS OF ENGINEERING –
AFTERNOON SESSION
Test 1
ANSWER SHEET

1. Ⓐ Ⓑ Ⓒ Ⓓ
2. Ⓐ Ⓑ Ⓒ Ⓓ
3. Ⓐ Ⓑ Ⓒ Ⓓ
4. Ⓐ Ⓑ Ⓒ Ⓓ
5. Ⓐ Ⓑ Ⓒ Ⓓ
6. Ⓐ Ⓑ Ⓒ Ⓓ
7. Ⓐ Ⓑ Ⓒ Ⓓ
8. Ⓐ Ⓑ Ⓒ Ⓓ
9. Ⓐ Ⓑ Ⓒ Ⓓ
10. Ⓐ Ⓑ Ⓒ Ⓓ
11. Ⓐ Ⓑ Ⓒ Ⓓ
12. Ⓐ Ⓑ Ⓒ Ⓓ
13. Ⓐ Ⓑ Ⓒ Ⓓ
14. Ⓐ Ⓑ Ⓒ Ⓓ
15. Ⓐ Ⓑ Ⓒ Ⓓ
16. Ⓐ Ⓑ Ⓒ Ⓓ
17. Ⓐ Ⓑ Ⓒ Ⓓ
18. Ⓐ Ⓑ Ⓒ Ⓓ
19. Ⓐ Ⓑ Ⓒ Ⓓ
20. Ⓐ Ⓑ Ⓒ Ⓓ
21. Ⓐ Ⓑ Ⓒ Ⓓ
22. Ⓐ Ⓑ Ⓒ Ⓓ
23. Ⓐ Ⓑ Ⓒ Ⓓ
24. Ⓐ Ⓑ Ⓒ Ⓓ
25. Ⓐ Ⓑ Ⓒ Ⓓ
26. Ⓐ Ⓑ Ⓒ Ⓓ
27. Ⓐ Ⓑ Ⓒ Ⓓ
28. Ⓐ Ⓑ Ⓒ Ⓓ
29. Ⓐ Ⓑ Ⓒ Ⓓ
30. Ⓐ Ⓑ Ⓒ Ⓓ

31. Ⓐ Ⓑ Ⓒ Ⓓ
32. Ⓐ Ⓑ Ⓒ Ⓓ
33. Ⓐ Ⓑ Ⓒ Ⓓ
34. Ⓐ Ⓑ Ⓒ Ⓓ
35. Ⓐ Ⓑ Ⓒ Ⓓ
36. Ⓐ Ⓑ Ⓒ Ⓓ
37. Ⓐ Ⓑ Ⓒ Ⓓ
38. Ⓐ Ⓑ Ⓒ Ⓓ
39. Ⓐ Ⓑ Ⓒ Ⓓ
40. Ⓐ Ⓑ Ⓒ Ⓓ
41. Ⓐ Ⓑ Ⓒ Ⓓ
42. Ⓐ Ⓑ Ⓒ Ⓓ
43. Ⓐ Ⓑ Ⓒ Ⓓ
44. Ⓐ Ⓑ Ⓒ Ⓓ
45. Ⓐ Ⓑ Ⓒ Ⓓ
46. Ⓐ Ⓑ Ⓒ Ⓓ
47. Ⓐ Ⓑ Ⓒ Ⓓ
48. Ⓐ Ⓑ Ⓒ Ⓓ
49. Ⓐ Ⓑ Ⓒ Ⓓ
50. Ⓐ Ⓑ Ⓒ Ⓓ
51. Ⓐ Ⓑ Ⓒ Ⓓ
52. Ⓐ Ⓑ Ⓒ Ⓓ
53. Ⓐ Ⓑ Ⓒ Ⓓ
54. Ⓐ Ⓑ Ⓒ Ⓓ
55. Ⓐ Ⓑ Ⓒ Ⓓ
56. Ⓐ Ⓑ Ⓒ Ⓓ
57. Ⓐ Ⓑ Ⓒ Ⓓ
58. Ⓐ Ⓑ Ⓒ Ⓓ
59. Ⓐ Ⓑ Ⓒ Ⓓ
60. Ⓐ Ⓑ Ⓒ Ⓓ

FUNDAMENTALS OF ENGINEERING – AFTERNOON SESSION
Test 2
ANSWER SHEET

1. (A) (B) (C) (D)	31. (A) (B) (C) (D)
2. (A) (B) (C) (D)	32. (A) (B) (C) (D)
3. (A) (B) (C) (D)	33. (A) (B) (C) (D)
4. (A) (B) (C) (D)	34. (A) (B) (C) (D)
5. (A) (B) (C) (D)	35. (A) (B) (C) (D)
6. (A) (B) (C) (D)	36. (A) (B) (C) (D)
7. (A) (B) (C) (D)	37. (A) (B) (C) (D)
8. (A) (B) (C) (D)	38. (A) (B) (C) (D)
9. (A) (B) (C) (D)	39. (A) (B) (C) (D)
10. (A) (B) (C) (D)	40. (A) (B) (C) (D)
11. (A) (B) (C) (D)	41. (A) (B) (C) (D)
12. (A) (B) (C) (D)	42. (A) (B) (C) (D)
13. (A) (B) (C) (D)	43. (A) (B) (C) (D)
14. (A) (B) (C) (D)	44. (A) (B) (C) (D)
15. (A) (B) (C) (D)	45. (A) (B) (C) (D)
16. (A) (B) (C) (D)	46. (A) (B) (C) (D)
17. (A) (B) (C) (D)	47. (A) (B) (C) (D)
18. (A) (B) (C) (D)	48. (A) (B) (C) (D)
19. (A) (B) (C) (D)	49. (A) (B) (C) (D)
20. (A) (B) (C) (D)	50. (A) (B) (C) (D)
21. (A) (B) (C) (D)	51. (A) (B) (C) (D)
22. (A) (B) (C) (D)	52. (A) (B) (C) (D)
23. (A) (B) (C) (D)	53. (A) (B) (C) (D)
24. (A) (B) (C) (D)	54. (A) (B) (C) (D)
25. (A) (B) (C) (D)	55. (A) (B) (C) (D)
26. (A) (B) (C) (D)	56. (A) (B) (C) (D)
27. (A) (B) (C) (D)	57. (A) (B) (C) (D)
28. (A) (B) (C) (D)	58. (A) (B) (C) (D)
29. (A) (B) (C) (D)	59. (A) (B) (C) (D)
30. (A) (B) (C) (D)	60. (A) (B) (C) (D)

FE/EIT

FE: PM General Engineering Exam

Appendix

VARIABLES

a = acceleration
a_t = tangential acceleration
a_r = radial acceleration
d = distance
e = coefficient of restitution
f = frequency
F = force
g = gravity = 32.2 ft/sec^2 or 9.81 m/sec^2
h = height
I = mass inertia
k = spring constant, radius of gyration
KE = kinetic energy
m = mass
M = moment
PE = potential energy
r = radius
s = position
t = time
T = tension, torsion, period
v = velocity
w = weight
x = horizontal position
y = vertical position
α = angular acceleration
ω = angular velocity
θ = angle
μ = coefficient of friction

EQUATIONS

Kinematics

Linear Particle Motion

Constant velocity

$$s = s_o + vt$$

Constant acceleration

$$v = v_o + at$$

$$s = s_o + v_o t + \left(\frac{1}{2}\right)at^2$$

$$v^2 = v_o^2 + 2a(s - s_o)$$

Projectile Motion

$$x = x_o + v_x t$$

$$v_y = v_{yo} - gt$$

$$y = y_o + v_{yo}t - \left(\frac{1}{2}\right)gt^2$$

$$v_y^2 = v_{yo}^2 - 2g(y - y_o)$$

Rotational Motion

Constant rotational velocity

$$\theta = \theta_o + \omega t$$

Constant angular acceleration

$$\omega = \omega_o + \alpha t$$

$$\theta = \theta_o + \omega_o t + \left(\frac{1}{2}\right)\alpha t^2$$

$$\omega^2 = \omega_o^2 + 2\alpha(\theta - \theta_o)$$

Tangential velocity

$$v_t = r\omega$$

Tangential acceleration

$$a_t = r\alpha$$

Radial acceleration

$$a_r = r\omega^2 = \frac{v_t^2}{r}$$

Polar coordinates

$$a_r = \frac{d^2 r}{dt^2} - r\left(\frac{d\theta}{dt}\right)^2 = \frac{d^2 r}{dt^2} - r\omega^2$$

$$a_\theta = r\left(\frac{d^2\theta}{dt^2}\right) + 2\left(\frac{dr}{dt}\right)\left(\frac{d\theta}{dt}\right) = r\alpha + 2\left(\frac{dr}{dt}\right)\omega$$

$$v_r = \frac{dr}{dt}$$

$$v_\theta = r\left(\frac{d\theta}{dt}\right) = r\omega$$

Relative and Related Motion

Acceleration

$$a_A = a_B + a_{A/B}$$

Velocity

$$v_A = v_B + v_{A/B}$$

Position

$$x_A = x_B + x_{A/B}$$

Kinetics

$$w = mg$$

$$F = ma$$

$$F_c = ma_n = \frac{mv_t^2}{r}$$

$$F_f = \mu N$$

Kinetic Energy

$$KE = \left(\frac{1}{2}\right)mv^2$$

Work of a force $= \int F ds$

$$KE_1 + \text{Work}_{1-2} = KE_2$$

Potential Energy

Spring $PE = \left(\frac{1}{2}\right)kx^2$

Weight $PE = wy$

$$KE_1 + PE_1 = KE_2 + PE_2$$

Power

Linear power $P = Fv$

Torsional or rotational power $P = T\omega$

Impulse-Momentum

$$mv_1 + \int F dt = mv_2$$

Impact

$$m_A v_{A1} + m_B v_{B1} = m_A v_{A2} + m_B v_{B2}$$

$$e = \frac{v_{B2} - v_{A2}}{v_{A1} - v_{B1}}$$

Perfectly plastic impact ($e = 0$)

$$m_A v_{A1} + m_B v_{B1} = (m_A + m_B)v'$$

One mass is infinite

$$v_2 = ev_1$$

Inertia

Beam $\quad I_A = \left(\frac{1}{12}\right)ml^2 + m\left(\frac{1}{2}\right)^2 = \left(\frac{1}{3}\right)ml^2$

Plate $\quad I_A = \left(\frac{1}{12}\right)m(a^2 + b^2) + m\left[\left(\frac{a}{2}\right)^2 + \left(\frac{b}{2}\right)^2\right] = \left(\frac{1}{3}\right)m(a^2 + b^2)$

Wheel $\quad I_A = mk^2 + mr^2$

Two-Dimensional Rigid Body Motion

$$F_x = ma_x$$
$$F_y = ma_y$$
$$M_A = I_A\alpha = I_{cg}\,\alpha + m(a)d$$

Rolling Resistance

$$F_r = \frac{mga}{r}$$

Energy Methods for Rigid Body Motion

$$KE_1 + \text{Work}_{1-2} = KE_2$$

$$\text{Work} = \int Fds + \int Md\theta$$

Mechanical Vibration

Differential equation

$$\frac{md^2x}{dt^2} + kx = 0$$

Position

$$x = x_m \sin\left[\sqrt{\frac{k}{m}}\,t + \theta\right]$$

Velocity

$$v = \frac{dx}{dt} = x_m\sqrt{\frac{k}{m}} \cos\left[\sqrt{\frac{k}{m}}\,t + \theta\right]$$

Acceleration

$$a = \frac{d^2 x}{dt^2} = -x_m \left(\frac{k}{m} \right) \sin\left[\sqrt{\frac{k}{m}}\, t + \theta \right]$$

Maximum values

$$x = x_m, v = x_m \sqrt{\frac{k}{m}},\ a = x_m \left(\frac{k}{m} \right)$$

Period

$$T = \frac{2\pi}{\left(\sqrt{\dfrac{k}{m}} \right)}$$

Frequency

$$f = \frac{1}{T} = \frac{\sqrt{\dfrac{k}{m}}}{2\pi}$$

Springs in parallel

$$k = k_1 + k_2$$

Springs in series

$$\frac{1}{k} = \frac{1}{k_1} + \frac{1}{k_2}$$

AREA UNDER NORMAL CURVE

$$\frac{1}{\sqrt{2\pi}} \int_0^z e^{-\frac{z^2}{2}} dz$$

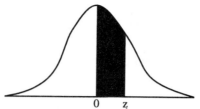

Z	0	1	2	3	4	5	6	7	8	9
0.0	.0000	.0040	.0080	.0120	.0160	.0199	0239	.0279	.0319	.0359
0.1	.0398	.0438	.0478	.0517	.0557	.0596	.0636	.0675	.0714	.0754
0.2	.0793	.0832	.0871	.0910	.0948	.0987	.1026	.1064	.1103	.1141
0.3	.1179	.1217	.1255	.1293	.1331	.1368	.1406	.1443	.1480	.1517
0.4	.1554	.1591	.1628	.1664	.1700	.1736	.1772	.1808	.1844	.1879
0.5	.1915	.1950	.1985	.2019	.2054	.2088	.2123	.2157	.2190	.2224
0.6	.2258	.2291	.2324	.2357	.2389	.2422	.2454	.2486	.2518	.2549
0.7	.2580	.2612	.2642	.2673	.2704	.2734	.2764	.2794	.2823	.2852
0.8	.2881	.2910	.2939	.2967	.2996	.3023	.3051	.3078	.3106	.3133
0.9	.3159	.3186	.3212	.3238	.3264	.3289	.3315	.3340	.3365	.3389
1.0	.3413	.3438	.3461	.3485	.3508	.3531	.3554	.3577	.3599	.3621
1.1	.3643	.3665	.3686	.3708	.3729	.3749	.3770	.3790	.3810	.3830
1.2	.3849	.3869	.3888	.3907	.3925	.3944	.3962	.3980	.3997	.4015
1.3	.4032	.4049	.4066	.4082	.4099	.4115	.4131	.4147	.4162	.4177
1.4	.4192	.4207	.4222	.4236	.4251	.4265	.4279	.4292	.4306	.4319
1.5	.4332	.4345	.4357	.4370	.4382	.4394	.4406	.4418	.4429	.4441
1.6	.4452	.4463	.4474	.4484	.4495	.4505	.4515	.4525	.4535	.4545
1.7	.4554	.4564	.4573	.4582	.4591	.4599	.4608	.4616	.4625	.4633
1.8	.4641	.4649	.4656	.4664	.4671	.4678	.4686	.4693	.4699	.4706
1.9	.4713	.4719	.4726	.4732	.4738	.4744	.4750	.4756	.4761	.4767
2.0	.4772	.4778	.4783	.4788	.4793	.4798	.4803	.4808	.4812	.4817
2.1	.4821	.4826	.4830	.4834	.4838	.4842	.4846	.4850	.4854	.4857
2.2	.4861	.4864	.4868	.4871	.4875	.4878	.4881	.4884	.4887	.4890
2.3	.4893	.4896	.4898	.4901	.4904	.4906	.4909	.4911	.4913	.4916
2.4	.4918	.4920	.4922	.4925	.4927	.4929	.4931	.4932	.4934	.4936
2.5	.4938	.4940	.4941	.4943	.4945	.4946	.4948	.4949	.4951	.4952
2.6	.4953	.4955	.4956	.4957	.4959	.4960	.4961	.4962	.4963	.4964
2.7	.4965	.4966	.4967	.4968	.4969	.4970	.4971	.4972	.4973	.4974
2.8	.4974	.4975	.4976	.4977	.4977	.4978	.4979	.4979	.4980	.4981
2.9	.4981	.4982	.4982	.4983	.4984	.4984	.4985	.4985	.4986	.4986
3.0	.4987	.4987	.4987	.4988	.4988	.4989	.4989	.4989	.4990	.4990
3.1	.4990	.4991	.4991	.4991	.4992	.4992	.4992	.4992	.4993	.4993
3.2	.4993	.4993	.4994	.4994	.4994	.4994	.4994	.4995	.4995	.4995
3.3	.4995	.4995	.4995	.4996	.4996	.4996	.4996	.4996	.4996	.4997
3.4	.4997	.4997	.4997	.4997	.4997	.4997	.4997	.4997	.4997	.4998
3.5	.4998	.4998	.4998	.4998	.4998	.4998	.4998	.4998	.4998	.4998
3.6	.4998	.4998	.4999	.4999	.4999	.4999	.4999	.4999	.4999	.4999
3.7	.4999	.4999	.4999	.4999	.4999	.4999	.4999	.4999	.4999	.4999
3.8	.4999	.4999	.4999	.4999	.4999	.4999	.4999	.4999	.4999	.4999
3.9	.5000	.5000	.5000	.5000	.5000	.5000	.5000	.5000	.5000	.5000

POWER SERIES FOR ELEMENTARY FUNCTIONS

$$\frac{1}{x} = 1 - (x-1) + (x-1)^2 - (x-1)^3 + (x-1)^4 - \ldots + (-1)^n (x-1)^n + \ldots,$$
$$0 < x < 2$$

$$\frac{1}{1+x} = 1 - x + x^2 - x^3 + x^4 - x^5 + \ldots + (-1)^n x^n + \ldots, \qquad -1 < x < 1$$

$$\ln x = (x-1) - \frac{(x-1)^2}{2} + \frac{(x-1)^3}{3} - \frac{(x-1)^4}{4} + \ldots + \frac{(-1)^{n-1}(x-1)^n}{n} + \ldots,$$
$$0 < x \le 2$$

$$e^x = 1 + x + \frac{x^2}{2!} + \frac{x^3}{3!} + \frac{x^4}{4!} + \frac{x^5}{5!} + \ldots + \frac{x^n}{n!} + \ldots, \qquad -\infty < x < \infty$$

$$\sin x = x - \frac{x^3}{3!} + \frac{x^5}{5!} - \frac{x^7}{7!} + \frac{x^9}{9!} - \ldots + \frac{(-1)^n x^{2n+1}}{(2n+1)!} + \ldots, \qquad -\infty < x < \infty$$

$$\cos x = 1 - \frac{x^2}{2!} + \frac{x^4}{4!} - \frac{x^6}{6!} + \frac{x^8}{8!} - \ldots + \frac{(-1)^n x^{2n}}{(2n)!} + \ldots, \qquad -\infty < x < \infty$$

$$\arctan x = x - \frac{x^3}{3} + \frac{x^5}{5} - \frac{x^7}{7} + \frac{x^9}{9} - \ldots + \frac{(-1)^n x^{2n+1}}{2n+1} + \ldots, \qquad -1 \le x \le 1$$

$$(1+x)^k = 1 + kx + \frac{k(k-1)x^2}{2!} + \frac{k(k-1)(k-2)x^3}{3!}$$
$$+ \frac{k(k-1)(k-2)(k-3)x^4}{4!} + \ldots, \qquad -1 < x < 1$$

$$(1+x)^{-k} = 1 - kx + \frac{k(k+1)x^2}{2!} - \frac{k(k+1)(k+2)x^3}{3!}$$
$$+ \frac{k(k+1)(k+2)(k+3)x^4}{4!} - \ldots, \qquad -1 < x < 1$$

TABLE OF MORE COMMON LAPLACE TRANSFORMS

$f(t) = L^{-1}\{F(s)\}$	$F(s) = L\{f(t)\}$
1	$\dfrac{1}{s}$
t	$\dfrac{1}{s^2}$
$\dfrac{t^{n-1}}{(n-1)!}; n = 1, 2, \ldots$	$\dfrac{1}{s^n}$
e^{at}	$\dfrac{1}{s-a}$
$t\, e^{at}$	$\dfrac{1}{(s-a)^2}$
$\dfrac{t^{n-1}e^{-at}}{(n-1)!}$	$\dfrac{1}{(s+a)^n}; n = 1, 2, \ldots$
$\dfrac{e^{-at} - e^{-bt}}{b-a}; a \neq b$	$\dfrac{1}{(s+a)(s+b)}$
$\dfrac{a\, e^{-at} - b\, e^{-bt}}{a-b}; a \neq b$	$\dfrac{s}{(s+a)(s+b)}$
$\sin at$	$\dfrac{a}{s^2 + a^2}$
$\cos at$	$\dfrac{s}{s^2 + a^2}$
$\sinh at$	$\dfrac{a}{s^2 - a^2}$

$f(t) = L^{-1}\{F(s)\}$	$F(s) = L\{f(t)\}$
$\cosh at$	$\dfrac{s}{s^2 - a^2}$
$\dfrac{1}{a^2}(1 - \cos at)$	$\dfrac{1}{s(s^2 + a^2)}$
$\dfrac{1}{a^3}(at - \sin at)$	$\dfrac{1}{s(s^2 + a^2)}$
$\dfrac{t}{2a}\sin at$	$\dfrac{s}{(s^2 + a^2)^2}$
$\dfrac{1}{b}e^{-at}\sin bt$	$\dfrac{1}{(s + a)^2 + b^2}$
$e^{-at}\cos bt$	$\dfrac{s + a}{(s + a)^2 + b^2}$
$h_1(t - a)$	$\dfrac{1}{s}e^{-as}$
$h_1(t) - h_1(t - a)$	$\dfrac{1 - e^{-as}}{s}$
$\dfrac{1}{t}\sin kt$	$\arctan\dfrac{k}{s}$

CONVERSION FACTORS - GENERAL

To convert from	To	Multiply by
Acres	Square feet	43,560
Acres	Square meters	4074
Acres	Square miles	0.001563
Acre-feet	Cubic meters	1233
Ampere-hours (absolute)	Coulombs (absolute)	3600
Angstrom units	Inches	3.937×10^{-9}
Angstrom units	Meters	1×10^{-10}
Angstrom units	Microns	1×10^{-4}
Atmospheres	Millimeters of mercury at 32°F.	760
Atmospheres	Dynes per square centimeter	1.0133×10^{6}
Atmospheres	Newtons per square meter	101,325
Atmospheres	Feet of water at 39.1°F.	33.90
Atmospheres	Grams per square centimeter	1033.3
Atmospheres	Inches of mercury at 32°F.	29.921
Atmospheres	Pounds per square foot	2116.3
Atmospheres	Pounds per square inch	14.696
Bags (cement)	Pounds (cement)	94
Barrels (cement)	Pounds (cement)	376
Barrels (oil)	Cubic meters	0.15899
Barrels (oil)	Gallons	42
Barrels (U.S. liquid)	Cubic meters	0.11924
Barrels (U.S. liquid)	Gallons	31.5
Barrels per day	Gallons per minute	0.02917
Bars	Atmospheres	0.9869
Bars	Newtons per square meter	1×10^{5}
Bars	Pounds per square inch	14.504
Board feet	Cubic feet	$\frac{1}{12}$
Boiler horsepower	B.t.u. per hour	33,480
Boiler horsepower	Kilowatts	9.803
B.t.u.	Calories (gram)	252
B.t.u.	Centigrade heat units (c.h.u. or p.c.u.)	0.55556
B.t.u.	Foot-pounds	777.9
B.t.u.	Horsepower-hours	3.929×10^{-4}
B.t.u.	Joules	1055.1
B.t.u.	Liter-atmospheres	10.41
B.t.u.	Pounds carbon to CO_2	6.88×10^{-5}
B.t.u.	Pounds water evaporated from and at 212°F.	0.001036
B.t.u.	Cubic foot-atmospheres	0.3676
B.t.u.	Kilowatt-hours	2.930×10^{-4}
B.t.u. per cubic foot	Joules per cubic meter	37,260
B.t.u. per hour	Watts	0.29307
B.t.u. per minute	Horsepower	0.02357
B.t.u. per pound	Joules per kilogram	2326
B.t.u. per pound per degree Fahrenheit	Calories per gram per degree centigrade	1
B.t.u. per pound per degree Fahrenheit	Joules per kilogram per degree Kelvin	4186.8
B.t.u. per second	Watts	1054.4
B.t.u. per square foot per hour	Joules per square meter per second	3.1546
B.t.u. per square foot per minute	Kilowatts per square foot	0.1758
B.t.u. per square foot per second for a temperature gradient of 1°F. per inch	Calories, gram (15°C.), per square centimeter per second for a temperature gradient of 1°C. per centimeter	1.2405

(continued)

To convert from	To	Multiply by
B.t.u. (60°F.) per degree Fahrenheit	Calories per degree centigrade	453.6
Bushels (U.S. dry)	Cubic feet	1.2444
Bushels (U.S. dry)	Cubic meters	0.03524
Calories, gram	B.t.u.	3.968×10^{-3}
Calories, gram	Foot-pounds	3.087
Calories, gram	Joules	4.1868
Calories, gram	Liter-atmospheres	4.130×10^{-2}
Calories, gram	Horsepower-hours	1.5591×10^{-6}
Calories, gram, per gram per degree C.	Joules per kilogram per degree Kelvin	4186.8
Calories, kilogram	Kilowatt-hours	0.0011626
Calories, kilogram per second	Kilowatts	4.185
Candle power (spherical)	Lumens	12.556
Carats (metric)	Grams	0.2
Centigrade heat units	B.t.u.	1.8
Centimeters	Angstrom units	1×10^8
Centimeters	Feet	0.03281
Centimeters	Inches	0.3937
Centimeters	Meters	0.01
Centimeters	Microns	10,000
Centimeters of mercury at 0°C.	Atmospheres	0.013158
Centimeters of mercury at 0°C.	Feet of water at 39.1°F.	0.4460
Centimeters of mercury at 0°C.	Newtons per square meter	1333.2
Centimeters of mercury at 0°C.	Pounds per square foot	27.845
Centimeters of mercury at 0°C.	Pounds per square inch	0.19337
Centimeters per second	Feet per minute	1.9685
Centimeters of water at 4°C.	Newtons per square meter	98.064
Centistokes	Square meters per second	1×10^{-6}
Circular mils	Square centimeters	5.067×10^{-6}
Circular mils	Square inches	7.854×10^{-7}
Circular mils	Square mils	0.7854
Cords	Cubic feet	128
Cubic centimeters	Cubic feet	3.532×10^{-5}
Cubic centimeters	Gallons	2.6417×10^{-4}
Cubic centimeters	Ounces (U.S. fluid)	0.03381
Cubic centimeters	Quarts (U.S. fluid)	0.0010567
Cubic feet	Bushels (U.S.)	0.8036
Cubic feet	Cubic centimeters	28,317
Cubic feet	Cubic meters	0.028317
Cubic feet	Cubic yards	0.03704
Cubic feet	Gallons	7.481
Cubic feet	Liters	28.316
Cubic foot-atmospheres	Foot-pounds	2116.3
Cubic foot-atmospheres	Liter-atmospheres	28.316
Cubic feet of water (60°F.)	Pounds	62.37
Cubic feet per minute	Cubic centimeters per second	472.0
Cubic feet per minute	Gallons per second	0.1247
Cubic feet per second	Gallons per minute	448.8
Cubic feet per second	Million gallons per day	0.64632
Cubic inches	Cubic meters	1.6387×10^{-5}
Cubic yards	Cubic meters	0.76456
Curies	Disintegrations per minute	2.2×10^{12}
Curies	Coulombs per minute	1.1×10^{12}
Degrees	Radians	0.017453
Drams (apothecaries' or troy)	Grams	3.888

(continued)

To convert from	To	Multiply by
Drams (avoirdupois)	Grams	1.7719
Dynes	Newtons	1×10^{-5}
Ergs	Joules	1×10^{-7}
Faradays	Coulombs (abs.)	96,500
Fathoms	Feet	6
Feet	Meters	0.3048
Feet per minute	Centimeters per second	0.5080
Feet per minute	Miles per hour	0.011364
Feet per (second)^2	Meters per (second)^2	0.3048
Feet of water at 39.2°F.	Newtons per square meter	2989
Foot-poundals	B.t.u.	3.995×10^{-5}
Foot-poundals	Joules	0.04214
Foot-poundals	Liter-atmospheres	4.159×10^{-4}
Foot-pounds	B.t.u.	0.0012856
Foot-pounds	Calories, gram	0.3239
Foot-pounds	Foot-poundals	32.174
Foot-pounds	Horsepower-hours	5.051×10^{-7}
Foot-pounds	Kilowatt-hours	3.766×10^{-7}
Foot-pounds	Liter-atmospheres	0.013381
Foot-pounds force	Joules	1.3558
Foot-pounds per second	Horsepower	0.0018182
Foot-pounds per second	Kilowatts	0.0013558
Furlongs	Miles	0.125
Gallons (U.S. liquid)	Barrels (U.S. liquid)	0.03175
Gallons	Cubic meters	0.003785
Gallons	Cubic feet	0.13368
Gallons	Gallons (Imperial)	0.8327
Gallons	Liters	3.785
Gallons	Ounces (U.S. fluid)	128
Gallons per minute	Cubic feet per hour	8.021
Gallons per minute	Cubic feet per second	0.002228
Grains	Grams	0.06480
Grains	Pounds	$\frac{1}{7000}$
Grains per cubic foot	Grams per cubic meter	2.2884
Grains per gallon	Parts per million	17.118
Grams	Drams (avoirdupois)	0.5644
Grams	Drams (troy)	0.2572
Grams	Grains	15.432
Grams	Kilograms	0.001
Grams	Pounds (avoirdupois)	0.0022046
Grams	Pounds (troy)	0.002679
Grams per cubic centimeter	Pounds per cubic foot	62.43
Grams per cubic centimeter	Pounds per gallon	8.345
Grams per liter	Grains per gallon	58.42
Grams per liter	Pounds per cubic foot	0.0624
Grams per square centimeter	Pounds per square foot	2.0482
Grams per square centimeter	Pounds per square inch	0.014223
Hectares	Acres	2.471
Hectares	Square meters	10,000
Horsepower (British)	B.t.u. per minute	42.42
Horsepower (British)	B.t.u. per hour	2545
Horsepower (British)	Foot-pounds per minute	33,000
Horsepower (British)	Foot-pounds per second	550
Horsepower (British)	Watts	745.7
Horsepower (British)	Horsepower (metric)	1.0139
Horsepower (British)	Pounds carbon to CO_2 per hour	0.175

(continued)

To convert from	To	Multiply by
Horsepower (British)	Pounds water evaporated per hour at 212°F	2.64
Horsepower (metric)	Foot-pounds per second	542.47
Horsepower (metric)	Kilogram-meters per second	7.5
Hours (mean solar)	Seconds	3600
Inches	Meters	0.0254
Inches of mercury at 60°F.	Newtons per square meter	3376.9
Inches of water at 60°F.	Newtons per square meter	248.84
Joules (absolute)	B.t.u. (mean)	9.480×10^{-4}
Joules (absolute)	Calories, gram (mean)	0.2389
Joules (absolute)	Cubic foot-atmospheres	0.3485
Joules (absolute)	Foot-pounds	0.7376
Joules (absolute)	Kilowatt-hours	2.7778×10^{-7}
Joules (absolute)	Liter-atmospheres	0.009869
Kilocalories	Joules	4186.8
Kilograms	Pounds (avoirdupois)	2.2046
Kilograms force	Newtons	9.807
Kilograms per square centimeter	Pounds per square inch	14.223
Kilometers	Miles	0.6214
Kilowatt-hours	B.t.u.	3414
Kilowatt-hours	Foot-pounds	2.6552×10^{6}
Kilowatts	Horsepower	1.3410
Knots (international)	Meters per second	0.5144
Knots (nautical miles per hour)	Miles per hour	1.1516
Lamberts	Candles per square inch	2.054
Liter-atmospheres	Cubic foot-atmospheres	0.03532
Liter-atmospheres	Foot-pounds	74.74
Liters	Cubic feet	0.03532
Liters	Cubic meters	0.001
Liters	Gallons	0.26418
Lumens	Watts	0.001496
Micromicrons	Microns	1×10^{-6}
Microns	Angstrom units	1×10^{4}
Microns	Meters	1×10^{-6}
Miles (nautical)	Feet	6080
Miles (nautical)	Miles (U.S. statute)	1.1516
Miles	Feet	5280
Miles	Meters	1609.3
Miles per hour	Feet per second	1.4667
Miles per hour	Meters per second	0.4470
Milliliters	Cubic centimeters	1
Millimeters	Meters	0.001
Millimeters of mercury at 0°C.	Newtons per square meter	133.32
Millimicrons	Microns	0.001
Mils	Inches	0.001
Mils	Meters	2.54×10^{-5}
Minims (U.S.)	Cubic centimeters	0.06161
Minutes (angle)	Radians	2.909×10^{-4}
Minutes (mean solar)	Seconds	60
Newtons	Kilograms	0.10197
Ounces (avoirdupois)	Kilograms	0.02835
Ounces (avoirdupois)	Ounces (troy)	0.9115
Ounces (U.S. fluid)	Cubic meters	2.957×10^{-5}
Ounces (troy)	Ounces (apothecaries')	1.000
Pints (U.S. liquid)	Cubic meters	4.732×10^{-4}
Poundals	Newtons	0.13826

(continued)

To convert from	To	Multiply by
Pounds (avoirdupois)	Grains	7000
Pounds (avoirdupois)	Kilograms	0.45359
Pounds (avoirdupois)	Pounds (troy)	1.2153
Pounds per cubic foot	Grams per cubic centimeter	0.016018
Pounds per cubic foot	Kilograms per cubic meter	16.018
Pounds per square foot	Atmospheres	4.725×10^{-4}
Pounds per square foot	Kilograms per square meter	4.882
Pounds per square inch	Atmospheres	0.06805
Pounds per square inch	Kilograms per square centimeter	0.07031
Pounds per square inch	Newtons per square meter	6894.8
Pounds force	Newtons	4.4482
Pounds force per square foot	Newtons per square meter	47.88
Pounds water evaporated from and at 212°F.	Horsepower-hours	0.379
Pound-centigrade units (p.c.u.)	B.t.u.	1.8
Quarts (U.S. liquid)	Cubic meters	9.464×10^{-4}
Radians	Degrees	57.30
Revolutions per minute	Radians per second	0.10472
Seconds (angle)	Radians	4.848×10^{-6}
Slugs	Gee pounds	1
Slugs	Kilograms	14.594
Slugs	Pounds	32.17
Square centimeters	Square feet	0.0010764
Square feet	Square meters	0.0929
Square feet per hour	Square meters per second	2.581×10^{-5}
Square inches	Square centimeters	6.452
Square inches	Square meters	6.452×10^{-4}
Square yards	Square meters	0.8361
Stokes	Square meters per second	1×10^{-4}
Tons (long)	Kilograms	1016
Tons (long)	Pounds	2240
Tons (metric)	Kilograms	1000
Tons (metric)	Pounds	2204.6
Tons (metric)	Tons (short)	1.1023
Tons (short)	Kilograms	907.18
Tons (short)	Pounds	2000
Tons (refrigeration)	B.t.u. per hour	12,000
Tons (British shipping)	Cubic feet	42.00
Tons (U.S. shipping)	Cubic feet	40.00
Torr (mm. mercury, 0°C.)	Newtons per square meter	133.32
Watts	B.t.u. per hour	3.413
Watts	Joules per second	1
Watts	Kilogram-meters per second	0.10197
Watt-hours	Joules	3600
Yards	Meters	0.9144

TEMPERATURE FACTORS

$$°F = 9/5 \, (°C) + 32$$

Fahrenheit temperature = 1.8 (temperature in kelvins) −459.67

$$°C = 5/9 \, [(°F) - 32]$$

Celsius temperature = temperature in kelvins −273.15

Fahrenheit temperature = 1.8 (Celsius temperature) +32

HANDBOOK of
**MATHEMATICAL,
SCIENTIFIC, &
ENGINEERING**
FORMULAS, FUNCTIONS,
GRAPHS, TABLES,
& TRANSFORMS

RESEARCH & EDUCATION ASSOCIATION

A particularly useful reference for those in math, science, engineering and other technical fields. Includes the most-often used formulas, tables, transforms, functions, and graphs which are needed as tools in solving problems. The entire field of special functions is also covered. A large amount of scientific data which is often of interest to scientists and engineers has been included.

Available at your local bookstore or order directly from us by sending in coupon below.

The
HANDBOOK of
ELECTRICAL ENGINEERING

Staff of Research and Education Association

Available at your local bookstore or order directly from us by sending in coupon below.

RESEARCH & EDUCATION ASSOCIATION
61 Ethel Road W., Piscataway, New Jersey 08854
Phone: (732) 819-8880

VISA   **MasterCard**

☐ Payment enclosed
☐ Visa   ☐ MasterCard

Charge Card Number

Expiration Date: _____ / _____
          Mo   Yr

Please ship **"The Handbook of Electrical Engineering"** @ $38.95 plus $4.00 for shipping.

Name _____

Address _____

City _____ State _____ Zip _____

Available at your local bookstore or order directly from us by sending in coupon below.

Available at your local bookstore or order directly from us by sending in coupon below.

REA's Test Preps
The Best in Test Preparation

- REA "Test Preps" are **far more** comprehensive than any other test preparation series
- Each book contains up to **eight** full-length practice tests based on the most recent exams
- **Every** type of question likely to be given on the exams is included
- Answers are accompanied by **full** and **detailed** explanations

REA publishes over 60 Test Preparation volumes in several series. They include:

Advanced Placement Exams (APs)
Biology
Calculus AB & Calculus BC
Chemistry
Computer Science
English Language & Composition
English Literature & Composition
European History
Government & Politics
Physics
Psychology
Spanish Language
Statistics
United States History

College-Level Examination Program (CLEP)
Analyzing and Interpreting Literature
College Algebra
Freshman College Composition
General Examinations
General Examinations Review
History of the United States I
Human Growth and Development
Introductory Sociology
Principles of Marketing
Spanish

SAT II: Subject Tests
Biology E/M
Chemistry
English Language Proficiency Test
French
German
Literature

SAT II: Subject Tests (cont'd)
Mathematics Level IC, IIC
Physics
Spanish
United States History
Writing

Graduate Record Exams (GREs)
Biology
Chemistry
General
Literature in English
Mathematics
Physics
Psychology

ACT - ACT Assessment

ASVAB - Armed Services Vocational Aptitude Battery

CBEST - California Basic Educational Skills Test

CDL - Commercial Driver License Exam

CLAST - College-Level Academic Skills Test

ELM - Entry Level Mathematics

ExCET - Exam for the Certification of Educators in Texas

FE (EIT) - Fundamentals of Engineering Exam

FE Review - Fundamentals of Engineering Review

GED - High School Equivalency Diploma Exam (U.S. & Canadian editions)

GMAT - Graduate Management Admission Test

LSAT - Law School Admission Test

MAT - Miller Analogies Test

MCAT - Medical College Admission Test

MECT - Massachusetts Educator Certification Tests

MSAT - Multiple Subjects Assessment for Teachers

NJ HSPT- New Jersey High School Proficiency Test

PPST - Pre-Professional Skills Tests

PSAT - Preliminary Scholastic Assessment Test

SAT I - Reasoning Test

SAT I - Quick Study & Review

TASP - Texas Academic Skills Program

TOEFL - Test of English as a Foreign Language

TOEIC - Test of English for International Communication

RESEARCH & EDUCATION ASSOCIATION
61 Ethel Road W. • Piscataway, New Jersey 08854
Phone: (732) 819-8880   **website: www.rea.com**

Please send me more information about your Test Prep books

Name _____

Address _____

City _____ State _____ Zip _____

REA's Problem Solvers

The "PROBLEM SOLVERS" are comprehensive supplemental textbooks designed to save time in finding solutions to problems. Each "PROBLEM SOLVER" is the first of its kind ever produced in its field. It is the product of a massive effort to illustrate almost any imaginable problem in exceptional depth, detail, and clarity. Each problem is worked out in detail with a step-by-step solution, and the problems are arranged in order of complexity from elementary to advanced. Each book is fully indexed for locating problems rapidly.

ACCOUNTING
ADVANCED CALCULUS
ALGEBRA & TRIGONOMETRY
AUTOMATIC CONTROL
   SYSTEMS/ROBOTICS
BIOLOGY
BUSINESS, ACCOUNTING, & FINANCE
CALCULUS
CHEMISTRY
COMPLEX VARIABLES
COMPUTER SCIENCE
DIFFERENTIAL EQUATIONS
ECONOMICS
ELECTRICAL MACHINES
ELECTRIC CIRCUITS
ELECTROMAGNETICS
ELECTRONIC COMMUNICATIONS
ELECTRONICS
FINITE & DISCRETE MATH
FLUID MECHANICS/DYNAMICS
GENETICS
GEOMETRY

HEAT TRANSFER
LINEAR ALGEBRA
MACHINE DESIGN
MATHEMATICS for ENGINEERS
MECHANICS
NUMERICAL ANALYSIS
OPERATIONS RESEARCH
OPTICS
ORGANIC CHEMISTRY
PHYSICAL CHEMISTRY
PHYSICS
PRE-CALCULUS
PROBABILITY
PSYCHOLOGY
STATISTICS
STRENGTH OF MATERIALS &
   MECHANICS OF SOLIDS
TECHNICAL DESIGN GRAPHICS
THERMODYNAMICS
TOPOLOGY
TRANSPORT PHENOMENA
VECTOR ANALYSIS

*If you would like more information about any of these books,
complete the coupon below and return it to us, or visit your local bookstore.*

RESEARCH & EDUCATION ASSOCIATION
61 Ethel Road W. • Piscataway, New Jersey 08854
Phone: (732) 819-8880

Please send me more information about your Problem Solver books

Name _____

Address _____

City _____ State _____ Zip _____

REA's Test Prep Books Are The Best!

(a sample of the <u>hundreds of letters</u> REA receives each year)

" I am writing to congratulate you on preparing an exceptional study guide. In five years of teaching this course I have never encountered a more thorough, comprehensive, concise and realistic preparation for this examination. "
Teacher, Davie, FL

" I have found your publications, *The Best Test Preparation...*, to be exactly that. "
Teacher, Aptos, CA

" I used your *CLEP Introductory Sociology* book and rank it 99% – thank you! "
Student, Jerusalem, Israel

" Your GMAT book greatly helped me on the test. Thank you. "
Student, Oxford, OH

" I recently got the French SAT II Exam book from REA. I congratulate you on first-rate French practice tests. "
Instructor, Los Angeles, CA

" Your AP English Literature and Composition book is most impressive. "
Student, Montgomery, AL

" The REA LSAT Test Preparation guide is a winner! "
Instructor, Spartanburg, SC

(more on front page)